Moms in Chief

Moms in Chief

The Rhetoric of Republican Motherhood and the Spouses of Presidential Nominees, 1992–2016

Tammy R. Vigil

 University Press of Kansas

Published by the University Press of Kansas (Lawrence, Kansas 66045), which was organized by the Kansas Board of Regents and is operated and funded by Emporia State University, Fort Hays State University, Kansas State University, Pittsburg State University, the University of Kansas, and Wichita State University.

Library of Congress Cataloging-in-Publication Data

Names: Vigil, Tammy R., author.
Title: Moms in chief : the rhetoric of Republican motherhood and the spouses of presidential nominees, 1992–2016 / Tammy R. Vigil.
Description: Lawrence, Kansas : University Press of Kansas, [2019] | Includes bibliographical references and index.
Identifiers: LCCN 2018046928
   ISBN 9780700627486 (cloth : alk. paper)
   ISBN 9780700627493 (ebook)
Subjects: LCSH: Presidential candidates' spouses—United States | Political campaigns—United States—History. | Rhetoric—Political aspects—History. | Motherhood—Political aspects—United States. | Women—Political activity—United States.
Classification: LCC HQ1391.U5 V54 2019 | DDC 320.082/0973—dc23.
LC record available at https://lccn.loc.gov/2018046928.

British Library Cataloguing-in-Publication Data is available.

Printed in the United States of America

10 9 8 7 6 5 4 3 2 1

The paper used in this publication is recycled and contains 30 percent postconsumer waste. It is acid free and meets the minimum requirements of the American National Standard for Permanence of Paper for Printed Library Materials Z39.48-1992.

For Andrew,
Once again.

Contents

Acknowledgments

I owe a large debt of gratitude to the heterodox women who struggled against social and political norms to open opportunities for those who followed. Working on a project like this offers many reminders of just how much women have done in an effort to gain social and political parity and how much more work remains.

I owe a hearty thank you to the editorial staff at the University Press of Kansas. I appreciate their interest in and support of this project as well as their tireless efforts to produce this book. Also, I am obliged to the individuals who reviewed the initial manuscript. Their comments in support of the monograph were heartening, and their recommendations were invaluable.

Most of all, I wish to thank Andrew L. Crick. This book would not be the same without his unending support in the research, writing, and editing stages. I appreciate his resolute character and exacting nature.

Introduction

Political Spouses and Presidential Campaigns

In March 2016, nude photos of Melania Trump taken fifteen years earlier circulated on the internet, and news articles detailing an alleged mental breakdown Heidi Cruz suffered in 2005 emerged online. The interest in these events was spurred by the political aspirations of each woman's husband; because their spouses sought the Republican presidential nomination, these women's pasts became fodder for gossip, rumor, and negative campaign messaging by the intraparty opposition. In both cases, the spouses were judged based on whether they would make an appropriate first lady of the United States, and in each instance the women were used in arguments against their husbands' candidacies.

Spouses played interesting and diverse roles during the 2016 presidential primary contests for both the Republican and Democratic candidates. Some contenders' partners, like Melania Trump, mostly appeared beside their spouses at various events without speaking or campaigning directly. Others, such as former US president Bill Clinton, acted as true surrogates by campaigning solo, holding rallies, and giving speeches without the candidate present. By the midway point of the primary season, whether voluntarily or otherwise, the spouses of all serious contenders for each party's nomination were a visible part of the contest and part of what many pundits considered dirty campaigning. Ted Cruz was accused of circulating the Melania photos, and Donald Trump threatened to reveal negative news about Heidi.[1] Internet sources criticized Jane Sanders, wife of Bernie Sanders, for her plain sense of style and accused her of financially ruining a college of which she was once president.[2] Decades-old charges against Bill became grounds for opposing Hillary.[3] In each instance, negative claims about the spouses were used to question the viability of the candidates. In cases in which the wife was criticized, her standing as a potential gender role model was the main point of concern: Was Melania Trump too racy? Was Heidi Cruz too emotionally unstable? When the candidate's husband was targeted, the candidate was questioned about her response to her spouse's bad behavior: Did Hillary Clinton condone or even inspire her husband's infidelity? Did she try to silence the women who claimed her husband had sexually assaulted them? In every case, the female, whether as the spouse or the candidate, was scrutinized for her standing as a respectable woman.

Campaigns frequently try to use the candidate's spouse as part of the packaging of the candidate. Including spouses in this way gives the press and the opposition implicit permission to discuss the politician's life partner. Even without this opening, the importance of the role the partner assumes if her or his spouse wins the presidential campaign invites public evaluation of the consort. After all, the helpmate to the president of the United States has the potential to wield a great deal of influence. Although mates assume this potentially powerful position without the explicit consent of the citizenry because no one votes for them directly, there is still a vetting process for the person who might attain the role. Despite the fact that there are no official criteria for judging spouses, the public and the press evaluate these individuals based on the ways they meet or fail to meet social expectations tied to traditional gender roles.

This book examines the ways mates (those married to successful as well as unsuccessful presidential candidates) contribute to the conversation regarding the expectations of presidential partners. These presumptions carry implications for citizens' conceptions of gender and sex roles, particularly about women as political actors. Of specific interest here is how assorted judgments offered by the press, portrayals by others (primarily various opponents of the candidates), and the spouses' self-depictions (through their own words) rely on, reinforce, or contest traditional gender norms. In particular, the following chapters examine the ways contemporary spouses conform to or challenge deep-rooted sex-based standards often ascribed to the first lady of the United States. The remainder of this introduction provides a brief summary of some ways presidential spouses have participated in campaigns, a discussion of the relationship between the constraints placed on presidents' spouses and the social construction of gender expectations for someone in that position, and a preview of the various questions explored throughout this book.

Nominees' Mates and the Battle for the White House

Contemporary pundits and politicians often publicly lament the negative insertion of mates into campaigns and complain about unfavorable assessments of these partners as though vetting a potential helpmate to the president is a recent and unsavory development. In fact, the United States has a long history of presidential nominees' spouses participating in campaigns and managing the inevitable criticism directed toward them. In some instances, the spouses voluntarily participate by attending campaign events and helping make their life partner seem accessible and relatable to potential voters. In other cases, they are dragged into campaigns and used in a negative manner by those opposing the candidate. Oftentimes individuals face a combination of these two scenarios. For more than two centuries, wives of nominees have sometimes been integrated into campaigns against their husbands, whereas at other times they have served as decided assets.

Wives and Negative Campaigns

One of the first examples of an opposing group negatively using a candidate's wife occurred in 1808. At that time, Dolley Madison, wife of presidential contender James Madison, was accused of having had an affair with incumbent president Thomas Jefferson.[4] Dolley Madison had often served as the White House hostess during the widowed Jefferson's administration, so the stories about an illicit romance were easy for some to believe. In the end, Dolley's popularity overrode the claims about her, and the gossip did not ultimately prevent James from winning the Oval Office. Still, the anecdote demonstrates how early in US presidential campaigning opponents began incorporating spouses in negative messaging.

In 1828, Andrew Jackson's wife, Rachel, was similarly used in a campaign against him. Early attempts to derail Andrew's candidacy focused on questions surrounding his wife's first marriage. Rachel Jackson was a divorcee—a relatively minor scandal at the time. The more damning allegation was that her first husband had delayed filing the legal documents dissolving their marriage until after she and Andrew exchanged vows. Although the facts exonerated Rachel (she had been assured the divorce was finalized long before marrying Andrew), the rumored bigamy led to many accusations regarding her lack of ethics and questionable morality. In addition, newspapers printed pointed stories about her rugged ways and accused her of unacceptable personal habits such as smoking a pipe, riding horses with a western saddle, and wearing clothes considered out of fashion.[5] Pointing to her lack of ladylikeness, many newspaper editors called on readers to vote for John Quincy Adams (Andrew's opponent) in order to avoid making Rachel the "head of the female society of the United States."[6] Andrew did win the presidency, but his wife never resided in the White House; she died a couple of months before he took the oath of office. Andrew blamed his wife's death on the Adams campaigners who attacked her and publicly proclaimed that he could "never forgive those murderers."[7]

Ida McKinley's health and mental stability became fodder for gossip and spurred criticism against her husband, William McKinley, in 1896. The speculation regarding her frailty and lack of fitness to serve as the president's helpmate became such a concern that William and Ida threw a two-day anniversary party to which they invited numerous newspaper editors and high-profile political figures. The entire thrust of the event was to give influential individuals the opportunity to personally observe Ida McKinley's health and vitality. The McKinleys hoped reports from their guests would curtail further opposition regarding her potential to be an adequate symbolic representation of the nation's women.[8]

By the twentieth century, opponents' negative use of spouses in campaigns became routine. Eleanor Roosevelt's awareness that her fear of public speaking could be a liability to her husband led her to take oratory and argumentation classes early during Franklin Delano Roosevelt's (FDR's) political career. Ironically, Eleanor Roosevelt's well-developed speaking skill later led Republican opponents to admonish her unladylike assertiveness during each of the 1932, 1936, 1940, and 1944 contests. In addition, whisper campaigns regarding various facets of her sexuality and chastising her friendship with African Americans recurred throughout her time as first lady and spiked during her husband's reelection campaigns. Some individuals lauded Roosevelt as something of a new or modern first lady,[9] and many others chided her for rupturing social convention through her purportedly masculine style.[10]

Sometimes choosing not to be part of a presidential campaign caused grief for the spouse of a politician. Theo Landon, wife of Republican Alf Landon, declined to participate in her husband's 1936 bid to unseat FDR. Citing her desire to protect her family's privacy and her need to care for the couple's children, Landon refused to appear at public campaign events and did not speak on her husband's behalf. The press admonished her for such unsupportive behavior. When she died in 1996, her *New York Times* obituary focused more on explaining her decision not to campaign and the onslaught of criticism it incited than any other facet of her life.[11]

In 1960, Jacqueline "Jackie" Kennedy was both praised for her beauty and class and faulted for being detached from average Americans.[12] Although the Camelot mythos surrounding her and her husband, John Fitzgerald Kennedy (JFK), appealed to many Americans, opponents highlighted the young Jackie Kennedy's expensive taste and preference for European goods and fashions in an effort to decrease her husband's popularity. In a few instances, adversaries tried to make the race a competition between the ostensibly all-American Patricia "Pat" Nixon, wife of Richard M. Nixon, and the foreign-seeming and aloof Jackie Kennedy.[13] Eventually, Kennedy's pregnancy offered a pretext to avoid participating in most of the general election contest, but it was no secret that she did not enjoy the campaign trail and preferred to remain out of the public eye whenever possible.[14]

The wives of major parties' nominees for the presidency have always faced scrutiny and have been used in a variety of negative ways. The later chapters in this book explore the criticisms leveled against contemporary spouses beginning in 1992 and continuing through the 2016 election. However, the life partners of presidential contenders are also deliberately used to contribute positively to their spouses' campaigns.

Wives as Campaign Assets

Even though it is common for candidates and spouses to complain about the negative use of mates in campaigns, throughout history many contenders have strategically included their spouses in efforts to win the presidency. The first three presidents' wives were not part of campaigns (George Washington was essentially drafted into office twice, so there was no campaign for Martha to support; John Adams's wife, Abigail, was caring for his ailing mother during his 1796 race and could not take time to campaign on his behalf; and Thomas Jefferson's wife, Martha, had died long before his two presidential bids), but by the fourth presidential election, spouses began to play an important role in campaigns by using social interactions to forward their husbands' political agendas. Dolley Madison epitomized this approach by winning electoral voters' support for her husband's candidacy while serving as a popular hostess in Washington, DC.

In the early 1820s, Louisa Adams, wife of John Quincy Adams, used open house receptions to court potential supporters for her husband's bid for the presidency. By attending legislative sessions on a weekly basis, she also became friendly with many political figures who would ultimately help decide the outcome of the 1824 election.[15] Despite the fact that she claimed to disdain politics, Louisa made many shrewd moves to aid her husband, including arranging social meetings with influential newspaper editors, connecting John Quincy with powerful businessmen, and even hosting a ball in honor of her husband's eventual political rival Andrew Jackson—an unsuccessful attempt to earn the general's endorsement for her husband. Despite her many obvious efforts to promote her husband, Louisa Adams openly asserted no personal ambitions for herself and argued she only entered political discussions to advocate for her husband.[16] She cast herself simply as a dutiful and supportive wife. Although Louisa's exact influence cannot be measured, the fact that John Quincy won the presidency in 1824 based on a decision by the House of Representatives (no candidate won a majority of Electoral College votes that year) meant her social campaigning might have swayed some key decision makers. Her efforts, however, did not help her husband overcome Andrew Jackson's challenge in 1828.

During the 1856 campaign, Jessie Fremont, wife of Republican candidate John C. Fremont, became a positive part of her husband's campaign. A well-known author and member of a powerful political family, Jessie Fremont was not shy about engaging in political conversations and making her opinions known. Members of the newly formed Republican Party viewed her as a strong asset to her husband. Many voters used envelopes with her picture on them to indicate their support for the couple, and others wore homemade ribbons championing "John and Jessie" for the White House.[17] Jessie was extremely popular and helped boost support for her husband, but it was not enough to secure victory; John lost the election to the bachelor Democrat James Buchanan.[18]

In the late 1800s, Mary Baird Bryan, wife of three-time Democratic nominee William Jennings Bryan, took a direct role in her husband's presidential efforts. She reportedly entered law school, finishing third in her class, for the primary purpose of assisting her husband.[19] She worked with him throughout his campaigns. She did the research for and helped write most of the campaign addresses delivered by the famed "boy orator."[20] In fact, Mary had a big hand in constructing her husband's 1896 Democratic National Convention (DNC) address, a speech so impactful that it helped William earn the party's nomination that year.[21] It is noteworthy that despite having worked diligently behind the scenes on behalf of her husband for several decades (including completing his autobiography),[22] her headstone at Arlington National Cemetery reads simply, "Wife and Helpmate."[23]

During the twentieth century, candidates for president became more active in their personal efforts to win the Oval Office. In many cases, spouses were strategically included in overt campaign events such as nominating conventions. In 1912, Helen "Nellie" Taft sat in the front row of the DNC in order to dissuade speakers from ferociously attacking her husband, William Taft, the incumbent president and presumptive Republican nominee.[24] Eight years later, Florence Harding, wife of Warren Harding, courted the press at the Republican National Convention (RNC) by giving interviews in the corridors of the convention hall and urging reporters to write about her husband's kindness, intelligence, and compassion toward children.

Despite the negative messaging often surrounding Eleanor Roosevelt, she was generally viewed as an asset to her husband's multiple presidential campaigns. When FDR's bid for a third term faced opposition at the 1940 DNC, supporters called on Eleanor Roosevelt to fly to the convention and assist them in securing the nomination on his behalf. Although she claimed to find direct campaigning unladylike, she acquiesced and appeared at the convention.[25] When she addressed the delegates on the convention floor, Roosevelt became the first spouse of a candidate to deliver an official national convention speech. Her address focused on unity building and argued for stability in times of uncertainty, yet not once did she mention FDR by name or office.[26] Thus, Roosevelt's speech was arguably more philosophical than political, allowing her to allay some of her own concerns about the social appropriateness of her engaging in open campaigning. Her approach did not prevent detractors from claiming she had overstepped appropriate social bounds for women and particularly for the first lady, but the speech did seem to help shore up support for her husband's third nomination.[27]

During the latter half of the twentieth century, the popularity of several candidates' spouses meant they became increasingly visible parts of campaigns and sometimes worked as independent campaigners. Richard Nixon's 1960 bid for the presidency was partially built around the popularity his wife, Pat Nixon, had earned during his vice presidency. The strategic "Pat for First Lady" campaign included official buttons, bumper stickers, and pennants. The movement focused on building housewives' support for Richard. A similar effort occurred in 1976 when "Vote for Betty's Husband" became a popular slogan for those supporting the incumbent Republican, Gerald Ford. Although the two appeals were similar in tone, a major difference between them was that the Pat Nixon campaign was a planned effort constructed by staffers, and the Betty Ford support was an organic, grassroots movement. As with Jessie Fremont in 1856, neither Pat Nixon (in 1960) nor Betty Ford was popular enough to help her respective husband win.

In 1964, Claudia Alta "Lady Bird" Johnson was such a well-liked and amiable first lady that campaign staffers sent her on a tour of the southern United States without her husband, Lyndon Baines Johnson. The "Lady Bird Special" traveled through eight states in four days, and she delivered a stump speech at each major stop. The excursion was intended to gain back support the president had lost for signing the Civil Rights Act and to urge acceptance of the legislation. The trip was generally considered a success.[28] Scholars also deem it significant because it helped expand the realm of influence for first ladies and candidates' spouses.[29]

These anecdotes offer only a small sampling of the ways wives of nominees have participated in presidential campaigns. Generally speaking, throughout the nineteenth and twentieth centuries, spouses of presidential contenders primarily acted as dutiful wives supporting their candidate husbands. Even when they had their own political perspectives and agendas, they most frequently portrayed themselves as serving an important but subservient function. This makes sense considering they were acting as campaign surrogates rather than as candidates themselves. However, presidential spouses are unique in that they are never simply proxies for the candidate but are part of the presidential package; should the proffered candidate win the election, the spouse, by virtue of marriage, assumes a high-profile position filled with potential social and political influence.

Presidential Spouses and Gender Roles

In 1797, as the second woman preparing to face the already daunting job of spouse to the president of the United States, Abigail Adams expressed concerns about the restrictive nature of the prominent position she was about to undertake. She wrote to her husband, president-elect John Adams, that the prospect of taking up the mantle of the president's spouse was like being "fastened up hand and foot and tongue to be shot at as our Quincy lads do at the poor geese and turkies [sic] and like the frog in the fable, sport to the boys was death to the frogs."[30] Fretting about assuming such a demanding role, Adams shows that the job of helpmate to the president has, from the very beginning, been viewed as a difficult and restrictive undertaking for the women whose husbands ascend to the Oval Office. Adams's remarks indicate that the public nature of the first couple is the primary concern; the press and the citizenry make sport of the president's spouse and the uncertainty and variability of expectations for people in that role make it difficult for the "frog" to emerge unscathed. Because there are no formally established criteria for evaluating a president's spouse, each helpmate is judged based on socially determined and pliable measures that alter as political and social standards do. The challenges facing a president's spouse make the individuals who have assumed this post particularly compelling objects of study.

The first ladyship is fascinating to scholars for a variety of reasons. It is a highly visible and potentially influential political position, yet its power is almost entirely rhetorically derived.[31] Lacking any certified mandate or delineation of official duties and limited by some governmental antinepotism laws, the job is highly malleable and subject to change based on the interests and abilities of each person thrust into it.[32] Because of the significant amount of potential influence this position has and the unique constraints placed upon it, the first ladyship is the subject of many studies by scholars in various fields. Historians often log the activities of women in this role and delineate the evolution of the duties associated with it.[33] Women's studies scholars investigate the ways these women influence perceptions of females in society.[34] Political scientists examine the impact these women have on the policies and perceptions of their presidential husbands and also their campaign-related activities.[35] Communication scholars share many of these points of focus but do so by analyzing the messaging by and about spouses of commanders in chief.[36]

This book includes elements of each of these types of inquiries and expands current research about this unique group of political participants in two specific ways. First, by including the spouses of both winning and losing presidential nominees from the two major US parties, this study broadens our understanding of the potential that candidates' spouses have to impact perceptions of women in the United States. Second, exploring the campaign messages by and about the spouses of contenders for the White House provides insights regarding the expectations and constraints faced by those who would be the helpmate to the person holding the nation's highest elected office. Of particular importance are the convention addresses nominees' spouses deliver to delegates and the nation. When these high-profile individuals frame their own experiences during such key political events, they influence public dialogue and contribute to the social reification of gender norms and standards.

In 1992, the proclaimed "Year of the Woman," particular attention was given to women as political actors.[37] Even though women had been influential in several election cycles between 1920 and 1992, the participation of women, as campaigners (for themselves and others) and as voters, reached a new apex that year.[38] Among the more visible changes in women's roles during the 1992 campaign was the addition of the spouse's speech at the RNC. For the first time in fifty-two years, the spouse of a presidential nominee delivered a full-length, prepared address to party delegates and the nation.[39] In an explicit attempt to earn support from female voters, Barbara Bush's RNC speech was designed to discuss issues campaign staffers thought women would care about. Her speech marked only the second time a spouse delivered a formal convention address. Between

Eleanor Roosevelt's DNC speech in 1940 and Bush's RNC talk in 1992, wives of presidential nominees primarily served as props for photo opportunities by standing on stage with their husbands during signature moments of the convention. In a slightly more visible role, both Pat Nixon in 1972 and Nancy Reagan in 1984 took the stage to be applauded for their time spent as first lady.[40] Although the addition of spouses to convention pageantry has raised women's political profile, as explained in detail throughout subsequent chapters of this book, their inclusion during conventions often reinforces traditional perceptions of women.

Convention speeches by spouses are a particularly useful lens for examining representations of women in the political sphere. Between 1992 and 2012 all nominees' spouses were women, and each was tasked with engaging female voters. Therefore, the ways these speakers presented themselves and women generally illustrated the prevailing interpretations of women by would-be first ladies and presidential campaign staffers. Furthermore, because the spouses' speeches delivered by women have followed a rather predictable pattern, including the use of specific strategies and appeals,[41] the address by the first male spouse of a nominee in 2016 provided new insight into the ways gender and sex roles inform this type of speech. Bill Clinton's DNC speech underscored the rhetorical difficulties and opportunities traditional gender-based understandings of citizens create when women pursue roles previously dominated by men and place men in positions historically occupied by women. Spouses' convention speeches from both parties usually highlight customary domestic roles for women, characterize women's political interests as focused primarily on the home, define women based on their relationships with others, and describe women as self-sacrificing and politically deferential. Those speakers who do not comply with traditional gender norms often receive unfavorable reviews by pundits and the public.[42] Because these speeches are so consequential, this book is organized around their emergence as a key piece of communication by and about candidates' spouses and American womanhood. For this reason, 1992 is the first election examined in the analysis chapters.

The political, social, and economic opportunities open to women have been in flux throughout US history. The development of the nation has been fraught with inequality of various sorts, and women have fought against multiple types of political restraint. Such struggles have included the battle for enfranchisement, attempts to reform coverture laws, and efforts to expand other forms of female political participation and representation. In many ways, women still have not overcome the false narrative that they are too fragile, too sensitive, or lack the intelligence necessary to engage fully in the public sphere. They are also often assumed to lack interest in politics. For women married to presidential contenders, these derogatory perspectives are obvious in the fact that no matter their individual knowledge and experience, their credibility as independent, full citizens is automatically diminished after their husbands enter the political arena.[43] Furthermore, the first lady's opinions on issues are frequently questioned and often dismissed[44] because "her marriage is perceived as abolishing her autonomy and thus her [political] effectiveness."[45] The social mores surrounding traditional femininity suggest that women be other-centered; lack personal ambition; and seek subordinate, supporting roles in their marital relationships.[46] All of these standards are consistently reinforced by the expected functions presidential spouses fulfill and the criticism they receive when they assert their own interests and power. This is why many women who have served as first lady have been "forced to disguise their political power by professing apoliticism."[47]

All first ladies who have tried to make use of the social and political power of their position have been reprimanded. Eleanor Roosevelt was accused of political overreach when she addressed the 1940 DNC even though she did not explicitly advocate for her husband,[48] and Rosalynn Carter was admonished for being too involved in efforts to expand mental health care—a new law was enacted in 1977 to try to block her from being named the chair of the President's Council on Mental Health.[49] These are just two of myriad examples of the opposition presidential spouses have faced for their political involvement. Oftentimes, past presidents' spouses have tried to temper the charges against them by limiting their own political activity to issues deemed feminine in nature—compassionate topics related to social well-being such as health care, education, child welfare, and drug abuse.[50] Yet this strategy has not stopped pundits, members of the opposing party, and the public at large from complaining when the spouse of a president extends her political reach beyond the standards of social acceptability.[51]

Being the spouse of the president does demand a certain level of personal subordination simply because of the importance and stature of the presidency. However, questions remain concerning how much of the deference necessary in the role is based on relative positioning and how much is based on the actual sex of the president's spouse. Past presidents' wives have been expected to emphasize their femininity, have had their political opinions discounted based on their relationship with the president, have been pilloried for political activity, and have had the types of topics they could address restricted by social mores. These are all characteristic restraints placed on women as political actors (not just political spouses, but women generally) throughout US history.[52]

The gender- and sex-based challenges first ladies face do not suddenly materialize at the time of a presidential inauguration. Throughout the primary and general election campaigns, spouses of presidential nominees develop public personas geared toward building electoral support not only for the candidates as prospective presidents but also for themselves as part of a potential first couple. Because contemporary candidates' life partners are almost required to participate in campaigns, their activities reveal a great deal about the couple and their perceptions regarding gender.[53] During their interactions with the press, their appearances with (and sometimes without) the candidates, and their own campaign speeches, nominees' spouses are expected to share personal anecdotes to humanize the candidate and provide voters a more intimate view of the person running for president.[54] These potential presidential helpmates also spend a lot of time auditioning to become the "first spouse."[55] The words they use and the activities they engage in during the campaign give voters a sense of the nominees' spouses' personalities and illustrate the types of pursuits the helpmates might undertake if given access to the White House. As becomes apparent in later chapters of this book, the outspoken campaigners are often faulted for seeming too ambitious and suffer from generally lower likability ratings than those who appear to support their spouses in a more traditionally feminine and subservient manner.

The ways modern spouses engage in campaigns demonstrate the established role requirements of a would-be presidential helpmate. From delivering campaign stump speeches to giving personal interviews to providing the press guided tours of their homes and participating in the quadrennial *Family Circle* cookie recipe competition, most activities reinforce established gender norms. The most viewed and analyzed campaign messages contemporary spouses deliver, their national nominating convention speeches, also tend to emphasize traditional sex roles. The potential for presidential nominees' spouses to influence discussions of gender and sex, particularly as they relate to political empowerment (or disempowerment), makes the study of these individuals important.

Depictions of Contemporary Candidates' Mates

This book expands upon previous research by scrutinizing the rhetoric regarding contemporary spouses of both successful and unsuccessful presidential nominees. In particular, it explores the continued influence of the republican motherhood ideal, a centuries-old conceptualization that views women as limited political actors, by interrogating the ways the press, the parties, and the candidates' spouses have embraced or challenged traditional sex-role stereotyping during the various presidential campaigns between 1992 and 2016. Applying rhetorical criticism to survey and compare messaging about candidates' consorts in a series of case studies, this analysis considers the positive and negative implications of the sustained reliance on conventional rhetoric to evaluate politically active modern women. The rhetorical assessments throughout the book provide qualitative critiques of the depictions of nominees' spouses that reveal influential recurring themes. The case-study structure encourages consideration of the social and historical contexts for the treatment of each set of presidential contenders' helpmates. Blending these methodologies makes possible a thorough understanding of the individual portrayals of particular people, the consistent as well as the changing elements of communication about spouses across time, and the broader implications of these representations for perspectives regarding women in the political realm.

The republican motherhood ideal, developed as a means of rhetorically placating women's expressed desire for political empowerment following the Revolutionary War without actually changing the status or duties of female citizens, frames women as domestically focused, self-sacrificial, deferential, and defined by their relationships with others. According to this view, women's domesticity is their primary means of contributing to the well-being of the nation. Chapter 1 summarizes the development of this trope across more than two centuries and traces its impact in a variety of eras and contexts. Chapters 2–8 examine the ways republican motherhood rhetoric is used in contemporary presidential campaigns to shape interpretations of women in general and to evaluate some of the most visible females in these contests. Approaching each pair of major party candidates' mates as part of a comparative case study in a given election cycle, every campaign-based chapter presents a thematic analysis of representative rhetoric regarding presidential contenders' consorts, including the content of news reports and entertainment media, comments by various party and opposition members, and speeches by the candidates' spouses. Each chapter offers detailed insights about the treatment of potential presidential helpmates in a particular campaign, and these revelations inform observations about the continuing impact of republican motherhood rhetoric that appear in the conclusion of the book.

The chapters wrestle with questions regarding how gender expectations are embraced and challenged through discussions about and by presidential contenders' spouses. In some cases, the queries revolve around tensions between conservative and progressive perceptions of appropriate female roles (see Chapters 2, 5, and 6). How is each point of view framed? Is one approach featured more positively than the other? Are there ideology-driven differences in the parties' representations of these spouses? Other chapters explore what happens when two spouses embody similar perspectives on womanhood, either progressive (see Chapter 3) or conventional (see Chapter 4). Are the women punished or rewarded for conforming to or contesting purported feminine norms? Portrayals involving a more complex nexus of intersecting variables provoke different inquiries. What happens when race becomes an additional factor in the strategic decision-making regarding a candidate's spouse, as it did in 2008 and 2012 (see Chapters 6 and 7)? Does accentuating the ways a candidate's mate meets expectations of traditional motherhood help overcome presumed racial and socioeconomic differences between the spouse and purported average Americans? If a candidate's spouse is an immigrant, does that affect applications of the republican motherhood ideal (see Chapters 5 and 8)? What happens when the spouse of the nominee is male (see Chapter 8)? Are the media presentations and self-depictions equally restrictive for male and female candidates' spouses?

How does the male consort negotiate the gender expectations put forth by the republican motherhood ideal, both for himself and his candidate-wife?

When individuals are thrust into the national spotlight during a presidential campaign because of their marital relationship with a major party's nominee, relying on a rhetorical strategy that emphasizes intimate personal connections makes strategic sense, and because of its deep-seated roots, references to the republican motherhood frame can be an effective persuasive tool on an individual level. Therefore, the continued prevalence of this trope is not surprising. However, its use is still highly problematic for women's pursuit of equal participatory citizenship. When the press, pundits, and assorted political operatives rely on such a narrow interpretation of politically active women, they reinforce an image of womanhood that denies female citizens the fully autonomous standing granted to men. In addition, when political spouses use republican motherhood rhetoric, they legitimize this restrictive point of view.

Although motherhood is an important and consequential activity for many women, the tendency to understand women politically as primarily motivated by maternal drives and wifely duties contributes to the classification of women as a special, homogeneous subset of the population. Instead of affording women the same standing as men by treating them as independent and diverse citizens, considering women fundamentally as mothers and wives automatically discounts their credibility on nonfamilial subjects, discourages overt expressions of personal ambition, and degrades their ability to advocate for themselves. The conclusion of this book discusses these and other implications of using republican motherhood rhetoric as a means of interpreting women in politics and outlines potential methods for encouraging journalists, pundits, and other political functionaries (including political spouses) to move beyond this unnecessarily restrictive interpretive frame.

Conclusion

Complaints about the confining nature of being a president's spouse trace back to the early days of the nation. Yet, as the summary above demonstrates, the challenges of having a matrimonial connection to the country's leader can begin long before election night. US history is replete with examples of presidential candidates' spouses being inserted into campaigns. Their negative and positive uses speak to the expectations and constraints placed upon candidates' spouses by virtue of their relationships with politically ambitious mates. Until 2016, the life partners of candidates were female, tying many of their duties to the social assumptions about women's proper roles in society. The emphasis on the feminine qualities of presidential spouses encourages many people to accentuate the importance of those same characteristics when considering women as political actors more broadly. Thus, the treatment of presidential candidates' spouses during campaigns provides valuable information about the gender- and sex-based assumptions still prevalent in US society when it comes to political empowerment.

The following chapters take a close look at the contemporary depictions of presidential nominees' spouses during the campaigns between 1992 and 2016. The biographies of each spouse provide a context for analyzing how each is portrayed during the campaign by the press, by the opposition, and, most tellingly, through her or his own words during the heavily viewed convention address. In each case, how the nominees' spouses embrace or challenge the traditional expectations set by the republican motherhood ideal and the ways others use these standards when critiquing these individuals highlight modern interpretations of spouses as politically active citizens and explore widely held perceptions about women as political actors.

1

Women as Citizens

The Emergence and Entrenchment of Republican Motherhood

During the late seventeenth and early eighteenth centuries, political philosophers began confronting problems with the dictatorial models of leadership that pervaded governmental structures. They questioned the legitimacy of birthright as grounds for the acquisition or retention of power and debated the potential for more representative styles of community rule. Consequently, leading thinkers of the time embraced the idea of republicanism, a type of government that relies on participation by community members and that gives citizens responsibilities related to the administration of public affairs. This form of elective government was applauded for its ability to empower citizens and liberate them from tyrannical rule. Members of a republic would not be subjected to taxation without representation, nor would they be treated as de facto children with kings or czars acting as all-knowing fathers making arbitrary decisions on the citizenry's behalf.

The ability to self-govern inherent in the republican perspective was particularly appealing to colonial revolutionaries in America during the mid-eighteenth century. Core tenets of republicanism formed the foundation for many arguments in the Declaration of Independence and for the representative democracy created first by the Articles of Confederation and later in the Constitution of the United States of America. The freedoms this form of government offers were innovative for the time, yet the application of republican ideals was initially quite limited. The biases and shortsightedness of revolutionaries led to a narrow interpretation of who constituted the citizenry and circumscribed the actual distribution of governmental authority during the early years of the United States. The right to vote or hold office was granted exclusively to males and in most cases only to white, male landowners or men of means. Colonial leaders excluded whole classes of individuals from direct governmental participation, including slaves, Native Americans, the poor, and assorted immigrant groups. Although early definitions of citizenship restricted access to power in a variety of ways, sex-based discrimination meant females of all races and classes were effectively prohibited from formal participation in government. Over time, perspectives did begin to shift, and so did ideas about citizenship for women.

This chapter examines the problems that arose from the initial disregard for women as citizens, the proffered rhetorical fix later dubbed the "republican motherhood" ideal, and the ways this notion still pervades contemporary portrayals of women as political actors. Specifically, the chapter considers the ways philosophical and praxis-based origins of women's expected roles in society helped justify women's initial exclusion from political activity; explains the emergence of the republican motherhood ideal and the progressive and regressive results of its prevalent application; delineates the enduring effects of the republican motherhood conceit, which include its use in feminist and antifeminist movements as well as how related rhetoric frames women as a special interest group rather than as independent citizens; and highlights how women have been depicted in modern presidential campaigns through the widespread use of politicized female caricatures and the portrayals of candidates' spouses. Every component of this chapter is important because each contributes to a comprehensive understanding of republican motherhood rhetoric, a concept that has covertly and overtly pervaded women's struggle to gain empowerment on many fronts and that continues to create barriers for female citizens as they battle for social and political equality.

Women's Early Exclusion from Politics

Thought leaders contemplating citizenship in developing republics were dismissive toward or held unfavorable views of women; hence, few credited them with the ability to participate as full and active citizens in a nation.[1] Those holding more sympathetic opinions about females also tended to depict them in restrictive ways that relied heavily on traditional sex roles. Even though their existence in the new republic afforded them some recognition as citizens from a social perspective, women were largely excluded from direct political decision-making, rendering them contingent citizens lacking direct access to governmental participation.[2] Customary approaches to family and social structures encouraged male leaders to ignore women's political needs and capacities and reinforced females' dependence on others. Although democratic principles were said to guide governmental practices, rarely did the initial beneficiaries of republican ideals extend opportunities for political involvement to others; females were particularly excluded. The philosophical and praxis-based constraints placed upon women explain many of the challenges they faced when seeking political empowerment.

Philosophical Perspectives

Plato's *Republic* far predates Enlightenment interests in republican government, yet the treatment of women in his hypothetical citizen-run polis is much more inclusive than that of seventeenth- and eighteenth-century philosophers.

By discussing women at all, Plato exceeds the consideration most of his later counterparts gave the putative fairer sex. In Book V specifically, Plato argues for basic equality between the sexes and claims that women should participate in the protection and development of the city-state in a manner identical to men.[3] Conceding that specific duties would likely require modification to account for differences in physical strength, Plato asserts that being female is not a disqualifying characteristic for citizenship.[4] Though he generalizes about the frailties of women and portrays females as paradoxically both equal to and lesser than males, Plato does build the case for women as individual contributors to the community and acknowledges that they have the ability to serve the polis in multiple ways. This progressive perspective was not very popular in Plato's day and seemed to fully disappear by the time Enlightenment thinkers began their own exploration of republicanism.

For most Enlightenment philosophers, women were inconsequential. Many tomes contemplating various forms of government simply ignored female citizens or dismissively equated them with children and people with mental or physical disabilities. For example, Robert Filmer's *Patriarchia; or the Natural Power of Kings,* published in 1680, avoids addressing historic female rulers and focuses on male dominance and power.[5] Theorists who did ruminate on women's roles in society often did so half-heartedly. In 1778 (Henry Home) Lord Kames wrote the 1,867-page *Sketches of the History of Man* and dedicated just 97 pages to women. Kames's short explication of the female sex argues that women did not need or want more influence than they had. In the book he writes that females lack the aptitude to make significant decisions and therefore should be prevented from participating in public deliberation.[6] Many of David Hume's writings from the mid-1700s and the anonymously published 1807 *Sketches of the History of the Fair Sex* extend this restrictive perception of women. In some cases, women's presumed inability to function outside the home was treated as a type of malady. Such a point of view allowed philosophers to frame men's control over women's lives as an act of pity and protection.[7] This sort of attention paid to females and the widespread belief that women were naturally unable to effectively wield power indicated a broadly dismissive attitude about women rather than an active malevolence toward them. However, other writers approached females in a more aggressive and openly hostile manner.

One of the clearest examples of an acrimonious attitude toward women comes from Jean-Jacques Rousseau in his mid-eighteenth-century writings. Throughout his work, he tends to belittle and degrade all females as feeble, untrustworthy, and incompetent. In *Emile,* the Frenchman depicts the ideal woman as a thoughtless servant toiling solely in support of a man (her father, husband, son, etc.). He maintains that most women do not meet his ideal and that they actually disrupt the proper development of men because females are frivolous by nature.[8] Their indulgent interests in fashion and gossip, he says, inevitably corrupt women and the men around them. Rousseau questions women's intellectual capacity and advises that females not be educated beyond the necessary skills for maintaining a household. He chastises learned women by calling them "masculine" and "unnatural," and he blames them for the destruction of the family.[9] Rousseau insists that parents should strictly control their daughters' social interactions in order to avoid distracting girls from their proper development as homemakers. These negative and repressive attitudes toward women are reinforced in his *Social Contract.* Rousseau's perspective provides the foundation for claims that educating women unravels the social fabric because it disrupts traditional family hierarchies.[10] Similarly negative opinions about women were propagated throughout the eighteenth and nineteenth centuries by other influential thinkers such as Edmund Burke.[11] Remnants of these arguments are still evident in twentieth- and twenty-first-century US politics.[12]

Not all philosophers examining citizenship and government were dismissive of or antagonistic toward women. Some made assertions in favor of women's importance and their ability to engage in decision-making. However, those who saw women as potentially effective political participants tended to temper their arguments or ground their perspectives in women's traditional roles.[13] John Locke, in his 1690 *Two Treatises of Government,* affirms that women have much to contribute to society, yet he considers women only as mothers and wives.[14] He applauds females' abilities to govern their children, but he does not discuss their existence as members of a larger government or their responsibilities as individual contributors to a nation.

The Baron de Montesquieu took a similar approach. In *The Spirit of the Laws,* printed in 1748, he calls for the education and enfranchisement of females by demonstrating that women's empowerment benefits their husbands and children.[15] Montesquieu states that females would, because of their giving nature, use their influence on behalf of families. He posits that if women were allowed to participate in government, their policy decisions would necessarily enhance the lives of men.[16] This perspective limits women's interests to domestic issues and devalues more broad-based political activity by females. It also maintains that women are other-oriented and dismisses the possibility for female citizens to self-advocate or show personal ambition outside the home.

Thomas Paine publicly championed more equitable treatment of women in society. In his 1775 article "An Occasional Letter on the Female Sex," Paine delineates numerous examples of how "Man, who has never neglected an opportunity of exerting his power . . . has always availed himself of [women's] weakness."[17] He details the struggles women face in myriad cultures and emphasizes their frequently constrained existence.[18] Yet even Paine, in rendering a sympathetic perspective on female suffering as a result of "law and custom," defends women's value by identifying their contributions to the state as "the sons and husbands they sacrifice" for the war effort.[19]

Many of the leading women thinkers of the era also presented socially restrictive pretexts for expanding women's public and political participation by focusing on women's place in the home. Catharine Macaulay offers a limited approach to female interests that mirrors that of Locke and Montesquieu when she argues for extending women's access to education based on the ways it would benefit the family.[20] Although permitting females to have access to regular schooling was a liberal proposition at the time, Macaulay's justification was grounded in the purportedly natural duties of women as nurturers. Relying on this customary perspective of women as primarily motivated by their traditional caregiver roles might have been a clever strategy intended to help make more progressive perspectives about women palatable to a wider audience. However, the persuasive assertions based on gender-stereotyped interests reinforced a narrow interpretation of women's potential as political participants.

Whereas many philosophers dismissed women as incapable of, unfit for, or uninterested in participating in politics, a few did make stronger cases for the education and development of women. Mary Wollstonecraft advocates for the treatment of women as full citizens in her 1792 publication, *A Vindication of the Rights of Women*.[21] She contends, "A woman's maternal duty was secondary to her primary moral and political responsibility to herself."[22] Wollstonecraft does succumb to the limits of the arguments of her day and considers masculine characteristics the superior ones all people should strive to develop; still, her claims concerning the problems associated with the perpetual subjugation of women over time and the need to combat the errors of history by developing more "masculine" women are compelling.[23] It is important to note that even though Wollstonecraft's overall position was extremely progressive, she also occasionally justified women's development as a way for them to be more effective mothers and wives.[24] Still, customary women's roles were not the only, or even the primary, rationale she used for expanding women's opportunities.

The Enlightenment inheritance of philosophical views on women's political participation in colonial American history mirrored social attitudes regarding females and reflected the practical limits placed upon women in their daily lives. As Montesquieu acknowledges, "Freedom or repression, equality or inequality in a state is a function not of its merely political organization, but of the structure of its personal and social life as a whole."[25] Practical and traditional applications of sex roles also hampered women's citizenship.

Praxis-Based Influences

Females during the colonial and postcolonial eras were generally considered in terms of their service roles to others. Not only did theorists like Locke and Montesquieu discuss women solely as mothers, wives, and daughters but the daily practices and interactions of the era also socialized men and women alike to regard females as domestically oriented and driven by the need to nurture others. A female owed her subsistence to a man tasked with providing for her until that responsibility was passed on to another man—usually from father to husband and possibly eventually to son. With women's social and economic identity largely dependent on their relationship to other people, leaders of the day often discounted the need to give women a political voice of their own and claimed that female interests were adequately addressed by males.[26] Women's political disenfranchisement within the republic was not just a product of theoretical arguments but also was deeply rooted in the customs and beliefs of the people of the time. Basic daily activities as dictated by religious teachings, restrictions placed on female education, and the legal status of women during the developmental days of the republic all stemmed from traditional assumptions regarding women's presumed proper role in society.

Although most perspectives on sex roles originate from the physical dominance of males in the human species, religious codification of appropriate roles institutionalized distinctions between male and female functions and substantiated beliefs about women's alleged inability to exercise leadership and control. For example, the Judeo-Christian origin myth contends that woman was derived from the rib of man's body. Females are described as a divine afterthought designed as helpmates and comforters of men. Thus, the theological justification for woman's very existence relegates females to a necessarily subservient nurturer role. In addition, biblical narratives center on how female errors in judgment, susceptibility to temptation, and ability to seduce men lead to their downfall. In the first book of the Bible, a woman eating fruit from the tree of knowledge results in humankind's expulsion from paradise.[27] Thus, many Christian denominations teach followers that women are inferior to men because of the circumstances of their creation; these faiths supply ample grounds for male dominance based on stories of detrimental female decision-making.

Scripture goes beyond implying woman's subordination to man based on narrative depictions. It also explicitly outlines a hierarchical relationship between the sexes. References to man being the head of the family offer a patriarchal perspective on leadership within the home. Passages such as "Wives submit yourselves to your own husbands, as unto to the Lord" and "The husband is the head of the wife, even as Christ is the head of the church" simultaneously establish a clear chain of command in the home and encourage believers to view male heads of households as infallible demigods.[28] Women are defined as servants of men in the same manner that the church serves Christ. The dominance of husbands is total, as the Bible makes evident in Ephesians 5:24 when it states, "Wives should submit to their husbands in everything."[29] The tenets of Christianity allow for indisputable and possibly tyrannical leadership in the home. Women are given some dominion over children through Old Testament commandments such as "Honor thy father and mother," but the overt placement of the father/husband as the ruler over his wife and children in the earlier passages robs women of any independent standing or empowerment.[30]

Religious interpretations of the proper role of men and women in society offered a pretext for excluding women from politics in the emergent republic and provided the foundation for arguments about the appropriate daily duties and life goals of women. During an era when economic production was largely agrarian, both men and women worked primarily at home, but there were clear sex-defined tasks.[31] Females helped as needed in the fields and tending the animals, but they were also responsible for keeping the house; cooking, cleaning, and rearing and caring for children were all part of the woman's domain.[32] Meanwhile, men conducted most of the major family business by negotiating prices for livestock and crops, purchasing or leasing land, determining the schedule for planting and harvesting, and hiring others to assist with the farm work when necessary.[33] Men were usually the public face of the family and were the decision makers of consequence. Women, although sometimes granted helpmate status, were often thought of as little more than companionable servants, and young females were raised with the expectation that their main goals in life were to become effective wives and mothers.[34]

In the early days of the republic, women's education was decidedly practical and designed to suit their anticipated future domestic roles. They learned about household management mostly by watching their mothers. Despite the fact that some middle- and upper-class women did learn to read or write, most females in the late 1700s could not even sign their names.[35] The idea of a literate woman was scandalous during that period because "domestic tradition condemned highly educated women as perverse threats to family stability."[36] The American Revolution sparked interest in education for females primarily because the increased public activity women engaged in during the war accentuated the need for both sexes to be prepared to conduct basic business practices during difficult times. In addition, the war created many widows and other women with no male family member on which to rely.[37] This social instability produced at least some awareness of the drawbacks of having one half of the population reliant on the other half. One of the most common arguments, however, for providing women at least some basic education (primarily in the form of increased literacy) was not grounded in their own protection and enhancement but in their ability to serve others. Sufficiently educated women made better companions for men and were better prepared to take charge of their children's education.[38]

In addition to the daily activities and education of women, the legal treatment of females during the development of the new republic also reflected a custom-based disempowerment of the female sex. The most blatant example of social disregard for women as individual actors was the concept of coverture, which referred to the legal loss of identity and property women suffered upon marriage.[39] Unless particular steps were taken to protect her premarital assets (e.g., entrusting them to a male relative), a woman's husband automatically became the de facto administrator of her possessions, be they money, real estate, or other valuables.[40] A husband had the right to oversee his wife's estate and to make legal transactions on her behalf and without her consent. The wife, because of coverture laws, had little recourse with respect to her husband's actions. Unless legally declared a feme sole, married women were not allowed to enter into contracts of their own or to manage their own financial lives.[41] Coverture was based on the assumption that women lacked the cognitive ability to make good decisions or comprehend contractual obligations. It also held that any married woman "could never be a fully independent 'free dealer' [because] she was always subject to some degree of covert manipulation and open intimidation" from her husband.[42] This legal barrier prevented many women from being able to sustain themselves. It also reinforced the archetypal notion of female helplessness by providing women few options beyond being reliant upon male protectors and providers.

The nascent American republic offered women few of the advantages bestowed upon members of a republican democracy. Because of philosophical biases and praxis-based restrictions, female members of society were actively excluded from the purportedly empowering new form of self-rule. For many women, the tyrannical leadership from which male members of society sought liberation was commonly recapitulated within the home; male heads of households were often as dictatorial as the kings and czars the democratic republic rebuked. With such oppressive religious foundations, philosophical support, and legal codification, women were discouraged from expressing personal ambition (outside of marrying well) and were socialized to expect little from life beyond the domestic realm. As time passed, though, views about women evolved, and so did their status as citizens. Progress was slow and difficult, but the American Revolution urged a reevaluation of women's perceived abilities, needs, and contributions to the state.

Women in Postrevolutionary America

During the American Revolution, as men went to war, women actively participated in public roles customarily closed to them. Mothers, wives, and daughters had to run farms and businesses while fathers, husbands, and sons were away. Women negotiated crop prices; hired, fired, and oversaw workers; and made decisions and commitments essential to the life and livelihood of the family.[43] Females proved their ability and willingness to engage in the community in ways previously outside their province. This led to a partial reevaluation of women's standing in society. As the new nation took shape, variations in the treatment of women from philosophical, educational, and legal perspectives emerged. Some interpretations broadened opportunities for women, whereas others solidified traditional, restrictive gender roles.

In the decades following the colonial fight for independence, a growing set of philosophers and thought leaders became more complimentary and progressive in their assessments of females. In 1843, Margaret Fuller published *Woman in the Nineteenth Century*. In it, she challenges the belief that man is the head of his wife, arguing, "God has given her a mind of her own."[44] Fuller also identifies a fundamental change occurring in society at that time. She claims, "Many women are considering within themselves, what they need that they have not, and what they can have, if they find they need it. Many men are considering whether women are capable of being and having more than they are and have, *and,* whether, if so, it will be best to consent to improvements in their condition."[45] This emerging interest in the wants, needs, and faculties of female members of society began to spur a reexamination of attitudes about women.

In his 1869 book *On the Subjection of Women*, an extended exploration of the socialized oppression of members of the female sex, John Stuart Mill argues that there is nothing to gain and much to lose for any society when half its citizens are ignored and their skills are stunted. He outlines the maltreatment of women and explains how the social and legal restrictions placed on females were at least partially, if not fully, responsible for shaping women into the seemingly feeble and dependent creatures they were criticized for being.[46] Mill critiques the hypocrisy of actively suppressing women's development, then pointing to their underdeveloped minds and bodies to rationalize denying them access to education and power. He explains, "No other class of dependents have had their character so entirely distorted from its natural proportions by their relation with their masters" as women have by their subjugation to men.[47] Mill's explication is detailed and multifaceted, including discussions of women's capacity to excel in many roles both in and out of the home. Unlike Locke's earlier arguments, Mill's do not tie women's political or public identity to their relational status, making his position highly progressive, even radical, compared with those of the theorists who preceded him. Even though Mill's assertions represent a shift in perspectives toward women, his was a minority viewpoint.

One area of women's lives that did show measurable change during the postrevolutionary era was access to education. With a new nation depending on an active and informed citizenry, the need to educate individuals became increasingly important. Both males and females benefited from this development, although not in equal measure and certainly not across all economic or racial categories.[48] Despite a boom in the construction of academies for women following the Revolution,[49] the curriculum for young women's education was limited because "the cultural world that women inhabited was practical, technical, and vernacular."[50] Whereas male education was intended to broaden knowledge and expand opportunities in the newly freed nation, most formal female schooling was geared toward improving girls' ability to someday function as mothers and wives;[51] hence, the curriculum tended to pay particular attention to interpersonal roles.[52] Benjamin Rush, a proponent of female education, asserted that women, as mothers, needed targeted formal education because they were the first teachers of children and could "train young patriots" if they "focused on the great subjects of liberty and government."[53] He also prescribed a course of study that included "English, writing and bookkeeping — [subjects] relevant to a woman helping her husband succeed."[54] Because women's domesticity was considered their vocation, female education was tailored toward preparing them for that role.[55] Teaching females to read, write, do basic math, and explore other subjects in a formal academic setting did mark an important modification in the scholastic opportunities available to women. However, the limitations placed on the topics females studied indicate that the social belief that "a learned woman was an unenviable anomaly"[56] still lingered long after the war ended. Many of the "anomalous" women who expanded their own knowledge beyond the stipulated restraints of the time subsequently helped push for further changes in the treatment of women and the opportunities open to them.[57]

In addition to granting women access to formal schooling, the widening acceptance of institutional instruction for both males and females helped women enter the workforce in a very specific way following the Revolutionary War. As educational systems developed, more teachers were needed, and educated women began to enter this field. Teaching was an acceptable profession for young, unmarried women because it allowed them to exercise their purportedly nurturing nature and prepared them to be experienced instructors for their presumed future children.[58] Teaching offered many women an initial entry point into employment outside the home, and as the nation became industrialized, young single women also sought work in factories and as office clerks.[59] The "canon of domesticity," however, set the expectation that these women would quit their jobs after they married and would then shift their attention toward childrearing and other duties focused on the home.[60]

The legal status of women was also modified following the Revolutionary War. Divorce and abandonment laws were eased, and restrictions against women who engaged in contractual agreements were reduced. With husbands missing in the war, many women were left in a type of legal limbo; they were unable to establish feme sole status because they were technically still married and thus prohibited from participating in business transactions on their own behalf. Without the permission to act as one's own legal agent feme sole standing supplied, the principle of coverture meant married but abandoned women, or women whose husbands were incarcerated as war prisoners or traitors, could not control their own property or the resources left to them.[61] Although many women benefited from coverture during the war (perceived as unable to hold political opinions of their own, they could not be charged with treason or treated as traitors), they did pay a steep price for their husbands' political activities when left legally unable to sustain themselves in their spouses' absence.[62] The problems associated with managing the impact of the war urged lawmakers to adjust particular rules related to obtaining a divorce and, in turn, earning the right to enter into legal contracts. Shortly after the war, many individual states began making marital dissolution easier, and records show that many women, and a few men, availed themselves of the opportunity to be released from burdensome relationships.[63]

Aside from shifts in laws regarding family structures, because women were socially understood as extensions or property of others rather than empowered individual citizens in their own right, as a class they suffered what some call "constitutional neglect" throughout the first century of the nation's existence.[64] Women had to contend with "legal fictions" (the social presumptions held by attorneys and judges) about females during any court proceedings.[65] These fictions relied on common stereotypes of females that viewed women as biologically inferior to men, morally pure and so in need of protection by a paternalistic court, and unable to deal freely because of the influence of a husband.[66] The third fiction, based on coverture, illustrates the long-standing habit of understanding women through their relationship to others rather than treating them as individual agents. These beliefs about females made it difficult for women to improve their legal standing for many decades.

The Revolutionary War provided the impetus for many social and political changes in the nation. The members of the burgeoning republic began to exercise newly won freedoms and negotiate the extension of rights and responsibilities to those considered citizens. As the country developed, larger questions regarding the definition of "citizen" had to be addressed. For example, governmental leaders explicitly argued about how to count slaves for the national census. In addition, a broader social debate was also occurring regarding the citizen status of the large number of the nation's occupants excluded because of their sex. As philosophical, educational, and legal attitudes toward women evolved, small windows of public participation began to open. Yet many of the old social perceptions of women created expectations that they retain their domestic focus. The eventual conceptualization of the ideal political role for women, an idea later deemed "republican motherhood," helped solidify particular social beliefs about females as political actors.

The Republican Mother as Ideal Female Citizen

The impact of women's participation in the public sphere during the Revolutionary War highlighted some hypocrisies between the principles espoused by the leaders of the new nation and the actual application of those ideals. Because females proved their ability to fulfill roles previously closed to them based on preconceptions about intellectual and physical inferiority, the postwar denial of women as full, empowered citizens underscored the "disparities between the men's assertion of 'rights' and 'equality' . . . and the dispossessed status of women."[67] Many American women felt they had earned the right to more concrete consideration as citizens, yet although for them the war "had been a strongly politicizing experience . . . the newly created republic made little room for them as political beings."[68] In fact, some leaders viewed politically incorporating women into the developing nation as detrimental to the growth of the country;[69] they believed men would take on new roles and challenges more willingly if women's duties and responsibilities remained predictably the same.[70] The desire to acknowledge women's wartime efforts in a manner that "sought no fundamental change in gender roles, but merely a rhetorical resolution" led to the emergence of the republican motherhood ideal as a frame for interpreting women's domesticity as political participation.[71]

The notion of republican motherhood as applied in the formative years of the nation was built on an interpretation of the "Spartan mother" from ancient Greece. For women in Sparta, political involvement in the city-state revolved around raising strong, patriotic sons who would directly contribute as members of the polis and daughters who would eventually produce new generations of loyal and competent male citizens.[72] Political accomplishments for women were earned vicariously through the valor and achievements of their husbands and sons.[73] For women in the nascent nation, many of whom had sacrificed their husbands and sons for its creation, this type of ideal had widespread appeal. It gave greater meaning to the losses they suffered, and it amplified their own contributions to a war that had largely been fought by men. It also required little or no adjustment regarding practical expectations of women.[74] Amplifying the political aspects of familiar duties provided some social stability in uncertain times. The politicization of women's roles in the emerging nation simply reframed women's actions at first; it did not initially expand or alter their long-established social position.[75]

Most definitions of republican motherhood emphasized women's labor on behalf of others as their primary and preferred means of participating in the country's development. One of the most important services women could render to the nation was to "raise the future generations of male citizens and . . . support their husbands in the sacrifices they made for the government."[76] The ideal female "was an educated woman . . . [who] placed her learning at her family's service."[77] As the "first and most important guardians and instructors of the rising generation," good republican mothers "would assure to the state the reproduction of virtuous citizens."[78] This meant that one of a patriotic woman's central tasks was to instill morality in her children and enforce it in her husband.[79] The same was true of civic virtue.[80] In this way, motherhood became "almost . . . a fourth branch of government, a device that ensured social control in the gentlest possible way."[81] Republican motherhood elevated the status of common female roles in a manner that made it appealing for women to embrace the canon of domesticity.[82] To be a patriotic woman was to be a good wife and an effective mother.

The fact that the republican motherhood ideal embraced the often-overlooked domestic work women performed and gave it national importance created paradoxical effects for women as political actors. The celebration of the wife and mother roles filled by most female citizens was encouraging to many women because it openly acknowledged their value. Because domesticity was such a fundamental component of most women's lives, this recognition seemed a positive step in women's evolution as political agents.[83] Even if not as empowering as enfranchisement (denied women for more than a century), republican motherhood rhetoric signaled an appreciation for women's private endeavors and eventually supplied grounds for expanding female participation in public discussions and political decision-making.

Although some positives emerged from the rhetorical embrace of this conceptualization of the ideal female patriot, there were also many enduring negatives. For example, the idea conflated the terms "woman," "wife," and "mother" and reified the already common social assumption that the highest calling for any female was to become a wife and a mother. This tendency to define women based on their relationships with others rather than as autonomous individuals (as men have generally been viewed) offered a narrow interpretation of women's interests and discouraged females from displaying self-interest and personal ambition—characteristics acceptable and often applauded in males.[84] Because of the manifold implications of republican motherhood, the concept has been simultaneously praised as a "feminist response to patriarchal politics"[85] and condemned as "a theoretical trap for women as citizens."[86]

Progressive Outcomes

The positive reading of republican motherhood draws attention to the significance of acknowledging women's societal contributions and demonstrates the ways in which the interpretive frame helped expand opportunities for women. Although the widespread postrevolutionary-era perspective held that men, as protectors of and providers for women, were the rightful political decision makers on their behalf, the rhetorical recognition of the importance of female contributions to the nation meant that political conversations did occasionally address issues of specific importance to women and encourage various discussions about their needs. It also meant that women were no longer politically invisible.

Making motherhood the focal point of the ideal female endowed this previously marginalized role with importance and underscored the value of those engaging in maternal activities. Instead of simply complying with a natural, biological imperative, engaging in domestic nurturing was considered politically and socially consequential. Many magazines and newspapers of the day bestowed high praise upon mothers, arguing, "The nation could not do without their service."[87] This complimentary attitude toward women's traditional obligations conferred status upon this dispossessed group. It also encouraged women to embrace their customary work and to interpret their domestic labor as a means of making significant political contributions.

Because the republican motherhood ideal made women duty-bound to protect and cultivate the home, it also provided the grounds for more progressive arguments about women's appropriate concerns and actions outside of the home. Women used the ideals of republican motherhood to press for their own advancement as a means of better fulfilling their expected feminine roles. Society generally accepted that a good republican mother needed to be educated for the sake of her husband and children, so many activists used this claim to press for more and better schooling for girls. Additionally, women argued that topics like child labor, health care, and sanitation directly affected domestic life and that their roles as mothers not only justified but required them to speak out and become involved in public policy debates. Many women asserted that their experience as mothers gave them credibility regarding domestic subjects and that denying them a political voice prevented women from effectively fulfilling their patriotic duties as understood through the republican mother frame.

Extensions of republican motherhood also underpinned many efforts in support of female enfranchisement. Advocates asserted that the right to vote was fundamental to women's ability to fulfill their domestic roles. Further relying on the tenets of republican motherhood, women also alleged that they would bring morality and civility to the political realm just as they did to the home.[88] Thus, the maternal interpretation of an idealized female patriot presented women a platform from which to enter public discussions. However, these positive uses of republican motherhood rhetoric do not mean that the concept was entirely, or even primarily, empowering for women.

Repressive Impacts

Commonplace descriptions of the ideal republican woman reveal a more repressive than progressive perspective on female citizenship. The republican mother concept painted a picture of the consummate female patriot as self-sacrificing, deferential, and defined by her relationships with others. These attributes appeared to complement women's traditional nurturing roles while accentuating the feminine qualities that tended to reinforce women's subordinate status. This approach opened a few avenues by which some women entered the public sphere, but it also limited the ways in which females could engage in political dialogue by circumscribing the acceptable interests and motivations for women as civic actors. By making maternal status the only grounds for women's political interests, republican motherhood offered a "comfortably ordered perspective, but . . . also erase[d] richness and complexity" from women's political life.[89]

In addition to prescribing limits to women's political interests by underscoring the importance of their maternal roles, the conceptualization of the ideal republican woman actively discouraged direct female participation in politics. Such social norms dissuaded females from seeking public influence too vigorously. "Political" women were depicted in popular culture and news reports as unattractive and unlikely to win a husband.[90] Rousseau's sallies against masculine women were often quoted to denounce female activists.[91] Additionally, many people argued that women did not need direct political participation because their personal relationships already gave them the opportunity to influence political thought and action; opinion leaders insisted that women could privately share their points of view on topics in a subtle feminine manner and effectually hold sway over the actions of male relations and friends.[92] Male and female philosophers alike claimed increased activity in the public sphere would come at the expense of women losing the "special type of influence" they had over men.[93]

Because women were expected to remain domestically centered, the ideal republican mother was necessarily deferential when it came to civic issues. Although she had some influence at home, "the republican mother did not demand rights for herself . . . she lived her political life by identifying with the interests of her husband and participated in the civic community through the exploits of her sons."[94] Such a perspective encouraged women to be politically quiescent and to hope that men, because "each has his wife, sister, or female friends, . . . [were] too much biased by these relations to fail of representing their interests."[95] Women who attempted to meet the obligations of the ideal female patriot accentuated their other-centric nature and muted their own political and public ambitions. They sacrificed their own physical and intellectual development and suppressed their own public interests in order to support the active citizenship of their husbands and sons. A good republican mother taught her daughters to do the same.

One of the most oppressive aspects of republican motherhood is that its emphasis on women's domesticity creates a conception of female citizenship based exclusively on women's relationships with others. Such interpretations of women forced female citizens to be understood not as individuals with their own interests, abilities, and rights but as homogenous and reliant on others for their functional motivation and political existence. Some scholars assert that the drive to understand women based on their relationships was grounded in the need to discern the sexual availability of females.[96] Identifying married women made it easier for men seeking mates to determine whether to pursue a particular female, gave husbands legal sexual dominion over their spouses, and created a social hierarchy among women.[97] Others contend that the historical contexts that have dominated women's lives made their personal connections to others (particularly through marriage) a primary means of political and economic survival, thus encouraging women to understand themselves through their familial associations.[98] In either case, the persistent tendency to conceive of women based primarily on their interpersonal relationships was a political hurdle their male counterparts did not face. Defining women based on their connections to others invited women and men alike to perceive females as dependent rather than independent persons and made it easy to discount their political efforts and marginalize their political voices.

Because republican motherhood was a rhetorical strategy used to allay charges of hypocrisy, not a legislative effort to concretely establish rights and duties of citizenship for women, the idea was open to multiple interpretations and applications. As a result, the conceptualization of the ideal female patriot had both positive and negative consequences for women as political participants during the early years of the American republic. Its influence and use, however, were not limited to the development of the nascent nation. Many elements of this rhetorical trope continue to pervade discussions of women's political rights and responsibilities today.

Enduring Effects

As women have struggled to establish themselves as full, participatory citizens in the United States, the idea of republican motherhood has been a mainstay both in efforts to expand rights and in attempts to stifle progress toward that goal. As explained above, women used elements of the idealized female patriot to press for entry into public conversation and to fight for the right to vote. Yet, even though the concept offered grounds for supporting women's political action, it also provided an attenuated footing for female participation. Because the rhetoric of republican motherhood defines women based on their reproductive abilities and their relational connection to others, it is a myopic view of females that pigeonholes women into maternal roles; it ignores those who do not or cannot subscribe to traditional gender expectations or else it treats them as unnatural and incomplete.

Modern women have technically earned equal status with men based on the established rights and responsibilities assigned full citizens of the nation (i.e., voting, paying taxes, etc.), yet components of republican motherhood continue to serve as a foundation for interpreting women's contributions and for assessing their abilities and interests. The enduring impact of this conceptualization of the ideal female patriot is evident in various feminist efforts, in antifeminist arguments, and in the consideration of women as a so-called special interest group in political dialogue.

Feminist Viewpoints. Women seeking equal rights and full citizenship have had a mixed relationship with the idea of republican motherhood. The concept brought attention to the important work women had been doing in the home for centuries. This encouraged women to regard their contributions as valuable and to see themselves as capable individuals within the context of the home. The confidence that came from the enhanced social status and increased education young women received because of assertions supported by republican motherhood helped create pockets of empowered women who began pressing for more rights and equal treatment for women. Although feminism itself began before republican motherhood became a widespread rhetorical category, the ideas related to female patriotism did expand opportunities for American women to become educated and to perceive themselves as more than just companionable servants to husbands or caretakers of children.

Feminism in the United States does not follow one distinct path. There are myriad branches with different focal points and a variety of alternate perspectives. Some feminist approaches reject the idea of republican motherhood as restrictive and isolating, arguing that the concept encourages an interpretation of "women . . . as bodies not minds, wombs not brains."[99] Other approaches acknowledge the historical importance of the frame but see the "cult of domesticity" as too narrow to afford women true independence or equality.[100] Domestic feminism promotes a decidedly laudatory take on republican motherhood, accepting many of the tenets of the idealized female patriot as a positive step for women.

Domestic feminism, sometimes also referred to as social feminism, traces its roots to the work of activists such as Catharine Beecher, Harriet Beecher Stowe, and Jane Addams, women who supported advancing women's education and political activity based both on the intellectual development of women for their own enrichment and the improvement of their ability to be effective homemakers.[101] Beecher and others pushed for education for females that would "render them the intellectual equals of their husbands, better mothers for their children, and experts in nutrition and hygiene."[102] Such a perspective amplified the ideals of republican motherhood by emphasizing a form of female advancement that accentuated the benefits men, children, and the nation gleaned from enhancing women's stature. This type of argument was extremely appealing "to a nation in which the institution of the family was considered crucial to social stability."[103] The domestic feminist approach embraced the positive aspects of republican motherhood and was considered innovative because it advocated marriage based on intellectual equality.[104] It also offered a first step toward domestic unions in which homemaking tasks were shared rather than divided along traditional gender lines.[105]

Domestic feminists did not stop at pushing for educational opportunities for women. They also insisted that domestic duties were vital to society and the nation and therefore should be treated as a vocation, or even as a verified profession. This led to the creation of "domestic science" courses in which students, primarily women, studied science-based hygiene protocols for the home, learned about balanced nutrition through cooking courses, and examined new processes in childrearing.[106] More strident feminist efforts suggested dramatic adjustments to family and neighborhood configurations in an effort to create more opportunities for women to seek development in and out of the home. These efforts included communal approaches to housework and childrearing.[107] Although the more extreme programs alleviated stress for some women, they still left the bulk of activities customarily considered feminine to females. Opposed to such radical changes, the domestic feminists functioned within the commonly accepted realm of republican motherhood and worked to create modifications within the existing system without upsetting the established social order. They were rewarded with an extensive national home economics curriculum, much of which still exists in various forms more than a century and a half later.[108]

The domestic science movement promulgated by this particular vein of feminists had paradoxical effects. On the one hand, it further legitimized the view of traditionally designated woman's work as difficult, worthy of respect, and a meaningful contribution to the nation. Creating training programs for women that fell distinctly within the domestic sphere did help demonstrate women's ability to take instruction, a capacity that could be put to use outside of the home as well. However, the movement also furnished ammunition for those opposed to opening new opportunities to women by illustrating that "the job of running a home was so all-encompassing that it could be mastered only over a lifetime and then with difficulty."[109] Such a claim allowed antifeminists to assert that women needed to concentrate squarely and solely on the home.

Antifeminist Arguments. Many traditionalists and antifeminists throughout the nineteenth, twentieth, and even early twenty-first centuries have relied upon the idealized version of the female patriot as the republican mother to support their perspectives. Pointing to purportedly negative impacts of feminism on domestic tranquility, social stability, and the health and well-being of children, people opposed to more expansive approaches to women's rights tend to blame progressive attitudes toward women and efforts to expand female opportunities as the primary sources of most contemporary social problems. Often based on nostalgic visions of a selectively remembered past, traditionalist arguments offer the idealized republican motherhood frame as a panacea for perceived national struggles.

Opponents to women's suffrage claimed they were protecting female purity and morality by keeping women out of usually raucous polling places.[110] Additional stances against extending the vote to women included assertions that a woman's attention should not be diverted from the home, that females' domestic service to the nation was more important than voting, and that women would lose their special influence over men if given enfranchisement. This last argument was sometimes articulated a bit differently, with critics complaining that because of the considerable influence women have in the home, giving females the vote would mean women would unfairly have double the political influence that men had.[111]

Although female enfranchisement was established via the nineteenth amendment in 1920, many attempts to mute women's contemporary political power still rely on interpretations of the republican mother as the ideal female citizen. Antifeminists often contend that marriage should remain women's central goal in life. They also allege that modern attempts at female empowerment lead to disappointing sexual relations and make marriage "elusive" for most women because many men do not want to marry professionally accomplished women.[112] Traditionalists blame working women, particularly mothers employed outside the home, for the disintegrating social fabric.[113] Some say that by ignoring their maternal obligations, women neglect to instill a proper sense of morality and civic duty in their children, thus creating generations of delinquents.[114] Others argue that when educated women forego motherhood altogether they deprive the nation of new generations of patriots and consumers, thereby harming the development of the country.[115] Females failing to live up to the ideals of republican motherhood are deemed selfish rather than self-sacrificing, assertive rather than deferential, and disconnected rather than relationally focused.

Other stands against women's civic equality emphasize familial happiness. Antifeminists have complained for decades that women's efforts toward social parity result in greater female dissatisfaction, which, in turn, prevents them from maintaining serenity in the home.[116] Because true republican women are tasked with making the home "a redemptive counterpart to the world,"[117] or a place where husbands can relax and escape the concerns of public life,[118] a traditionalist approach encourages women to minimize domestic discord. As a means of chastising progressive women, some antifeminists still reference Rousseau's warnings that educated, publicly active women are the primary reason for most of society's ills.[119]

In the latter part of the twentieth century, opposition to the Equal Rights Amendment (ERA) exploited traditional views of ostensibly proper women as self-sacrificing, deferential, and defined by their relationships with others to encourage defeat of the controversial bill. ERA opponents claimed that its passage would prevent women from being able to leave the workforce to care for their children;[120] that equality meant breaking up families because women would be drafted into military duty;[121] that women would have access to abortions,[122] thereby violating the core defining characteristic of republican motherhood (namely to become a mother); and, again, that women would lose their special influence over men if granted constitutionally protected citizenship equal to that of men. Although most research indicates that the defeat of the ERA was largely a result of voters motivated by perceived economic self-interest, the rhetoric of republican motherhood certainly colored the arguments of ERA opponents.[123]

The concept of the idealized female patriot as mother has formed the foundation of many political stances, some that have benefited women's political empowerment and some that have suppressed it. One of the most enduring impacts of the rhetoric of republican motherhood is the treatment of female members of society as a single, homogenous political body.

Women as a Special Interest Group. Because women were initially conceived of as apolitical beings understood solely in relation to the men or children in their lives and not as individual autonomous citizens the way males were, when females experienced a political awakening they did so as part of a preconceived "sisterhood" defined primarily by their relationships with other women.[124] There was, and still is, a presumption that all members of this class had strikingly similar experiences.[125] With males (particularly white males of means) serving as the default standard for what constitutes a citizen, all others seeking access to the rights and privileges associated with civic participation became classified as special subsets of people with particular shared interests. Sometimes the concerns of these factions coincided with those of the original class of male citizens, and other times they collided. Although women made up a basically equal share of the population as men, their longtime subordinate status as contingent rather than participatory citizens led to their being granted a "separate and dependent citizenship"; women rhetorically and politically became part of a special interest group rather than discrete individual citizens with varied interests.[126] This sense of category-based female citizenship is apparent in the ways women are considered in political discourse.

Much of the dialogue regarding women's political interests and motivations still relies upon the republican motherhood ideal. The fact that women's issues are a rather restricted set of topics that still concentrate on domesticity illustrates part of the problem that arises from a special interest group status that is tied to sexuality and fertility.[127] For example, discussions of women's health usually revolve around reproductive rights even though more women die annually of heart disease than of any other cause.[128] Heart health, respiratory diseases, diabetes, and strokes are major health problems for women, yet they make up a very small part of the political conversation about women's health care.[129] Because heart attacks, strokes, and to a lesser extent diabetes were long ago framed as "men's diseases," a large amount of federal funding has gone into research regarding their effects on men, but similar research on women lags far behind.[130] For men, displays of virility help portray a sense of power, but political stature is not tied to the number of offspring a man produces or the manner in which his children are raised. Additionally, legislation regarding male reproduction is rarely if ever a concern in national politics. The treatment of women as mothers, in essence and in function, emphasizes their procreative capacities at the cost of their individual personhood.[131]

Although breast and ovarian cancers do receive national attention and federal research funding, the vast majority of governmental focus on women's health is directed toward reproductive issues and features debates over access to birth control and abortions. Discussions of these subjects often include claims that frame each method of reproductive control as a means of allowing women decision-making power over the creation of new citizens and question whether women should possess this power.[132] Many arguments opposing the legalization of abortion and proposing limitations on access to birth control originate in religious beliefs; they prioritize the rights of the fetus and assert that the legal interests of unborn potential patriots (half of whom are male) are more important than those of the actual living citizens (all of whom are female) who bear them.[133] Women who opt to exercise control over their own bodies and to affect their perceived contributions to the nation by limiting their offspring are depicted as unpatriotic and unnatural.[134] Legislation intended to impede women's individual reproductive choices is just one way that classifying women together in one homogenous, role-based special interest group allows for the development of "policies that regard women's role as mothers as central to their societal contribution[, thus] fundamentally link[ing] full citizenship with motherhood."[135]

Women's treatment as a special class of citizens is also evident in other types of legislation and political sparring. In the early twenty-first century, many state-level legislative efforts were specifically intended to harm women and restrict women's rights as citizens.[136] The laws in question dealt with restricting abortion, limiting the availability of various forms of contraception, and defunding Planned Parenthood (an organization that offers reproductive counseling and health care).[137] These legislative proposals all consider women's rights primarily based on females' potential procreative capabilities. Liberal groups claimed conservative factions were waging a "War on Women."[138] The slogan provided a shorthand way of referencing efforts to create legal barriers for women seeking autonomy, justice, and equal access. Additional political conversations regarding the war on women concentrated on cases of sexual assault and other violence against women.[139] In arguments reminiscent of the republican motherhood ideal that made women responsible for the morality of men, legislators cautioned against aggressive punishments for sexual assault in the military by claiming male perpetrators were influenced by a "hormone level created by nature"[140] and female victims failed to discourage the attacks.[141]

Gender-based wage discrimination was one area of the war on women that did not rely heavily on the republican motherhood ideal for its foundational arguments.[142] Instead, legislative efforts to decrease protections against pay discrimination concentrated on the economic impact of women in the workforce and dealt with questions regarding the relative value of work done by females. Many of the disagreements surrounding equal pay emphasized issues connected to the historical devaluation of a particular career after women entered it en masse.[143] However, a few groups who supported decreasing wage protections did point to women's occasionally erratic employment as a result of motherhood choices as the reason for sex-based pay differentials.[144]

Treating women as a special interest group defined primarily in terms of socially prescribed maternal duties rhetorically homogenizes politically diverse individuals and invites infighting among members of this category. Because not all women embrace motherhood as their defining characteristic or life purpose, this restrictive vision of female citizens creates tensions among women. Those who fulfill the functions of a mother in a traditional sense often receive the most political support and face the least direct criticism.[145] However, they frequently perceive themselves as devalued in comparison to working mothers and career women who have no children.[146] Women who have children and work outside the home often complain about the public stigma and political shaming that blames them for any number of problems plaguing society.[147] Women who choose not to have children frequently explain that they are depicted as selfish, incomplete, and somehow fundamentally flawed.[148] Women who cannot give birth biologically and decide not to adopt face social and emotional hurdles as well. Interpretations of female citizenship as contingent upon relational and reproductive status cast women in a narrow, unsatisfactory frame.

Although the shared consciousness of women as defined by their sex did help establish the need to espouse women's rights and to address issues of particular concern to female citizens, the treatment of women as actual or potential mothers continually reifies sex-based distinctions in citizenship.[149] As long as women are viewed, and view themselves, as a special interest group, a difference will exist where "men are rational, rights-bearing citizens while women's citizenship [is] 'relational, role-oriented, and difference-based.'"[150] The continued belief that all women are, or wish to be, mothers, and that motherhood is the primary base of experience for female citizens, hampers the political growth of women, robs them of their ability to show ambition and self-interest, and silences women who do not meet the purportedly natural criterion of women as self-sacrificing nurturers.

Modern Presidential Campaigns and the Status of Women

The republican mother ideal has always been a rhetorical construct meant to acknowledge the contributions women make through their traditional roles within the home. Although it was originally intended as a means of addressing the philosophical disconnect between the inclusive claims of a developing representative government and the actual disenfranchisement of half of the new American nation's population, the flexibility of this rhetorical tool resulted in its being used in a multitude of progressive and regressive ways. Even though many changes have occurred regarding women's access to both legitimate and informal political power, the republican motherhood ideal still influences interpretations of women as political and social contributors in subtle as well as overt ways.

Conversations about the status of female citizens are ongoing and can rise to the forefront of public consciousness at any time, yet in the contemporary United States, every four years consideration of the status of women reaches a climax as politicians, pundits, and political scholars (in fields such as history, gender studies, political science, and communication) emphasize the possible impact women might have on the US presidential election. Direct appeals to potential female voters often pervade the rhetoric of particular campaigns. Many contemporary portrayals of women as political agents by the press, politicians, and various women in the public sphere rely heavily on allusions to different facets of republican motherhood, sometimes to the benefit and other times to the detriment of women as a whole. Modern presidential elections thus provide particularly telling representations of females as political actors.

Major Female Tropes

The female voting bloc has been characterized in ways that usually highlight traditional roles for women and underscore how women do or do not fit customary expectations. In the 1980s, conservatives chided the unacceptable behaviors of putative "welfare queens."[151] Claimed to be an entire class of women who bore children not out of patriotic duty but out of a selfish desire to earn more government aid, these women were usually presented as single women of color with no education.[152] The rhetoric surrounding these females derided them as unfit mothers and unworthy citizens living off the taxes paid by "honest, hardworking Americans."[153] They were portrayed as undesirable women because they did not fit the model of republican motherhood; they were said to be self-absorbed and unable to teach their offspring the moral and civic principles necessary to be productive citizens.[154]

Rhetorical depictions of women in the late 1980s and early 1990s took a more positive turn, yet still embraced republican motherhood standards. Conservative messaging during the 1988 campaign concentrated on the idea of "family values" as a means of proactively supporting traditional sex-based roles. By the 1992 contest, campaigners from both parties tried to expand the idea of family to include multiple types of nontraditional structures including single parents, grandparents raising grandchildren, adoptive families, and other domestic arrangements. However, amid this effort to understand alternate roles within a family, a spotlight remained on the importance of a maternal force as a nurturing presence.

The 1996 presidential race witnessed the rise of "soccer moms" as a shorthand characterization of women voters. The term reflected a view of women as middle-class suburban housewives whose primary point of self-identification was maternally based.[155] Adopting attributes of domestic or social feminism, these women tended to wield political power in a manner directly related to issues that affected the home.[156] The antithesis of the much maligned "welfare queens," "soccer moms" were viewed favorably because they were seen as self-sacrificing females defined and motivated by their relationships with others, especially their kids. During the 2008 campaign, the "hockey mom" emerged as a variation on the soccer mom designation with an implied increase in women's tenacity and toughness, particularly regarding their protection of their children.[157] These modern representations of women appear powerful and positive, yet they are troubling because they encourage interpretations of females as a homogenous group and continue to conflate the terms "woman" and "mother." Each of these tropes restricts female citizens to relational roles and limits their ability to fully participate in public life as autonomous individuals.

Presidential Nominees' Spouses

As explained in the introduction, the mates of presidential candidates have played an active role in US politics for almost as long as there have been national campaigns for the presidency. Many of the expectations placed upon presidential spouses have been and continue to be built around traditional roles women have filled. The socially prescribed behaviors for these consorts tend to reify the ideal of republican motherhood. Although some presidents' mates have certainly challenged and expanded perceptions of women because of their actions as first ladies, the wives of presidents and presidential contenders tend to underscore characteristics usually described as feminine and emphasize their own conventional experiences as wives and mothers in order to highlight their husbands' masculine qualities.[158] During campaigns, the wife of a presidential nominee becomes "another piece of evidence, testifying to his fitness for office" and must consider the ways her messaging and self-presentation impact perceptions of her husband.[159] Nominees' partners are used to help solidify support from particular constituents by depicting themselves in a manner the campaign believes voters will embrace. By virtue of their public actions, all first ladies to some extent "shape expectations of what women can properly do,"[160] making the first ladyship a site for the "symbolic negotiation of female identity."[161] The unofficial battle between spouses vying for the role of presidential helpmate also contributes to interpretations of American womanhood.

The actions of and criticisms about first ladies and candidates' spouses prompt a great deal of debate regarding proper female roles in society and particularly regarding women as political agents. Most scholars agree that political wives tend to have their own political and social identities subsumed by those of their mates[162] and that the women who have taken up the first lady mantle have generally had their own substantive knowledge and professional qualifications discounted largely because of their husband's political standing.[163] The same holds true for nominees' mates. Such treatment of women married to presidential contenders relies heavily on the republican motherhood ideal that women be deferential characters with little interest in political issues that have no overt connection to the home and family. However, the diminishment of their credibility as autonomous individuals does not render presidential helpmates powerless. Instead, many have found ways to use their ability to gain the public's regard to advocate for particular issues and causes. Because their power is primarily rhetorically derived, some scholars refer to the communication-based influence these women wield as the "first lady pulpit."[164] Although early first ladies were viewed primarily as the "national hostess," several subsequent first ladies have used their connection to the president and the attention they garner from the press to increase their political activity.[165]

Through speeches, public forums, and other carefully planned events, many modern first ladies have advocated for key political and social movements. They have promoted equality by supporting civil and women's rights movements, argued for improving physical and mental health access, developed anti-drug-abuse campaigns, increased highway beautification efforts, and made several attempts to enhance children's health. Legislative actions such as the Anti-Deficiency Act of 1884 (which restricted voluntary government service), the White House Personnel Act of 1978 (which made the president's spouse a de facto public official subject to the constraints of all public officials), and other federal antinepotism laws require the president's spouse to be cautious and clever in how she or he engages in political action surrounding any issue.[166] However, possibly more constraining than the legal limitations political spouses face are the social ones. Societal norms that often reinforce conventional republican motherhood ideals force presidential helpmates to rely on their rhetorical savvy when the media spotlight is placed on them.

Presidential contests are quite instructive when it comes to the status of women. The chapters that follow closely examine individual election cycles from 1992 to 2016 and the ways campaign coverage and messaging portray individuals married to presidential nominees. The results indicate that even as women have made great strides toward full citizenship, they are still politically hamstrung by interpretations of their political interests as informed by the ideal of republican motherhood.

Conclusion

The second first lady of the United States, Abigail Adams, wrote to her husband, "Remember, all men would be tyrants if they could. If particular care and attention is not paid to the ladies we are determined to foment a rebellion, and will not hold ourselves bound by any laws in which we have no voice, or no representation."[167] She was cautioning against the dismissal of women as participatory citizens in the new nation. Rather than heeding such warnings, the founders largely ignored females in the official construction of the government. As a result, women have continually had to struggle for "equitable treatment . . . that does not . . . [demand] assimilation or acceptance of stereotypic 'feminine' roles as the price of full participation in U.S. society."[168]

Republican motherhood began as a means of rhetorically managing the hypocritical distinction between male revolutionaries' fight for equality and representation and the disenfranchised role of women in society. The idealized female was a mother and wife whose life was dedicated to the moral and civic education of her children. True republican mothers did not advocate for themselves unless improving their own situation would enhance their ability to serve others more effectively. Based on this ideal, all women were considered mothers (actual or potential) first, wives second, and social servants third. There was no room for personal ambition (political or otherwise) in this glorified version of traditional female roles. Essentially, the republican mother epitomized a romanticized version of long-established social norms and expectations for women. Unfortunately, even though the plasticity of the republican motherhood ideal allowed some women to use the concept to forward a progressive political agenda, and others used it to justify their conventional existence and retain their customary domesticity, this image of the ideal woman patriot painted all female citizens with one broad maternal brush and limited the ways in which women would be understood for centuries.

The United States has had difficulty outgrowing the rhetorical construct early leaders of the nation created to avoid upending domestic life during the country's developmental years. Elements of republican motherhood have influenced political messaging throughout the nation's history and still pervade political discussions about women, particularly during presidential campaigns. Contemporary criticism of assertive and educated women creates challenges for women seeking equal opportunities in the public sphere. Mother-based tropes employed as shorthand interpretations of women's concerns stereotype female citizens in ways that limit their perceived competencies. Modern political and religious figures frequently blame learned women and working mothers for destroying traditional family structures. These conventional beliefs about women's roles in society present shortsighted perspectives about women that encourage men and women alike to perceive females as a special subgroup of society with narrowly defined homogenous interests. Although republican motherhood rhetoric can be used to positively press women's political interests, it still tends to offer a restrictive view of women as political actors. Thus, its use by and about high-profile political females warrants close attention and scrutiny.

2

Barbara Bush and Hillary Rodham Clinton

The Year of the Woman (1992)

The 1992 election marked a milestone in American women's journey toward political equality. That year, four women won US Senate seats, the most victories for female candidates in a single year up to that point. For the first time in history, two female senators represented one state, when Barbara Boxer and Dianne Feinstein both won in California.[1] Furthermore, twenty-four new women earned US House of Representatives seats. When the 103rd Congress was sworn in, forty-seven House members were women, a substantial increase over the twenty-eight female representatives in the 102nd Congress.[2] Some pundits claimed this uptick in women's political activity occurred because the controversial 1991 US Senate confirmation hearings for Clarence Thomas to serve on the Supreme Court underscored problems stemming from a dearth of females in powerful governmental positions.[3] Although the hearings and other political scandals might have spurred some activity, it is more likely that a series of short-term election issues combined with several long-term trends (including shifts in demographics, the continued impact of women's rights efforts, and changes in the economy) were largely responsible for the expansion of female political involvement.[4]

The surge in female electoral achievements led the media to label 1992 "The Year of the Woman." Many female leaders of the time disliked the phrase and argued it belittled consequential advancements in females' participatory citizenship by casting women's growing political activity as little more than a fluke.[5] Even though such criticisms were understandable, this shorthand reference to the prominence of females during that election drew direct attention to women's sustained underrepresentation and pursuit of political empowerment. The term also highlighted the significance of 1992 in the evolution of US politics by describing it as a key moment when women's desire for an active role in government translated into the notable attainment of numerous influential political positions.

Despite some complaints about the terminology, the Year of the Woman was generally viewed as a positive step in women's ongoing movement toward equal rights and fully enacted citizenship. However, that does not mean everyone embraced the success of female politicians. Because the majority of women running for office were Democrats, some high-ranking Republicans made ill-advised comments regarding female candidates. During one of the 1992 presidential debates, the moderator asked contestants about the increased number of female contenders for elected office. Whereas the Democratic challenger, Bill Clinton, responded, "There are special experiences and judgments and backgrounds and understandings that women bring to this process," the incumbent, President George H. W. Bush, said, "Let's see how they do. I hope a lot of them lose."[6] Although this statement was likely a jest indicating that he did not wish to see Democrats of any sex win Senate seats, the tone-deaf nature of the answer was problematic in an election cycle where women were considered an extremely important voting bloc.

During the seven decades between female national enfranchisement and the Year of the Woman, the role of women in society changed dramatically, and so did their tendency to vote. In 1992, approximately 7.3 million more females cast ballots than males did.[7] Understanding the growing power of this group, savvy politicians regularly discussed topics considered "women's issues" and paid more concentrated attention to female constituents. Campaigns made more direct appeals to women and deployed more female surrogates to advocate for party candidates. On the presidential level, nominees' wives were an integral part of each contender's persuasive efforts. The treatment of these specific women throughout the general election by the press and the parties highlights the tensions women faced at that time and underscores the relative benefits and drawbacks of republican motherhood rhetoric as applied to and by these candidates' spouses.

The 1992 Presidential Nominees' Spouses

The presidential election during the Year of the Woman offered the nation an interesting set of contrasting options. The top-of-the-ticket contest included the incumbent, George H. W. Bush, an esteemed statesman who had been a part of national politics for several decades, and Bill Clinton, a young saxophone-playing governor with a reputation as a bit of a philanderer. The running-mate competition pitted the boyish Vice President Dan Quayle, well known for his numerous gaffes while in office (including famously misspelling "potato" during an elementary school visit), against Senator Al Gore, a longtime politician with a serious and somewhat wooden persona. Even the unofficial race for the first ladyship included two seemingly antithetical figures in the affable, white-haired, pearl-wearing First Lady Barbara Bush and the ambitious, professionally accomplished, pantsuit-donning attorney Hillary Rodham Clinton. In addition, a third-party candidate earned enough initial support in the polls to win a place in the presidential debates. Ross Perot, an eccentric billionaire from Texas, was a viable contender and an alternative to mainstream candidates, but his degree of support failed to yield even one Electoral College vote. His running mate and spouse received little attention and were not treated, by the press or opposition, in a comparable way to those of the Republican incumbent or the Democratic challenger. Although various 1992 electoral characters provide interesting fodder for analysis during the Year of the Woman, the wives of the two major party presidential nominees are of concern here.

Born in New York City on June 8, 1925, Barbara Pierce (later known as Barbara Bush) was the third of four children. Raised in relative comfort during the Great Depression, Pierce was physically active in her youth. She was a swimmer and a tennis player who also enjoyed bike riding. She began her education in the public system but completed high school at a private residential program in South Carolina. She met George H. W. Bush at a Christmas dance in 1941. The two married on January 8, 1945. Barbara Bush briefly worked at a department store, a nuts-and-bolts factory, and a campus bookstore before settling into a home-focused life.[8] She spent most of her adulthood following her husband to various locations as he developed his career. She bore six children, including one who died of leukemia at just two years of age.

Barbara Bush was the first lady of the United States during the 1992 presidential campaign. As first lady, and previously as the wife of the vice president, she had been on the national stage for more than a decade at the outset of the race. However, she had spent her early life in considerably more private pursuits.[9] Her formal education ended when she dropped out of college after just one year, making her the only first lady since Marie "Mamie" Eisenhower not to have completed postsecondary schooling or formal vocational training.[10] Barbara married George when she was nineteen years old, and her primary occupation throughout the next several decades of her life was as a stay-at-home mother to the couple's children. Her life "was strictly confined to the traditional responsibilities of motherhood and housekeeping, as well as . . . teaching Sunday school and volunteering for the . . . YMCA, United Way, and hospital."[11] Her later public activity was a direct result of her husband's political ambitions. As he sought various positions in government, she outwardly performed the role of a compliant wife but privately furnished her husband strategic advice.[12] By 1992, she had seen her husband through two unsuccessful Senate races (1964 and 1970), two successful bids for a US House of Representatives seat (1966 and 1968), one failed attempt to win the Republican presidential nomination (1980), two campaigns as the vice presidential nominee (1980 and 1984), and the 1988 presidential contest. Although she had previously acted in a supportive behind-the-scenes role, because of her popularity, she became a strategic and public part of her husband's 1992 reelection efforts. Her outward persona throughout her time as a public figure continually emphasized her domesticity by drawing particular attention to her roles as an acquiescent wife, nurturing mother, and doting grandmother.

Hillary Diane Rodham, known throughout the 1992 campaign as either Hillary Clinton or Hillary Rodham Clinton, was born in Chicago on October 26, 1947. The eldest of three children, Rodham was a bright and active child. She was a Girl Scout, became a National Honor Society member, participated in student government, and belonged to a Methodist youth group. After high school she attended Wellesley College. In 1969, she enrolled in Yale Law School, where she met her future husband, Bill Clinton. After earning her JD in 1973, she did postgraduate work at the Yale Child Studies Center. In 1974, she accepted a position teaching law at the University of Arkansas in Fayetteville to be closer to Bill. The couple married on October 11, 1975, and had a daughter in February 1980.

Hillary Clinton was one of the most politically active and professionally accomplished spouses of any presidential nominee in history. Like Mary Baird Bryan, the Democratic challenger's wife a century earlier, Clinton held a law degree. Unlike Bryan, who studied law for the sole purpose of aiding and promoting her husband, Clinton's education and career development were motivated by her desire to use her intellect to make her own distinct impact on the world.[13] Clinton remained professionally active throughout her marriage; she continued to practice law while raising her daughter and during her husband's political campaigns for the US Congress and for the governorship of Arkansas. While the first lady of Arkansas, she became the first woman to earn a full partnership with the prestigious Rose law firm.[14] For twenty-four years, Clinton's salary exceeded her husband's pay until he won the White House and she ceased her paid professional work.[15] Clinton's outward persona downplayed her domestic duties and prioritized her competence outside of the home.

The biographical differences between Barbara Bush and Hillary Clinton are striking when viewed through the lens of republican motherhood and its expectations that women be other-centric, self-sacrificing, primarily concerned with domesticity, and deferential to masculine authority. Bush's publicly touted life story accentuated her strong and consistent embrace of the duties customarily attributed to a domesticity-driven female patriot. She sought only the formal education necessary to function as an effective homemaker, she married young, she produced and cared for several offspring, and she dedicated her life to supporting her husband throughout his numerous professional and political ventures. She relinquished her right to pursue her own professional development to care for her spouse and children.[16] Bush uprooted the family multiple times to support her husband's career ambitions and lent her assistance when needed during his various campaigns. As evidence of her patriotic mothering, two of her male children, George W. and Jeb, sought political office, winning governorships and contending for the presidency (George W. twice winning the highest office). Barbara Bush outwardly embodied the ideals of republican motherhood in a decidedly explicit fashion.

Hillary Clinton, in contrast, attained academically equal status with her husband, developed her own individual career, sought bold professional opportunities for herself, and functioned for many years as the primary breadwinner for her family. She established her career before having only one child and continued to work when her daughter was young. Although Clinton's life choices veer away from conventional enactments of republican motherhood, her professional career skirted along more mother-oriented lines. The primary focus of her work was improving conditions for children; during her early professional life she specialized in legal issues related to compassionate topics such as access to health care, desegregation, education, and ending child abuse and neglect. Therefore, despite the fact that she challenged the tenets of republican motherhood in her personal life, Clinton did not fully countermand all characteristics of the ideal female patriot in her work life.

Both Barbara Bush and Hillary Clinton were quite active during their husbands' 1992 efforts to win the White House. Each woman served as a surrogate campaigner, appearing at events with and without her spouse.[17] Clinton essentially went through an unofficial national vetting process as she actively participated in her husband's Democratic primary contest throughout the spring; Bush was less consequential in the early stages of her husband's reelection bid because the Republican nomination was effectively settled by January, when the incumbent won the New Hampshire primary. Each woman received a great deal of attention (Clinton throughout the primaries and Bush during her time as first lady); therefore, both women had clearly established public personas. The attention paid to the wives of both major parties' nominees increased at and after the national conventions. Bush and Clinton were each interviewed by numerous press outlets, delivered their own campaign speeches, and participated in countless photo opportunities. Both women also gave their husbands strategic as well as tactical advice. Bush's subtle, yet persuasive, endeavors reinforced her nickname, the "Silver Fox."[18] Clinton's vocal participation in planning meetings and strategy sessions led to concerns that she would become a kind of copresident if her husband won.

As spouses of presidential contenders, these women faced many of the same challenges and opportunities as did past nominees' wives, but they also received a great deal of attention and criticism because of the prominent role each assumed during the campaign. The manner in which the press, the opposition, and the spouses themselves portrayed these women underscored the social expectations of presidential spouses and illustrated the restrictive frames placed on prominent female citizens during the Year of the Woman. These renditions also demonstrated the utility, positive and negative, of republican motherhood as a rhetorical device.

Representations of Barbara Bush and Hillary Clinton

Perceptions about both Bush and Clinton were driven by a combination of factors influencing each woman's public image. The media often provided simplified or exaggerated descriptions of the candidates' spouses that were nonetheless quite impactful. The parties and their various members also put forth complimentary and oppositional readings of the two women. Additionally, each of the ladies contributed to the construction of her public persona through her own words and actions. All three sources of information about these women relied heavily on the rhetoric of republican motherhood ideals to evaluate them.

Media Depictions

Media representations of Barbara Bush and Hillary Clinton during the 1992 campaign reveal stark differences in the ways each was interpreted and judged. Part of the variation in treatment was because of their husbands, part can be attributed to their biographies, and part was a result of their individual interactions with the press and the public. Although specific coverage varied based on the particular outlet and the priorities of those offering sketches of these women, the candidates' spouses were frequently and consistently reported on in a way that amplified the differences between their personal and professional life choices: Bush was purported to be a kind and patient grandmother figure who deferred to her husband and prioritized others' needs above her own, whereas Clinton was presented as a decisive "modern woman" who sought power and attention outside of the home and allegedly showed contempt for women who chose more domestically centered lives.

The press and the public were quite familiar with Barbara Bush before the 1992 presidential contest. She had served as the visible, but not especially vocal, wife of the vice president for eight years and had been the sitting first lady of the United States for more than thirty-six months by the time the campaign got into full swing. Bush's personal charm and willingness to stay out of her husband's business were the focal point of many news reports about the first lady. Stories about Bush often reminded readers of her "practice of not speaking out on policy matters" and the fact that "Mrs. Bush has declined to state her own views . . . for years."[19] Media outlets touted her as the president's "secret weapon," credited her with being the "kinder, gentler half of the White House," and deemed her the president's "public social conscience."[20] Many pundits pointed to her popularity as a key to her husband's potential reelection. Bush's 1992 public opinion ratings rank her as the most popular nominee's spouse of the modern era.[21]

Barbara Bush became more vocal as the 1992 campaign wore on, yet her seemingly newfound public assertiveness did not cause a major shift in her media-rendered persona. A few articles pointed out a change in her routinely deferential demeanor, but even her fiercest critics in the press excused her sup-posedly surprising behavior. Highlighting her "shift [away] from her American Queen Mum image"[22] and comparing her seemingly new political involvement to that of Nancy Reagan,[23] most news reports still framed Bush's actions as those of a dutiful wife supporting her husband.[24] A decade or more after the Bushes left the White House, a different, more aggressive image of Bush as the first lady emerged,[25] but during the 1992 campaign most stories relied heavily on narra-tives that contrasted "everyone's grandmother,"[26] Bush, against the "overbearing yuppie wife from hell,"[27] Clinton.

Long before her husband announced his presidential candidacy, Hillary Clin-ton faced challenges in the press based on her activism and her seeming distaste for roles commonly ascribed to women. One month into her time as the first lady of Arkansas, the press began criticizing Clinton for not using her husband's last name, for choosing to continue practicing law, and for not fitting "the image that we have created for the governor's wife."[28] She was later accused of costing her husband votes during his reelection bid by refusing to temper her progres-sive manner and reputedly unorthodox viewpoints.[29] Similar charges arose dur-ing the 1992 campaign and helped form the basis for many of the comparisons between Clinton and Bush. The press frequently portrayed Clinton's modern perspective negatively.[30] News outlets claimed she "offended some voters early on with her ambition, fierce independence, and seeming disdain for homemak-ers."[31] Reporters reinforced this interpretive lens by continually describing her as "the outspoken wife of the Arkansas Governor"[32] or the "high-powered lawyer wife of the Democratic nominee."[33] Even the most charitable stories about Clin-ton characterized her as "by no one's standards a meek woman."[34] Journalists used her work on behalf of women and children to accentuate her purportedly ambitious nature, writing that she was "the chairman of the board of the Chil-dren's Defense Fund and earn[ed] at least three times her husband's $35,000 an-nual Governor's salary."[35] Dozens of less sympathetic articles made comparisons between Hillary Clinton and Lady Macbeth.[36]

In the spring of 1992, Hillary was heavily criticized when a story broke about an alleged long-term affair Bill had with a woman named Gennifer Flowers. Af-ter initially joining in a denial of the accusations, then sitting by her husband as he confessed his transgressions, she dutifully defended her husband, showed unwavering support for him and his candidacy, and touted the strength of their marital bond.[37] Even though these are exactly the types of actions the repub-lican motherhood ideal would encourage from a good wife, rather than prais-ing her for her conventionality, the press lambasted her. Reporters claimed the governor's wife was a hypocritical feminist for excusing her husband's actions and questioned whether her marriage was a genuine loving union or something more akin to a business arrangement.[38]

Although some pundits stated that "a coequal couple in the White House is a little offensive to men and women,"[39] deemed Hillary Clinton a "Rorschach test for the culture and its changing attitudes toward women,"[40] or declared that she had been "victimized by social expectations and political traditions that are still remarkably sexist,"[41] most journalists generally blamed the Democrat's public image problems squarely on her personality. Some proclaimed that Clinton's low favorability ratings were a result of her being "grating, abrasive, and boastful," whereas others faulted her for "pushing too hard" the idea that her marriage was an equal partnership.[42] During the campaign, media watchdog groups argued that the press was "fixat[ed] on a few anecdotes and quotes about Hillary Clinton's views about marriage and domestic work, and [used] traditional and often conservative vocabulary . . . to discuss these issues."[43] Essentially, news coverage repeatedly emphasized the ways in which Clinton violated the ideals of republican motherhood. They cast her as assertive rather than deferential, self-centered rather than other-focused, and intent on disrupting purportedly normal home life. This starkly contrasted with the portrayal of Bush as a grandmotherly first lady who occasionally violated the norms associated with womanhood but did so only to buttress her husband's patriotic actions.

Throughout the 1992 campaign, media outlets regularly compared the spouses of the presidential candidates and frequently, if unwittingly, used republican motherhood rhetoric as the basis for evaluating the women. One of the most overt comparisons designed to assess these spouses' domestic skills came from *Family Circle* magazine in response to a quip by Hillary Clinton. During the Democratic primary, she responded to questions about her active professional life by remarking, "I suppose I could have stayed home and baked cookies and had teas . . . but what I decided to do was fulfill my profession."[44] The statement ignited a firestorm of criticism as news media accused Clinton of belittling homemakers. Although she explained that her answer had been unfairly abbreviated and apologized for the apparent slight, many media outlets and GOP party members repeatedly pointed to the comment to underscore Clinton's seeming distaste for feminine domesticity. *Family Circle* used the putative gaffe to promote its magazine by challenging the spouses of the nominees to a "cookie bakeoff." The magazine printed cookie recipes attributed to Clinton and to Bush. Readers voted on which was the best.[45] News outlets reported the results in a manner that highlighted the perceived home life of the participants,[46] including stories of each recipe's origination, tales of the women baking with or for their families, and details of individuals testing the recipes at home.[47] A snide observation regarding Margot Perot's failure to participate hypothesized that she "ordered in her cookies."[48] In the end, Clinton's chocolate chip cookie recipe prevailed. This victory, however, did little to repair the damage caused by her earlier statement. The cookie bakeoff has since become a quadrennial event in which all candidates' spouses are expected to participate.

Talk radio, a combination of news and entertainment media, was another space in which both candidates' wives were frequently contrasted with one another in ways that relied heavily on republican motherhood rhetoric. Much like in other media forums, Barbara Bush's ensconced image as a dutiful, deferential homemaker was frequently cited and often provided grounds for praise by hosts and callers alike. Her standing as a mother and grandmother was lauded, and her willingness to support her husband's professional and political efforts was touted as the ideal action of a "good" woman. This was particularly true on conservative shows. More liberal on-air personalities occasionally questioned Bush's standing as a role model for modern women or called her a first lady for a different era, but rarely did anyone openly chastise her life choices or political actions. The same was not true for Clinton.

Conservative talk radio programs served as an outlet for both hosts and callers to vent frustrations about the changing role of women. Hillary Clinton, as the embodiment of the modern woman, became a key target for participants' vitriolic rants. She was criticized over the airwaves by sports figures and private citizens for everything from her appearance to her use of her maiden name and from her unwillingness to stop working when her daughter was born to the fact that she earned more money than her husband.[49] Clinton was charged with emasculating her spouse, and some program participants claimed she wanted to do the same for the entire nation. One of the most negative frames placed on Clinton because of her unwillingness to conform to established feminine norms came from conservative radio host Rush Limbaugh. Arguing that the Democratic nominee's wife was trying to ruin the fabric of society by destroying the traditional family structure, Limbaugh branded Clinton a "femi-nazi," a term the polarizing radio personality frequently used to identify purportedly troublemaking women pushing for a change in the established gender hierarchy.[50] Limbaugh frequently warned listeners of the dangers posed by an ostensibly power-hungry first lady and overtly favored a woman who "knows her proper place" over "flag waving man haters."[51] Guests and callers rallied around the image of Clinton as an extremist and an enemy, making crude assertions about her perceived sexuality (or even lack thereof) and joking about the potential changes a progressive couple might bring to the White House. Limbaugh and others cast her as a fear-inspiring witch who would eventually destroy the nation.

Media representations of Barbara Bush and Hillary Clinton routinely highlighted the ways each met or failed to meet the presumed requirements of a proper first lady and often reinforced a preference for political wives who are deferential, who are other-oriented, and who embrace widely accepted features of femininity. Many visual renditions of the two wives played up the distinction between the conventionally ladylike appearance of Bush and the modern woman image of Clinton. The contrast between Bush's dresses and Clinton's pantsuits rendered the latter the more masculine woman, recapitulating the criticisms of educated women leveled by Jean-Jacques Rousseau more than two centuries earlier when he wrote that a learned woman "is always trying to make a man of herself," thus rendering herself unnatural and foolish.[52] Somewhat ironically, political satires did occasionally frame Bush in unflattering ways by casting men to play the first lady in order to highlight her sturdy stature and relatively deep voice.[53] The attitudinal difference between the reputedly affable and sincere Bush and the ostensibly aggressive and overly ambitious Clinton accentuated issues of likability that plagued the latter throughout her public life. In both cases, representations of these women featured the ways each embodied or challenged the standard norms of womanhood.

The media's reification of gender norms espoused by republican motherhood illustrates the complexities of this rhetorical tool. On the one hand, the comparison of women from different generations and backgrounds drew attention to the changing roles of women in society; by highlighting these differences, the media encouraged discussions about the various tensions women in the early 1990s faced regarding old-fashioned and modern expectations. The familiar version of feminine patriotism offered a common vocabulary for the conversation. On the other hand, by directly favoring a more restrictive view of women, media outlets reinforced an interpretation of females that made their desire for expanded participation as active citizens seem unusual, negative, and contrary to their supposed natural drives.

Party Portrayals

Much like the depictions offered by media outlets, the parties on both sides of the 1992 campaign put forth dramatically different interpretations of the nominees' spouses. Not surprisingly, each party tried to draw attention to the positive attributes of its own candidate's wife. The Republicans touted Barbara Bush's likability and framed her as the ideal role model for American women. The GOP held up Bush as an iconic, patriotic, and genial female. The Democrats, similarly, lauded what they viewed as the favorable features of their nominee's spouse. Hillary Clinton was promoted as a first lady for a new era, and her professional accomplishments and competencies were, at least during the early parts of the campaign, presented as assets for a potential presidential helpmate. These positive portraits of the women by their respective camps are to be expected, but each campaign's treatment of the opponent's wife reveals a negative use of these women reminiscent of the manner in which nominees' spouses like Dolley Madison, Rachel Jackson, and others were unfavorably inserted into their respective husbands' campaigns (see the Introduction).

During the 1992 primary season, the Democratic Party's nominee had been under fire for his past treatment of women. The concerns had revolved around extramarital sexual relationships, and the Democratic candidate needed to avoid arousing controversy regarding his views on women. Therefore, during the general election campaign, Bill Clinton did not engage in much direct criticism of Barbara Bush. Hillary Clinton also had to steer clear of attacking the first lady because, having already been chastised for purportedly insulting housewives, she could not risk further alienating those who perceived her as holding "anti-housewife" sentiments. Democratic campaign staff and other surrogates were primarily responsible for constructing the opposition's interpretation of Barbara Bush. However, the first lady's popularity with a wide range of voters prevented most Democrats from openly chiding her. There was little to gain from denouncing an amiable, aging woman who had made expanding literacy the cornerstone of her social platform and who had largely refrained from commenting on political issues throughout her public life. Yet the 1992 campaign was not fully devoid of oppositional assessments of the first lady.

The few negative assertions Democrats made regarding Barbara Bush were subtle jabs that cast her as a relic of the past who, like her husband, was out of touch with the modern era and the average American's experiences. Many of these covert critiques occurred in Democratic National Convention (DNC) speeches that highlighted the new challenges women faced balancing work and home life. When Democratic vice-presidential nominee Al Gore praised the work of Hillary Clinton, celebrated the Year of the Woman, and touted his mother's graduation from law school forty-six years before, some pundits contended that he was making a veiled slight against the less-educated Bush.[54] However, the vague nature of each presumed insult ostensibly directed toward the first lady left its specific meaning open to interpretation. Gore did applaud women's professional accomplishments, but nothing in his address provided a direct snub against homemakers, women without professions, or the first lady.

After the conventions, as Barbara Bush became an increasingly vocal part of her husband's campaign, Democrats began to question the sincerity of her supposed deferential nature and hinted that her kindly demeanor masked a more aggressive personality. Some operatives pointed to her 1984 description of Geraldine Ferraro, in which she called the vice-presidential nominee a "four-million dollar . . . I can't say it, but it rhymes with 'rich,'" as evidence of the more mean-spirited nature of the first lady.[55] Democrats also negatively framed Bush by complaining about her joining fellow GOP members in overt criticisms of Hillary Clinton.[56] They claimed Bush's remarks violated her earlier statements in which she said she disdained political attacks on candidates' families. Although some Democrats tried to paint Bush as duplicitous, the first lady's deeply entrenched public persona effectively muted most charges against her.

During the 1992 general election, and even a few months before it officially began, Hillary Clinton was labeled "the woman Republicans love to hate."[57] The GOP aggressively argued that the Democratic nominee's wife was antifamily. This depiction began early and took many forms but was most powerfully articulated by GOP chair Rich Bond. He warned voters, "Hillary Clinton . . . believes kids should be able to sue their parents rather than helping with the chores they were asked to do. She's likened marriage and the family to slavery. She has referred to the family as a dependency relationship that deprives people of their rights."[58] This statement goes beyond assailing Clinton for failing to fulfill the type of feminine role espoused by the republican motherhood ideal; it describes her as a subversive agent proactively trying to prevent others from fulfilling their patriotic duties through the role of homemaker.

Bond's claims, based on a 1974 *Harvard Education Review* essay penned by Hillary Clinton, were actually taken out of context. Scholars in the field declared at the time that the article's contents had "become the source of both unfair and distorted portrayals as well as over statement [*sic*] and exaggeration."[59] Although the original essay "does not advocate certain positions but rather reviews the positions of others and sets them within a broader theoretical framework," the characterization of Clinton based on Bond's statements was often repeated and became a central part of the Republican argument against her husband.[60] At the 1992 Republican National Convention (RNC), Patrick Buchanan echoed Bond's argument during his "culture war" speech. Casting Clinton as a dangerous potential copresident in the address, Buchanan reiterates the false narrative: "Hillary believes that 12-year-olds should have a right to sue their parents, and she has compared marriage as an institution to slavery—and life on an Indian reservation."[61] He goes on to protest, "This, my friends, this is radical feminism. The agenda that Clinton and Clinton would impose on America: abortion on demand, a litmus test for the Supreme Court, homosexual rights, discrimination against religious schools, women in combat units. That's not the kind of change America needs. That's not the kind of change America wants."[62] Throughout the remainder of the speech, Buchanan dubs the potential Democratic administration "Clinton and Clinton" when talking about domestic issues and the morality of the country. He demonizes Hillary Clinton and hints that her inappropriate equal partnership with her husband would result in widespread immorality across the nation.

Other RNC speakers were less direct in their criticism of Clinton but still alluded to her inability to satisfy the traditional standards of femininity long expected of a first lady. In his address, Pat Robertson uses republican motherhood rhetoric in an implied comparison between Barbara Bush and Hillary Clinton. He tells the audience, "We have a first lady, Barbara Bush. She's a gracious lady, a devoted wife, a dedicated mother, and a caring grandmother. . . . I don't care what the polls say. Nobody can convince me that the American people are so blind that they would want to replace Barbara Bush as first lady."[63] Marilyn Quayle, wife of the vice president, took a similar approach when she spoke at the RNC. Rather than directly attacking Clinton, throughout the speech Quayle uses republican motherhood ideals to paint the lives and desires of most women as dramatically different from those purportedly touted by Clinton. Quayle contends,

"Most women do not wish to be liberated from their essential natures as women. Most of us love being mothers and wives, which gives our lives a richness that few men or women get from professional accomplishments alone."[64] She goes on to call her marriage a "true partnership," mocking Clinton's often-repeated description of the Democratic couple's union as an equal partnership.[65] Quayle then highlights her own willingness to give up a law career in order to support her husband's political aspirations. Although she never directly chides Clinton, Quayle asserts that a good woman happily sacrifices her own needs and desires for her family. The implication, of course, is that Clinton does not meet the basic criteria of a good wife or mother, and therefore she cannot be a good woman or a good citizen.

During the 1992 campaign, former president Richard Nixon offered one of the most unabashedly conservative critiques of Hillary Clinton by any Republican Party member. Explicitly relying on republican motherhood rhetoric, Nixon pilloried Clinton for not assuming a servile persona. He explained, "If the wife comes through as being too strong and too intelligent, it makes the husband look like a wimp."[66] He went on to praise Barbara Bush as a model wife who did not upstage her husband and argued, "Many Americans are put off by a male politician who does not seem as strong as his wife."[67] Alluding to past political figures and sounding reminiscent of Rousseau's warning that educating female children too much renders them unattractive,[68] Nixon proclaimed, "Intellect in a woman is unbecoming."[69] He said specifically, "Hillary pounds the piano so hard that Bill can't be heard. You want a wife who is intelligent, but not too intelligent."[70] This seemingly archaic perspective on the role of women as dutiful and compliant supporters asserts that a woman's patriotism should be demonstrated by the subordination of her own interests to the deeds of her husband and sons.

Even Barbara Bush eventually joined the GOP attacks on Hillary Clinton. Repeating the inaccurate claim that the Democratic candidate promised a co-presidency should he be elected, Bush buttressed criticisms by her husband and others when she declared the Democratic nominee's wife's views fair game for robust discussion.[71] This marked a significant reversal for Bush, who had previously admonished Bond and others for attacking the opposing candidate's mate.[72] Although her actual utterances against the spouse of the Democratic challenger were mostly indirect, Bush did ultimately condone the Republican strategy of "keep[ing] the focus on Hillary versus Barbara."[73] After the contest was over, Bush again changed her tune and defended her successor. In December, she scolded the White House press corps for its treatment of Clinton and advised reporters to "give [Clinton] a chance to make her own mistakes"[74] before attacking her.

The ways opposing parties treated the spouses of presidential nominees in 1992 mirrored previous campaigns throughout history as republican motherhood rhetoric dominated the critiques by both sides. For the Republicans, Hillary

Clinton's purported unwillingness to behave in a manner consistent with orthodox femininity and her alleged distaste for domesticity made her an unfit role model for the women of the nation. Somewhat paradoxically, the Democrats, who had initially argued in favor of a more progressive interpretation of female citizenship, ended up simultaneously lambasting Barbara Bush both for embracing restrictive gender roles and for not truly fitting the mold of a republican mother after she began campaigning more aggressively. Democratic surrogates portrayed Bush as out of touch with modern women and the challenges they faced and insisted that the dutiful and docile wife persona established by Bush was really a facade.

In both cases, the Republicans and Democrats measured Bush's and Clinton's fitness to be the first lady of the United States based on republican motherhood ideals, which reinforced the notion that women's political activity should fit comfortably within the confines of traditional domesticity. The parties made these women an unusually large part of the discussion of presidential politics. However, the bulk of the conversation focused on setting appropriate limits to their public influence and political power.

Self-Presentations

Throughout the 1992 election season, the wives of the Democratic and Republican nominees for president were publicly and privately active in their husbands' campaigns. Both were interviewed numerous times (with and without their spouses), delivered remarks at rallies, and participated in planning and strategy sessions. Through their rhetorical activities, each woman developed and promoted her own version of her public persona. Like the depictions from the media and the opposition, the self-presentations forwarded by these women were strikingly different.

Barbara Bush put forth a public face generally consistent with her well-cultivated image as an ideal wife. She often refused to comment on controversial topics, discounted her own credibility, deferred to her husband or other key males when asked for her opinion, and touted her role as a mother and grandmother when called upon to discuss herself. During campaign interviews, Bush dodged questions about her own accomplishments and listed her husband, children, and grandchildren as the primary sources of her personal pride.[75] Yet, her seemingly deferential public attitude was strategically used to help humanize her husband and to provide an amiable counterbalance to the personable challenger, Bill Clinton.[76] Nowhere was this more evident than at the RNC, where Bush's acquiescent, dutiful spouse persona and her standing as a model republican woman earned her a prime-time spot at the podium.

On August 19, 1992, Barbara Bush became the first spouse of a major party nominee to deliver a full address to the delegates of a nominating convention since Eleanor Roosevelt's 1940 speech to the DNC.[77] Bush's address was touted as one of the hallmark moments of the Republican gathering. The first lady gave a fully prepared address that some pundits called a "speech of adoration"[78] for her husband and that set the tone for many future convention speeches by candidates' spouses.[79] Her address was intended to help humanize her husband, firm up support from the Republican base, and invite new voters to identify with the Republican nominee. Bush's self-depictions throughout the address illustrate a strong embrace of republican motherhood ideals; she casts herself as a model of feminine domesticity and lauds her husband's "softer side."

Throughout her speech, Bush accentuates her adherence to established expectations of women in the political realm through self-deprecating statements and personal anecdotes. She disparages her own abilities as a speaker and rejects her credibility as a national political figure when she jokes, "You know, there's something not quite right here, speeches by President Ronald Reagan, President Gerald Ford, Secretary Jack Kemp, Senator Phil Graham, and Barbara Bush."[80] By not including her own title as the first lady of the United States, Bush presents herself as a common woman among the esteemed, experienced, and credible men. This move highlights her allegedly apolitical perspective and invites audience members to view her as an "ordinary" American. As the only woman among this list of respected speakers, Bush also devalues the standing of women among the political elites of her party. She downplays the importance of her address when she argues, "I'm here not to give a speech, but to have a conversation, and most of all, to thank hundreds of communities across the country for . . . the chance to meet so many American families and be in your homes."[81] Here, Bush discounts her own political perspective and highlights the domestic elements of her experience as the first lady.

Although her address had been one of the most anticipated moments of the RNC and was promoted by convention planners as an example of the party's homage to women, throughout the speech Bush identifies herself only as a deferential wife and a dutiful mother. She portrays herself as an exemplary American woman by emphasizing attributes that coincide with archetypal interpretations of appropriate female patriotism. Early in her speech, she reflects on the difficulties of raising children, sympathizing with those "determined to teach their children integrity, strength, responsibility, courage, sharing, love of God, and pride in being an American."[82] Stressing that patriotism should be taught in the home, a value espoused through republican motherhood rhetoric, Bush then launches into stories of her own family. Each tale underscores her traditional marriage by showing her husband's compassion and strength and spotlighting her actions as a wife and mother. She talks of George H. W. Bush working long hours in the oilfield, yet "he always had time to throw a ball or listen to the kids."[83] In the meantime, she "carpooled, was a den mother, and went to more Little League games than I can count."[84] As a family, she explains, "we went to church; we cheered at

Fourth of July picnics and fireworks, and we sang carols together at Christmas."[85] Barbara Bush paints a picture of a Rockwellian family in which each member dutifully assumes a conventional role.

Bush reinforces her standing as a deferential wife throughout the address, always accentuating her husband's virtues, sometimes at her own expense. This happens when she tries to exemplify her husband's kindness by sharing an anecdote about disciplining the children. She reminisces, "Once, when one of the boys hit a baseball through the Vanderhoff second-story window, I called George to see what dire punishment should be handed out and all he said was, 'The Vanderhoff second-story window, what a hit.'"[86] This tale undermines Bush's own standing as a matriarch. She reveals her inability to assign punishment and her willingness to surrender her parental authority to her husband. Later in the speech she gives him credit for the quality of their familial solidarity, calling the fact that "his children still come home" his accomplishment rather than theirs.[87] Although she talks about herself primarily in motherly or grandmotherly terms, Bush does not take any credit for her contributions to their family.

Bush continually relied on republican motherhood rhetoric in her representation of herself during her time in the public eye, so it is no surprise that this practice continued throughout the 1992 campaign. The self-deprecating lines in her RNC speech and in interviews made her seem unthreatening and demonstrated her lack of personal political ambition; her tendency to express her own opinion on issues by referencing her husband highlighted a desire to appear apolitical and deferential, and her focus on families and children when she did address political topics emphasized her domesticity. Bush embodied ideal female patriotism as portrayed in early US history. Her popularity during the 1992 campaign indicates that many Americans approved of this perspective on women and the purported spectator role in politics it assumes for them. Bush's Democratic counterpart cultivated a wholly different public persona.

Hillary Clinton's proffered public image evolved during the Democratic primaries and into the general election. At first, she described herself as a progressive, independent woman and equal partner to her husband. On morning talk shows and other outlets, Clinton highlighted her experiences chairing state commissions and leading task forces; she presented her time in Arkansas as a model for her potential role as a politically active first lady. Clinton clearly intended to engage in governmental affairs more directly than Bush, but she narrowly prioritized issues related to the home when delineating her interests. She frequently talked about her decades-long work on improving education and health care for kids and pointed to the initiatives she had led to protect abused women when outlining her planned agenda should her husband win the White House.

Early on, Clinton framed herself as representing a generational change among women. She argued that her perspective and experiences reflected an evolution in the United States because "the kind of opportunities women are coming into . . . are really so broad and deep that we should all be willing to take responsibility and to do what we can to further the causes we believe in."[88] She also cast herself as a champion of all women, arguing, "Women need to have some sense of solidarity and to respect the choices that each of us make."[89] In fact, the complete version of her ostensibly controversial comments about staying home and baking cookies actually acknowledged the multitude of decisions females confront throughout their lives.[90] Although Clinton did not explicitly embrace republican motherhood ideals in the same manner Bush did, she did concentrate on domestic issues and did not openly disparage women who made more conventional choices, contrary to media and opposition claims about her. However, the distinction between Clinton's earlier and later self-portrayals indicates the extent to which external factors influenced her publicly enacted persona.

Clinton, as stated previously, played a very active role in her husband's presidential campaign. However, after many "confusing" run-ins with the press, Clinton tried to adapt her public image.[91] She became less assertive and adopted a more obliging demeanor after the contest shifted toward the general election. Clinton did not deliver an address to the 1992 DNC for at least two reasons associated with her media- and opposition-driven public persona. First, because the DNC occurred before the RNC, had Clinton delivered a full speech, she would have been the one to break with tradition by being the first spouse since 1940 to do so instead of Bush. She would have also been the first candidate's wife who was not a sitting first lady to address such a gathering. Although Clinton was a precedent-setting spouse in many ways, speaking in this context would have provided additional fodder for those framing her as pushy, aggressive, and overly ambitious. Voters uncomfortable with a progressive potential first lady did not need additional reminders of her assertiveness. Second, because phrases like "two-for-one" and "copresidency" were being used to criticize Bill Clinton's candidacy, Democratic strategists were wary of giving Hillary Clinton too visible a role at the DNC. Instead, she was relegated to more conservative-seeming duties and photo opportunities that included handing out cookies to attendees. These actions were framed as Clinton's attempt to become "a new, more digestible version of a campaign spouse."[92]

During the latter part of the campaign, Clinton tried to embrace the republican mother ideal in an effort to rehabilitate her public image. She made more frequent references to and appearances with her daughter, publicly enacting a motherly role. She downplayed her potential activity in a Bill Clinton administration, framing her involvement simply as a way to help her husband. Clinton also softened her physical appearance by changing her hair, makeup, and some of her clothing. As though following an old-school, patriarchal playbook, Clinton tried to appear "more maternal, domestic, average, likeable."[93] Republican motherhood rhetoric offered clear strategies for Clinton to use when refurbishing her public persona. By recasting herself as more deferential, family-focused, and self-sacrificial, the Democrat's wife disappointed some more progressive voters but earned new support for her husband's candidacy. The familiar symbolism of republican motherhood made Clinton's alterations easy to interpret, yet the shift in attitude caused pundits to question her authenticity.[94]

Throughout the 1992 primary and general elections, Clinton tried to paint herself not as an opponent of orthodox femininity but as a representative of modern transformations in women's lives and duties. She did not contradict the tenets of republican motherhood, but she did challenge its assumptions by attempting to expand accepted norms. By discussing purportedly feminine topics such as health care and education, she retained a domestic focus. However, she expressed her own opinion, at times openly (if gently) disagreed with her husband, and challenged male figures when necessary. It is important to remember, though, that Clinton's political activity was geared toward supporting her husband. Every interview, speech, and personal appearance was part of a concerted effort to advance her husband's political career; like most political spouses and women assuming traditional roles, she subordinated her own interests to aid her husband. Clinton never fully embraced or rejected republican motherhood ideals, but her own self-depiction reflects a complex reliance on the rhetoric surrounding long-standing views of the proper enactment of female patriotism.

The strategic use of components of the republican motherhood trope by Barbara Bush and Hillary Clinton typifies the dual nature of the rhetorical tool. For Bush, consistently framing herself as the ideal female patriot earned her a prime speaking spot at the Republican Party's national nominating convention. Her submissive public image allowed her to break new ground for political spouses by expanding the accepted boundaries of their participation in the public sphere. For Clinton, initial failure to judiciously embrace heteronormative gender roles caused enduring problems for her and her husband. Her inability to adequately consider the entrenched nature of republican motherhood ideals early on led to dramatic shifts in her public persona later in the campaign. These changes left many voters wondering about her sincerity. Clinton's relationship with republican motherhood ideals typifies the struggles of all women battling for new political ground in the United States.

Conclusion

The Year of the Woman was a perplexing time for American females. Women candidates for office were more accepted and more successful, women voters and the issues they were assumed to care about received more positive attention, and there were more women campaign surrogates giving voice to women's concerns. In many ways, dominant models of womanhood seemed to be changing regarding female political activity. However, when it came to the spouses of the two major party candidates for president, entrenched expectations regarding femininity played a major role in the way each was measured and judged. Both Barbara Bush and Hillary Clinton were evaluated based on their actual and assumed enactment of archetypal femininity.

Republican motherhood is a paradoxical rhetorical tool with deep historical roots. Because the common characteristics usually assigned to female patriots — that they be deferential, other-centric, self-sacrificial, and domestically focused — are so entrenched in political dialogue and expectations about women, republican motherhood standards are easy to apply when evaluating someone who might become the "symbol of American womanhood" by assuming the mantle of first lady of the United States.[95] In 1992, Bush and Clinton appeared antithetical in so many ways that their approach to femininity seemed an important and inevitable point of comparison. Accentuating their differences, those evaluating the nominees' spouses largely framed the more conservative perspective espoused by Bush favorably and treated Clinton's more progressive view with skepticism. Unfortunately, these depictions provided voters little more than simplified caricatures; the public received shorthand interpretations of complex women rather than nuanced representations that explored the social and political challenges each woman actually faced.

Although there were positive and negative aspects to the portrayals of Bush and Clinton, continually interpreting both spouses in such a narrow manner restricts our understanding of women as political beings. Despite the fact that Bush publicly embraced the role of submissive wife and apolitical female, she also eventually took strong stands on topics such as abortion and openly contradicted and even scolded male GOP party leaders. She supported heterodox family structures and occasionally addressed ostensibly male political topics such as national security and the military. Likewise, even though Clinton was cast as an elitist and ultrafeminist who disdained many aspects of republican motherhood, she worked tirelessly on compassionate topics often labeled "feminine" issues, subordinated her political and professional interests to those of her philandering husband, and praised motherhood as one of her proudest accomplishments.

Neither Bush nor Clinton fully embodied the ideals of traditional female patriotism, and neither wholly rejected them. In truth, both women reflected the complex decision-making and intense social pressures all American females of the era encountered. Yet a narrow view of womanhood, even during this supposedly progressive election cycle, is evident in the way republican motherhood rhetoric pervaded the depictions of these women and the choices each made in her own presentation of herself. In 1996, the spouses of the presidential nominees were two women whose biographies were more comparable because both were career-oriented women. However, the 1996 depictions of Hillary Clinton and Elizabeth Dole retained many of the elements of the presidential candidates' mates' portrayals in 1992.

3

Hillary Rodham Clinton and Elizabeth Dole

Dutiful (and Accomplished) Wives (1996)

The midterm election cycle that followed the Year of the Woman became known as the "year of the angry, white male."[1] Lashing out against the political strides made and attention garnered by women, men in 1994 voiced irritation and anger at purportedly being disregarded and took to the polls to express their frustrations.[2] Despite this pushback, the number of women pursuing national elected office during the 1996 election was comparable to that of 1992. Two fewer females sought Senate seats, and six more battled to become members of the US House of Representatives.[3] As a result of the election, women gained four spots in the House[4] and retained the nine previously won in the Senate.[5] Without a new surge in participation, there was no particular increase in media coverage of women candidates. However, there was a noticeable change in the way presidential nominees, their campaign surrogates, and the press conceived of women in 1996.

One of the most sought-after sets of voters during the presidential election was a new category of citizen labeled the "soccer mom." This articulation of women cast them as primarily white, married, middle-class, suburbanite mothers.[6] The soccer mom was a "superparent"; she was first and foremost motivated by her duties as a mother but tried to "have it all."[7] This conceptualization of the female voter emphasized a woman's domesticity by basing her identity on her familial relationships, featuring her tendency to put others' needs ahead of her own and focusing on her desire to effectively fulfill childrearing responsibilities.[8] Although this type of female was envisioned as a working parent, discussions about these women generally dismissed their professional endeavors and treated their employment outside of the home as a burden women assumed in addition to fully attending to their families.[9] Political operatives as well as members of the press assumed the soccer mom's political decision-making was entirely grounded in her perspective as a matriarch. The soccer mom, as depicted in presidential rhetoric of the time, was the epitome of the modern republican mother.

The impact of the soccer mom figure in 1996 was reminiscent of the pros and cons of republican motherhood rhetoric during its developmental stages (see Chapter 1 for more information on the evolution of republican motherhood). On the one hand, talking about these types of women acknowledged the largely unrecognized domestic labor many women were performing, underscored the pressures modern women faced to prioritize their familial responsibilities above their careers, and bestowed political importance on mothers and mothering. On the other hand, the term made personal associations the primary source of political identity for female citizens and disempowered women who were not wives and mothers.[10] Rather than addressing the complexities of women as political citizens with a wide range of experiences and interests, the notion of the soccer mom reinforced a narrow view of females not just generally as mothers but as a particular subset of mothers who led somewhat privileged lives.[11]

Democratic candidates and surrogates paid a great deal of attention to the rhetorically constructed collective of soccer moms throughout the 1996 general election campaign, making the trope appear to represent a much larger segment of the population than it actually did. The media spotlight on this group (more than two hundred news stories appeared about soccer moms in 1996) likewise raised the perceived importance of women voters thus conceived.[12] The popularity of this contemporary republican mother ideal shaped the political perception of women during the 1996 campaign because female citizens were understood almost exclusively in terms of their relational responsibilities, and individual women were judged based on this updated version of a traditionally patriotic lady.

Although neither of the presidential nominees' wives fully met the criteria for a soccer mom, both were pressured to appear as though they were a part of this category. First Lady Hillary Rodham Clinton and the challenger's wife, Elizabeth Dole, were often compared to or themselves used elements of this restrictive interpretation of women. This chapter examines the ways these women were portrayed by others and depicted themselves throughout the campaign. It also explores the role republican motherhood rhetoric played in assessments of their past achievements as well as of their fitness to act as the first lady of the United States.

The 1996 Presidential Nominees' Spouses

The 1996 presidential election included a slate of familiar faces. The Democratic incumbent, Bill Clinton, and his sitting vice president, Al Gore, squared off against a pair of well-respected long-term Republican legislators with Senator Bob Dole at the top of the GOP ticket and Representative Jack Kemp as his running mate. Once again, the Texas billionaire Ross Perot ran as a Reform Party candidate, but as in 1992, he failed to earn a single Electoral College vote. The presidential race was not closely contested. In weekly Gallup surveys, Bill Clinton generally amassed support from more than 50 percent of potential voters, whereas Bob Dole struggled to stay above 40 percent.[13] Dole's Gallup numbers did not surpass Clinton's after mid-January 1996. Clinton's anticipated victory resulted in a relatively sedate campaign that decreased general interest in the contest and participation in it. For the first time since 1924, less than 50 percent of the voting age population showed up at the polls.[14]

One area of the presidential competition that earned significant attention and that raised a great deal of discussion was a part that included no certified voting; the unofficial battle for first lady of the United States drew interest from the press, the parties, and the voters. Unlike the 1992 contest, which pitted two seemingly antithetical figures against each other, the women married to the 1996 presidential contenders were quite similar. Hillary Clinton and Elizabeth Dole were both successful career women with noteworthy achievements outside of the home. Yet, as will become evident throughout this chapter, this does not mean the women were described analogously and contrasted accurately, or that either managed to avoid evaluations rooted in republican motherhood rhetoric.

The two spouses of the major party candidates in 1996 had almost identical backgrounds. Both were Ivy League–trained attorneys who had politically ambitious husbands, and each woman had her own publicly touted interests and professional pursuits. They each married later in life than the average for their age cohort, and neither made mothering the cornerstone of her life. Although a broad-strokes assessment of their lives indicates that these women had more in common than Hillary Clinton and Barbara Bush did in 1992, a more detailed look at their experiences up to the 1996 campaign provides much-needed context for the comparisons and portrayals of each that emerged during that contest.

By the outset of the Democratic primaries, Hillary Clinton had been the sitting first lady of the United States for almost three years (see Chapter 2 for more information on her early biography). Battling image problems ingrained in the minds of the public since the 1992 campaign and grounded in her failure to meet the established standards of femininity set for a politician's wife, Clinton nevertheless became an active part of her husband's administration at the outset of his presidency. She led a committee tasked with reforming the nation's health-care system and failed in a dramatic fashion. Critics pilloried Clinton's involvement in policy development and chided her political activity by calling it an overreach of power by the president's spouse. In addition, Clinton became embroiled in various scandals during the early part of her time as the White House matriarch. As a result, she earned the dubious distinction of obtaining the lowest favorability ratings of any sitting first lady since the inception of modern polling.[15] As a politically savvy person, and wishing to avoid costing her husband votes in his reelection bid, Clinton sought to rehabilitate her public image soon after what many called her "health care debacle."[16]

As she had done late in the 1992 campaign, Clinton used several cues from republican motherhood rhetoric to soften her public persona and emphasize her more conventional feminine characteristics. She began referring to herself more frequently as "Mrs. Clinton," occasionally dropping her maiden name but never abandoning it altogether (until around 2000 when she ran for the US Senate).[17] Clinton focused on performing the ceremonial duties of the first lady and significantly curtailed but did not cease her efforts to influence policy. She highlighted her work on behalf of children and attended events with her daughter to underscore her status as a mother. She also published a book about children and childrearing, *It Takes a Village*. By the time the 1996 election was fully under way, Clinton had tried to shift the public's attention away from her failures and her feminist perspective, but the public was not quick to forgive or forget.[18] In 1996, her favorability rating sat at less than 50 percent, and 45 percent of poll respondents held unfavorable views of her.[19]

Mary Elizabeth "Liddy" Hanford, later known as Elizabeth Dole, was the daughter of a North Carolina flower vendor father and a civic-minded mother. She won recognition for her social, academic, and public service achievements as an undergraduate student. She was voted both the May Queen and the Leader of the Year while at Duke University, then went on to earn a law degree at Harvard. Her personal charm and intellectual competence carried over into her professional career, and she was given the nickname "Sugar Lips" for her ability to gain support from her male counterparts.[20] In 1972, she met Bob Dole, the then newly divorced US senator from Kansas. She was thirty-nine when they married two years later; it was her first marriage and his second. Unlike Hillary, who kept her maiden name for many years after marrying Bill, Elizabeth assumed Bob's last name immediately following their wedding. The couple had no children together. Although Bob had a daughter from his previous marriage, Robin was twenty-one when the couple wed. Thus, Elizabeth Dole lacked any extended mothering experience.

The 1996 Republican contender's wife was no stranger to politics. After law school, Dole held various political positions in Washington, DC. She campaigned for Lyndon Baines Johnson and served in his administration before switching political parties, became Richard Nixon's deputy assistant for consumer affairs in 1969, and served as the director of the White House Office of Public Liaison before Ronald Reagan nominated her to be his secretary of transportation. George H. W. Bush later named Dole secretary of labor, making her the first woman to hold two separate cabinet posts under two different presidents. In 1991, she began leading the American Red Cross, a post from which she took a leave of absence during her husband's 1996 campaign.

The political and occupational activities these women engaged in showed Clinton as more inclined toward republican motherhood ideals than Dole. Clinton's public efforts had always been oriented around helping children and women, and her issues of interest (education, health care, etc.) were topics considered feminine because of their compassionate nature and direct link to the home and family. Dole, in contrast, had focused on what are usually regarded as more masculine pursuits. Even if her attempts to increase safety features in automobiles might arguably be family-friendly, neither of her signature governmental roles (in transportation and labor) dealt with traditional womanly concerns. Her work with the American Red Cross, however, fell into the purportedly female realms of improving health and providing comfort.

The 1996 presidential election marked a turning point for spouses of presidential candidates. For the first time, the résumés of the wives of both nominees reflected a dramatic shift away from homemaker experiences and toward more career-minded endeavors. Although the personal histories of both Clinton and Dole contravened conventional gender expectations, the rhetoric of republican motherhood still dominated many depictions of these women proffered by the press, the parties, and the women themselves.

Representations of Hillary Clinton and Elizabeth Dole

Throughout the 1996 campaign, treatment of the presidential nominees' spouses relied heavily on archetypal interpretations of females. The media highlighted the experiential similarities between the professionally accomplished women and underscored their personality-based differences. The parties tended to concentrate on describing the women in a manner that promoted orthodox perceptions of the proper duties of a presidential helpmate. Both groups used republican motherhood rhetoric to frame the public's understanding of Clinton and Dole. The women also relied heavily on elements of this trope to emphasize how their attitudes and actions corresponded to the historical model of a good woman to foster electoral support for their husbands.

Media Portrayals

The press provided an interesting and perplexing sketch of the two wives of the 1996 presidential contenders. Whereas media portraits of Clinton were most often based on the deeply ensconced images established throughout the 1992 campaign and her time as first lady, portrayals of Dole were a bit more challenging to develop. Unlike in 1992, when Barbara Bush offered a counterbalance to Clinton that easily suggested stories comparing the spouses' attitudes toward domesticity, Dole's commonalities with the sitting first lady forced reporters to look for and amplify different sorts of distinctions. Despite having a wealth of potential new directions in which to take the coverage of these women, most journalists still seemed preoccupied with how each embraced or rejected attributes associated with the republican motherhood ideal.

Having established an image of Clinton during the 1992 campaign as an ambitious career woman who disdained homemakers, the media revived that caricature during the 1996 contest. With three years of high-profile White House activities to point to, reporters simply added updated evidence to their original interpretation that cast Clinton as unlikable, insincere, and untrustworthy. Most coverage of the first lady began by describing the "travails of Hillary Rodham Clinton."[21] Calling her "the lodestone of [the] administration" because she seemed embroiled in endless controversy, correspondents often reminded voters of Clinton's so-called gaffes during the 1992 campaign by recycling old news footage and repeatedly replaying her comments seeming to disparage housewives.[22] They also mixed in new stories of questionable behavior by the first lady. To portray her as disingenuous, some commentators directly equated her attempts to alter her image in 1994 and 1995 to her ostensibly inauthentic "late campaign makeover" in 1992; they implied that her focus on traditional values and presumed female interests was an example of savvy political gameplay rather than a reflection of her true self.[23] In addition, news outlets more frequently referred to Clinton by her maiden and married names in 1996 than in 1992. By stressing her unorthodox decision to retain her maiden name, the press reminded voters of her previously cultivated persona as a forcefully independent woman despite her many efforts to highlight her own domesticity.

The press also resuscitated stories about Bill Clinton's ill-advised 1992 campaign theme, "two-for-one," as an opening to discuss his wife's public failures and shortcomings since becoming the first lady.[24] Hillary Clinton was chided for "trying to redefine the office" of the first lady of the United States by directly influencing national public policy.[25] The health-care reform failure coupled with her involvement in at least two high-profile scandals (the Whitewater investment scheme and Travelgate, the alleged firing of White House travel office employees to replace them with political supporters) led many media commentators to rail against affording first ladies unchecked power. Clinton's responses to these accusations of misconduct earned her both a subpoena to testify before a special Senate panel and a reputation as a dishonest and evasive politician. She was dubbed a "congenital liar . . . compelled to mislead, and to ensnare her subordinates and friends in a web of deceit."[26] Three years in the White House did little to improve Clinton's media-driven identity and instead transformed her image from an unlikable forceful feminist to a dangerous mendacious manipulator.

A consistent theme across media depictions of Clinton was that she did not fit the expectations of an old-fashioned female patriot. Much like in 1992, reporters in 1996 used the rhetoric of republican motherhood to frame Clinton's alleged duplicity as unfeminine. Critics claimed she was not the "gracious hostess, good mother, and loyal, supportive helpmate" a president's wife should be.[27] Instead of being deferential, other-oriented, and interested in creating a comfortable home, Clinton was presented as self-serving, ambitious, and intent on forging her own political path. However, the press did concede that of the two presidential candidates' spouses, Clinton was "the soccer mom of the pair" who, before becoming first lady, "went grocery shopping and to . . . baseball games."[28] She was also credited with "firmly hitch[ing] her wagon to her husband's star."[29] In contrast, Dole "never had children" and "was a player with a portfolio before she met Bob."[30]

The news media treated the GOP candidate's wife with a mix of respect and bemusement. Almost every story about Elizabeth Dole contained an overt comparison to Hillary Clinton in terms of the women's professional accomplishments. Assessments frequently credited Dole with having the more acclaimed résumé, then quickly moved on to contrast Dole's charm with Clinton's abrasiveness. Dole was described as a "steel magnolia"[31] who wielded an "iron hand in a velvet glove."[32] Although Dole was reportedly very strategic and driven to succeed, journalists declared that her ability to appear accommodating increased her likability among political pundits and Washington elites.[33] Commentators identified her southern manner and ostensibly deferential behavior as key to her occupational prowess; the press described her approach as more personable than that used by Clinton. One story asserted that as an intelligent southern belle, "she was taught to defer to men, even beguile them, but rarely challenge them."[34]

Media coverage of Dole mentioned her political credentials and her ability to influence others, yet most stories still concentrated primarily on her adherence to traditional gender roles. Although aware she was not a mother, the press accentuated the ways Dole met the spousal elements of the republican motherhood ideal by subordinating her interests to those of her husband and by supporting but not exerting control over Bob. Quick to point out the numerous times Dole had resigned or taken a leave of absence from a job in order to work on one of her husband's campaigns, reporters portrayed her as graciously self-sacrificial. Also, recalling depictions of Barbara Bush in 1992, journalists talked about Dole as her husband's moral conscience,[35] maintained that she helped him appear more personable,[36] and argued that she provided behind-the-scenes strategic and tactical advice during his political campaigns.[37] Elizabeth Dole was considered "her husband's not-so-secret weapon."[38]

Even as they acknowledged that she was a "national figure in her own right," some correspondents still tried to mute Dole's individual success.[39] Journalists gave her husband credit for her political talent by arguing that her effectiveness was largely a result of the fact that no one wanted to upset the wife of the Senate majority leader.[40] They also downplayed her influence over her husband's decision-making by relating tales underscoring Bob's independence from his wife and illustrating her loyalty and subordination to him.[41] Reinforcing expectations long established by conventional conceptions of female patriotism that placed women in subservient positions, the press was careful to be clear: "For all of Mrs. Dole's accomplishments . . . no one would mistake her for [Bob's] equal."[42]

On the whole, in spite of the women's professional similarities, the news media generally played up the differences between Clinton and Dole in a way that framed the latter as a deferential wife who embraced several of the elements of republican motherhood despite her career-mindedness and presented Clinton as a domineering and duplicitous partner who rejected orthodox family structures even though her own life was actually much more domestically focused than Dole's. In addition, each woman's occupational enterprises were often a source of adverse coverage. Each received attention for scandals related to her political and professional activities; as Clinton was bombarded with accusations about Whitewater and Travelgate, Dole was charged with exploiting conflicts of interest in order to advance her efforts at the American Red Cross and to secure paid speaking appearances.

Other media generally amplified the representations of Hillary Clinton and Elizabeth Dole put forth by news correspondents. Entertainment programs such as *Saturday Night Live* questioned Clinton's motherly self-image by impersonating her as stiff and uncomfortable around children[43] and mocked Dole's folksiness by exaggerating her repeated self-depiction as "a simple woman and loving wife, not . . . an over-ambitious feminist by the name of Hillary Clinton."[44] Editorial cartoonists often used images of Clinton "elbowing her husband aside," and late-night talk-show hosts made almost as many jokes about the first lady as about the president.[45] Talk radio outlets tended to pay more negative attention to Clinton than they did in 1992, with Rush Limbaugh's program and listeners reviving and intensifying their previous critiques of her (see Chapter 2).[46] Dole did not receive as much or as vitriolic attention as Clinton, yet questions about both Dole's sincerity and the GOP discounting her professional success arose on some liberal call-in shows.

Despite the fact that neither woman fit the mold of a traditional housewife, media descriptions of Clinton and Dole during the 1996 campaign still relied heavily on republican motherhood rhetoric. Comparing the two women with the updated version of the ideal female patriot (i.e., the soccer mom) was a means of referencing and discussing entrenched interpretations of women's proper roles and motivations. The trope acknowledged the work women often did outside the home, even if those efforts were depicted as a distraction from domestic responsibilities, and both Clinton and Dole epitomized the difficulties most women faced trying to balance familial and career-based expectations. Although republican motherhood rhetoric did not accurately encapsulate the lives of the 1996 presidential nominees' wives, its continual appearance in stories about them did help goad pundits into conversations about the changing status of women in society. Still, the fact that the press forced these women into a stereotype that did not fit them, then questioned the sincerity of their endeavors to meet outdated and arbitrarily imposed standards, created a rhetorical space in which neither woman could be her genuine self. The reliance on republican motherhood rhetoric also tempered potentially valuable exchanges about the prospect of fully empowered and engaged female actors.

Party Depictions

The two major parties had similar strategies when it came to their portrayals of presidential spouses during the 1996 campaign. Both the Democrats and Republicans tried to represent their own candidate's wife as illustrative of the typical experiences of most American women. Neither party accentuated the achievements of its nominee's consort. Instead, each party directed attention toward the domestic activities of the woman married to its candidate. The same, however, was not the case when dealing with the opposition. Both parties repeatedly referenced the professional credentials of the opponent's wife. The Democrats and the Republicans used republican motherhood rhetoric a great deal when offering the public shorthand characterizations of each candidate's wife.

Because she seemed something of a scandal magnet, Clinton's public participation in the 1996 campaign was much different than in 1992. She was "only seen (but not heard) in proper 'helpmeet' photo-ops like the Atlanta Olympics."[47] Campaign strategists endeavored to distance her from the health-care defeat and minimize perceptions of her influence over her husband's administration by emphasizing her conventionally feminine attributes. She traveled with her daughter, Chelsea, competed in the second-ever *Family Circle* first lady cookie recipe contest, gave reporters tours of the White House, and hosted luncheons for the spouses of sitting senators. Clinton's main contribution to her husband's reelection campaign was through fund-raising.[48] She was, however, given a prime-time speaking spot during the Democratic National Convention (DNC). Strategists argued that the national stage would allow her to further refurbish her public image. By shifting attention toward Clinton's exploits as a mother and a wife, the Democrats strove to accentuate her traditionalism without overtly discounting her feminist history.

When it came to the opposition, the general Democratic strategy during the 1996 campaign was to avoid direct attacks. The fact that the Democratic incumbent was far ahead in the polls meant there was little to gain from a barrage of negative messages about the aging war veteran topping the Republican ticket. There was even less to achieve by fervently critiquing his wife. Bill Clinton rarely mentioned Elizabeth Dole, and Hillary Clinton generally spoke favorably about her Republican counterpart. She complimented Dole's long record of public service, praised her as a trailblazer for women, and implied that the two were kindred spirits from different generations. She framed Dole as a role model for career-oriented women. This, however, is not to say that there were no Democratic efforts to insert Dole negatively into the 1996 contest.

Much like in 1992, surrogate Democratic campaigners offered more criticisms of the opponent's wife than either of the Clintons did. Political operatives pointed to Dole's standing as a Washington insider and the scandals attached to her work as indicators that she was not the submissive wife she often portrayed herself to be. Democratic operatives painted her as "duplicitous"[49] and "disingenuous"[50] because of the distinctions between her professional track record and her claims to hold mainstream values. Some Democrats applauded Dole's assertion that she would remain the president of the American Red Cross should her husband be elected by calling it a progressive or feminist move. Others chided the idea as fraught with potential ethical conflicts. In both cases, the intent was to spotlight characteristics of Dole that conservative voters might find unappealing. The Democrats subtly but clearly used Dole's occupational endeavors as points of criticism even when they seemed to be complimenting the Republican candidate's wife.

The GOP took a similar approach to characterizing its nominee's spouse. The Republicans employed familiar elements of republican motherhood rhetoric to emphasize Dole's conservative values and downplay her extensive résumé. Campaign surrogates deflected attention away from her impressive professional accomplishments as a political operative and redirected it toward her standing as a charming and supportive wife. By frequently alluding to her willingness to interrupt her own high-powered career by resigning or taking leaves of absence to help her husband pursue his goals, campaigners underscored Dole's deference to her husband and her willingness to subordinate her interests to his. Framing her career aspirations as secondary to those of her husband made her appear more conservative than her own biography indicated and burnished her credentials as a more orthodox female patriot than Clinton. Although each party cast its candidate's spouse in terms of her adherence to republican motherhood ideals, the GOP's use of Dole was different than the Democrats' handling of Clinton; rather than being relegated to photo ops and other low-consequence events, Dole became an active part of the campaign by giving numerous interviews and speeches as well as by appearing solo in television ads.

The Republicans developed a two-pronged approach to framing Hillary Clinton. First, they launched direct attacks designed to reinforce the image of Clinton as power hungry, off-putting, and untrustworthy. Republican operatives continually referenced Clinton's failed health-care reform efforts to demonstrate her overly ambitious nature, to illustrate flaws in her character as a leader, and to reify her manipulative image.[51] Republicans also pointed to her seeming evasiveness when questioned about the Whitewater and Travelgate controversies as evidence of her dishonesty. Some GOP members simply chided Clinton for her personality, arguing, "There's just something about her that pisses people off."[52] To combat Clinton's self-asserted maternal persona during the 1996 campaign, Republicans criticized her book, *It Takes a Village,* by claiming it furthered her antifamily agenda by absolving mothers of their responsibility for the care and well-being of children.

The second component of the GOP's anti-Clinton strategy involved pointedly comparing Elizabeth Dole's potential first ladyship to Hillary Clinton's actual time in the White House. Bob Dole often stated his intent to limit his wife's political activity should he win the presidency. He specifically told voters, "When I'm elected, she won't be in charge of health care . . . or in charge of anything else."[53] Some reporters argued that his protests against her potential involvement became so frequent and fervent that they made the potential first lady sound intellectually challenged.[54] Even Elizabeth Dole herself said she would never attempt to influence an issue as consequential as health care.[55] The GOP nominee's wife repeatedly critiqued the first lady in several interviews, implying that even if Clinton ostensibly did not understand the limitations of the role of the president's spouse, Dole did.

Each major party's treatment of the presidential candidates' wives in 1996 illustrates the difficulties political women often face. In this year when both nominees' mates were professionally accomplished individuals, each party chose to commend the conventional aspects of its own candidate's spouse and reprove the opponent's consort for her failure to embrace traditional femininity. By highlighting Clinton's standing as a mother and her interest in family-oriented topics, the Democrats employed republican motherhood rhetoric to reestablish her reputation and decrease the potential impact of her scandals on her husband's reelection campaign. The Republicans tried to do much the same thing with Dole by accentuating her purportedly deferential nature and hoping her "beguiling charms . . . overshadowed her drive, discipline, and pursuit of power."[56] While touting the ways their own candidate's mate met old-fashioned standards of femininity, each party also used the political and public activities of the opposing nominee's wife to criticize her. Conflicts of interest became points of censure for Clinton and for Dole, making the case that each woman's work outside the home not only hampered her public stature but also endangered her husband's political career.

The parties' reliance on republican motherhood rhetoric in 1996 seemed inappropriately restrictive considering the qualifications of the candidates' wives, yet the trope provided time-tested guidance for campaign strategists trying to encourage voters to develop positive perceptions of the most visible women in the presidential campaign. Because it acknowledged established perspectives held by numerous voters, men and women alike, referencing this narrow view of women's roles encouraged citizens to identify with these women on a personal level. However, the republican motherhood lens also contravened interpretations of women as competent political agents by treating female participation in politics as inherently negative. Democrats proffered an understanding of Clinton, and of women generally, as motivated by maternal drives. Republicans used

Dole to stress the idea that even strong, competent women should be submissive to their husbands. Democrats paradoxically disparaged Dole both for not being an orthodox wife (and not a mother at all) and for not embracing a more feminist public persona. Republicans condemned Clinton for pretty much every action she did or did not take.

Self-Representations

As established throughout this chapter, Hillary Clinton and Elizabeth Dole were experienced political actors who made strategic choices regarding their public personas. Through interviews, campaign ads, photo opportunities, and other campaign activities, each candidate's spouse carefully crafted an image of herself she thought Americans would find appealing. This is not to say that the self-representations were disingenuous but that Clinton and Dole chose to accentuate particular elements of their lives and downplay others in order to encourage positive identification building between themselves and potential voters. For each woman, this meant relying heavily on republican motherhood rhetoric. Elements of this narrow comprehension of female citizenship were emphasized in several of their campaign activities and were particularly prominent in their national convention addresses, the most widely viewed campaign performances by these women.

Clinton was a far less vocal part of her husband's 1996 campaign than she was in 1992. In an effort to mitigate her potentially adverse impact on the incumbent's reelection, Clinton gave few political speeches or interviews of her own (although she did occasionally appear with her husband). When she did speak out, it was to praise her husband's positive actions and attributes, to promote her book, and to illustrate her standing as a modern American mother. Almost every interview or public commentary focused on compassionate topics such as education and protecting children from assorted dangers. In August, she accepted "a fresh chance in the national spotlight" when she took the stage at the Democratic National Convention (DNC) in Chicago to advocate on behalf of her husband.[57]

Clinton's address at the 1996 DNC encapsulates her efforts to redefine herself ahead of her husband's potential second term. Using republican motherhood rhetoric throughout the oration, Clinton endeavors to overcome her problematic public image by emphasizing her actions as a conscientious mother and a proud, supportive wife. She refers frequently to her experiences as a parent and purports to speak as a representative of American women. Clinton never directly discusses her career achievements and only casually mentions her professional activity when referencing the challenges working parents confront. Instead, she concentrates on issues commonly considered feminine because of their direct connection to home and family. The first lady describes herself as the embodiment of the modern republican mother concerned first and foremost with the welfare of others (children, husband, etc.).

In her DNC speech, the first lady casts herself as a working mother with many of the same experiences and concerns most American parents have. She relays brief tales of her and the president's personal life, always understating her employment record and giving prominence to her maternal status. Clinton makes nine references to her daughter, Chelsea, during the speech and uses her child as a justification for her own political interests. She explains how her husband was "with me when Chelsea was born, in the delivery room, in my hospital room, and when we brought our baby daughter home," and then she uses that experience to argue for expanded hospital stays for new mothers.[58] She shares an anecdote about how, as a worried mom, she was not able to sleep the one night her daughter spent in the hospital after a tonsillectomy in order to broach the subject of offering better health insurance options for families. She laments her daughter's eventual departure for college to comment on our collective potential to make the future better for all children. Clinton makes it clear that mothering has always been her priority when she tells listeners, "There has been no experience more challenging, more rewarding, and more humbling than raising our daughter."[59]

In addition to explicitly and repeatedly referring to her child, Clinton also paints herself with a traditional brush by emphasizing her marital relationship. The first lady says "my husband" as often as "the president" when referring to him. She tells the audience about the couple's upcoming twenty-first wedding anniversary to underscore the longevity of their marriage. Clinton also speaks about the couple's shared experiences, using phrases such as "Bill and I will celebrate" and "Bill and I are fortunate" to accentuate their bond.[60] Aside from one reference to "what I've been doing for more than twenty-five years," Clinton never really presents herself as an independent being politically, socially, or otherwise.[61] Instead, she is Bill's wife or Chelsea's mother. She never verbally acknowledges her position as the first lady of the United States, does not remark on her experiences as an attorney, and only occasionally alludes to her book because it aligns with the major theme of the speech, helping children and families.

In addition to identifying herself almost exclusively based on her relationships with others, Clinton also uses republican motherhood rhetoric by restricting her speech to domestic topics. Her presentation, intended to help expand her husband's appeal and revamp her public persona, broaches issues clearly and directly affecting families. Clinton opens her address by claiming, "I want to talk about what matters most in our lives and in our nation, children and families."[62] She then discusses the challenges new mothers face, the stresses of being a working parent, and the importance of promoting adoption and supporting those who adopt children. She also speaks about education, community involvement, and the necessity for all people to have access to effective health care. When addressing each topic, Clinton carefully inserts her own experience as appropriate and outlines her husband's actions in that area. For example, speaking about how "raising kids is a full-time job," Clinton depicts herself as an ordinary parent by arguing, "We [working parents] are stretched thin."[63] She then demonstrates her knowledge of the challenges folks raising children encounter by delineating the many duties they assume. She uses this explication to justify her husband's support for legislation offering flex-time employment options. Clinton argues, "We have to do whatever it takes to help parents meet their responsibilities at home and at work."[64]

During the address, Clinton also discounts her own standing as a skillful professional. As with Barbara Bush's self-deprecating use of humor in 1992, Clinton opens her 1996 speech by humorously outlining some of the advice she had received while preparing for her presentation. The idea that Clinton needs help with her speech is itself a bit discrediting to the first lady. However, the odd nature of the suggestions she references, such as appearing "with Bindi, the child-saving gorilla" and "to cut my hair, color it orange, and change my name to Hillary Rodman Clinton" (a reference to then-popular NBA star Dennis Rodman), makes it seem as though others perceived the address as a superficial event in which style would triumph over substance.[65] Clinton, as Bush did in 1992, redefines her address as something other than a political oration. Clinton tells the audience, "I wish we could be sitting around a kitchen table, just us, talking about our hopes and fears about our children's futures."[66] The desire for a comfortable and intimate conversation prioritizes interpersonal relations over deliberative political debate. Here, she laments her inability to speak personally with individual audience members and frames the types of informal political exchanges women are presumed to prefer as centered on relationship building.

In her DNC address, Clinton depends heavily on republican motherhood rhetoric and continually alludes to elements of the soccer mom trope. She identifies herself primarily in terms of her relationships, highlights her interest in subjects that affect the home, uses motherhood to justify her political activity, and diminishes her own standing as a competent and independent political actor while praising her husband's public actions. Clinton's self-portrayal casts her as an exemplar of the modern republican mother by acknowledging contemporary shifts in women's assumed responsibilities, yet maintaining domesticity as their primary focus. Elizabeth Dole sought to do the same thing, but she had to be more creative because of her lack of maternal experience.

Dole's efforts to manage her public image included a mix of strategies that both embraced and contested established elements of republican motherhood. On the one hand, Dole seemed eager to depict herself as a dutiful wife supporting her husband's aspirations without seeking power for herself. As explained earlier, she engaged in critiques of Hillary Clinton that required Dole to discount her own desire to influence national policy in spite of an apparent lifelong interest in policy development and advocacy. She also yielded to her husband and his publicly stated positions whenever asked about her stance on an issue. She talked often about her devotion to Bob and deflected attempts to discuss her own political accomplishments.

Although Dole tried to appear like an ordinary wife, not all of her actions aligned with the expectations of the traditional conception of women as deferential political actors who are primarily interested in domestic pursuits. Early in the presidential contest Dole announced that she would continue her professional commitments if her husband won the presidency; she would resume her post as the president of the American Red Cross rather than participate in her husband's administration or focus on the ceremonial duties assigned to the president's spouse. Her declaration was groundbreaking. No other nominee's mate had made such a definitive statement regarding her intended future employment. Choosing an occupation over domesticity clearly challenged the feminine norms proffered through republican motherhood rhetoric.

During the 1996 Republican National Convention (RNC), Elizabeth Dole became the first person to deliver a prime-time address as the wife of a presidential challenger. Both Eleanor Roosevelt and Barbara Bush had been sitting first ladies when they spoke to delegates at their husband's respective conventions (as was Clinton when she addressed the DNC days after Dole's speech). Following in the footsteps of the popular Bush, Dole gave a speech designed to showcase her husband's "softer side" that contained many brief narratives intended to provide a more personal understanding of the potential future president.[67] Through the speech, Dole also offered audience members a lens through which they could interpret her.

Even though she is not a mother, Dole's RNC address portrays her as a woman who embraces multiple characteristics of republican motherhood. Her intent throughout the talk is to illustrate the accomplishments and positive attributes of her husband (not surprising given that the speech is a campaign oration promoting her husband's candidacy), and she often does so at her own expense. While she tries to boost her husband's appeal with stories of his kindness and generosity, several stories strategically position her as a supportive and deferential wife who subordinates her own ambitions in order to promote her husband's endeavors. Dole crafts this conservative public persona specifically to attract voters.

Dole begins her address claiming to "break with tradition" by leaving the podium and walking among the delegates on the convention hall floor.[68] Although she challenges expectations relative to such speeches, she had often employed this type of delivery when speaking in smaller settings throughout the Republican primary season.[69] Dole's rationale for her unique style is twofold. In the speech she explains, "I'm going to be speaking to friends and . . . I'm going to be speaking about the man I love, and it's just a lot more comfortable for me to do that down here with you."[70] Turning the presentation into a seemingly interactive conversation, Dole's delivery distinguishes the speech from the usual political oration in a way that mimics Bush's stated desire to engage in a conversation and amplifies the perceived importance Dole places on establishing interpersonal relationships. As a politically accomplished woman known for her ability to beguile and charm others, she uses a speaking style that complements her public persona. In addition, her emphasis on interpersonal connections reinforces the idea that women's political power is, or should be, grounded in their coy ability to influence others relationally (see Chapter 1 for more about women's presumed special influence).[71]

During her recitation of stories dedicated to revealing the kindheartedness of her husband, Dole further projects a republican mother persona by depicting herself as an acquiescent wife adjusting to the priorities of her mate and providing the support necessary to help him achieve his goals. She talks about her husband deciding to start a foundation for people with disabilities, changing plans for their shared birthday celebration, and inviting people to Thanksgiving without telling her. In each instance, rather than displaying any agency or ambition of her own, Dole simply adapts to the desires of her husband and helps make sure the foundation is started, the celebration is organized, and the dinner is planned (violating the republican motherhood ideal of a domestically inclined wife, Dole indicates that the Thanksgiving dinner was held at a restaurant; she did not cook it herself). Dole does not speak about her own actions or aspirations but casts herself as a supporting character in her husband's life.

Throughout the address, Dole mentions her career only one time. In an effort to highlight her husband's sense of humor, Elizabeth describes how Bob introduced her for her Senate confirmation hearing when she was nominated for secretary of transportation. She tells listeners, "My husband introduced me, and you know what he did to me? He sort of did a takeoff on Nathan Hale. 'I regret that I have but one wife to give for my country's infrastructure.'"[72] Although the intent was to allude to a famous historic patriot and to illustrate Bob's colorful personality, the tale disempowers Elizabeth by emphasizing her marital relationship over her professional credentials. The story also implies that Bob allowed his wife to assume this public position rather than that she sought and earned it as an independent individual. The seemingly harmless joke and the retold story portray Elizabeth Dole as a dutiful and yielding spouse; she needed her husband's permission to engage in public service, and her husband had the right to give her (in service) to others.

Hillary Clinton and Elizabeth Dole both played up the ways they met the expectations set by the republican motherhood ideal throughout the 1996 presidential campaign. These women's reliance on the historically established characteristics of an ideal female patriot is clear in their nomination convention speeches. Even though a narrow view of women as submissive and deferential political actors did not accurately describe either candidate's spouse, the fact that each wife assumed foregrounding these attributes would win her and her husband support from voters indicates that many Americans still perceived women in predominantly traditional ways in 1996. By accentuating preferred feminine characteristics, each woman bolstered this restrictive interpretation of female citizenship by making it seem credible in an era of increased political empowerment and activity for women. However, the use of this trope was not entirely negative.

These women used rhetorical devices connected to republican motherhood to expand accepted conceptualizations of political dialogue, topics, and actors. By defining conversations "around a kitchen table" as having the potential to affect politics and by including love and personal character as valuable metrics in a presidential campaign, Clinton and Dole tried to legitimize exchanges and concerns usually linked to women.[73] Also, by using a national platform to discuss the impact of political decision-making on issues such as balancing work and home life, medical treatment for new mothers, and adoption, these women reframed subjects often considered personal or family matters as important political concerns. Although Clinton and Dole shortchanged themselves by downplaying their own abilities and interests, they did invite ordinary Americans to perceive ostensibly personal struggles as part of bigger problems calling for political attention and united action. Thus, although republican motherhood rhetoric reinforced a limited understanding of women, their interests, and their abilities, its use by the spouses of the presidential contenders in 1996 did help widen the scope of appropriate political concerns and expand some ideas about what constitutes meaningful political participation.

Conclusion

The 1996 presidential election was simultaneously very different from and similar to the 1992 contest regarding the treatment of women. It was distinct because the dominant depiction of female citizens included an explicit acknowledgment of women's increased movement into the workforce. The soccer mom conceit articulated the stresses women experienced balancing work and home life. However, women's domesticity remained the focal point of this modernized version of republican motherhood. Just like in 1992, political dialogue regarding women in 1996 interpreted women predominantly as wives, mothers, or motherly beings motivated by the needs of others, usually their children and husbands.

Like most American women, neither Clinton nor Dole actually fit the mold of the soccer mom. Based on their biographies, both were more career-minded than the characterization allowed. Yet the press, the parties, and the women themselves offered the public renditions of Clinton and Dole that prioritized the ideals of republican motherhood. Relying on the deep-rooted cultural expectation that women be deferential, self-sacrificing, and other-focused, much of the political conversation surrounding the nominees' spouses argued for and against the fitness of each woman to fulfill the symbolic role-modeling responsibilities of the first lady of the United States based on an outdated understanding of women's "proper" position in society. The results of evaluating these women based on standards set by a centuries-old rhetorical device originally designed to placate women's desire for autonomous political standing without fundamentally altering their actual participation were paradoxical.

The presentation of Clinton and Dole as professionally proficient women who managed to have personal lives and loving marital relationships did add a level of complexity to the public perception of women as political actors. Rather than reifying a dichotomous approach that sketched women as either fiercely independent careerists or entirely family-oriented housewives, the soccer mom trope accounted for both the cultural shifts that allowed some women to choose to develop independent careers and the economic pressures that propelled others begrudgingly into the labor market. Showing the nominees' spouses confronting a variety of tough decisions and balancing their own needs with those of their families drew attention to the sacrifices many women of the time were making and opened a dialogue about the stresses female citizens faced every day. The pressure placed on each candidate's wife to embody an idealized version of womanhood mirrored the difficulties women encountered when trying to meet externally imposed standards of femininity while exploring new opportunities as autonomous individuals. Therefore, the use of republican motherhood rhetoric relative to Clinton and Dole inspired more considered deliberation regarding women's continued struggle to establish their political and personal identities. Although the conversation did at least allow for the possibility that women were a more diverse and capable group than the most conventional portrayals suggested, it still leaned heavily toward prioritizing the perspectives of mothers and wives.

Downplaying the political activities and accomplishments of Clinton and Dole, whether by the press, party members, or the wives themselves, meant discounting the contributions of these highly active women. Reframing politically prominent females to accentuate their position as doting wives diminished the importance of their participation in the public sphere and impeded arguments promoting more visible and consequential political involvement by women. In addition, the fact that the press and the parties highlighted scandals related to each woman's professional actions underscored the supposed inappropriateness of female public activity. Clinton's Whitewater and Travelgate problems and Dole's alleged conflicts of interest with the American Red Cross provided pundits and the press (and opposition party operatives) evidence to argue that a woman's employment outside of the home had the potential not only to negatively affect her own reputation but also to harm the patriotic efforts of her husband. The implied argument was that these powerful women in fact lacked the ability to function effectively beyond the domestic realm and that their ambitions were detrimental to their families and the nation. Making these talented women seem incompetent or ill-intentioned undermined their credibility and provided support for limiting women's authority to more traditional spheres.

The republican motherhood ideal is a deeply entrenched interpretation of womanhood. Rhetoric governed by this frame is so pervasive that even when it is not the most appropriate lens for understanding and evaluating politically prominent women, it still dominates discussions about women and their political roles. Even in revised form, as in the case of the soccer mom, the idealized American woman in 1996 was still expected to be other-centric, self-sacrificing, and deferential. Thus, the reliance on republican motherhood rhetoric continued to discount women's ability and desire to function as autonomous, individual citizens. In 2000, as will become clear in the next chapter, the candidates' wives were neither as professionally accomplished nor as politically seasoned as Clinton and Dole, yet the depictions of the presidential nominees' spouses were still strikingly familiar.

4

Tipper Gore and Laura Bush

Quintessential Republican Mothers (2000)

The 2000 presidential contest was memorable for a number of reasons, including the fact that it was one of the more tumultuous contemporary elections. The
primaries appeared to be nastier than usual, particularly on the Republican side,
as leading candidates spread racist rumors about challengers, robo-calls flooded
potential voters with negative messaging, and party-sponsored opinion polls offered respondents a wealth of misinformation. The general election was dominated by talk of Social Security lockboxes and "nucular strategery."[1] The final
count resulted in incumbent Vice President Al Gore winning the popular tally
and Texas governor George W. Bush securing just enough Electoral College votes
to win the White House. Tabulation troubles in Florida, dubbed the problem of
the "hanging chads" because of punch ballot abnormalities, led to a legal battle
over the reported results. A Supreme Court ruling finally brought the battle to a
close almost six weeks after Election Day.

Because of the protracted conclusion to the presidential race, little attention
was paid to some of the important gains made by women during this momen-
tous election. In many ways, the results marked a new but largely unrecognized
Year of the Woman. State contests sent more women to the US Senate than ever
before, with the total number of female senators breaking double digits for the
first time. Thirteen female senators were part of the first Congress of the new
millennium, including former first lady Hillary Clinton as the new junior senator from New York. Furthermore, California and Maine each sent only female
senators to Washington, DC, that year. In the US House of Representatives, 62
female politicians served alongside their 373 male counterparts. Of the 209 total women who had served in the US Congress up until that point, 75 sat in the
107th.[2] Sizeable support by women voters helped female candidates secure wins
in the US legislature and in state gubernatorial races.[3] Yet, as women continued
to make strides toward increasing their overall participation in government, the
presidential race underscored a distinct gender gap.

The battle for the White House, with two major parties and five established
third-party groups fielding contenders, included one woman and twenty-nine
men. Elizabeth Dole, the lifelong political operative who had gained national
popularity as the well-liked wife of Republican presidential nominee Bob Dole

during the 1996 election (see Chapter 3), announced her candidacy in the summer of 1999. She earned high poll ratings but failed to raise sufficient campaign contributions to sustain her bid until the start of primary voting. She withdrew from the race in October 1999 and turned her attention toward attaining one of North Carolina's US Senate seats (winning a spot in 2002). Her candidacy drew attention to women's political aspirations and raised questions about whether a woman could ever feasibly win the Oval Office.

In 2000, as with most presidential contests, issues of sex roles and expectations became an overt part of the national dialogue, yet the topic was less prominent that year than it had previously been. Elizabeth Dole's brief run piqued some interest in women's political roles, and some candidates used women's issues to earn attention. However, the pursuit of the soccer mom vote was less intense and, with the polarizing Hillary Clinton busy running for a Senate seat, fewer politicians and their surrogates felt compelled to make the role of women in society a topic of debate. In addition, the histories and personalities of the two wives of the major parties' presidential nominees did not invite the kind of discourse prompted by spouses during previous contests. The potential presidential helpmates were less prominent in the campaign and appeared to openly embrace republican motherhood ideals. The various portrayals of the women poised to become the new feminine face of the nation reveal the desired characteristics associated with American womanhood at the turn of the century.

The 2000 Presidential Nominees' Spouses

The 2000 presidential contest featured a variety of familiar contenders. Vice President Al Gore won the Democratic nomination after a three-month primary battle against New Jersey senator Bill Bradley. Gore, who tried to distance himself from incumbent President Bill Clinton, chose longtime Connecticut senator and vocal Clinton critic Joe Lieberman as his running mate. The Republicans had a heated primary race, at the end of which the eldest son of the forty-first president of the United States won the top spot. George W. Bush chose former US secretary of defense Richard "Dick" Cheney to round out the GOP ballot. With decades of legislative and executive experience dominating each ticket, none of the major party nominees were new to the national stage. The spouses of the presidential hopefuls were also relatively well-known figures even though neither of the candidates' mates was as vocal or active as Barbara Bush, Hillary Clinton, or Elizabeth Dole. As the second lady of the United States, Tipper Gore had been in the public eye for many years, and, as the first lady of Texas, Laura Bush had earned a great deal of largely positive attention, but neither woman had been subjected to the kind of vetting potential first ladies usually endure.

Mary Elizabeth Aitcheson, later known as Tipper Gore, was born on August 19,

1948, in Washington, DC. Her mother, Margaret, nicknamed her "Tipper" after a character in a nursery rhyme, and the name became her primary moniker throughout her life. Her youth was scarred by her parents' abusive relationship and subsequent divorce.[4] Being the child of what was referred to then as a broken home made her the target of many schoolyard taunts. She claimed the experience enhanced her ability to empathize, sparked her interest in psychology, and led to her later work as an advocate for others.[5] In high school, she played multiple sports and was a drummer in an all-girl rock band. She met Al Gore at the senior prom in 1965. They began dating the next day and married five years later. She earned two degrees in psychology, a bachelor's from Boston University in 1970, and a master's from Vanderbilt in 1975. Tipper Gore briefly worked as a newspaper photographer during the early years of her marriage and bore four children between 1973 and 1982. During the early 1990s, she was diagnosed with and treated for depression following a near-fatal accident involving her son.[6]

By the mid-1970s, Gore left her professional work in order to raise her children and support her husband's political aspirations. She began acting as a campaign surrogate and aid during her husband's successful 1976 congressional bid. As the wife of a US representative and later a US senator, Gore took up social causes related to traditionally feminine issues. She helped organize the Congressional Wives Task Force, cofounded Families for the Homeless, and raised awareness and funding for mental health initiatives. Perhaps her most famous crusade was geared toward protecting children from what she deemed inappropriate entertainment content. Working with the Parents Music Resource Center (PMRC), Gore fought to get the music industry to put warning labels on albums that contained lewd lyrics. She also pushed for a television program rating system similar to the one used to identify adult-themed movie content. Although opponents of labeling called Gore a cultural terrorist and an advocate for censorship, her efforts resulted in the implementation of a voluntary system of warnings indicating the age-appropriateness of media content.[7] Her work with the PMRC was politically valuable to her husband; it helped him claim the family values mantle generally appropriated by Republicans. Gore's public activities helped her husband earn an invitation to join the Democratic presidential ticket in 1992.[8]

Laura Lane Welch, later known as Laura Bush, was born to Harold and Jenna Louise Welch in Midland, Texas, on November 4, 1946. Her father was a real estate developer, and her mother kept the books for the family business. Laura Bush credits her parents for her love of reading, noting that they instilled in her an appreciation for books when she was quite young.[9] By all accounts, her home life was ostensibly more stable than Tipper Gore's was, yet a tragic event defined her youth. At the age of seventeen, she was out for a drive when she ran a stop sign and struck and killed a close friend who was driving another car. She was not charged in the accident, nor was she seriously injured, but she later said the event had a dramatic effect on her personal outlook on life.[10] She graduated from high school several months later, earned a bachelor's degree in education from Southern Methodist University in 1968, and worked as an elementary school teacher. In 1973, she obtained a master's degree in library science from the University of Texas at Austin and became a librarian in Houston. She later relocated to Austin.

Laura Welch met George W. Bush at a friend's home in the summer of 1977, and they married four months later. Laura Bush subsequently ceased her own professional endeavors and began assisting her husband with his ultimately unsuccessful 1978 congressional campaign. She later helped her husband as he toiled in support of his father's 1980 presidential (which eventually turned into a vice presidential) bid. In 1981, Bush gave birth to twin daughters and became a full-time mother. In order to help with George H. W. Bush's campaign, in 1988 the family relocated to Washington, DC. They remained there through the early 1990s. Bush and her family returned to Texas following the 1992 election. When her husband won the Texas governorship and was inaugurated in 1995, Bush became a conventional first lady of Texas. Although she did not host many formal events, she did perform most of the ceremonial duties of the governor's spouse and addressed issues that aligned with purportedly acceptable feminine interests. She advocated for women and children, took an interest in health care, and promoted literacy.

The biographies of both Tipper Gore and Laura Bush typify a modern version of the ideal republican mother. In each case, the candidate's spouse gained the education necessary to be a fitting partner to her husband and to care for her children. Each woman also ceased individual professional pursuits to support her husband's political ambitions. They each embraced traditionally feminine issues, defended the choice to assume a domestic focus, and justified their public engagement by asserting their interests as mothers. Gore and Bush embodied republican motherhood ideals by prioritizing the needs and desires of their husbands and their children above their own. Unlike Clinton and Dole, neither Gore nor Bush had to downplay her professional accomplishments in order to appear to meet the ideals related to conventional female patriotism. The life each woman had led fit the vintage feminine model; therefore, republican motherhood rhetoric was an obvious tool many individuals used when discussing and evaluating this pair of political spouses.

Representations of Tipper Gore and Laura Bush

The lived experiences of the wives of the 2000 presidential nominees invited an assessment that focused on their traditional lifestyles. Their domestically oriented backstories corresponded positively with the common practice (as demonstrated in every chapter of this book) of journalists and party leaders to interpret candidates' spouses using historically entrenched gender norms. In this case, however, rather than pitting two contrasting images of womanhood against each other (as in 1992) or trying to force the women to fit the mold of customary female patriotism (as in 1996), various renderings of Gore and Bush celebrated traditional feminine roles and accentuated the ways each woman filled her maternal and spousal responsibilities. The women were promoted as icons of femininity because of their conventional perspectives.

Media Coverage

After two election cycles filled with controversial and politically active spouses, in 2000 the press faced a set of presidential nominees' wives who were relatively scandal free and who avoided the spotlight whenever possible. Although some stories negatively highlighted Gore's efforts to get warning labels on entertainment content or revisited the tragic consequences of Bush's auto accident as a teenager, both were routinely and positively depicted as appropriately feminine potential first ladies. The most common media portrayals defined the women based on their relationships with others, particularly singling out their roles as supportive wives and protective mothers. Yet for each woman the press emphasized slightly different characteristics of the republican mother ideal.

During the 2000 campaign, the press was quick to cast Gore as the quintessential political spouse by building on the public image created during her time as the vice president's mate. Reporters characterized Gore as self-sacrificial and family oriented. She was the "archetypal pretty blond politician's wife"[11] with an "All-American cheerleader look"[12] who provided unwavering assistance to her husband and whose primary occupation was caring for the couple's four children. Stories often explained Gore's advanced education and limited professional experience either by joking that her degrees in psychology helped her manage and understand her husband[13] or by tying her past studies to her political causes.[14] The media also frequently underscored her decision to quit working altogether after her husband decided to enter politics. Gore was described as knowing her role and fulfilling it dutifully, and her two main goals, as delineated by journalists, were to humanize her husband and to protect children (hers and everyone else's).[15]

As vice president of the United States, Al Gore had played the straight man in contrast to Bill Clinton's playboy for eight years by the time of the 2000 contest. In comparison with the more gregarious incumbent, he had earned a national reputation for having a stiff, serious persona often considered wooden or robotic.[16] Yet, when paired with the congenial and vivacious Tipper, Al came across as much more personable; together the two were pronounced a "popular Washington power couple."[17] Tipper Gore was credited with bringing out the charismatic side of her husband.[18] When the press queried her about her husband's stern persona, she responded by sharing stories that revealed the vice president's flare for romance and his softer side. She called her husband playful and "sexy," talked about his sexual prowess, and implied he slept in the nude.[19]

Gore's personal disclosures were intended to offer a supposedly more accurate image of her husband, but her preoccupation with his sexuality became a point of critique against his campaign. Journalists argued that sharing such intimate details about her marriage was a strategic political ploy that smacked of desperation.[20] Because most Americans were largely unfamiliar with (or unconvinced of) the purportedly amorous side of the Gore couple, when the two engaged in a somewhat passionate televised kiss on stage during the 2000 Democratic National Convention (DNC), it became big news and received lots of mixed coverage by various media outlets.[21] The most cynical interpretations of the embrace called it a calculated exchange intended to send a message about Al Gore's fidelity that would further distance him from the philandering Bill Clinton.[22] More sympathetic reports called it an awkwardly spontaneous moment between dedicated life partners.[23] In the end, the kiss proved a memorable interaction of little political consequence that provided more useful fodder for entertainment programs than for undecided voters.

Although some commentators took issue with the intimate nature of Tipper Gore's attempts to reshape her husband's public persona, most reporters did not censure her for the remarks. To the press, Gore had long been "the antidote to her stuffy husband, Lucy to his Ricky Ricardo."[24] She had also occasionally demonstrated her "raucous side and . . . authentic subversive streak."[25] Known for taking pictures of photographers assigned to capture images of her and having once spontaneously jumped fully clothed into Lake Michigan to surprise journalists covering the 1996 DNC, Gore had developed a mostly positive relationship with the press over the years.[26] She had a reputation for going off script and for defying expectations in lighthearted and relatively innocuous ways; therefore, to the press, Gore occasionally sharing personal insights about her husband was not out of character. Instead, commentators asserted that the continual effort to draw attention to the candidate's sex appeal was a sign of the campaign taking advantage of Gore's amiable nature in an ill-advised manner.

In addition to framing Gore as a charming and spontaneous potential first lady who offered a counterbalance to her husband's rigid personality, the press routinely focused on her standing as a conventional wife and mother. Most stories about Gore began by detailing her feminine attributes and her domesticity. She was a woman who "had married her high school sweetheart, settled on a farm . . . sewn the dining-room drapes, planted the vegetable garden,"[27] and resigned herself to having only four children after hoping for six. She was complimented for earning a master's degree, then praised for choosing her children and husband over her own career ambitions. Reporters commended her willingness to engage in campaign activities on her husband's behalf, though she preferred a life of privacy for herself and her children. The press depicted Gore as motivated by her concern for her family and her regard for others rather than by her own needs or desires.

Members of the media positively framed Tipper Gore by contrasting her with First Lady Hillary Clinton. It is not uncommon to highlight distinctions between potential first ladies and those who previously filled the role, but this juxtaposition specifically pitted the traditional ideals of femininity embodied by Gore against the reportedly heterodox perspective touted by Clinton. Gore was said to be "in manner and bearing . . . an anti-Hillary . . . [whose] self-described advocacy role more echoes Barbara Bush's push for literacy than Hillary Clinton's lead role in the debate on overhauling health care."[28] Journalists claimed that "with their four sunny children, [the Gores are] seen as having a happier, more genuine relationship than the Clintons."[29] Gore was credited for her children's cheerfulness; reporters claimed the kids' happiness was a result of Gore's protectiveness and aptitude as a mother.[30] Meanwhile, the fact that she bore four kids (compared with Clinton's one) was extolled as a mark of the sincerity of her maternal desires and an indication of her husband's virility. As a dedicated mother unmoved by professional or public ambition and willing to constantly be "changing plans and making compromises to promote a husband's career," Gore was cast not only as a counterbalance to her husband's personality but also as the antithesis of the progressive sitting first lady.[31]

The press also promoted a favorable image of Gore as a traditional politician's spouse by interpreting her political actions through a republican motherhood lens. News stories about her work championing various causes connected her social interests to familial responsibilities. Gore's desire to help the homeless was allegedly sparked by her children's compassion for a destitute mother and children they had met in Washington, DC.[32] Her interest in mental health, originally grounded in her childhood experiences with a mentally ill mother as well as her studies in psychology, was often connected to the depression Gore suffered after her son's near-death accident in 1989.[33] Perhaps the most overt links the press made between Gore's public action and her maternal duties were in reference to her work regarding media warning labels. Most coverage of her actions with the PMRC emphasized her drive to protect kids from inappropriate content by empowering parents to make informed decisions on behalf of their children.

Overall, Gore was generally treated kindly by the press in large part because of her adherence to the expectations set by the republican motherhood ideal. News reports cast her as an educated woman who used her knowledge to nurture and sustain her husband and children, sublimated her own ambition, and prioritized others' needs above her own desires. Concerned with her children's well-being and the well-being of others, she purportedly used her access to political power to draw attention to issues that helped protect families. Her interests fit well within the boundaries of acceptable feminine concerns. To the news media,

Gore was the ideal female patriot and an exemplary politician's wife, but she was not the only nominee's spouse presented as a consummate republican mother during the 2000 campaign.

It is not surprising that with such comparable family-oriented biographies, Tipper Gore and Laura Bush received similar treatment from the press. Like Gore, Bush was depicted as an ideal mate for a presidential candidate, and reporters highlighted how she epitomized conservative feminine attributes. Stories underscored her willingness to sacrifice her own interests to buttress her husband's ambitions by discussing her short-lived professional career and her participation in her husband's political endeavors. Bush was portrayed as primarily fulfilling the two complementary roles of wife and mother. As a wife, Bush was characterized as her husband's moral compass by adding both discipline and compassion to his life. As a mother, Bush was said to be concerned with protecting her daughters and promoting traditionally feminine and family-friendly public causes.

News coverage of Bush frequently began by spotlighting her hesitance to become a public figure, followed by a brief delineation of the multiple contributions she had made to her husband's personal and political life. Journalists described Bush as liking "being home, reading books, and taking care of [the couple's] twin daughters" and touted her as principally motivated by domesticity.[34] Several articles about the first lady of Texas reinforced this image of her by sharing an often-repeated anecdote about Laura agreeing to marry George only after he promised she would never have to deliver a public address on his behalf (a deal that was broken shortly after he announced his 1978 congressional run).[35] Reporters dubbed Laura Bush a "political wallflower"[36] and a "reluctant show stealer"[37] and contrasted her tentativeness engaging in public discourse against her vast experience as a campaign aide; one story argued that she had participated in more national campaigns than most paid consultants of the time.[38] Members of the media framed her evolution from a quiescent housewife into an effective campaigner as the action of a spouse driven to champion her husband even when his needs contravened her desires.[39]

In addition to pointing out her willingness to abandon her preferred lifestyle in order to help her husband achieve his goals, the press also applauded Bush for meeting the historically established requirements of a good wife by instilling a sense of social responsibility in her husband and children. Many news stories that claimed Laura had helped George quit drinking in 1986 underscored a key example of her moral guardianship.[40] Although the specific details about how she confronted the problem varied, most versions of events labeled Bush as motivated to protect her family, including saving her daughters from witnessing her husband's bad behavior and preventing her husband from ruining his future political career. News outlets also highlighted Bush's efforts to protect her daughters' privacy. Commentators credited Bush with giving her children a relatively normal life despite the attention generally foisted upon family members of politicians and depicted her maternal activities, such as her tenacious insistence that her children be left out of the limelight, attend public school, and be shielded from politics as much as possible, as those of a woman with a proper focus on her home and family.[41]

The emphasis on her domesticity led many reporters to contrast Bush with Clinton. The comparisons were variously obvious and subtle. On many occasions, reporters specifically urged Bush to draw distinctions between herself and the sitting first lady by questioning Bush about whether she would ever run for elected office,[42] asking her to explain her vision of the proper role of a politician's wife,[43] and querying the extent to which she involved herself in legislative initiatives as the first lady of Texas. Bush generally demurred when pushed to make direct judgments about Clinton's life choices but drew clear distinctions between her version of womanhood and that portrayed by Clinton. Members of the press were less reserved in their juxtapositions, calling Bush the "anti-Hillary[, who] comes across as bright but unthreatening—a reluctant but dependable political wife who's dedicated to her husband's campaign simply because she loves him, and not . . . because she's interested in the spotlight."[44] Framing Bush as the antidote to a claimed fatigue of progressive femininity induced by Clinton, the press presented traditional republican motherhood as the gold standard of behavior for political wives.[45] Journalists reinforced the idea that good female consorts of presidential candidates should be submissive, accommodating, and supportive. By doing so, reporters implied that these same attributes were also lauded in women generally.

Bush was also viewed as an ideal female helpmate based on her limited but feminine-focused set of political interests. Her concern with social issues such as feeding the homeless, assisting struggling mothers and children, and helping those battling AIDS aligned with the tendency for female political actors to prioritize topics related to the home, health, and the well-being of others.[46] According to news reports, Bush spoke most passionately about education and literacy, topics on which she had personal and professional credibility. In much the same way reporters linked Gore's discussion of mental health initiatives with her educational background in psychology, commentators invariably tied Bush's work advancing literacy and early childhood education to her time as a schoolteacher and librarian. Her public advocacy for such issues aided her husband's campaign. By promoting topics associated with the home and family, Bush was regularly credited with adding the compassion to her husband's "compassionate conservatism" campaign mantra.[47]

Gore and Bush contributed to their husbands' campaigns in many ways, including by engaging in events that celebrated traditional feminine attributes. They visited hospitals and schools, and they gave interviews about their home lives. Both women also participated in the *Family Circle* cookie bakeoff. This round of the contest was less heavily reported than previous competitions, but the style of coverage was similar. Accentuating the orthodox feminine roles each woman played throughout her life, stories documenting the competition contained anecdotes about the women learning to make cookies when they were young, accounts of them baking for their families, and brief tales of them teaching their daughters the recipes.

Unlike in past campaigns, in 2000 entertainment media largely ignored the candidates' wives. Although occasional references to one or the other were part of daytime talk-show discussions of the candidates or late-night comedic monologues, Tipper Gore and Laura Bush were relatively invisible compared with Barbara Bush, Hillary Clinton, and Elizabeth Dole. Following the nominating conventions there was a short-lived spike in the attention entertainment outlets paid to the spouses, but even then it was primarily about Gore and mostly directed toward her husband. The Gores' on-stage kiss became a conversation point on talk radio, offered grounds for many jokes on television and in editorial cartoons, and was reenacted as part of an opening monologue for *Saturday Night Live.* Satirical and sketch comedies frequently lampooned George W. Bush, but they rarely discussed Laura Bush. When the candidates each appeared on *Oprah,* a popular daytime talk show of the era, each man mentioned his wife, framing her as an ideal helpmate and an effective mother. Overall, entertainment media represented Tipper Gore and Laura Bush in the same manner as the press did; the women were given modest attention, were discussed largely in reference to their husbands, and were praised for their embrace of traditional feminine roles.

Using the rhetoric of republican motherhood to demonstrate their self-sacrificial natures, their dedication to their husbands, and their maternal drives, the news and entertainment media portrayed Gore and Bush as ideal spouses. The presentations varied only by degree. Each was said to add a missing element to her husband's persona; Gore brought spontaneity and fun to counteract her husband's purportedly wooden manner, whereas Bush contributed a sense of orderly structure and compassion to her husband's unpolished and politically conservative demeanor. Although each enhanced her husband's appeal, neither wife appeared controlling or inappropriately influential.

For all of the talk of a liberal media bias that surrounds most presidential campaigns, the press certainly seemed to prefer female mates of candidates that promoted a conservative view of American womanhood. Neither Gore nor Bush was questioned about her decision to give up her professional pursuits to care for her husband and children. Instead, both were praised for the sacrifices they made and for their willingness to suppress their own needs and to overcome their own fears to dutifully promote their husbands' political agendas. With both women variously described as a counterpoint to the controversially progressive Clinton, the 2000 news coverage of the nominees' wives provided a clear commentary that favored a more conservative perspective regarding women's proper roles. According to the press, these wives epitomized proper femininity by offering a modern instantiation of the republican motherhood ideal.

The media depictions of Gore and Bush are consequential because they foster a particular point of view regarding women and their position in society. Some commentators argued that coverage of the conventional perspectives of these two particular women gave respect and reverence to a style of womanhood ignored or denigrated during the two previous campaigns. In actuality, this familiar point of view regarding women has never really been disregarded and was not in 1992 or 1996 either. Because republican motherhood has proven to be the default standard by which presidential candidates' wives are judged by most of the mainstream press, traditional femininity is continually presented as the preferred perspective on American womanhood. The media portrayals of Gore and Bush reinforced a homogeneous interpretation of women that favored female domesticity and overlooked the multiple other individual aptitudes and interests women have.

Furthermore, the fact that these outwardly more docile women were rewarded with positive treatment by the press created a model for other women. Future spouses of nominees who wished to avoid controversial coverage had templates for establishing palatable public personas, and female candidates for office received cues regarding the attributes they should highlight in campaigns. Chapters 6 and 7 of this book indicate that the partiality and positive press given women who embrace the republican motherhood ideal inform the strategies used by future potential first ladies. In addition, this type of media coverage confirms submissiveness, dutifulness, and self-sacrifice as desirable traits in women generally.

Party Portrayals

In 2000, each of the two major political parties in the United States embraced the idea that its standard-bearer's wife exemplified a contemporary version of a traditional approach to womanhood because it meant the campaigns could reap the potential rewards of a useful female surrogate without facing the consequences of an overassertive helpmate. Both Gore and Bush were well-educated women who willingly chose to forego professional opportunities to raise children and support politically ambitious husbands. These women were important political operatives whom party leaders strategically deployed to help reach specific target audiences. The women were also used to highlight aspects of their husbands' lives and personalities that other party faithful could not comfortably discuss. Because Gore and Bush had similar public personas, it was difficult for the opposing party to critique one without implicating the other. Therefore, the parties viewed these traditional women as able to generate a great deal of favorable attention for the campaign while offering few discernable drawbacks.

Both the Democrats and Republicans showcased their own nominee's mate as the ideal ambassador to stay-at-home moms, a subset of American voters party leaders presumed important. Because of the comments by Clinton in 1992 that some interpreted as denigrating mothers who did not work outside of the home (see Chapter 2) and the 1996 emphasis on soccer moms who balanced work and home life (see Chapter 3), stay-at-home mothers were a part of the electorate some party members claimed had been largely ignored or dismissed for several election cycles. Democrats and Republicans alike tried to capitalize on this group's apparent neglect by framing their own candidate's spouse as ostensibly one of them. The Democrats used Gore to redefine the soccer mom by including in that voting bloc women like her who were publicly active but had no official employment outside the home. Trying to broaden the Democratic appeal from specifically targeting working moms to addressing all mothers, Gore regularly talked about the need to juggle many different aspects of life when caring for children and a husband no matter one's employment status. She often delineated the struggles she faced as a busy mom and related them to the challenges mothers of all sorts confronted on a daily basis. Gore tried to cast a wide net by building bonds of identification with both working and stay-at-home moms.

The Republicans knew their appeal to female voters was not as strong as that of the Democrats, but they viewed Bush as their means for solidifying support among conservative women and for syphoning some votes away from the opposition. Her background amplified her appeal to women who shared her outlook on womanhood, and the fact that she had been a Democrat before marrying George W. Bush enhanced her credibility when using her maternal perspective to outline the distinctions between the parties. Taking a traditional stance on sex roles, GOP leadership assumed that women, whether stay-at-home moms or working mothers, were primarily concerned with caring for and educating their children. Therefore, party leaders presented Bush's focus on literacy and education as a way to widen their appeal to various types of mothers. Republican strategists believed Bush could garner enough goodwill to help enhance her husband's image. This is part of the reason party leaders aggressively promoted her speech at the 2000 Republican National Convention (RNC).[48]

In addition to winning over female voters, party leaders considered Gore and Bush key to helping shape their husbands' public personas. Because candidates' wives are routinely judged as a reflection of their husbands' decision-making and they are an important part of the nation's representative first couple, the mates' outward image frequently affects voters' perceptions of and support for candidates.[49] The fact that both spouses seemed to complement their husbands in temperament and attitude meant the parties used Gore and Bush to illustrate that their husbands blended reason and passion when selecting a mate; passion was the unexpected element for Al Gore, whereas reason was the unanticipated component for George W. Bush. The wives also helped temper criticisms of their husbands by underscoring their ability to influence their spouses without controlling them; Gore got her husband to be more personable, and Bush helped her husband to be more compassionate. The helpmates presumably provided the public a behind-the-scenes glimpse at the would-be presidents' true character.

One aspect of the 2000 campaign many voters appeared to find refreshing was the lack of attacks each party volleyed against the opposing candidate's spouse. Two election cycles filled with constant pillorying of Hillary Clinton and a fair amount of censuring of Barbara Bush and Elizabeth Dole appeared to leave all life choices women made vulnerable to critique. However, the fact that Tipper Gore and Laura Bush had lived somewhat parallel lives neutralized both parties' ability to chastise the choices of the opponent's wife; condemning the competitor's mate would require either reproving the decisions of their own nominee's spouse or being conspicuously hypocritical. A few Republican Party members made mention of Gore's mental health challenges, and a couple of Democrats alluded to Bush's auto accident as a teenager, but those types of negative portrayals were rare and not sustained. The fact that Gore's most controversial work, her effort to require warning labels on entertainment content, aligned more with Republican priorities than Democratic ones disarmed potential GOP assaults and broadened her appeal among conservative voters. Meanwhile, Bush diligently guarded against saying or doing anything that could be construed as inappropriate or tendentious.

The parties made heavy use of republican motherhood rhetoric and not only upheld but glorified the ideals of old-fashioned female patriotism through their treatment of the spouses during the 2000 election. By presenting these women as ancillary characters defined by their connections to others rather than as autonomous actors with a range of interests, skills, and opinions, the parties reduced Gore and Bush to second-class citizens who relished the safety and security of a home-focused life and relied on others to protect their political interests. The parties used the nominees' spouses to legitimize a point of view that contends women prefer to be domestically oriented. Because both parties' strategic use of the wives directed the women's messaging specifically toward mothers, female citizens were almost exclusively conceptualized as primarily assuming maternal roles. The lack of diverse perspectives between the spouses and the parties meant that customary views of womanhood dominated discussions about the proper functions females should fulfill. In addition, the dramatic decrease in vitriolic attacks on opponents' spouses rewarded women for embracing republican motherhood ideals.

As a simple reflection of the actual lives the spouses had lived and a part of the larger pattern of institutions holding modern women to conventional standards of femininity, the reification of established gender norms by the parties and the press helped solidify expectations that women restrict themselves to traditional roles. So did the manner in which Gore and Bush portrayed themselves.

Self-Depictions

It is not surprising, given the backgrounds of both Tipper Gore and Laura Bush, that the spouses of the presidential candidates in 2000 self-identified as traditional, family-focused wives. Throughout the primary season and during the general election, Gore and Bush both tended to avoid attracting too much attention and still fulfilled the obligations of a nominee's spouse. When the women were put into the spotlight, they stayed true to their well-cultivated personas. They defined themselves in relation to others, accentuated their general submissiveness, and underscored the sacrifices they made to aid their husbands. They embraced conservative views of female patriotism and employed republican motherhood rhetoric to emphasize their orthodox perspectives on womanhood.

Almost without fail, when either Gore or Bush participated in interviews with various media outlets, common topics of discussion included their personal relationships, their preferences for spending time at home, and either explicit or implied comparisons to Clinton. Each woman often talked about her decision to forego developing a professional career to focus on raising children and supporting her husband. Although they frequently cited motherhood as the most rewarding part of their lives, Gore and Bush spent more time discussing their husbands' standing as fathers than their own parental activities. The two presidential contenders' consorts cast themselves as ideal helpmates. Nowhere was this more evident than in each woman's participation in her party's national nominating convention. Their particular activities at the quadrennial gatherings were quite different, but their self-descriptions were quite familiar.

At the 2000 DNC, Gore played the part of a traditional nominee's wife. Even though the emerging norm was for candidates' spouses to address delegates and the nation during a televised prime-time address, a trend started by Barbara Bush in 1992 (see Chapter 2) and continued by Hillary Clinton and Elizabeth Dole in 1996, Tipper Gore did not deliver a full address. She posed for photo opportunities and prerecorded a video message instead of delivering her own full-length live speech. Her speaking role was limited to narrating a video about her husband and their life together and introducing him for his nomination acceptance address. Tipper Gore's sparse verbal activity recalled the days when political wives were seen but not heard at conventions. The content of her brief messages also reinforced a view of female citizenship that tied it to maternal and spousal functions.

Gore received an almost three-minute ovation by DNC audience members when introduced by her daughter as "one of the coolest people you'll ever know . . . my mother, Tipper Gore."[50] Gore then provided a two-minute-and-twenty-five-second lead-in to a video comprising selections from the family photo album. Her brief opening commentary delineated her husband's qualifications for the presidency from a family-oriented perspective. In it, Tipper characterizes Al's public service as time spent "fighting for America's working families" and describes him as a loyal "husband, father, and grandfather . . . [who] will always be there for your family."[51] By emphasizing the personal side of her husband and avoiding mentioning his nonfamilial political work, Gore establishes her perspective as a devoted wife. Her decision to focus on his interest in family life and his ability to effectively fulfill patriarchal duties indicates that Gore considered familial fidelity an important credential for a potential president.

According to Gore, her tribute video to her husband was intended to reveal his personal side and to get audience members to see the vice president "in a way [they] may not have seen him before."[52] The goal was to reframe the candidate, but several aspects of Gore's narration reinforce her self-depiction as an encouraging and steadfast spouse instead of revealing much about her husband. For example, talking about their early courtship, Gore delineates the numerous efforts she made to solidify their relationship. She explains how she traveled to Massachusetts (with her grandmother as a chaperone) to visit him at college, she eventually moved to Boston to be near him, and she made trips to Tennessee to meet his family. She also shares several brief anecdotes about the couple's life as newlyweds that highlight their assumption of typical sex roles. He enlisted in the military, and she learned proper laundry protocol. In the video, Gore represents herself as loyal and attentive to his needs but does not share whether he responded in kind.

When Gore talks about her husband's budding political career, she uses an active voice (e.g., "he listened," "he met," "he fought," etc.), but when she discusses her contributions to their growing family, her style becomes decidedly passive (e.g., the children "were born"; she did not bear them). She also frequently talks about the kids as belonging to her husband. She speaks about "Al putting his family first" and "making time for his children."[53] By using the term "his" as opposed to "ours," Gore gives her husband ownership over the group rather than indicating a partnership between the parents. Such an approach assures that she does not appear overly assertive and turns attention toward the nominee while depicting herself as compliant and deferential.

At the end of the ten-minute video, Gore introduced her husband. Upon taking the stage, he grabbed her and gave her the now-famous kiss mentioned previously. There is no way to accurately assess the sincerity of the embrace, yet the video footage shows an awkwardness that indicates Gore likely did not expect as impassioned a greeting as she received. However, the visuals also illustrate a quick adaptation by Gore as she adjusted her response. On stage, Gore yielded to her husband's desires, called attention to his presumed virility, and provided a glimpse into his personality in a manner befitting a conventionally good wife. Throughout her time at the DNC, Gore reinforced her image as a traditional woman happy to fill a subservient role and who showed no indications of having her own ambitions beyond the domestic realm.

Bush took a more active role in the 2000 RNC. Following in her mother-in-law's footsteps as well as those of Hillary Clinton and Elizabeth Dole, Laura Bush delivered a full-length address on the second night of the gathering. Although the convention planners had indicated that there would be no keynote address, some pundits identified Bush's speech as the de facto keynote (others claimed Colin Powell's opening night oration was the true keynote).[54] The speech afforded Bush the opportunity to more formally introduce herself to the nation, to appeal to female voters, and to humanize her husband by offering personal insights into his character. In the speech, Bush depicts herself as the epitome of republican motherhood and promotes its ideals as essential to American womanhood.

The self-introductory elements of Bush's 2000 RNC speech are generally entwined with her tales about her and her husband's personal history; the only exception is her discussion of her professional life, which occurs early in the address. Joined on stage by many schoolchildren at the outset of the speech, Bush acknowledges her work as a teacher and librarian. She tells listeners, "I have never had this many people watch me give a speech before, but I feel very at home here in this classroom setting. Education is the living room of my life."[55] This passage underscores her comfort with children and situates her profession in terms of a home. The line draws attention to her premarital employment and her enduring concern for kids. It also begins to cast her in terms of a potential national mother figure. A bit later she talks about deciding to become a teacher when she was in the second grade, explaining, "Growing up I practiced teaching on my dolls. I would line them up in rows for the day's lessons."[56] Yet, in spite of her declared lifelong passion and drive to be a teacher, Bush abandoned her career upon marrying in order to assume the positions of traditional housewife and campaign aide.

Bush's brief references to her short-lived time in the workforce reinforce a limited interpretation of her interests and abilities because they remain squarely within a purportedly feminine realm. She does not discuss her individual accomplishments or the joys of pursuing her childhood passion. Instead, Bush describes herself as uncertain and filled with self-doubt in the classroom. She complains, "Many of my second, third, and fourth grade students couldn't read, and frankly I'm not sure I was very good at teaching them."[57] Rather than emphasizing positive elements of her work or underscoring her skills, she calls attention to her inability to function effectively as a professional. She follows this line with a call for better teacher training and a reference to her husband's plans for enhancing educator preparedness. Bush uses her brief career (approximately four years teaching and four more as a librarian) to promote the republican motherhood ideal by undermining her competence in order to promote her husband's agenda. As a traditional wife of a politician, Bush's professional aptitude is considered less important than advancing her husband's political aspirations.

Bush also uses her career to highlight her relationships and establish her own potential future actions. She presents herself as a teacher (along with her husband) to her daughters, and she reminds listeners, "George spends EVERY night with a teacher."[58] Bush promises that if she were to be first lady she would "make early childhood development one of my priorities, and George will strengthen Head Start to make sure it's an early reading and early learning program."[59] Avoiding taking the spotlight entirely away from her husband, Bush mentions her own intentions and delineates her husband's related endeavors. Her plans for herself are vague, whereas her husband's ideas are concrete and actionable.

Although she references her work outside the home, Bush primarily portrays herself as a dutiful and deferential wife during her RNC speech. Mirroring elements of Barbara Bush's 1992 convention address (see Chapter 2), Laura Bush almost exclusively depicts her own motherhood as a by-product of her husband's parental activities. Every anecdote she shares involves "George and Laura" as parents or George as father but never just Laura as mother. Bush talks about how "George and I have been blessed throughout our 23 years of marriage. . . . He was elected governor, we moved to Austin with our then 13-year-old twin teenagers, and since then, we've been through dating, driver's licenses, prom night, and just a few weeks ago, high school graduation."[60] She shares tales of her husband's interactions with his daughters, including him reading stories to the twins and "turning story time into a contact sport," but she provides no similar anecdotes about her actions as a mother.[61] Unless she makes it part of a "we" statement, such as, "We wanted to teach our children what our parents taught us,"[62] Bush does not claim an independent parenting role for herself. Although Bush does include herself more directly than Gore did by using "we" and "our" instead of "him" or "his," in her own version of the story of her life, Bush rhetorically disappears as an autonomous being after she marries her husband.

In her RNC speech, Bush embodies orthodox feminine patriotism by rendering herself in a subordinate relational position and accentuating her functionality as a helpful wife. Admittedly, because the speech is a campaign oration championing her husband's presidential bid, it makes sense that the candidate should be the focal point. Still, Bush marginalizes both her professional work and her own motherly role by privileging her husband's political agenda and paternal influence. Bush thereby reinforces traditional hierarchies within the home in a manner typified by the republican motherhood ideal.

In addition to portraying herself in conventional terms, Bush also favors traditional female roles for all women during her address. Her discussion of female citizens tends to conflate the terms "woman," "wife," and "mother." She does this in part because she is trying to appeal directly to many American women who might have felt ignored or belittled during Clinton's time as first lady. She speaks generically of women only once in the entire oration, asserting, "The President of the United States of America is MORE than a man—or a woman, as I hope the case will sometime be."[63] This reference is a passing argument in favor of women's political advancement. However, this one line is overshadowed by Bush's twenty remarks about children, five allusions to family, and three specific statements about wives and mothers. Her comments regarding children generally underscore her interest in governmental initiatives designed to increase literacy or improve health care for kids. Her attention to wives and mothers focuses on their need to fulfill their responsibilities to their husbands and children. Throughout the speech, Bush keeps women's purported interests within the domestic sphere. Because she is expressly trying to attract votes from certain females, she (and her speechwriters) assumes that the targeted women share her political perspective and prioritize home life in much the same way she does. However, the absence of any acknowledgment of less traditional female activity limits discussions of womanhood and defines all women based on old-fashioned norms.

Both Gore and Bush stayed true to their well-established public personas as traditional wives whenever participating in the 2000 campaign and particularly during their respective parties' national nominating conventions. Both women emphasized their willingness to sacrifice their own aspirations in support of their husbands' political ambitions, kept attention focused on their husbands, humanized the candidates, and restricted their own professed interests to issues commonly considered within the feminine realm. In contrast to the 1996 candidates' spouses, who had to contort themselves and their records to try to fit an image they did not match, Gore and Bush personified the republican motherhood ideal for most of their adult lives. They were able to naturally and comfortably portray themselves as having a conservative outlook on womanhood and wifedom.

Although the self-depictions of Gore and Bush seemed to provide a narrow and restrictive view of women, they did represent a segment of female citizens who might have felt criticized for their decisions not to enter the work world. For women who preferred a life of domesticity, the 2000 election provided a confirmation that the broadening opportunities for women in society also included the option of choosing not to pursue a career and, instead, to seek out a more orthodox lifestyle. By celebrating their own embrace of republican motherhood, Gore and Bush recognized the valuable work stay-at-home mothers were doing, and, mirroring the actions of early domestic feminists (see Chapter 1), they reminded listeners that a maternal perspective could add valuable insights to the political realm.

Despite the potential positives associated with the self-portrayals put forth by Gore and Bush, the conversations about womanhood elicited by their depictions were harmful to women's pursuit of political equality. By relying on their standing as wives and mothers to establish their credibility, these women provided high-profile evidence that legitimized the perception of women as ancillary citizens dependent on others for their political identity.

Conclusion

Many aspects of the 2000 presidential election were historic and unusual, yet as far as the spouses of the major party nominees were concerned, the campaign was about as conventional as any modern contest. After eight years of progressive discussions regarding women's political aptitudes and interests centered around the appropriate role of both sitting and prospective first ladies, the wives of both the Democratic and Republican candidates offered a traditional image of femininity. Tipper Gore and Laura Bush embodied a modern version of republican motherhood through their lived experiences, their campaign activities, and their self-depictions. Neither spouse overtly criticized women who chose to build professional lives, and each was careful to frame her own choices as right for her, but the manner in which both women talked about womanhood was quite restrictive. The fact that Gore and Bush highlighted their own traditionalism invited the parties and the press to do the same. Therefore, conversations about two of the most visible female political actors in 2000 were steeped in republican motherhood rhetoric.

Whether a reflection of deep social conservatism when it comes to women or a referendum against the generally more progressive, independent, and politically assertive Clinton, Gore and Bush earned revealing poll numbers during the 2000 campaign. Reaching 57 percent, Gore's pre-DNC favorability score was the highest, excluding sitting first ladies, of any nominee's spouse between 1992 and 2016.[64] Her unfavorable ratings were the second lowest among these women at 18 percent; Bush had the lowest unfavorable score with just 8 percent of all respondents indicating they had negative opinions about the GOP candidate's wife.[65] Gore's net favorability is third highest among all spouses (sitting first ladies included) within this time frame, and Bush is sixth on the list.[66] Bush's standing might be tied to the fact that most voters claimed to have no opinion of the eventual first lady before her appearance at the RNC, and her general election participation during this cycle was fairly muted.[67] Overall, these wives, who created no notable controversies and earned largely favorable press coverage, garnered more praise and less derision from potential voters than most nominees' spouses of the past quarter-century.

Republican motherhood rhetoric provided a useful and appropriate tool for describing and evaluating Gore and Bush. By focusing on these women's obligations as compliant and encouraging wives, the press, the parties, and the women themselves helped illustrate the importance of the background assistance many women provide to their spouses. The traditional approach to womanhood and to female patriotism gave voice to the interests of women who had chosen a more conventional lifestyle and who had felt displaced by a changing world in which women were increasingly expected to pursue careers of their own no matter their personal preferences. Thus, coverage of Gore and Bush empowered a subset of female citizens by demonstrating that women could exert influence through their husbands and by engaging in civic activism that enhanced rather than interfered with their domestic responsibilities. Echoing the earlier domestic feminists and relying on the original application of republican motherhood ideals, explications of Gore and Bush as gender role models acknowledged homemaking as a valuable means of contributing to society and categorized wifedom and motherhood as useful types of female political activity.

Still, in addition to the few potential positives that came along with this emphasis on conventional feminine roles for presidential partners, there were also substantial drawbacks. By casting Gore and Bush as direct opposites of Clinton, and by favoring the more docile spouse approach, the press, the parties, and the wives themselves implied that conservative perspectives on women were more acceptable and appropriate than progressive ones. Supportive and submissive spouses who embraced long-established gender norms were treated more kindly than those who broke with expectations, were more assertive, or showed any personal ambition. Furthermore, rewarding the quiescent mates with more positive news coverage and fewer opposition party attacks provided behavioral cues for future potential first ladies. As later chapters of this book indicate, many subsequent candidates' mates paid attention to the implications of the 2000 campaign and heeded the lessons proffered by the spouses' treatment during this election cycle. The reinforcement of republican motherhood ideals by the press, the parties, and the spouses effectively encouraged many (though not all) political spouses to curtail their own potentially progressive views of females and instead celebrate motherhood and wifedom as the core characteristics of womanhood.

Nominees' spouses in contests that followed the 2000 campaign often preemptively adapted their public images prior to their spouses becoming presidential contenders to abide by the restrictive expectations republican motherhood rhetoric promotes. Although some spouses continued to test the boundaries of presumed propriety, perhaps believing society had genuinely become more progressive and willing to accept (or at least accommodate) assertive female voices, the majority incorporated republican motherhood rhetoric into their own self-depictions. In 2004, the press and the parties accentuated the different approaches to womanhood taken by the brash billionaire businesswoman Teresa

Heinz Kerry and the conservative, demure First Lady Laura Bush. As happened in 1992, the distinctions between candidates' spouses and their approaches to femininity became a major point of contention throughout the election. The next chapter explores how republican motherhood rhetoric influenced these women and continued to pervade discussions surrounding American womanhood early in the new century.

5

Laura Bush and Teresa Heinz Kerry

The All-American Wife and the Assertive Heiress (2004)

The first presidential election of the twenty-first century was less contentious than the last contest of the twentieth. As had happened many times before, an incumbent president faced a reasonable challenger in a battle of philosophies and perspectives that invited lively debate about the future of the nation. Nevertheless, the 2004 election was significant because of its historical context; it was the first presidential competition following the terrorist attacks on September 11, 2001. Much has been written about the actual events occurring on September 11 and their subsequent impacts. For this chapter, the most relevant ensuing consequence was a marked change in political dialogue during the 2004 election. National security, military preparedness, and the nation's international responsibilities became major topics of concern for the first time in many election cycles, and the presidential candidates were frequently evaluated based on leadership qualities associated with traditional masculinity.

The 2004 presidential election was also notable for changes in the communication technologies used during the campaign. The internet, which had been growing in common public use for about a decade at that point, was a relatively new tool campaigners began to experiment with just after the turn of the century. Political operatives started creating websites promoting specific candidates and covering particular issues in the hope of capitalizing on the relatively broad reach and low costs the new medium offered. Democratic candidate Howard Dean is often credited with having run the first digital presidential campaign during the 2004 primaries.[1] Dean was ultimately unsuccessful, yet his efforts laid the foundation for a new type of electioneering. The internet's impact, though, was not limited to candidates' use of it; the new communication platform became a device through which traditional and nontraditional sources disseminated information. Mainstream media began migrating onto the new forum, and alternative online news and opinion sources provided additional interpretations of the political events, actors, and issues of the day. The internet fundamentally changed the way people interacted with the world around them, making 2004 a pivotal year for communicative evolutions in presidential politics.

For women, the 2004 presidential election was an intriguing one. Females continued to improve their representation in government by winning more national leadership positions. The 109th Congress included eighty-five women. Female membership in the legislative body increased to almost 16 percent from the previous high of 14 percent.[2] In addition, although the gap in candidate preference between males and females was less dramatic than during previous campaigns, there was an interesting variation among subdivisions of women.[3] Women as a whole backed the Democratic nominee, John Kerry, over incumbent President George W. Bush by 10 percent, but white women (particularly married mothers) supported the president. As a group, white women endorsed Bush over Kerry by a margin of almost 11 percent.[4] The noticeable difference indicated that, despite often being treated as a homogeneous bloc, women actually held a variety of disparate views on candidates.

Because national security dominated much of the political conversation in 2004, the discussion of women's position in society was less prominent than in 1992 or 1996. Still, women's political aptitude was more widely debated than in 2000 for an assortment of reasons. First, as a result of her high-profile activities on behalf of the state of New York following the September 11 attacks, Hillary Clinton's name was being tossed around as a potential future presidential candidate. Second, unlike in 2000, when the candidates' spouses were near mirror images of each other and were accommodating wives who showed little ambition of their own, the mates of the 2004 nominees were apparent polar opposites who represented distinct perspectives on women's social and political roles. Both factors propelled discourse about women as political actors and presented republican motherhood ideals as the primary means for evaluating women.

The 2004 Presidential Nominees' Spouses

The cast of characters on the ballot in 2004 was a fairly standard mix of individuals. President George W. Bush retained his vice president, Dick Cheney, as his running mate. Although both had been controversial throughout their first term, they faced no serious challengers during the Republican primary and easily secured the GOP nomination. John Kerry, a decorated Vietnam War veteran and longtime senator from Massachusetts, battled several challengers for the top spot on the Democratic ticket, including his eventual running mate, North Carolina senator John Edwards. The electoral matchups were unsurprising. The wives of the nominees, though, were the most distinctive individuals among the high-profile political actors during the contest. The informal but very real battle of the candidates' spouses matched the quiescent First Lady Laura Bush against the brash and bold Teresa Heinz Kerry.

Laura Bush moved into the White House with her husband on January 20, 2001. She had been a reliable but relatively modest part of her husband's 2000 presidential campaign (see Chapter 4 for more on her early life and her political participation in 2000). The subdued early months of her first ladyship underscored her intent to remain unobtrusive. She gave a few interviews about her transition to Washington, DC, and appeared by her husband's side during requisite public events. She initially declared education and literacy the focus of her public endeavors and later added women's health to the list. Bush's role as the first lady took a dramatic turn on September 11, 2001, when she assumed a national mother persona and became the de facto "comforter in chief" to citizens devastated by the terrorist attacks. In the weeks following the incident, Bush organized fund-raisers for victims' families, visited hospitals housing the injured, and sent messages of encouragement to the nation when speaking with the press. The tragedy sparked Bush's interest in issues related to women and equality, particularly drawing her attention to the oppressive treatment of females in the Middle East.

During Bush's initial tenure as first lady, she became a markedly more enthusiastic advocate for women and developed women's wellness initiatives in the United States and abroad. Her efforts on behalf of the National Heart, Lung, and Blood Institute's Heart Truth campaign helped increase knowledge about the impact of heart disease on women. She also traveled abroad to learn more about women's lives outside of the United States. Bush spoke out on the plight of Iraqi and Afghani women using various public platforms, including once taking over the president's national weekly radio address to draw attention to the issue. Despite the fact that some critics claimed Bush's willingness to condemn the mistreatment of women in other nations while turning a blind eye to sex-based inequality in the United States was hypocritical, her activities helped enhance her public image and garnered her high favorability ratings.[5]

Bush's public undertakings throughout her time as first lady marked a significant departure from her previously proclaimed preference for living a serene, family-focused lifestyle. As explained in Chapter 4, Bush had been a rather demure, subservient, and compliant wife throughout her adult life and had embraced a great many attributes of the republican motherhood ideal. Although her increased interest in women's issues and her willingness to speak out on behalf of the causes she deemed important demonstrated a bit of empowerment on Bush's part, these actions were, in fact, still part of her overall embrace of old-fashioned female patriotism. She discussed issues that fit neatly within the feminine realm because they dealt with women, the family, and the domestic sphere. In addition, her activities were generally prompted by a desire to aid her husband; she spoke as an extension of her husband rather than as an independent political actor and used her perceived credibility, consistency, and compassion to build positive perceptions of him and his administration.

Teresa Heinz, known throughout the 2004 presidential campaign as Teresa Heinz Kerry, was the second wife of the Democratic presidential nominee, John Kerry. She was born Maria Teresa Thierstein Simões-Ferreira in Mozambique on October 5, 1938. She was raised along with her sisters in a comfortable home in an upscale Portuguese colonial community. She earned a bachelor's degree from the University of Witwatersrand in 1960 and a master's degree from the University of Geneva's School of Translation and Interpretation in 1963. She then moved to the United States and became an interpreter at the United Nations (UN). Fluent in five languages, Simões-Ferreira was a successful translator who interacted with many political figures.

In 1966, Simões-Ferreira married Henry John Heinz III, heir to the H. J. Heinz Company, and became a naturalized citizen of the United States. She had three sons with him. Teresa Heinz was an active stay-at-home mother who remained politically engaged while raising her children. She participated in philanthropic endeavors, advocated on behalf of women, supported environmental activism, and championed her husband's political ambitions (helping him win one of Pennsylvania's seats in the US House of Representatives and eventually the US Senate). At an Earth Day event in 1990, Henry Heinz introduced his wife to then Massachusetts senator John Kerry. The next year, Henry died in a helicopter crash. As a new widow, Teresa declined to run for her husband's Senate seat and instead took over the Heinz family's philanthropic organizations.

Heinz was serving at the behest of President George H. W. Bush as a member of the US State Department's delegation at the UN Earth Summit in 1992 when she saw John Kerry again. They began dating a few months later and married in 1995. John was a lifelong Democrat and Teresa a registered Republican. Yet despite their differences, Teresa enthusiastically supported John's political aspirations.

Although she had married two influential men, Heinz was a well-known political powerhouse in her own right. In 2001 she was named one of Pennsylvania's most politically powerful women.[6] She was elected a fellow of the American Academy of Arts and Sciences, received honorary doctorate degrees from twelve institutions of higher education, and was a trustee of both the Brookings Institution and the Carnegie Institute. She frequently championed causes related to the environment and women's economic security and maintained a consistent interest in promoting health and wellness. In 2003, she was awarded the Albert Schweitzer Gold Medal for Humanitarianism. Heinz's accomplishments made her one of the most publicly active spouses of any contemporary presidential nominee.

Heinz's experiences generally did not align with the expectations established by the republican motherhood ideal. Even though she was married, had children, supported the political aspirations of each of her husbands, and championed traditionally feminine causes, she maintained her own voice, defined herself in terms of her independent interests, and commanded resources that allowed her to set her own political priorities. She developed her own political aptitude, asserted power not often wielded by women in the public sphere, and was not reticent about expressing her own points of view. Admittedly, her prowess was predicated upon her ability to manage a financial fortune she had inherited from her first husband, but her adroit administration of those funds and her confident appropriation of the power the money provided were entirely hers. Still, Heinz did find it necessary to make certain accommodations during the 2004 presidential contest to manage the constraints associated with conventional views of American womanhood.

Prior to her husband's announcement of his candidacy, Heinz unofficially added his last name to her own. She proclaimed, "My legal name is still Teresa Heinz. Teresa Heinz Kerry is my name . . . for politics. Just so people don't ask me questions."[7] Unlike Hillary Rodham Clinton, who explained her use of her maiden name based on her professional accomplishments, yet subsequently claimed the Clinton moniker in earnest, Heinz Kerry was blunt and unapologetic about her name modification. She acknowledged the need to yield to certain customs but capitulated begrudgingly. She justified the retention of her legal name, saying, "Teresa Heinz is what I've been all my growing-up life, adult life, more than any other name. And it's the name of my boys. . . . So that's my legal name."[8]

In addition to adding her second husband's name, Heinz Kerry showed fidelity to him by changing her political affiliation and registering as a Democrat at the outset of the 2004 election season. The fact that she waited to do so until the beginning of his campaign rather than when they married indicated that the shift was a purely political decision intended to defuse charges that she did not truly support her husband's political perspectives. In contrast, Laura Bush changed her political party registration almost immediately upon marrying and often said she became a Republican by marriage. Based on their lives prior to 2004, Bush seemed a sincere manifestation of republican motherhood, whereas Heinz Kerry appeared to strategically take cues from the antiquated approach to attenuate criticism rather than out of a genuine embrace of old-fashioned female patriotism.

Bush and Heinz Kerry were two very different individuals. Bush was a relatively accommodating wife who had dedicated her life to supporting her husband. Heinz Kerry was an ambitious and worldly woman who had long acted as an independent agent in the public sphere. As Bush was learning to embrace political power, Heinz Kerry brandished her influence with the ease that comes from decades of practice. While Bush was becoming aware of gender inequities around the world, Heinz Kerry was globally recognized as a champion of the oppressed. Despite their differences, neither woman could escape public vetting that frequently employed republican motherhood rhetoric; the 2004 presidential race tested each woman's ability to fit into the well-defined parameters of an archetypal model of female citizenship.

Representations of Laura Bush and Teresa Heinz Kerry

The obvious dissimilarities between Bush and Heinz Kerry made republican motherhood rhetoric a viable tool for the press and the parties to use when comparing and contrasting the nominees' spouses. With coverage remarkably similar to that of Barbara Bush and Hillary Clinton in 1992, the mainstream press proffered a narrative that cast Laura Bush as the embodiment of accepted norms of womanhood and Teresa Heinz Kerry as an atypical and rebellious female. The parties mimicked these portrayals by alluding to republican motherhood when bolstering and critiquing the nominees' spouses. In their self-presentations, Bush painted herself as a model American female, whereas Heinz Kerry tended to avoid stereotyping herself in conventional terms.

Media Treatments

Laura Bush was relatively well liked by the press and often earned positive coverage as a "gracious, gentle, and noncontroversial" first lady.[9] Called a "role model for all Americans,"[10] Bush was praised for being "America's grief counselor"[11] following the September 11 attacks as well as for her earnest interest in children's literacy and women's treatment around the world. Many news stories about Bush that circulated during the 2004 presidential campaign focused on her "image as a traditional wife and mother"[12] and described her as "well-liked, grounded, and authentic."[13] Even though most pieces revered Bush for many of the same characteristics accentuated during the 2000 campaign, other articles noted a change in the first lady.

Arguing that Bush had evolved from a "cool Marian the Librarian . . . into a hot Mary Matalin," journalists remarked on the first lady's more vocal role in her husband's reelection campaign.[14] Although a few stories hinted that Bush's time in the White House might have generated experiences that inspired her to use the first lady pulpit in more meaningful ways, most coverage tied her increased activity to her lifelong status as a compliant wife. Many in the press claimed Bush's willingness to "shed her cozy, nonpartisan public image" in order to defend her husband's record was primarily motivated by a desire to help him secure a second term.[15] Building on the good-wife persona established throughout her life, some commentators insisted Bush's transformation into a "sharp-edged, tart-tongued, defensive protectrix" was a result of her wifely devotion rather than a personal political awakening.[16]

In addition to outlining the differences between the Laura Bush of 2000 and the more polished political operative she became in 2004, the press also continually compared the sitting first lady with her predecessor. Juxtapositions between Bush and Clinton took many forms. Some stories about Bush used lead-ins such as "Mrs. Bush may lack the dynamism and ambition of former first lady Hillary

Clinton, but . . . "[17] and "Unlike her immediate predecessor Hillary Rodham Clinton . . . "[18] Other comparisons involved full stories outlining the distinctions between the women and their approaches to the first ladyship.[19] Just as during the 2000 election, the reported divergence between Bush and Clinton almost always boiled down to their enactment of American womanhood. Bush was once more cast as the "un-Hillary: a traditional wife and mother, who embraced only the most uncontroversial causes in public policy."[20] Although Clinton's purportedly negative characteristics were not always explicitly delineated, they were always implied by the ostensibly positive descriptions of Bush. These depictions of Bush as the "Perfect Wife"[21] in contrast to the allegedly flawed Clinton also frequently formed the foundation for media assessments of voters' philosophies on women generally and about their specific attitudes toward Bush and Heinz Kerry.[22]

The media repeatedly framed Bush as the converse of Clinton and charged Heinz Kerry with being an older and more established version of the former first lady. Although most comparisons between Heinz Kerry and Clinton were based on their outward embrace of feminist ideals, their outspoken natures, and their professional assertiveness, the one area in which the two women had the most in common was likely their contentious relationship with the press. Both women tussled with journalists throughout their husbands' campaigns. Clinton was pilloried for her comment about staying home and baking cookies, and Heinz Kerry was lambasted for telling a reporter to "shove it."[23] The mainstream media seemed disinclined to embrace either woman and, just as it had been with Clinton in 1992 and 1996, the press was usually unforgiving of and uncharitable toward Heinz Kerry throughout the 2004 campaign.

Most news stories about Heinz Kerry began with a summary of her extraordinary wealth and the power she wielded because of it. She was described as "rich, clever, outspoken (in several languages) and she's got money . . . lots of it. . . . Heinz Kerry runs her own discrete show in support of her husband. She has her own schedule, her own staff in Washington, and her own private plane."[24] Heinz Kerry's independence and affluence were reinforced multiple times, though rarely in an approving manner. Writers called her an unusual political spouse, pointing out that she "refuses to suppress her élan or subordinate her character"[25] and "doesn't wear campaign buttons and sometimes even forgets to introduce herself as a presidential candidate's wife."[26] Although some writers conceded that Heinz Kerry might have been appealing to certain groups of voters, particularly women who found her assertiveness and self-assurance refreshing, she was most often chastised for ignoring the expected behaviors of a traditional candidate's spouse. Unlike Bush, who was portrayed as quashing her own needs and concealing her beliefs in order to promote her husband, Heinz Kerry was accused of being decidedly self-important, berated for making her right to freely express herself a "feminist issue,"[27] and censured for failing to adequately fawn over her husband.[28]

Despite the frequent representations of Heinz Kerry breaking with traditional expectations of candidates' wives, her media image was not entirely iconoclastic. Commentators were quick to point out her history as a stay-at-home mother during the women's movement of the 1970s. The press accentuated her apparent embrace of domesticity to question the authenticity of her public persona as a progressive woman. Some reports underscored her desire to be viewed as a tireless caregiver and a champion of the "discounted women of the Third World"[29] and contrasted it against her exacting standards as the manager of Heinz family funds and her own claim to be a demanding mom.[30] Although Heinz Kerry was recognized by some as having "tastes, pieties, and hobbies . . . of a traditional, if not Victorian, lady," her brashness and her wealth became points of derision many in the press used to illustrate the differences between her and purportedly average American women.[31]

In 2004, the media often pitted Bush and Heinz Kerry against one another despite the women's own apparent desire to avoid engaging in a contrived spousal competition. The women were pointedly asked about each other and usually did not say anything controversial. However, the relentless questions demanding self-comparisons did result in Heinz Kerry eventually commenting on the difference between herself and the first lady. She explained, "I don't know Laura Bush. But she seems to be calm, and she has a sparkle in her eye, which is good. But I don't know that she's ever had a real job—I mean, since she's been grown up."[32] This remark created a stir among reporters and was viewed as a slight against homemakers. Heinz Kerry went on to insist that her own experiences in life were "a little bit bigger—because I'm older" and contended, "It's not a criticism of her. It's just, you know, what life is about."[33] She ended up issuing a public apology to the first lady a few days later and spent several weeks clarifying her views about the value of homemakers and caregivers.

The press argued that Bush and Heinz Kerry made very different contributions to their husbands' campaigns. Bush's offerings were more positively framed than Heinz Kerry's were. Bush was described as bringing a sense of equanimity, compassion, and orderliness to the presidential pair that helped combat her husband's supposed recklessness. She also added an intellectual element to the White House that her husband could not feign. According to many pundits, Bush provided a counterbalance to the nominee that allowed many women to justify supporting the incumbent president. Heinz Kerry, in contrast, was occasionally credited with helping win over older women who had been widowed or who sought new opportunities later in life, but she was more often denounced for building barriers between her husband and potential voters. Commentators viewed her wealth and her appreciation for expensive items as reminders of the fiscal and experiential gap that stood between the billionaire and her husband and the bulk of Americans.[34] As one writer put it, Heinz Kerry "serves to highlight how very not average the Kerry family is."[35] By most metrics, the press considered her a potential liability to her husband's political ambitions, whereas it painted Bush as an asset to the president's campaign.

The wives of the 2004 presidential contenders were more visible in entertainment media than those during the 2000 contest. Both participated in interviews on daytime talk shows, with and without their husbands, and each submitted a recipe for the quadrennial *Family Circle* cookie bakeoff. Bush was a frequent guest on late-night talk shows and had earned a few fleeting moments of attention in comedic monologues. In these forums she was rarely criticized, but her good-wife standing did occasionally provide points of humor. When visiting shows such as *The Tonight Show with Jay Leno,* Bush mostly offered lighthearted commentary about life in the White House and discussed her own interests in literacy and women's health. Heinz Kerry, however, was frequently chastised on various entertainment programs. Her citizenship and patriotism were questioned on conservative talk radio, her wealth was mocked in satirical and sketch comedies, and her assertive attitude was a common point of ridicule. One *Saturday Night Live* skit ridiculed Heinz Kerry for scaring off voters by sounding "crazier than a tomcat in a bag of squirrels," and the show's faux Bill Clinton advised a fake John Kerry to "ditch the wife."[36]

The mainstream press was rather predictable in its treatment of the candidates' wives in 2004. However, the rise in popularity and use of the internet meant there were other sources of commentary regarding Bush and Heinz Kerry. The relatively new communication medium gave more people and groups a virtual megaphone with which to express their points of view. As a result, these women were discussed in a multitude of ways. Online versions of mainstream news sources tended to simply repeat the offline narratives explained above. Alternative news and opinion websites offered points of view sometimes based on fact and other times grounded in rumor and conjecture. On some sites Bush was praised as the model all-American woman and as a paragon of domesticity, yet on others she was accused of being a drug dealer and setting back progress by the women's movement. Some forums lauded Heinz Kerry for her purportedly pioneering ways, whereas others condemned her for any number of reasons from her accent to her wealth to her unwillingness to conform. The online treatment of these women often revealed more about the authors of the articles than about the women themselves.

Press representations of Bush and Heinz Kerry relied heavily on republican motherhood rhetoric. By evaluating the women based on their performance as loving mothers, dutiful wives, and self-sacrificing individuals, news and entertainment media reified archetypal standards of womanhood. Casting Bush as the good wife, willing to give up her own time and preferred lifestyle to support her husband's pursuit of a second term in office, reporters idealized the modern manifestation of republican motherhood principles. Despite her increased political activity, Bush was still depicted as quiescent, unassuming, and motivated by her domesticity. According to the press, Heinz Kerry was a wealthy and powerful woman unwilling to self-abnegate to aid her husband. No matter how her other attributes might align with traditional female patriotism, her refusal to succumb to the basic expectations of submissive political spouses meant she could not be a true republican mother. Disinclined to acquiesce to restrictive standards for American womanhood, Heinz Kerry was demonized by many and was identified as a contributing factor in her husband's electoral loss.[37] Overall, there was no doubt which female style the news media preferred. The traditionally feminine Bush received more favorable attention than the heterodox Heinz Kerry.

The press treatments of Bush and Heinz Kerry illustrate some problematic trends regarding the portrayal of candidates' spouses that also affect perceptions of women as political actors. The reliance on old-fashioned standards for assessing these women reinforces the idea that a good woman's proper place is in the home or standing behind a great man. The inability for commentators to update their interpretations of women and depict them in a variety of ways means the press fails to appropriately account for the wide range of experiences and expertise females might have. Providing such narrow representations of womanhood hinders female citizens' efforts to gain equal footing across a wide range of arenas, including politics. When reporters treat prominent women as ancillary to the political process and chastise them for trying to expand their participation outside of the domestic sphere, they legitimize an archaic division of labors and interests that makes it difficult for women to assert their rights as autonomous individuals.

The fact that so many news stories depended on antiquated views of womanhood when discussing Bush and Heinz Kerry seems to indicate either that the roots of the republican motherhood ideal are so deeply entrenched that it appears the natural approach to evaluating women, or that maintaining familiar story lines is more important to media commentators than accurately describing the richness of women's lived experiences. Despite the alleged liberal bias the media proffers, its treatment of presidential nominees' spouses reveals a profoundly conservative inclination when it comes to women and politics. The journalists who continue to write about candidates' wives using republican motherhood as the preferred measure of femininity do a grave disservice to all American women by implying that women should only strive to fulfill conventional and subservient roles.

Party Representations

Each political party routinely tries to make the most positive use possible of its presidential nominee's spouse during a campaign. The 2004 presidential contest was no different. By accentuating specific attributes of Bush and Heinz Kerry, and by employing them in particular kinds of ways, the Democrats and

Republicans revealed mildly different perspectives on the perceived appropriate role of women in presidential politics. The way each party treated its own candidate's spouse and the mate of the opposing party underscored the indelible nature of republican motherhood ideals and the tendency to continually reify outdated standards for female participation in politics.

Like those of her mother-in-law more than a decade before her, Bush's likability ratings far exceeded those of her husband, making her a valuable asset to the Republican Party. Campaign strategists were eager to capitalize on Bush's appeal and used her in myriad ways throughout the 2004 campaign. In addition to the multiple live events Bush attended with her husband, the party also included her in many television ads. In the commercials, she spoke on a wide range of issues, always grounding her commentaries in her experiences as a wife and mother. Online, she was part of just one ad, the only positive commercial her husband's campaign put on the internet.[38] Republican strategists also planned solo rallies, fund-raisers, and media appearances designed to showcase the popular first lady. Yet even when she appeared without her husband, Bush constantly reaffirmed her persona as a deferential and even reverential wife.

The GOP leaders viewed the charming and gracious Bush as an essential tool for winning over women voters of various types. Her interest in literacy and education was seen as a draw for intellectually minded females, her focus on health initiatives for women and children appealed to mothers, and her newfound personal voice was strategically amplified to ingratiate her with more liberal women who, party leaders hoped, would appreciate her interest in women's treatment around the world. Furthermore, by avoiding discussions of polarizing topics, Bush appeared to be "above the rough-and-tumble of the political fray."[39] This gave her comments more weight with women who disliked the often negative tone of presidential politics. Identified as the fourth most powerful woman in the world in 2004, Bush and her well-cultivated good wife persona were assets the Republicans tried to capitalize on during the campaign.[40]

GOP members exclusively used republican motherhood frames when describing the first lady. They tied her interest in women's health to her nurturing nature and argued that her concern for others was the mark of a good mother and made her a good woman. She was called the president's number one surrogate and his most effective defender.[41] Party leaders contended that, as his lifelong companion, she knew him best and represented his interests most cogently. The Republican strategy was for Bush to earn the trust and support of American women and then transfer that goodwill to her husband. While party members worked hard to help buttress Bush's purported everywoman image based on her experiences and actions as an ideal female patriot, a second part of the GOP's strategy to bolster her appeal was to create a clear contrast between the first lady and the woman who might replace her.

Republicans were not shy about negatively injecting Heinz Kerry into the

2004 presidential campaign. GOP strategists built covert and overt messaging that portrayed the Democrat's wife as unusual. They continually pushed stories about Heinz Kerry's differences from average Americans. Because she was a foreign-born naturalized citizen, surrogate campaigners often questioned Heinz Kerry's patriotism. They also underscored her distinctive perspective by challenging her ability to understand the lives of people the Republicans considered real Americans. Highlighting the frequent awkwardness of the affluent heiress's interactions with others, the opposition likened Heinz Kerry's appearances at campaign stops in the midwestern United States to those of "a debutante at a tractor pull."[42] Additionally, her accent and occasional ill-advised and unusual word choice (e.g., calling herself an African American) gave the Republicans concrete examples of her inability to assimilate after decades in the United States.

Challenging Heinz Kerry's trustworthiness, Republican party spokespeople were quick to point out her many decades as a key GOP figure in Pennsylvania politics. They insisted that her switch to the Democratic Party was disingenuous and politically mercenary. Party members accentuated her extreme wealth, implied that her political influence was unladylike, and made her philanthropic work seem like an ambitious pursuit of power. Republicans frequently used the fact that she had married two wealthy and powerful men as a sign of her aggressive desire for self-promotion.[43] By traditional standards of femininity, Heinz Kerry was, according to Republican-driven messaging, not a good wife and thus could not be considered a good woman. These depictions of the Democratic nominee's mate were an attempt to discourage voters from building points of identification with Heinz Kerry and her husband. Denigrating Heinz Kerry by accentuating her ostensibly unfeminine behaviors was an integral part of a broader narrative designed to make the Democratic couple appear peculiar, aloof, and out-of-touch with the interests and needs of the electorate. Heinz Kerry's outspoken nature and unwillingness to play the role of the docile political spouse reinforced the GOP's messaging and provided plenty of ammunition for the party's attacks against her.

The Democratic Party had a much more difficult time employing images of Heinz Kerry and Bush during the 2004 campaign than the Republicans did. The unpredictable and strong-willed Heinz Kerry was determined not to allow herself to be manipulated by her husband's handlers. She hired her own staff, kept her own schedule, and by many accounts made it difficult for campaign strategists to manage her actions or image.[44] Democratic Party leaders tried to promote her assertiveness as a positive trait and maintained that she reflected the strength and determination of all American women. They framed Heinz Kerry's bold outspokenness as a refreshing change from the doublespeak that usually pervades national politics. They presented her occasionally unvarnished delivery as a sign of her sincerity and honesty.

In some ways, the Democratic treatment of Heinz Kerry broke with the trend of presenting presidential nominees' spouses using republican motherhood rhetoric. She was portrayed as strong, independent, and knowledgeable about a number of wide-ranging topics. Her ability and willingness to discuss traditionally masculine issues such as economics, world affairs, military actions, and national security from the multiple perspectives of a businessperson, a philanthropist, a lifelong activist, a world traveler, and a mother and grandmother made Heinz Kerry's participatory citizenship more akin to the autonomous type generally afforded males. According to some party leaders, her credibility extended beyond the relational realm dictated by an archaic approach to female patriotism.

Despite its apparent progressiveness, the Democratic depiction of Heinz Kerry was not entirely heterodox. There were still many efforts to accentuate the ways she embraced mainstream femininity. She was urged to participate in conventional endeavors most wives of nominees engaged in, including the cookie recipe contest. Heinz Kerry played the doting wife on news and entertainment programs; gave interviews focused on her experiences as a mother; and frequently served, as most political spouses do, as a prop in a variety of photo ops. Heinz Kerry's husband also tried to help her appear like a more traditional wife. In words that evoked images of the more home-focused wives of the 2000 campaign, he described his wife as "a private person, even shy; hitting the campaign trail isn't her first choice for how to spend her time."[45] However, rather than characterizing her political activity as motivated by her duty to him, he explained his wife's political participation by saying "she's committed to doing this because the issues are so important."[46] Still, even though there were attempts to underscore some of the ways Heinz Kerry conformed to traditional expectations of womanhood, the party provided a rather broad-minded interpretation of the would-be first lady.

The Democrats faced a bit of a challenge in critiquing their opponent's spouse during the 2004 presidential campaign. Bush was quite popular among many Americans, so directly attacking the congenial woman who had established a largely apolitical public persona would have caused Democrats to appear unkind and overly aggressive. Moreover, because the Democratic nominee was having difficulty securing support from women, a group that historically supported liberal candidates, by chiding Bush the Democrats would have risked alienating stay-at-home mothers and "security moms," a new version of soccer moms concerned about terrorism following the September 11 attacks.[47] Although a few seemingly rogue Democratic proponents did level charges against Bush intended to degrade her standing as a moral guardian and role model, those efforts were inconsistent and were not part of a coordinated strategy by the party as a whole. The only sustained effort the Democrats made to inject Bush negatively into the campaign was one that eventually backfired.

Democratic operatives questioned Bush's integrity and sincerity by declaring that her political participation was not a reflection of her own interests and decision-making but was based on strategic choices made by Republican leadership. Essentially, the Democrats alleged that Bush was little more than a pawn in her husband's political game and that his advisors were the architects of her purported political awakening. Even though it is not unusual for opposing parties to claim a political wife is disingenuous, in this instance the rebuke simply reinforced Bush's quiescent wife persona, an image based on the conventions of republican motherhood, to which the US electorate regularly responds in a favorable fashion. Reminiscent of the Democratic efforts to reproach Barbara Bush in 1992, the party's assertions against Laura Bush in 2004 were limited and ineffectual.

Both the Republican and Democratic Parties incorporated republican motherhood rhetoric into their efforts to use the spouses of the presidential nominees throughout the 2004 contest. The Republicans were more impactful than the Democrats were. By highlighting the ways Bush embodied the orthodox characteristics of an ideal female patriot and denouncing Heinz Kerry's inability to fit the archetypal norms of American womanhood, the GOP capitalized on citizens' deep-rooted beliefs about the appropriate role of women in society. Conversely, the Democrats offered voters a complex picture of Heinz Kerry that contravened expectations set for political wives in the United States. Although this multifaceted perspective was more reflective of the true nature of most women, it was an image that challenged common beliefs and ran counter to the oversimplified media image of the preferred female spouse. The uniqueness of the Democratic representations of Heinz Kerry supported the Republican charge that she was atypical and thus untrustworthy.

The parties' depictions of Bush and Heinz Kerry are troubling because they seem to indicate that, when it comes to politically prominent women, an oversimplified rendition of womanhood is preferable to a more complex representation. Both parties' treatment of Bush fortified the idea that women should be other-centric. By commending Bush for her reputedly apolitical nature and her willingness to avoid self-advocacy, the Republicans sent a clear message about their ideal form of femininity. The Democrats tacitly condoned this approach by not openly critiquing the first lady's seeming self-abnegation. In addition, Heinz Kerry being framed as problematic, not only by Republicans but also by Democrats who complained about her unwillingness to be "handled," indicated that assertiveness and wide-ranging competence were troublesome traits for a politician's wife and for women generally. Although the Democrats did provide a more encompassing understanding of womanhood through their depictions of Heinz Kerry, the awkwardness with which this was done hints at a potential lack of earnestness in the party's purportedly progressive view of femininity. The fact that her own husband accentuated her domesticity rather than praising her extensive expertise in diverse fields supported the notion that women, no matter their other interests or talents, should keep focused on the home. Despite their seemingly different views of the presidential contenders' wives, both major political parties advocated, explicitly and implicitly, for an outdated and oversimplified version of American womanhood in 2004.

Self-Depictions

Bush and Heinz Kerry were both apparently enthusiastic participants in the 2004 presidential campaign. The women gave interviews to press correspondents, visited morning news programs, appeared on daytime talk shows, and spoke at fund-raisers and political rallies. Whether with her husband or solo, each woman's words and deeds helped solidify her public persona. Although both women provided a more nuanced picture of themselves than the media or the parties allowed for, even their own self-presentations made use of republican motherhood rhetoric. Both Bush and Heinz Kerry employed the trope, but they did so in distinctly different ways and to different degrees.

Bush had a well-defined public persona going into the 2004 election. Considered the perfect wife by many, she reinforced that image through the political messages she delivered on behalf of her husband. She frequently based her own credibility on her position as a wife and as a mother to twin daughters. She rarely asserted her own rights or interests as an independent citizen when broaching political topics of the day. Her concerns were couched in the language of motherhood as she addressed children's health and the treatment of women in foreign countries. The only time Bush broke out of established wife and mother roles was when she defended her husband's specific education initiatives. She justified his "No Child Left Behind" policy from the perspective of a former schoolteacher. Of course, because teaching has long been considered a suitable profession for women and is frequently linked back to women's duties as mothers and nurturers (see Chapter 1), Bush's references to her time in the classroom also accentuated her embrace of traditional femininity. It seems Bush so fully enacted the ideals of republican motherhood that every aspect of her perspective, even her work outside the home, reinforced an orthodox approach to womanhood.

Bush's 2004 address to the Republican National Convention (RNC) provides concrete examples of the ways she framed her public image and discussed women during the president's reelection campaign. She opens her speech with a tale about the early days of her life with him. Tying the present to the past and reminding listeners of the couple's long marriage, she says, "I am enjoying this campaign. It's reminded me of our very first one, 25 years ago. George and I were newlyweds. . . . You learn a lot about your husband when you spend that much time in a car with him."[48] Her brief narrative about their early life together demonstrates her willingness to adapt her interests to meet his needs and establishes her credibility based on her fealty as a wife. By emphasizing what she learned about her husband rather than what they learned about each other, Bush places the relationship-building duties on herself as the female spouse. She essentially argues that for two and a half decades she has been gathering knowledge about her husband and therefore should be considered an authority on his character and actions. His credibility is based on his actions, whereas hers is based on her lengthy study of him.

In addition to taking on the relational duties in her marriage, Bush assumes responsibility for building personal connections with the audience when she redefines the speech as a replacement for conversations she might have with individual audience members. She explains that her address contains information she would reveal "if we sat down for a cup of coffee or ran into each other at the store."[49] Barbara Bush, Hillary Clinton, and Elizabeth Dole had each used this strategy when they delivered addresses at their respective nominating conventions; Laura Bush used this approach in 2000 as well. This tactic attempts to depoliticize what is clearly a political message. Despite the fact that it appears folksy and charming, reframing the speech in such a fashion actually decreases the political power of the woman delivering it. Although she seems to be increasing her perceived likability and making herself more accessible, Bush is actually discounting her standing as a political agent and limiting her argumentative strength by aligning her comments with the types of exchanges frequently disregarded as idle chatter and gossip. The tendency to recast these speeches in this manner implies that women should not engage in political dialogue and degrades the value of their contributions. Furthermore, Bush's reconceptualization of the speech underscores her preference for building relationships rather than expressing her individual political perspective. She reifies stereotypes about women's functions in society.

Throughout the speech, in order to succinctly delineate her husband's interests and accomplishments, Bush lists a number of topics she maintains she could speak on at length, including education, tax relief for small businesses, stem cell research funding, health care, and increased home ownership in the United States. Never expounding more than a sentence or two on each, Bush quickly identifies national security as her central talking point. Although taxes, research funding, economics, and national security are traditionally considered masculine issues, Bush's treatment of each does not challenge gender normative perspectives. She only briefly mentions most of the purportedly male topics and does not extrapolate on any of them. The full extent of her consideration of the economy is that "home ownership in America, especially minority home ownership, is at an all-time high."[50] She clarifies that the president's stem cell research funding would allow "science to explore its potential while respecting the dignity of human life."[51] By injecting judgments about the compassionate nature of her husband's actions, Bush highlights her feminine perspective on subjects usually associated with male interests.

When Bush discusses national security, she does so from a decidedly relational perspective that amplifies her traditional womanliness. Framing national security as "the issue that I believe is most important for my own daughters, for all our families, and for our future," Bush makes the country's protection a familial topic rather than a military one.[52] Instead of addressing the strategic elements of the actions her husband ordered or the international effects of his decisions as commander in chief, Bush emphasizes the domestic impact of both the September 11 terrorist attacks and the nation's response to them by providing detailed narratives about the sacrifices made by the families of armed forces personnel. She tells the story of a mother whose sons were deployed overseas and states, "Their mother, Cindy, stands watch too, with worry and prayer."[53] Alluding to the tenets of the republican motherhood ideal, Bush describes Cindy's actions using martial terminology and insists that a mother's work and worry are patriotic acts.

A second specific example Bush uses to spotlight the impact military duty has on the family is a bit more complex. It begins as an unconventional illustration that breaks with long-standing gender norms by focusing on a husband and father struggling with his wife's deployment to Iraq. Although the tale is somewhat progressive in its initial explication of sex roles, it quickly alludes to customary divisions of labor within the home when Bush jokes about the husband's inability to effectively do laundry in his wife's absence. In the end, the story becomes an homage to past wives of servicemen as Bush relays the man's sentiment that he was learning "what our soldiers' wives have known for generations: hope and grief and perseverance."[54] Even Bush's attempt to chronicle women's roles in society in a more enlightened manner relies on an acceptance of and reverence for orthodox gender roles. Even though the stories are not about her personally, they do reveal a perspective that sees women primarily as caregivers and homemakers as they acknowledge some changes in society.

In the latter half of her 2004 RNC speech, Bush specifically reflects on her time in the White House in a manner meant to cast her husband in a positive and personal light. As she comments on key moments of her husband's presidency, Bush emerges as a supportive but ultimately passive wife. She remembers "some very quiet nights at the dinner table" and how she "listened many nights as George talked with foreign leaders on the phone, or in our living room, or at our ranch in Crawford."[55] Bush was "sitting in the window of the White House, watching as my husband walked on the lawn below" and "was there when my husband had to decide" to send troops into Iraq.[56] Yet in none of her tales is she a confidant, a sounding board, or even a source of solace for her husband. By standing watch during consequential moments without playing a role of any significance, much like the military mother in her earlier tale, Bush enacts the republican motherhood ideal by being present but not participative.

Bush's 2004 RNC speech is a bit more progressive than her 2000 address. In it, she includes women in more forward-thinking ways, such as acknowledging their ability to function as small business owners and active military personnel. She also discusses the international push for more freedoms for women in Afghanistan and Iraq. Yet throughout the speech Bush portrays herself in a decidedly traditional manner. She speaks as a proud wife lauding her husband's accomplishments and character. She downplays her own authority and characterizes her interests as limited, if not in scope, then in perspective; she talks about even the most masculine issues in customarily feminine terms. Bush defines herself based on her relationships with others, mostly as a wife and later in the speech as a daughter, and she denudes her own political power by discounting her ability to act as an autonomous political being.

Heinz Kerry created a multifaceted public persona for herself throughout her time as the Democratic nominee's wife. Her ability to explore a wide range of topics from a variety of perspectives meant she continually reframed her public persona. In some cases, she underscored her lifelong advocacy for others by talking about her participation in anti-apartheid rallies as a student in South Africa as well as her philanthropic work. At other events, she addressed economic issues and highlighted her skills as a businesswoman. Heinz Kerry also gave interviews during which she emphasized her maternal experiences by sharing her tough, yet loving, parenting philosophy. The Democratic candidate's spouse distinguished herself from many of the previous nominees' wives by creating a complex and progressive self-depiction. Her public image was not easily encapsulated in a simple caricature and did not fit the traditional model of womanhood. Therefore, it is not surprising that when it came time to more formally introduce herself to the nation during her speech at her husband's nominating convention, Teresa Heinz Kerry did not follow the example set by others and painted a portrait of herself distinctly different from that of Barbara Bush, Elizabeth Dole, Laura Bush, and even Hillary Clinton.

At the 2004 Democratic National Convention (DNC), Heinz Kerry was one of the principal speakers on the second night. As with most spouse speeches, Heinz Kerry's nationally televised DNC address reached the largest audience she faced during the entire campaign. Because candidates' wives had been giving speeches for several election cycles at this point, there were clear expectations for the content of the speech. Heinz Kerry was tasked with humanizing her husband, sharing insights about their personal life and his character, introducing herself to the nation, and illustrating how she would fulfill the role of first lady of the United States.[57] In the end, she did accomplish some of the goals typically associated with the spouse's speech (though not in expected ways), but she did not meet all of them. Although the historic keynote address delivered by then US

Senate candidate Barack Obama later that same night overshadowed her speech, Heinz Kerry's DNC oration is important because it illustrates her divergence from other potential first ladies. She intentionally challenged republican motherhood ideals.

Heinz Kerry's address begins with the standard salutational comments that often occur at the outset of such orations. In this case, Heinz Kerry starts by thanking her son for introducing her. She says, "Thank you, Christopher. Your father would be very proud of you and your brothers."[58] This simple verbal gesture is a bit more unconventional than it seems at first. Christopher's father was Henry Heinz III. Therefore, Teresa Heinz Kerry opens her speech in support of John Kerry by invoking the memory of her deceased first husband, a well-liked Republican senator. Coupled with the several times she had called Henry Heinz III the love of her life while campaigning for John Kerry, this reference to her first husband countermands Teresa Heinz Kerry's ability to claim the mantle of a dutiful and doting spouse. This allusion to her first husband subtly reminds listeners that her children are not the candidate's offspring and that she had pledged fidelity to another man before marrying John Kerry.

In addition to breaking with tradition by referencing her previous spouse before mentioning her candidate-husband, Heinz Kerry asserts her own independent voice in other ways throughout her address. Hinting at her reputed boldness, she tells listeners, "By now I hope it will come as no surprise that I have something to say."[59] Illustrating her intelligence and worldliness, she then welcomes listeners in Spanish, French, Italian, and Portuguese. Although she does express gratitude for "the opportunity to stand before you and to say a few words about my husband, John Kerry," she does not explicitly define herself primarily as his wife.[60] This is evident when, after stating that her purpose is to explain "why I firmly believe that he should be the next president of the United States," she launches into a discussion of her own nationality and citizenship status.[61] Rather than describing her courtship with John Kerry or their life together, she speaks about her life in Mozambique, her participation in anti-apartheid marches, and her experiences during the battle for civil rights in Africa. Heinz Kerry mentions her husband and her father but ultimately defines herself through her actions rather than her relationships, breaking with the traditional republican motherhood imagery most candidates' wives embrace.

The issues Heinz Kerry raises throughout her speech and the manner in which she broaches topics also distinguish her from other wives of nominees. She talks openly about US citizenship and the responsibilities it carries. Using her experiences as an advocate for others and as an immigrant herself, Heinz Kerry declares, "I have a very personal feeling about how special America is, and I know how precious freedom is. It is a sacred gift, sanctified by those who have lived it and those who have died defending it."[62] She then pushes for gender equality without equivocation or qualification. Alluding to the first amendment of the US

Constitution, she contends, "My right to speak my mind, to have a voice, to be what some have called 'opinionated,' is a right I deeply and profoundly cherish. And my only hope is that, one day soon, women—who have all earned their right to their opinions—instead of being called opinionated, will be called smart and well-informed, just like men."[63] Pushing for female empowerment, Heinz Kerry directly challenges the ideals of old-fashioned feminine patriotism, which make women's enactment of citizenship contingent on their relational connections to men.

Heinz Kerry's DNC speech contains some elements reminiscent of prior spouses' addresses, but even these passages tend to challenge traditional gender norms. Like many of the wives who had delivered convention speeches before her, Heinz Kerry reframes the talk as part of a conversation rather than a political oration. Unlike her predecessors, Heinz Kerry does not redefine the event in a disempowering manner that implies nervousness or a preference for intimate exchanges. Instead, she describes the presidential campaign as a conversation about shared values and invites the audience to participate in the broader dialogue in order to work "towards the noblest purpose of all: a free, good, and democratic society."[64] Heinz Kerry uses a common characteristic of the spouse's speech but does so in a manner befitting her assertive style.

The Democratic nominee's wife also meets an established expectation for this type of speech when she applauds maternal activities. Appreciating her own mother by praising her "warmth, generosity, wisdom, and hopefulness, and thank[ing] her for all the sacrifices she made on our behalf, like so many other mothers," Heinz Kerry links maternal behaviors with characteristics usually associated with republican motherhood, such as being self-sacrificial and caring for others.[65] However, rather than focusing on motherhood as the main role women play, Heinz Kerry maintains maternity is just one of many aspects of womanhood. Her very next line moves the conversation toward a more global empowerment of women not tied to their childbearing status. She argues, "I want to acknowledge and honor the women of this world, whose wise voices for much too long have been excluded and discounted. It is time . . . for the world to hear women's voices, in full and at last."[66] Teresa Heinz Kerry's address contains the second fewest references to mothers of any individual spouse's convention speech given between 1992 and 2016 (Melania Trump's brief address has only one), but it mentions women more times than the addresses by Barbara Bush, Hillary Clinton, Elizabeth Dole, and Laura Bush (in 2000) combined. Heinz Kerry is careful not to conflate the terms "woman," "wife," and "mother" as most presidential contenders' mates before her did.

Heinz Kerry delivered one of the most divergent spouse's speeches of the modern era. In it she displayed a sensitivity to the oppression women have faced, showed a willingness to express herself, and discussed issues of various sorts from multiple perspectives rather than relying heavily on her maternal experience as her defining frame. She accentuated the bold public persona previously established in the press and by the parties. Heinz Kerry did not embrace the compliant wife image expected of purportedly good political spouses. Instead, she challenged many existing gender norms and put forward a self-depiction that embodied a progressive view of women as independent political actors.

Bush and Heinz Kerry gave the public very different self-portrayals during the campaign and particularly through their respective speeches at the nominating conventions. Although Bush's treatment of women generally was more expansive than in 2000, her self-presentation was still quite heavily tied to archetypal expectations of female patriots that idealize women who are other-centric, docile, and defined by their relationships. Heinz Kerry, in contrast, challenged the established expectations of femininity by defining herself based on her own actions and experiences, expressing her own point of view, and refusing to reductively combine the categories of woman, wife, and mother. Bush embraced republican motherhood and used its rhetoric to provide voters a familiar frame to understand her as a public figure; Heinz Kerry challenged the public to expand its view of women and womanhood by offering a heterodox female figure and proclaiming her right to operate as an autonomous citizen. In the end, whether accepting or challenging established norms, both women still had to contend with the traditional and restrictive views of American womanhood that pervade interpretations of women's political and social roles.

When it came to creating overt public images of themselves, each woman treated listeners as though they were a reflection of herself. Bush approached her audience as if it was very conventional but was experiencing a somewhat delayed political awakening, and Heinz Kerry considered the citizenry more progressive, accepting, and open-minded about the abilities and interests of all of its members. In the end, it appears Bush had a more accurate understanding of the US electorate. Bush was applauded for increasing her awareness of the struggles women faced, and Heinz Kerry was censured for her decades of actual activity on behalf of oppressed females (and others). Based on the reactions to their respective personas, it seemed that the public still preferred the rhetorical recognition of women as citizens to the actual empowerment of female residents just as it did when postrevolutionary era women were given republican motherhood rhetoric in lieu of a formal place in the new government.

In addition, the fact that Heinz Kerry's perceived power and diverse set of interests and abilities became liabilities indicates that well-roundedness and professional competence might be desirable character traits in a leader, but not in his wife. Her willingness to challenge the norms associated with self-portrayals of candidates' spouses created a situation in which she (and her husband) was punished for openly demonstrating the various kinds of potential influence active and empowered female citizens could have. Because Bush was rewarded for a modest increase in political consciousness and Heinz Kerry was admonished for her more direct political engagement, the overarching message became one that encouraged women to exhibit caution when showing an interest in politics. This was generally true for women and specifically the case for future candidates' spouses.

Conclusion

Republican motherhood rhetoric pervaded the depictions of the presidential nominees' spouses in 2004. Because the first lady has customarily been considered an icon of American womanhood, attitudes about the president's spouse and those who might assume that role reveal much about the public's ideas regarding women. It seems that year the electorate was not especially open-minded. A survey conducted during the summer showed that, although some younger folks and people residing in urban areas liked the idea of a more progressive first lady, most citizens preferred presidential consorts to be more conservative and to fill more conventional roles.[67] Many US citizens agreed that a first lady should not hold a job and should not act as an advisor to the president but that she should serve as the official hostess at White House events.[68] Whether that is a result of nostalgia associated with the role or if it is a reflection of an underlying desire to maintain more traditional gender roles in society, regressive attitudes toward first ladies certainly influence judgments about potential presidential helpmates and speak to prevailing social interpretations of womanhood.

For Bush and Heinz Kerry, many people's desire for mainstream femininity among political wives was evident in their respective standing in public opinion polls. Bush, one of the most traditional mates to a contemporary presidential candidate, was wildly popular. Her net favorability rating of 57 percent in 2004 was second among all would-be first ladies since 1988.[69] Conversely, Heinz Kerry, labeled less orthodox than even Hillary Clinton, was rated lowest among all nominees' spouses until Melania Trump in 2016 (see Chapter 8).[70] In fact, until 2016, no candidate's mate other than Heinz Kerry had earned a negative overall rating. Though commentators argue about the influence presidential consorts might have on voter decision-making, it is clear that having a spouse with low ratings creates additional hurdles for any candidate.[71]

Bush gained perceived power by enacting the tenets of republican motherhood. Meanwhile, Heinz Kerry's refusal to contort herself to fit the archetypal mold of the ideal female patriot and her unwillingness to sublimate her needs and interests to aid her husband made her one of the least liked potential first ladies in modern history. Bush's seemingly apolitical nature gained her favorable media coverage, whereas Heinz Kerry's independence made her the target of criticism among many journalists and commentators. Although the two women shared common experiences as stay-at-home mothers and both advocated on behalf of women, the press and the parties cast the two as diametric opposites. The woman embracing more traditional perspectives on womanhood in 2004 was rewarded, and the one challenging established norms was punished.

The clear message emerging between 1992 and 2004 regarding candidates' wives was that the nominees' spouses who tended to be self-sacrificial, to unquestioningly support their spouses, and to avoid controversial topics or issues (i.e., those who most enthusiastically embraced republican motherhood ideals) faced less scrutiny and earned more public acclaim than those who reflected more complex and assertive aspects of American womanhood. This repeated lesson offered an informative template for Cindy McCain and Michelle Obama as they took up the mantle of would-be first ladies during the 2008 presidential campaign. As becomes clear in the next chapter, both women embraced key elements of republican motherhood, but for very different reasons.

6

Cindy McCain and Michelle Obama

Revering Wifedom and Motherhood (2008)

The 2008 US presidential election was certainly historic. For the first time since 1928 no incumbent or former president or vice president earned his party's nomination (in 1968 Richard Nixon, a nonincumbent former vice president, attained the top GOP spot). In addition, the two major political parties fielded an uncommonly diverse slate of primary competitors. Combined, they produced twenty candidates, including one woman, two African American men, and seventeen white males. After months of battling, the top three aspirants made up a distinctive group. The oldest nominee ever selected, John McCain, secured the Republican nomination by early March. Barack Obama, the first African American to successfully contend the Democratic primaries, eventually beat out Hillary Clinton, the first woman to amass nationwide support and win more than 1,000 delegate votes. Clinton conceded on June 7, 2008, ending the most effective presidential bid by a woman up to that time.

Even though it was ultimately unsuccessful, the former first lady's pursuit of the Democratic nomination was noteworthy for a number of reasons, not the least of which was that it increased dialogue surrounding women's ability to participate in politics and govern at the highest level. With no real female predecessor to provide guidance and cautionary advice, Clinton relied heavily on the same strategies many male candidates had used. She engaged in debates on a variety of topics, used her experience as a US senator to build her credibility, and vigorously attacked her opponent with both overt and covert messaging. Her candidacy was relatively traditional in many ways, with the evident exception of her being a heterodox candidate because of her sex. Despite the fact that she employed common campaign tactics, Clinton was frequently lambasted for her style of electioneering. The charges made against her were often related to the same republican motherhood–based critiques she endured as the wife of a candidate and as the first lady (see Chapters 2 and 3). Although plenty of legitimate complaints were made about Clinton's leadership style, criticisms grounded in entrenched gender norms simply reified the stereotypical expectations of women that encouraged female citizens to abdicate their individual right to self-advocacy. However, Clinton's ability to withstand a barrage of attacks throughout the contentious primary season and emerge as a true contender inspired many women to become more active political participants.

Women as a whole continued to take on increasingly visible roles in politics in 2008. The Republicans nominated a female vice presidential candidate for the first time when they selected Alaska governor Sarah Palin to round out the GOP ticket. Additionally, ten women joined the sixty-four females already in the US House of Representatives.[1] The results of the election also meant that the new US Senate would contain an all-time high of seventeen women. With ninety-one females in national legislative leadership positions following the 2008 election, and many more taking on significant positions in the new administration, women's political participation continued to grow in important ways. In the contest, more women than ever before cast a ballot, with more than 70 million women voting in the presidential election.[2]

In 2008, women were a substantial part of one of the most diverse US elections in modern history. However, it was not just the official candidates who contributed to the conversation regarding women as political actors; the spouses of the presidential contenders did as well.

The 2008 Presidential Nominees' Spouses

The 2008 presidential election included a cast of characters unlike any that preceded it. The Republicans nominated former prisoner of war (POW) and long-time Arizona senator McCain. He had been a major player in the Republican Party for decades and had previously tried to become his party's standard-bearer. In an ostensibly cynical move that some argued underestimated female members of the electorate, McCain picked Palin, a novice to national politics, as his running mate in an effort to win over disaffected women frustrated by Clinton's loss. On the Democratic side, one-term Illinois senator Barack Obama became the first African American to earn a position on a major party's presidential ballot. Senator Joe Biden, a respected Democrat from Delaware who had served for thirty-six years and had foreign relations experience, was a predictable choice for Obama's potential vice president. The fascinating mix of individuals associated with the national campaign extended beyond the formal candidates because many surrogates advocated for the prospective presidents. Two of the most relevant and interesting of these were Cindy McCain and Michelle Obama, the wives of the men headlining each party's ticket.

Cindy Lou Hensley, now Cindy McCain, was born on May 20, 1954, in Phoenix, Arizona. Her father was a wealthy beer distributor, and her mother was a stay-at-home mom. Cindy was the only child of her parents' union, but she had two half-sisters, one from each parent's prior marriage. She was a junior rodeo queen and a high school cheerleader, and she was named the best dressed among her high school classmates in 1972.[3] She attended the University of Southern California, where she earned a bachelor's degree in education in 1976 and a master's in special education in 1978. After graduate school, she became a special education teacher in Avondale, Arizona.

Cindy Hensley was a "pretty 24-year-old teacher" when she met John McCain at a cocktail party in 1979.[4] A naval officer, McCain was married but separated from his wife at the time. In spite of his marital status and age (he was seventeen years older than she was), there was "instant chemistry" between them.[5] After signing a prenuptial agreement that would protect her family fortune and waiting for a month to pass after his divorce was finalized, Cindy married John on May 17, 1980. Following their wedding, Cindy McCain quit working as a teacher and pursued her desire to build a large family. After suffering several miscarriages, she gave birth to the couple's first child in 1984. She eventually bore two additional children, and the couple later adopted one more. John McCain had three kids from his first marriage, bringing the total number of children to seven. Cindy McCain recruited family members and employed outside help to assist with the large brood.

In 1982, Cindy McCain began actively promoting her husband's political efforts. She canvassed neighborhoods on his behalf and helped him win a seat in the US House. She initially moved to Alexandria, Virginia, to be by her husband's side as he began his legislative career. However, she returned to Arizona before the birth of the couple's daughter in 1984, claiming that Washington, DC, was not a good place to raise a family. Cindy and John visited each other on weekends, but they spent a great deal of time apart. Nevertheless, she continued to organize fund-raisers for his political campaigns and supported his career from afar. She also occasionally worked for her father's company and eventually assumed the title of chair of Hensley and Company. McCain also engaged in various philanthropic endeavors, such as founding and traveling with the American Voluntary Medical Team.

McCain became entangled in a national controversy in the late 1980s, when her husband was accused of corruption for intervening on behalf of a financier named Charles Keating, Jr., under federal investigation for fraud. Keating was a friend and business partner of Cindy McCain's father, and she, working as a bookkeeper, was unable to account for trips the McCains took on Keating's private plane. Although her husband was eventually reprimanded for bad judgment but cleared of any legal improprieties for his role in what became commonly known as the "Keating Five" affair, the stress of the incident contributed to McCain's addiction to prescription drugs. She began using painkillers after having back surgery but continued to take them, she said, to ease the emotional pain of the scandal.[6] She eventually sought help for her drug problem and presumably had it under control prior to her husband's decision to run for president of the United States. Her addiction was a frequent topic of discussion during her husband's presidential bids in 2000 and in 2008.

On January 17, 1964, Michelle LaVaughn Robinson, now Michelle Obama, was born in Chicago, Illinois. Her father was a city water plant employee who suffered from multiple sclerosis, and her mother was a full-time homemaker who eventually became a secretary for a catalog store. Michelle had one older brother. She described her youth as "a very stable, conventional upbringing."[7] An academically gifted student, she attended a selective magnet high school ninety minutes from her home. She was on the honor roll and became a member of the National Honor Society. After high school, she majored in sociology and minored in African American studies at Princeton University. She graduated cum laude in 1985. Three years later she earned a JD from Harvard Law School.

Michelle Robinson spent much of her time during her undergraduate years and in law school advocating for minority groups. At Princeton she researched the intersection of race, class, and educational opportunity. While at Harvard, she fought for increasing the number of minority faculty members on campus and worked for the Harvard Legal Aid Bureau. After law school, she returned to Chicago and specialized in marketing and intellectual property law for the prestigious Sidley & Austin law firm. A year later she met her future husband, Barack Obama, while at work; she had been assigned to mentor him during his time as a summer associate. The two began dating and married on October 3, 1992, one year after she had entered the public sector. The couple waited to build their family but eventually had two daughters, one in 1998 and the other in 2001. Meanwhile, Michelle Obama continued to develop her professional career. She was an assistant to the mayor of Chicago, helped develop Public Allies (a leadership training and mentoring group), and became the associate dean of Student Services at the University of Chicago. In 2002, she was hired as the executive director of Community Relations and External Affairs for the University of Chicago Hospitals, and three years after that she was named their vice president of Community and External Affairs.

Obama was professionally active as her husband pursued his political aspirations. She split her time between fulfilling her professional obligations and her maternal responsibilities while aiding in her husband's statewide races. With help from family members, Obama was able to balance her home and work life as her husband served first as a community organizer, then as a state representative, and eventually as a US senator. Even though she was part of his political endeavors, she did not curtail her professional activities to assist her husband's efforts until 2007, when the family began to prepare for his presidential bid. Obama developed a full résumé and was considered "an independent player in Chicago" long before her husband became a rising political star.[8] Yet, like most spouses of serious presidential contenders, she substantially adapted her lifestyle and outward persona to participate in and contribute to her husband's national campaign.

Cindy McCain and Michelle Obama have two very different backgrounds. McCain is a wealthy woman with little professional experience who travels extensively and cares for a large family. Obama is an Ivy League–educated professional from a working-class family who pursued opportunities for career development and still found time for her children. Despite their differences, the women share some experiences. Both earned an advanced degree before meeting their future husbands, had children a few years after marriage, and relied on others for help raising their kids. The women also give back to their communities: McCain supports medical volunteerism, and Obama is a mentor to young people. Both women's biographies reflect the complexities of modern women's lives. Prior to the 2008 election, McCain and Obama both met and challenged standard expectations of womanhood in different ways.

McCain seemed, on the surface, to embody the established feminine ideal. She studied for a profession traditionally acceptable for females, gave up her career upon marrying, and dedicated much of her life to assisting her husband and raising his children. McCain also encouraged her husband's patriotic exploits. She worked on his political campaigns, attended and organized fund-raising events, and when he was elected to Congress initially moved with him to Washington, DC. Later, McCain sacrificed time with her mate in order to care for their children, thereby allowing her husband to serve his nation relatively unimpeded by familial responsibilities. She proved herself a self-sacrificial woman preoccupied with maternal endeavors. Conversely, Obama appeared to enact a more progressive style of womanhood. She earned degrees from elite universities, built a varied and distinguished career, and established financial and political power of her own. She also earned more money than her husband did throughout the early part of their life together. Thus, Obama appeared to challenge the expectations of republican motherhood throughout most of her life. However, the two women were neither fully conventional nor entirely progressive. McCain refused to comingle her financial resources with her husband's, adopted a daughter largely without her husband's permission, and engaged in purportedly unladylike actions such as driving racecars. Obama celebrated and prioritized motherhood, mentored young people, and championed her husband's political ambitions.

The lives McCain and Obama lived prior to the 2008 presidential campaign epitomized contemporary American womanhood. They both blended customary and nontraditional aspects of femininity in different ways. Yet when it came to the campaign, the manner in which the press, the parties, and the women themselves portrayed their experiences became much more one-dimensional. Descriptions of the women relied heavily on republican motherhood rhetoric;

the women were both praised for meeting and chastised for breaking with entrenched norms of femininity. Although the women tried to use the well-established trope to create appealing public personas, they were not always successful because they were not the only ones shaping the narrative.

Representations of Cindy McCain and Michelle Obama

McCain and Obama were relatively active participants in the 2008 presidential contest. Both attended rallies, gave speeches, raised funds, posed for photo ops, and gave numerous interviews with various media outlets, although Obama was considerably more vocal than McCain and more frequently appeared solo at planned events. Together, the two received a lot of attention. The press, the parties, and the wives used republican motherhood rhetoric to shape public perceptions of both women. Even though previous chapters of this book show that it is not unusual for representations of candidates' spouses to be based on entrenched ideals of femininity, the manner in which these standards were used to interpret McCain and Obama illustrates interesting differences in the strategic application of this frame.

Press Treatments

By the time the 2008 campaign had begun in earnest, the internet was a prevalent means of communication for many Americans. Most mainstream news sources had migrated content to websites, and new online information outlets had established themselves as reputable sources of political commentary. Alongside sites containing verifiable news, less trustworthy sources also appeared. The wives of the presidential nominees had to contend, to differing degrees, with a broader variety of information sources evaluating them in widely divergent ways. Media representations spanned from hypertraditional to ultraprogressive, depending on the outlet. Yet republican motherhood rhetoric still undergirded most press coverage.

News media generally portrayed McCain using three distinct lenses. She was an extremely wealthy heiress who used her fortune to aid her husband, a nurturing person whose maternal drive spilled over into her humanitarian work, and a supportive but long-suffering wife who made many sacrifices for her husband and children. These interpretations contained both positive and negative elements. In some cases, members of the press posited an image of the former rodeo queen that made her look like the embodiment of conventional femininity, and at other times they made her appear to be a disingenuous fraud who employed elements of the republican motherhood trope as a mercenary political ploy.

As with Teresa Heinz Kerry in 2004, the press often began profiles of Cindy

McCain by describing her purportedly unearned financial resources. Most news stories began by identifying McCain as the heiress of an estate valued at more than $100 million. Many articles also delineated the benefits of such wealth to both McCain and her husband. Reporters explained how John McCain "lives in a luxury high-rise condominium in Arlington, Va., owned by his wife," and she "owns their condos in Phoenix, San Diego, and Coronado, Calif., and their vacation compound near Sedona, Ariz."[9] Counting eight to ten homes and thirteen cars among Cindy McCain's possessions, reporters accentuated the lavish lifestyle of the would-be first lady and emphasized the comforts she enjoyed because of her father's business acumen. In stories also reminiscent of the press treatment of Heinz Kerry, journalists occasionally scorned McCain for her indulgent tastes by citing the price of her clothing or remarking on the expensive breaks she took from campaigning.[10] The press critiqued McCain by claiming that her money made her experiences distinctly different from those of most voters.

Yet unlike Heinz Kerry, who was reprimanded by the press for exerting the independence that resulted from her inherited wealth and was considered an atypical woman because of the political influence her money afforded her (see Chapter 5), McCain was often praised for using her money to sustain her husband's patriotic endeavors and to engage in humanitarian efforts around the globe. Members of the press repeatedly presented McCain as her husband's benefactor. Crediting her with having "invented John McCain," reports were quick to point out that his political career would have been short-lived had it not been for his wife and her family's funding.[11] His first campaign for Congress was nearly bankrupt, and "tens of thousands of dollars in loans to his campaign from [Cindy] McCain bank accounts helped him survive."[12] Commentators claimed McCain was eager to assist her husband when his ambitions required fiscal fortification. In general, the press interpreted McCain's monetary contributions in two paradoxical ways, one that reinforced her image as a sympathetic and customary spouse and another that countermanded that view. First, journalists argued that Cindy's use of her own funds to buttress John's career was an enactment of her traditional femininity because it highlighted her willingness to provide any assistance possible to allow her husband to pursue an active role in government. Reporters argued that, coupled with her more hands-on work on John's campaigns, providing money was a sign of Cindy's dedication to her husband and her desire to help him achieve his goals.

The second frame applied to McCain bankrolling her husband's political aspirations was less laudatory. News stories cast McCain as a deceptive person who subsidized her husband's activities as a means of flexing her own political muscle. These articles questioned the legality of her help and made it sound as though she essentially bought him a powerful seat in government. Such tales referenced her connection to the Keating Five scandal, pointed out her reluctance to release her tax returns (which she filed separately from her husband), and cited Federal

Election Commission investigations into past campaign loans.[13] Part of McCain's purported duplicity came in the form of queries into the nature of her marriage. Reporters referred to the couple's union as one that "mixed business and politics from the beginning" and pointed out that "her connections helped him launch his political career."[14] Depicting the union as one designed to give the Hensley and McCain families more access to power, commentators questioned the sincerity of McCain's outward persona as "a brittle, blond cipher . . . [with] a perpetually demure and deferential presence."[15] Many media figures called McCain's inheritance the means by which the would-be first lady controlled her husband. This depiction ran counter to the submissive spouse image promulgated by the republican motherhood-based characterizations of McCain.

In addition to focusing on her wealth, journalists wrote about McCain's maternal drive and its many manifestations. This approach made mostly positive use of the old-fashioned female patriot archetype. Such articles and video clips referenced McCain's desire for a large family by pointing out that she was an only child—a story that was only partially true because she had two half-sisters—with a privileged but lonely upbringing. Stories about McCain's willingness to sacrifice time with her husband to give her kids what she perceived to be the best childhood possible cast her as a giving mother with deep concern for others. Tales that presented her as a good mom who cared for the family as her husband was serving his nation clearly aligned McCain with the more conservative spouses of presidential nominees while simultaneously framing her as a de facto "single mother during the week."[16] Her dedication to her family marked McCain as a conservative woman fulfilling customarily feminine duties.

Several news outlets delineated the range of McCain's philanthropic efforts and portrayed them as a reflection of her nurturing nature. The press used the fact that she supported endeavors linked specifically to women and children's health care, a so-called feminine political issue that corresponded with an interest in domesticity, to characterize McCain as a compassionate woman whose concerns fell well within the bounds of orthodox republican motherhood. Some stories explicitly tied her humanitarian efforts to her experiences as a mother, arguing that her relief work in places such as Rwanda and Bangladesh was sparked by her identification with suffering mothers and her understanding that "you would do absolutely anything to help your child."[17] Almost every mention of her work helping children included the tale of McCain adopting her daughter Bridget from Mother Teresa's orphanage; this repeated story directly linked McCain's motherly instincts and desires to her volunteerism.

The third frame news media offered regarding McCain was that of a long-suffering but loyal wife. These stories frequently began with a summary of the courtship between Cindy and John that included details of the dissolution of his first marriage, a description of Cindy as a "twenty-four-year-old beauty," and a recounting of the age difference between her and her husband.[18] Reports frequently attempted to dispute McCain's claims that she and her husband were a happy and content couple. Contrasting the image of "the blonde standing alongside her gregarious husband, lips fixed in a practiced smile, ice-blue eyes serene and adoring, but inscrutable" against the woman who spent much of her married life ostensibly as a single mother who endured being "far away from her husband during difficult moments, including two of three miscarriages," journalists routinely portrayed McCain as a somewhat pathetic character struggling to maintain her dignity.[19] News stories also reinforced Cindy's dutiful wife persona by describing how she consistently discounted rumors about John's suspected infidelity; she reportedly denied the allegations and repeatedly called John a "man of great character."[20]

Some members of the press represented McCain as an ideal wife willing to make personal sacrifices to allow her husband to serve his nation by likening her to military wives whose husbands were deployed overseas. Others questioned the veracity of her commitment to her husband by noting that she had "prepared herself for a largely independent life"[21] and that she had been the mastermind behind both her life in Arizona and his in Washington, DC.[22] In both representations, the press compared McCain's actions with those of an ideal political spouse. The first version found her fulfilling the historically idealized role of a dutiful spouse, whereas the second portrayed her as corrupting wifedom for her own benefit. In either view, McCain's treatment by the press continually referenced the standards set by the republican motherhood ideal.

The press portrayed Obama, wife of the Democratic candidate, in a complex fashion throughout the primaries and the general election. As with McCain, Obama was also depicted as neither wholly embracing nor fully challenging the standards of conventional womanhood, and applications of republican motherhood rhetoric in evaluations of her seemed to vary based primarily on the motives of the reporter and the proffered story line. Analyses of Obama's enactment of femininity were grounded in a multitude of factors, including her physical appearance, her relationship with her husband, and her perceived effectiveness as a working mother. She was, to many in the press, "a type we've rarely seen in the public eye, a well-educated woman who is a dedicated mother, successful in her career, and happens to be black."[23]

Many news stories about Obama presented her in a manner that both accentuated and questioned her femininity. Addressing her physical presence, most articles stressed her stylish manner of dress by talking about her clothing and comparing her to Jacqueline Kennedy.[24] She was considered a trendsetter with daring tastes and was both applauded and denounced for occasionally showing off her bare arms (her arms were the subject of many media stories). Although several commentators complimented Obama's wardrobe, they periodically did so by adding qualifiers regarding the body she dressed. Such coverage explained that "though she is stylishly appointed, she is not dainty."[25] Journalists repeatedly discussed her height, writing that "she verges on six feet, and her firm-hold Jackie O. coiffure adds a few inches to the top."[26] Obama's stature, along with her athletic physique and strong arms, was routinely used to cast her as unusual and unfeminine. One reporter bristled at efforts to degrade Obama, arguing, "Some people . . . seem desperate to find a negative quality in her: She's too big, too masculine, too much like a drag queen."[27]

When addressing her physical features, mainstream media tended to avoid overtly mentioning Obama's race. Some reporters did initially note the historic nature of her being the first African American spouse of a major party's presidential nominee or discussed her familial roots and ties to slavery, but after the primary race began in earnest only a few stories explicitly mentioned her skin color. Those that did were usually about race relations in the United States, and they tended to underscore the importance of imagery emerging from the Obamas' standing as a prominent couple.[28] A few articles addressed her skin tone as a political appeal, contending that the fact she "is quite dark may have endeared Barack to black female voters who might otherwise have voted for Hillary Clinton."[29] More often, reporters addressed Obama's racial heritage by delineating her work exploring race-related issues. For example, her Princeton senior thesis on minorities who attend elite educational institutions created a stir among political commentators; it was misquoted in several news stories and was used to portray Obama as a woman who "simmers with undigested racial anger."[30] Also, without explicitly mentioning the color of her skin, some political pundits did inject race into their assessments of the would-be first lady by using racially charged phrases such as calling her Barack's "baby mama" (a derogatory term for an unwed mother usually applied to a low-income African American or Hispanic woman)[31] and attempting to soften assertive critiques of her by denying they were efforts at "lynching" the first lady.[32]

In addition to the physical descriptors they assigned Obama, members of the media presented a mixed interpretation of the Democratic nominee's wife by discussing her biography in different ways. Some commentators emphasized her intelligence and tenacity in a manner that chided her for being personally ambitious and disputed her standing as a good woman. They outlined the salaries she commanded at various jobs and depicted her pay as either inappropriately high (implying that she was paid more because of her political connections or her race) or as emasculating to her husband.[33] Thus, her professional acumen was repeatedly presented as a sign that she rejected traditional femininity. However, not all news stories presented Obama's professional accomplishments in a negative manner. Several progressive commentators claimed Obama's achievements made her a role model for young women, particularly females of color.[34] These articles argued that Obama's educational attainment and professional success in the face of her modest origins and the systemic obstacles she faced related to her race and sex made her an iconic figure whom both Democrats and Republicans should respect. Casting her as a female African American version of a Horatio Alger–type mythic hero, some members of the press turned critiques of Obama as a "striver" into positive depictions.[35] Other reporters argued that Obama's willingness to step away from her lucrative professional work to use her talents in support of her husband's political aspirations indicated that she truly was a self-sacrificing and encouraging spouse.

Reporters who said Obama's intellectual skill made her a helpful wife sometimes referenced her participation in the development of her husband's campaign as evidence of her utility. Journalists acknowledged that she was originally ambivalent about the idea of her husband running for president and was wary of putting their family through such an ordeal.[36] News stories about her involvement in the campaign vacillated between painting her as truly a partner and presenting her as a meddling or domineering wife. The more charitable treatments applauded Obama's initial concern for her family's well-being and her willingness to suppress her own ambitions to help her husband achieve his goals; the more critical ones alluded to Hillary Clinton's problematic 1992 image and proclaimed that Michelle was Barack's "bitter half."[37]

The media did offer an interpretation of Obama that accentuated her domesticity by focusing on her status as a mother. Her maternal drive took different forms but was a key part of most stories about her. She was "a successful working mother, but an ambivalent one" who "more than anything . . . seems to enjoy talking about her husband and her daughters."[38] Assertions about her dedication to her family were constantly reinforced with explanations of both her work on behalf of her husband and her insistence that campaigning not interfere with her responsibilities as a mother. Journalists pointed out, "Michelle campaigns about twice a week—she'll appear at one public event per city, then a fund-raiser, and hop back to Chicago to see her kids before they fall asleep."[39] Obama's focus on her family dominated stories about her, whereas her Ivy League education and professional accomplishments produced sporadic and rather brief coverage; by the end of the campaign some journalists acknowledged but did not necessarily question the "momification" of the potential first lady.[40]

The news media most often framed Obama as a model of contemporary American motherhood. Commentators detailed many of the choices and sacrifices she made as a working woman and "doting mother of two."[41] Journalists explained her efforts to juggle her work schedule with her home life, the ways she prioritized her daughters' needs, and the stress her many commitments placed on her romantic connection with her husband. In most portrayals, Obama embodied the daily challenges of average American women more so than most of her predecessors. Unlike other women who had assumed the spotlight as prospective first ladies, Obama did not indulge in the perceived luxuries, such as hiring nannies, many of the wealthier stay-at-home moms did. The press emphasized that she managed to have a career and children because she relied on family members to help care for her daughters. Obama appeared to be an ordinary woman despite her extraordinary achievements.

Both McCain and Obama participated in the media exchanges that have become the norm for wives in modern campaigns. They did interviews, stood as props in photo ops, visited schools and hospitals, and attended rallies and fundraisers. They both also engaged in actions that highlighted their domesticity. The McCain campaign website contained a link to what were purportedly McCain's favorite family recipes, and Obama contributed to the digital version of the *Obama Campaign Family Cookbook*.[42] They each also participated in the *Family Circle* first lady bakeoff, with McCain's recipe for oatmeal-butterscotch cookies winning and stirring controversy when she was accused of stealing it from the Food Network website. Reporters claimed McCain's pilfering of the recipe was a reflection of her pampered lifestyle and questioned her skills as a wife and mother.[43] The women's femininity was explicitly tied to their homemaking ability, and failure to demonstrate adequate skills was viewed as problematic.

Entertainment media were a bit lopsided in their treatment of McCain and Obama. Perhaps because she was more active in her husband's campaign and was more vocal with, without, and about her husband, Obama received more attention on talk shows and on comedic programs. For example, both women appeared on a female-oriented show called *The View,* but McCain was briefly included at the end of an interview with her husband and Obama was the main guest in a solo appearance. Obama also appeared by herself on a satirical program called *The Colbert Report* and other shows. Although Obama was criticized in some late-night monologues and was castigated on conservative talk radio, her personal appearances in entertainment venues tended to cast her in a favorable but domestically focused light. Most questions posed to the intelligent and accomplished woman emphasized her responsibilities as a wife and a mother. Even the spoof of Michelle performed on *Saturday Night Live* underscored her loving relationship with Barack.[44] Conversely, McCain's treatment by non-news media was rather restrained and usually emphasized her wealth. On *The View* she was asked few questions but was queried about how many houses she owned. When John and Cindy McCain appeared as themselves in a *Saturday Night Live* skit, Cindy McCain did not utter a single word; her part involved simply smiling and modeling gold jewelry.[45]

The media treatment of McCain and Obama was generally more varied and somewhat more nuanced than the portrayals of past spouses of presidential candidates. Still, even as press representations of the two women included different perspectives, the vast majority still relied heavily on the well-established trope of republican motherhood, which ties female patriotism to submissive domesticity. Both McCain and Obama were judged for their ability to serve as good wives and mothers, for their willingness to be deferential, and for how they upheld established gender norms. The range of individuals unofficially vetting the potential presidential consorts meant that applications of these metrics varied, but the measures were still based on historically grounded and restrictive views of womanhood that presumed female citizenship was contingent upon relational connections.

Media assessments of McCain and Obama reinforced the long-standing assumption that women should shun personal ambition and sacrifice their own needs and interests in support of their husbands and children. Such coverage highlighted these women's maternal and marital responsibilities and downplayed their other societal contributions, including their professional accomplishments. By pushing often-repeated story lines favoring conventional femininity among candidates' wives, the press publicly touted motherhood and wifeliness as essential characteristics of American womanhood. The media offered female citizens role models that discounted the importance of women's personal achievements and instead accentuated ladies' work on behalf of others, forcefully suggesting that proper American women should be other-centric and self-abnegating rather than acting as autonomous political actors in their own right and on their own behalf.

Party Depictions

In their uses and representations of the wives of the 2008 presidential prospects, the Republican and Democratic Parties were relatively consistent with those of past elections. In general, both sides tried to present the spouses of their standard-bearers in ways party leaders believed would appeal to voters. To different degrees, each party also tried to depict the opponent's wife in a manner that discouraged voters from building an affinity for or identification with her. Many of the strategies both parties used in relation to the candidates' mates relied heavily on customary views of womanhood and traditional assumptions about female patriotism.

The Republicans cast McCain as a loyal, dutiful, and relatively demure helpmate. Using similar tactics to the ones employed for their depictions of Laura Bush in 2000, GOP leaders often kept Cindy McCain out of the spotlight and only occasionally arranged for her to make solo appearances. Republicans proclaimed her shyness as the reason she rarely gave full speeches at large rallies. When she did speak, McCain usually touted her husband's strong character and his competence as a father.

Because the GOP had a woman on the ballot, its need to use the nominee's mate to appeal to a wide range of females was markedly lower than it had been in previous campaigns. Palin, a mother of five children, including one who has Down syndrome, was used to appeal to working moms, mothers of special needs children, and hockey moms (the 2008 variation on soccer moms). Vocal, active, and eager to address crowds of voters, Palin drew more attention than McCain did and allowed the party to limit McCain's verbal participation in the campaign. However, McCain was not entirely unneeded. Compared with the gregarious and daring vice presidential candidate, McCain was a quiet and calm presence. Whereas Palin might attract more assertive women, McCain was more alluring to conservative and circumspect women.

The Republicans' strategy regarding candidates' wives also included actively critiquing the Democratic standard-bearer's spouse. The GOP framed Obama as unpatriotic, unusual, and unladylike. They presented her as a stereotypical angry black woman by playing up her complaints about the US political system, claiming that she was critical of the country as a whole and saying she harbored disdain toward white Americans.[46] GOP members made pointed remarks about her appearance, used subtle but racially charged words to describe her, and accentuated her advanced education in a manner that differentiated her from purportedly average Americans. In some cases, Republicans made Obama's pursuit of the American dream appear threatening by characterizing her accomplishments as an effort to subvert white masculinity. She was said to be too ambitious for a woman and particularly for a woman of color. Obama was simultaneously censured for acting too white and being too black. She was also chided for being overbearing in stature and attitude. In general, the GOP strategy relied on deep-seated assumptions about femininity that presume whiteness, daintiness, and powerlessness are the preferred core characteristics of a proper woman. Republicans presented McCain as epitomizing such feminine qualities and Obama as embodying none of them.

The Democrats faced an interesting dilemma when trying to paint a particular picture of Obama. Even though she was professionally experienced at impression management and public relations, Obama would get irritated at the prospect of being "asked to subsume her personality, to make herself seem duller and less independent than she is, even in the service of getting her husband elected president of the United States."[47] This sometimes made it difficult for campaign staffers to manage the would-be first lady. Her willingness to speak on almost any topic and to assert her own point of view, in the words of her husband's chief strategist David Axelrod, "occasionally [gave] campaign people heartburn."[48] Rather than fighting to change Obama's mind, the Democrats worked around her by framing her outspokenness as a positive characteristic. Party leaders talked about her as a refreshing change from the prim and proper Bush and contrasted Obama against the ostensibly more standoffish McCain. Democrats portrayed Obama as a sort of "everymom" figure who worked hard, was resourceful, and spoke her mind. They played off her occasional gaffes as a sign of her sincerity by arguing that her mistakes made her more human and, therefore, more relatable.

Democratic operatives attempted to present the highly educated and professionally accomplished Obama as a revised version of the ideal republican mother by simply acknowledging her time as a working mom. They celebrated the ideals of the trope by emphasizing her willingness to sacrifice her professional growth to support her husband and underscoring her zealousness when it came to protecting and caring for her children. Party members still defined Obama based on her relationships with others by continually discussing her as a loving wife, a caring mother, and an appreciative daughter. They also highlighted the fact that although she harangued her husband for forgetting to take out the trash, when it came to big decisions (such as running for president) she deferred to him even if she disagreed with him.[49] Democrats argued that Obama was like most ordinary American women. Because they focused on her home life more than her professional achievements and frequently referred to her humble origins, the Democrats used Obama to reify republican mother ideals rather than challenge them.

The Democrats carefully played up Obama's embodiment of diversity as a means of increasing her appeal. She was seen as able to connect with voters across race and class lines, and "in a presidential campaign that . . . included discussions of race and gender, [she had] a singular vantage point at the intersection of the two."[50] Party leaders used Obama to humanize her husband and to make the somewhat aloof candidate appear well grounded and connected to the experiences of average Americans. Her approachable style "play[ed] well with a broad swath of the electorate."[51] Unlike the Republicans, who used their candidate's spouse in a limited capacity, the Democrats increased Obama's appearances throughout the general election and saw her as significantly improving her husband's likelihood of winning over large masses of voters that included women generally and women of color specifically.

As is often the case, the Democrats engaged in fewer attacks on the opponent's wife than the Republicans did. A few party members discussed McCain in derogatory terms, but there did not appear to be a large-scale plan to denigrate the Republican nominee's spouse. The charges against McCain included references to her drug addiction and the scandal surrounding it, queries into the sincerity of her purported devotion to her husband, and mentions of her potentially illegal loans to his early campaigns. Many of the charges Democrats made against McCain encouraged voters to question her moral fiber and her ability to adequately judge her husband's character. None of these attacks were sustained in any notable fashion. Because the Democrats held a pretty substantial lead in polls leading up to the election, there seemed little to gain from harshly judging the opponent's spouse. The Democrats' negative messaging focused squarely on George W. Bush, John McCain, Sarah Palin, and other GOP leaders.

The major parties tended to follow the same strategies they had in past elections when it came to depicting the wives of the nominees. On both sides, this meant foregrounding traditional feminine qualities. For McCain, the emphasis was on attributes that made her a good woman who stood behind a great man. She was portrayed as sympathetic, deferential, and dutiful. Obama was presented as self-sacrificing and encouraging, but not as a servile woman.

Democrats relied on republican motherhood rhetoric to interpret Obama just as Republicans did for McCain, but the Democrats tried to reinterpret some of the characteristics of a feminine patriot to account for Obama's assertiveness. The GOP, meanwhile, used allusions to conventional assumptions about femininity to cast Obama in a negative light. The Republican efforts to actively critique their opponent's spouse were more concentrated and coordinated than those of the Democrats, yet many attacks made clear use of republican motherhood rhetoric. In both cases, the parties' presentations demonstrated that customary gender expectations remained the norm by which women in the political sphere were judged and implied that the same criteria were applicable for women overall. According to the major parties, being a good woman and a proper patriot required female citizens to downplay their individual accomplishments and abilities in favor of accentuating their maternal and marital fealty.

Self-Portrayals

The wives of the presidential contenders provided their own self-depictions through various public appearances. In interviews, at rallies, and during their other interactions with voters, each woman helped shape her own persona. Although McCain and Obama both held advanced degrees and were powerful people in their own right, the images they both chose to craft accentuated elements of archetypal femininity. Both women employed a great deal of republican motherhood rhetoric in their personal portraits.

McCain presented herself to the public as her husband's loyal and dutiful supporter. Her penchant for standing silently by her husband, smiling, applauding, and nodding in agreement with him made her a model political spouse reminiscent of an earlier era. She was careful never to publicly disagree with her husband. She spoke of his character, of his dedication to his family and nation, and of her own service as a mother and aid worker, but she avoided delving into issues of national or international policy or addressing potentially controversial subjects. McCain frequently deflected attention toward her husband and framed herself as a proper old-fashioned female patriot.

On September 4, 2008, McCain gave her most viewed speech of the campaign when she addressed delegates and a national audience at the Republican National Convention (RNC). As the spouse of the party's presidential nominee, she was given a prime speaking spot. Like all other spouses' orations, her talk had been touted as an opportunity for voters to get to know the potential first lady. This chance to introduce herself to the nation was particularly important for McCain because preconvention polls showed that one-third of registered voters held no opinion of her and another 20 percent held an unfavorable view.[52] The address gave McCain an opening to potentially win over members of the electorate and to earn some public goodwill. Her decision to emphasize her customary femininity indicated that she (along with campaign strategists and speechwriters) believed these characteristics would most effectively appeal to voters.

McCain's RNC speech contains many elements that define her in terms of her relationships. Beginning with her opening line, McCain depicts herself foremost as a mother and wife. She tells audience members, "I would like to introduce you to the seven reasons John and I are so happy as a family," and then she proceeds to present the couple's children.[53] From the start, she explicitly ties her happiness, both as a person and as a wife, to her maternal standing. McCain contends, "Nothing has made me happier or more fulfilled in my life than being a mother."[54] Later, she claims that her maternity altered her sense of being and purpose. She reveals, "The great moment of clarity was when I became a mother. Something changed in me. I would never see my obligations the same way again."[55] This essential shift in perspective dominates McCain's self-perception and her interpretation of womanhood.

McCain assumes her maternal experience is a convincing point of credibility for her assessments about politics and presidential leadership. She argues that as a mother and as John McCain's wife, she is uniquely qualified to outline his presidential credentials because his being "a loyal and loving and true husband, and a magnificent father" make him a good candidate for the highest elected office.[56] McCain specifically lists among her husband's attributes that he is "the most marvelous husband and friend and confidant, a source of strength and inspiration, and also the best father you could ever imagine."[57] She argues that, as a father, "in that most sacred role, he brought to our children his great personal character, his lifelong example of honesty, and his steadfast devotion to honor."[58] Not only does McCain paint her husband as the quintessential paternal figure, but she also frames fatherly characteristics as essential governmental leadership qualities.

McCain also lauds the credentials of her husband's running mate based on Palin's parental status. The would-be first lady describes the GOP vice presidential nominee as "a reform-minded, hockey-mommin', basketball-shooting, moose-hunting, salmon-fishing, pistol-packing mother of five."[59] This initial characterization relies primarily on the governor of Alaska's maternal experiences as its driving force. McCain underscores her focus on motherhood as women's dominant attribute by recounting her and Palin's commonalities, saying, "As a fellow hockey mom myself and a Western conservative mother, I couldn't be prouder."[60] In her political assessments, McCain relies on parental attributes as criteria for evaluating others.

Throughout the address, McCain prioritizes domesticity for herself and for women generally. The term "mother" appears more times in McCain's talk than in any other spouse's convention speech before hers; the word "woman" occurs half as often. When she talks generally about women, she frames them primarily as mothers. McCain talks about "mothers with no choice but to send their children to unsafe and underperforming schools" and tells the audience the story of Ernestine, whom she introduces as "a mother like myself . . . [who] was made to watch appalling havoc wreaked [on] her family."[61] In such cases, females are regarded for their maternity; women are portrayed as worried mothers, and Ernestine is defined by her maternal commonality with McCain and her experiences relative to her familial connections. Perhaps the most obvious of McCain's applications of standard feminine ideals to women generally comes when she argues, "Women have always sought a husband with an eye to what kind of father that man would be."[62] Here, McCain makes all women's central goal motherhood "no matter how accomplished in other fields."[63]

McCain clearly promotes a conventional perspective regarding American femininity. Although she does reference women in nontraditional gender roles, these comments are simply a series of lines about "men and women" that sound perfunctory alongside her broader discussion of men's actions and women's duties. For example, she mentions men and women in the military but only specifically outlines the contributions her husband, her father, and her son made as sailors and soldiers. Yet when she talks about the men and women of the American Voluntary Medical Teams, McCain provides detailed examples only of women caring for and nurturing sick and injured children. There are clear distinctions between male and female responsibilities that run along heteronormative lines in McCain's proffered interpretation of the world. She presents herself as devoted to meeting stereotypical standards for a female patriot and takes for granted that other women are equally dedicated to upholding similar norms.

Obama's self-depiction also relied heavily on republican motherhood ideals and clearly emphasized the value of maternal devotion and spousal loyalty. Throughout Obama's time in the public eye, she adopted a persona that promoted her interest in domesticity and downplayed her professional accomplishments. She used similar tactics as Hillary Clinton and Elizabeth Dole did in 1996 (see Chapter 3) and took care to avoid discussing her career; instead, she publicly celebrated her maternal and spousal perspectives as her greatest source of political credibility. She did this in interviews, campaign speeches, and even in the purportedly personal emails sent to voters who registered on her husband's website. Obama's campaign messaging liberally but strategically applied republican motherhood rhetoric. Although Obama fully embraced the trope in descriptions of herself, she did not paint all women with the same restrictive rhetorical brush. Her address at the 2008 Democratic National Convention (DNC) provides a representative sampling of ways she blended conservative and progressive views of womanhood.

Obama creates a relatively normative feminine persona for herself throughout her 2008 DNC speech. In it, she defines herself very clearly in terms of her relationships with others. Her opening remarks construct a personal portrait based entirely on her familial linkages. She tells the audience,

I come here tonight as a sister, blessed with a brother who is my mentor, my protector, and my lifelong friend . . . as a wife who loves my husband and believes he will be an extraordinary president . . . as a mom whose girls are the heart of my heart and the center of my world . . . as a daughter, raised on the South Side of Chicago by a father who was a blue-collar city worker and a mother who stayed at home with my brother and me.[64]

Every aspect of Obama's initial self-introduction relies on her association with others to build her identity. In contrast, Obama never mentions her Ivy League education and barely touches on her work outside of the home. In fact, all of her professional exploits are summed up in one line of the speech when she explains, "I left a job at a big law firm for a career in public service, working to empower young people to volunteer in their communities."[65] Obama frames herself as deriving meaning and purpose from her connections to others rather than from her efforts as an independent and autonomous person despite the fact that so much of her biography foregrounds her self-sufficiency.

Obama's maternal perspective is a dominant aspect of her public persona. At different points during her 2008 DNC speech, she particularly underscores how her status as a mother influences her view of the world. Early on, she says that her daughters are "the first things I think about when I wake up in the morning and the last thing I think about before I go to bed at night. Their future—and all our children's future—is my stake in this election."[66] Here, Obama not only highlights her concern for her own children but also adopts a national mother persona by showing regard for all the nation's children. Later in the speech she talks about the values she and her husband learned and try to share with their daughters. After delineating their established beliefs, Obama argues, "Barack and I . . . want our children and all children in this nation to know that the only limit to the height of your achievements is the reach of your dreams and your willingness to work hard for them."[67] Again, Obama extends her parental perspective to include all children, not just her own daughters. The eventual first lady uses this maternal point of view to discuss multiple topics throughout the address.

It is important to note that Obama's assumption of a motherly persona is entwined with her position as a supportive wife. Not only does she employ the same sorts of adoring commentaries about her husband as previous nominees' spouses did but also she builds an image of her husband that shapes him into an admittedly flawed person who is nevertheless a perfect mate. Michelle casts Barack as an idealist with strong values and high hopes, as a hard worker who overcame challenging times, and as an embodiment of the American dream. She also paints him as an overly cautious father who occasionally makes mistakes but strives to raise his daughters as best he can. One of the most interesting aspects of Michelle's depictions of Barack is not what they say about him but what they say about her and their marriage. Unlike Barbara Bush and Laura Bush, each of whom portrayed her marriage as a standard patriarchy, Michelle Obama's relationship with her husband is presented as a partnership. Michelle presents "Barack and I" as equal familial decision makers and highlights her own parental experiences more than many of the past wives did. Although she does deflect attention to her husband and focuses primarily on his achievements (as would be expected for a campaign address by a surrogate speaker), Michelle Obama does not devalue her own interests and does not sacrifice her standing as a mother to elevate her husband's position as a father the way Barbara Bush did in 1992 and Laura Bush did in 2000.

In addition to emphasizing her maternal perspective, Obama also acknowledges the importance of mothers other than herself. She praises her own mother as "a sustaining force for our family," applauds Barack's mom, "a single mother who struggled to pay the bills," and talks about "the mother [Barack] met who was worried about her child in Iraq."[68] She also opines on how future mothers will "tell their own children about what we did together in this election."[69] Still, although she commends mothers and stresses their contributions and concerns, Obama breaks with common applications of republican motherhood rhetoric by not fully conflating the terms "woman," "wife," and "mother." Instead, she rhetorically allows other women to exist outside of the relational ties that bind her. She includes both men and women as caregivers, breadwinners, members of the military, and community volunteers. She argues that faith in the American dream is "the same conviction that drives the men and women" of the nation.[70]

Throughout the campaign, Obama offered the public a view of herself that highlighted her maternal perspective in a way that accentuated her alignment with orthodox assumptions about American womanhood and women's roles as helpful nurturers, yet she did so without circumscribing perspectives on women as a whole. Instead, she created her persona by blending conservative and progressive appeals. The fact that, as the first African American woman to potentially become the first lady of the United States, Obama was unique among nominees' spouses meant she needed to build rhetorical bridges between herself and others that accentuated their similarities. Republican motherhood rhetoric offered Obama the ability to tap into historically and socially established expectations of womanhood that allowed her to confirm her connection to and bolster her commonalities with women of the past and present.

Obama's careful use of the rhetorical device demonstrates how the republican motherhood trope could actually help forward a somewhat paradoxical agenda. On the one hand, reminiscent of Sojourner Truth's argument in her famous "Ain't I a Woman?" speech, Obama expands interpretations of the types of women who can serve as an icon of American womanhood by encouraging Americans to view women of color in the same way they do white women.[71] However, in spite of her modest success touting this particular progressive perspective, the would-be first lady still favors an interpretation of femininity that is extremely restrictive. By highlighting her own enactment of traditional womanhood, Obama validates presumptions regarding femininity historically used to curtail women's political activity.

Obama redefined expectations associated with the first ladyship and challenged assumptions about difference and diversity through her use of republican motherhood rhetoric. However, even though it might be a useful means of spotlighting similarities, the rhetorical strategy still reinforces a limited perspective of women as political actors. Obama mitigated the impact by not applying it to women at large and by finessing some elements of the established trope (such as portraying her marriage as a partnership), yet the fact that archetypal views of femininity create such apparently meaningful connections indicates that old-fashioned assumptions still dominate contemporary gender norms.

During the 2008 presidential campaign, McCain and Obama depicted themselves in similar but not identical ways. Both defined themselves based primarily on their relationships to others, emphasized the importance of motherhood in their lives, and dutifully attempted to humanize their husbands by accentuating personal elements of the candidates' character. They both relied heavily on republican motherhood rhetoric to frame their own public image. Although they referenced the same ideal to develop their outward personas, how they used it and to whom they applied it differed significantly, illustrating that the rhetorical device is multifaceted and flexible even though it ultimately presents a constrained view of women as political actors.

Conclusion

The biographies of McCain and Obama represent an amalgam of shared experiences with past political spouses. Cindy McCain is a woman who inherited extreme wealth (like Teresa Heinz Kerry), quit the work she had been educated for upon getting married (as did Laura Bush and Tipper Gore), and made her husband's political career a central focal point of her life (again, similar to Laura Bush and Tipper Gore). Obama is an Ivy League–educated woman with an independently established career (as are Clinton and Dole) who had developed her own political power (as had Dole and Heinz Kerry) and who put her own professional development on hold to assist her husband's presidential bid (again, like Clinton and Dole). Both McCain and Obama were mothers, as were all of the contemporary mates before them except Dole. McCain, an affluent and active woman of the West who literally rolled up her sleeves and physically pitched in as an aid worker in third-world countries, and Obama, an African American woman from a working-class family who worked hard to achieve the American dream, were clearly multifaceted women who had much in common with others.

They both embodied the complexities of modern American womanhood despite the one-dimensional depictions offered by the press, the parties, and even themselves.

As happened in 1992, 1996, 2000, and 2004, republican motherhood rhetoric dominated dialogue about and by candidates' wives throughout the 2008 election. Even as a new and more diverse set of voices in the media approached entrenched standards of femininity in different ways, coverage regarding McCain and Obama still presumed audience members understood and accepted traditional gender norms and therefore kept this archetypal view at the forefront of conversations about American womanhood. The parties maintained their habitual patterns of touting their own nominee's spouse and chiding the opponent's mate, basing both on historically rooted expectations of purportedly acceptable female roles.

The manner in which both McCain and Obama employed republican motherhood rhetoric was quite revealing. McCain, a fairly independent woman, presented herself as a compliant wife with little to say beyond applauding her husband's character. She professed motherhood to be a key element of her life and figured it was equally central to all women's lives. McCain depicted men as fully engaged political actors and women as mere spectators. Obama's self-application of republican motherhood rhetoric illustrated the strategic use of the trope in an effort to build bridges between people of supposed difference. She confirmed her (and her husband's) standing as an average American by spotlighting her actions as an encouraging wife and loving mother.[72] Although Obama did not limit other women to orthodox roles, her own embrace of presumed female characteristics did prioritize domesticity as a dominant attribute of American womanhood.

Between 1992 and 2008, US presidential campaigns included discourse about American female citizenship that took multiple forms and was fueled by different political and sociohistorical factors. Yet the two things that remained consistent across these discussions were that the potential first ladies played a key part in depicting the status of women in the United States and that the republican motherhood ideal still served as the general starting point for these exchanges. Learning from the successes and challenges others experienced, it seems that by 2008 most of the wives of presidential candidates began carefully shaping their public personas with an eye toward appeasing voters' apparent desire for a conventional first lady. By the start of the 2012 campaign, dialogue regarding the candidates' spouses almost fully conflated the categories of "wife," "mother," and "woman" (with a few notable and important exceptions). As Chapter 7 explains, the press, the parties, and the contenders' mates framed the informal contest between Michelle Obama and Ann Romney as a battle to be the ultimate "mom in chief."

7

Michelle Obama and Ann Romney

Battling for Mom in Chief (2012)

The 2012 election was noteworthy for American women as political actors for several reasons. First, the contest marked a significant differential between male and female candidate preference; women overwhelmingly supported the incumbent, President Barack Obama, and men backed the Republican nominee, Mitt Romney.[1] In addition, female citizens illustrated their political aptitude as candidates. Women earned more seats in the US legislature in 2012 than they had in any previous election. One hundred and two women were sworn in as part of the 113th US Congress; there were a record twenty female senators and eighty-two women members of the US House of Representatives.[2] Women also secured several executive positions. After the states' swearing-in ceremonies, five US governors (incumbents and newcomers) were women.[3]

The 2012 contest also marked the third time in four election cycles that the field of major party presidential contestants included a woman. Michele Bachmann, a US representative from the state of Minnesota, pursued the Republican nomination. An Iowa native, Bachmann earned support from more than 25 percent of participants in the 2011 Iowa straw poll, and she beat out all of her male opponents.[4] Nevertheless, by January 5, 2012, Bachmann had suspended her campaign after failing to break 5 percent in the official Iowa GOP caucuses.[5] Although several factors contributed to Bachmann's decline in popularity, one that stood out in the context of this analysis was the evaluation of her standing as a dutiful wife. Alluding to the ideals of republican motherhood, a moderator asked Bachmann during one Republican primary debate whether as president she would be submissive to her husband.[6] The question highlighted the tensions between the conservative view of womanhood, which demanded that females be deferential and quiescent, and the necessarily progressive perspective required for a woman to become the nation's political leader. Faced with the dilemma of either alienating party members who held conventional views of womanhood or admitting that as the president of the United States she would yield to her husband's wishes, Bachmann tried to redefine the term "submissive" by claiming that the phrase was synonymous with showing respect.[7] The answer did not satisfy reporters, and the issue of her wifely fealty dogged her for the remainder of her time in the campaign.

Despite women's continued political gains, the most memorable and widespread discussions of women throughout the 2012 presidential contest still primarily revolved around the familiar theme of women as mothers and wives. Although the tendency to conceive of women primarily in terms of their procreative ability and their enactment of traditional feminine roles was well established long before this particular campaign, the 2012 election highlighted the seeming preference for domestically focused women. No new catchphrase such as "soccer mom" or "hockey mom" emerged to describe idealized female voters (see Chapter 1 for more on maternal tropes in politics), yet the emphasis on women as deferential reproducers and nurturers was still a significant part of the campaign. This perspective was evident not just in the vetting of the one female presidential candidate but also through the representations of the spouses of the eventual nominees. Michelle Obama and Ann Romney, the two most visible women associated with the presidential race, became locked in a very public if unofficial battle to establish themselves as the ultimate version of American womanhood. Each made her case by accentuating her embrace of maternal and marital roles.

The 2012 Presidential Nominees' Spouses

During the 2012 election, the first African American president defended his seat and his record. A few candidates challenged him during the early Democratic primaries, but none posed a serious threat to the incumbent. President Obama retained Vice President Joe Biden as his running mate. The Republican Party initially fielded ten candidates, including one African American man and one woman. Former governor of Massachusetts Mitt Romney won the GOP nomination and selected Paul Ryan, US representative from Wisconsin, to complete the ticket. The tenor of the overall campaign was particularly negative, and both parties engaged in vitriolic attacks on the opposition. The presidential candidates' spouses generally injected more positivity into the campaign, but even they did not escape the contest unscathed; each woman received a blend of criticism and praise. Much of the discussion surrounding these women was based on their perceived ability to act in accordance with historically established expectations for presidential helpmates.

Michelle Obama's initial time in the White House reinforced the public image she, the party, and the press tried to build of her during the latter portion of the 2008 campaign (see Chapter 6 for more on 2008 and Obama's biography). Having suspended her professional activities prior to her husband's initial presidential bid, as the first lady of the United States Obama ceased all paid work outside the home and focused her energies on purportedly more feminine pursuits. Obama championed initiatives that appeared uncontroversial, including assisting families of military personnel and urging children to exercise and eat healthy foods. She usually avoided commenting on divisive political topics, frequently talked about her daughters, and consistently expressed her concern for the children of the nation. Obama occasionally lamented the restrictiveness of life in the White House but used her mild complaints to highlight her willingness to support her husband and to underscore how her and her family's sacrifice afforded the nation positive leadership.

As the first lady, Obama was routinely discussed in many of the same ways she had been during the 2008 campaign. The press often talked about her personal appearance, frequently commenting on her physique (particularly her arms) and her fashion sense. She was praised for some of her sartorial choices and ridiculed for others, but she was widely considered a trendsetter and an influential woman. With favorability ratings consistently in the mid- to high sixties, she was a popular first lady but was not free from censure. For example, Obama's decision to champion children's health was generally but not universally applauded. Even though attempting to get kids to engage in physical activity and consume more fruits and vegetables should be a politically benign issue, Obama's critics took umbrage with her effort to assume a national mother persona and lambasted the first lady for allegedly supporting the creation of a so-called nanny state; she was accused of trying to limit Americans' freedom to choose to be unhealthy. This was particularly true when Obama pushed for reforms that increased the nutritional quality of school lunches.

Throughout her husband's first term in office, Obama used the media to continue to cultivate the "everymom" persona she had established during the 2008 general election. She appeared on daytime talk shows to promote her initiatives and engaged in playful banter that cast her as an amiable person with the same needs and concerns as most American mothers. She shared stories about her husband and children or about the children she had met across the nation. She talked about her difficulties in getting her own kids to eat their vegetables and told tales about urging her husband to stop smoking. Her anecdotes were the kind many mothers and wives could relate to, and they made Obama seem like an ordinary woman in an extraordinary position. To many citizens, Obama was an accessible and relatable first lady.

Ann Lois Davies, later known as Ann Romney, was born on April 16, 1949, in Detroit. She was raised in Bloomfield Hills, Michigan. Her father was a businessman and local politician, and her mother was a homemaker who raised Ann and two sons. As a young person, Ann enjoyed riding horses, occasionally helped out at her father's machinery plant, and attended private school. In 1965, she formally met her future husband, Mitt Romney, at a school dance. Shortly thereafter, they watched the movie *The Sound of Music* on their first date.[8] The two became informally engaged after his senior prom in 1965. Mitt soon left Michigan to attend

Stanford University, and Ann stayed behind to finish high school. During that time, she converted from her Episcopalian faith to the Church of Jesus Christ of Latter-day Saints so she could share her future husband's religion. Ann graduated from high school in 1967 and attended Brigham Young University (BYU). Mitt left Stanford to complete his Mormon missionary assignment in France.

Though she at one point tried to dissolve their long-distance relationship, Ann eventually agreed to marry Mitt upon his return to the United States. The two were wed in a civil ceremony on March 21, 1969, and held a religious ritual at the Salt Lake Temple in Utah soon afterward. He transferred to BYU to study alongside his new bride, and the couple welcomed their first son in 1970. He graduated in 1971 and moved the family to Massachusetts. She gave birth to the couple's second son that year. She continued to work on her bachelor's degree while raising the children and keeping house as he simultaneously pursued graduate degrees at Harvard Business School and Harvard Law School. She finished her BYU bachelor's degree in 1975, using credits earned in Massachusetts. She bore three more sons between 1975 and 1981.

Much like Tipper Gore and Laura Bush, Ann Romney was a stay-at-home mom who dedicated much of her life to being a conventional female mate. She spent a great deal of time and energy encouraging her husband as he tried to conquer both the business and political worlds. She did so by caring for the children and preventing familial concerns from impeding his professional progress. As Romney nurtured a houseful of boys, volunteered at the church, and engaged in various philanthropic efforts, she also showed some political ambition of her own. In 1977, she campaigned to become a town meeting representative in Belmont, Massachusetts, and won. Twenty years later, when her husband unsuccessfully challenged Massachusetts senator Ted Kennedy, she participated in the campaign and dutifully supported her spouse. During that contest, she received praise from conservatives for her enactment of old-fashioned womanhood but was generally considered a liability to her husband because she appeared extremely deferential and naive.

In 1997, Romney was diagnosed with multiple sclerosis. Using a blend of mainstream and alternative treatments, she managed the symptoms of the disease and maintained an active lifestyle that included equestrianism and volunteerism. By 2002, Romney was well enough to help with her husband's successful campaign for the governorship of Massachusetts. As the first lady of the state, Romney kept a relatively low profile but did advocate for multiple sclerosis awareness and headed a new office designed to help faith-based groups earn federal grants. In 2007, shortly after her husband announced his intention to run for president, Romney was diagnosed with breast cancer. It was a noninvasive form, and a lumpectomy removed the disease. Even though her health issues limited her activity, Romney still participated in some events during the 2008

Republican primaries and stood by her husband when he conceded the nomination to John McCain. Four years later, Mitt would try again. At that point, Ann became a much more visible part of his efforts.

Michelle Obama and Ann Romney had dramatically different backgrounds but similar outward personas at the outset of the 2012 presidential campaign. Obama was an Ivy League–educated attorney with years of varied professional experiences, and Romney was a stay-at-home mom who had earned a degree but never put it to professional use. Obama came from a lower-middle-class family, and she and her husband struggled for years to develop economic stability; Romney's family was upper middle class, and she and her husband initially lived off the sale of stocks they were given as a wedding gift. The one thing the women did have in common was the fact that both were mothers. Although they were different even in that regard—Obama was a working mom juggling responsibilities in and out of the home, whereas Romney was a stay-at-home mom with a primarily domestic focus—their motherly duties became the centerpiece of both women's public images.

Obama's first few years in the White House emphasized her roles as wife and mother. She stood dutifully by her husband, rarely disagreed with him on issues of substance, and sacrificed her ability to live a less public life in order to support him. Obama appeared simultaneously to be an average mother preoccupied with her own daughters' well-being and a national mother figure concerned with the health and welfare of the nation's children. She was the consummate female patriot because she was defined by her relationship to others, deferential to her husband, and self-sacrificial. So was Romney, who offered a lifetime of evidence that she was the epitome of republican motherhood. Committed to her husband from an early age, she adapted herself almost entirely to meet his needs and desires, including changing her religion, moving her family across the country, and delaying the completion of her college education to support his pursuit of advanced degrees. She devoted her life to domesticity and made motherhood a central part of her personal identity. Romney was dedicated to buoying her husband's aspirations and nurturing her sons. She also appeared to be extremely compliant and unwilling to act as an autonomous individual.

Obama and Romney were the two highest profile women in the 2012 presidential campaign, and each had an outward persona that prioritized restrictive perspectives on femininity. By emphasizing their dedication to familial responsibilities, their tendency to acquiesce to their husbands' desires, and their self-sacrificial natures, the candidates' spouses encouraged a view of female citizenship that placed women in subservient, other-centric, home-based positions. Although each woman showed occasional signs of assertiveness, they both personified a modern version of traditional womanhood. During the race, the press and the parties relied on republican motherhood rhetoric to assess both

Obama's and Romney's fitness to serve as the first lady of the United States, and the women employed the same trope to build their own personas.

Representations of Michelle Obama and Ann Romney

The 2012 campaign demonstrated how the press, the parties, and the women married to presidential candidates continued to apply republican motherhood rhetoric to presidential spouses. The historical perspective that approaches women as ancillary rather than primary citizens fit the orthodox public personas Obama developed as the first lady and Romney established throughout her life. These archetypal views of femininity led to oversimplified portrayals of Obama and Romney as well as of female citizenship.

Press Depictions

By the outset of the 2012 presidential campaign, the internet had established itself as a dominant form of media. Whether by desk- or laptop computer, smartphone, iPad, or other device, many Americans received their news and entertainment through myriad online outlets. The wide range of available sources allowed for the expression of many more diverse opinions and perspectives regarding political figures. However, when it came to dialogue about the wives of the presidential nominees, the underlying framework for most conversations still relied on conventional standards of femininity.

On the whole, media coverage of Obama was much kinder in 2012 than in 2008. She had adopted a relatively nonthreatening and very likable persona as the first lady, and her relationship with the press became more congenial. Although many news reports referenced tense moments from the previous campaign, those events were largely used as a negative contrast to highlight Obama's purportedly more acceptable and positive participation in her husband's reelection bid. Arguing that "Michelle Obama has burnished her standing by taking a traditional course," some journalists recognized the strategic benefit of a first lady acting in accordance with widely accepted gender norms.[9] This sentiment echoed across much of the 2012 press treatment of Obama. News stories consistently pointed out her tendency to avoid controversial topics, labeled her public appearances as safe and friendly, and claimed she "kept her head down, raised her daughters, rarely responded to criticism, and managed to become a style icon without seeming shallow or overly concerned with appearances."[10] Even though they sometimes called her "modern, striving, scrappy, edgy, [and] ironic,"[11] the press most often framed Obama as "always charming, warm, and gracious . . . like Laura Bush."[12] Rather than being an unpredictable force in need of careful management, as some commentators characterized her in 2008, the first lady was now considered "a popular public figure with bipartisan appeal"[13] and a decided asset to her husband.[14]

Although Obama was at times called "intimidatingly smart and accomplished," the press normally downplayed her intelligence in favor of accentuating her standing as a concerned mother and a helpful wife.[15] Obama's motherliness was by far the most prominent element of her media persona. Her actions were repeatedly discussed as those of a mom who worried about her own kids and the nation's children. Her agenda as first lady was described as filled with "projects with a maternal focus."[16] Reporters argued that her concern about her daughters' health led to her decision to plant a White House vegetable garden,[17] motivated her advocacy for improving the content of school lunches, and sparked the creation of her "Let's Move!" program.[18] The press highlighted Obama's domesticity by portraying her as a caring and nurturing mom.

Commentators also presented Obama as a traditional woman by underscoring her actions as a dutiful wife. They regularly delineated the personal and professional sacrifices she made to promote her husband's patriotic endeavors. Journalists wrote about her reluctance to relinquish her family's privacy, indicating that in the end Barack's ambitions were more important to Michelle than her own peace of mind. Pundits routinely alluded to her abdication of her own career to work on behalf of her husband. Media figures also applauded her strategic appropriation of republican motherhood characteristics. Calling Obama's public reframing "from dogged lawyer to loving mother and wife"[19] a "canny decision by a wise woman with her eye on the big picture,"[20] many reporters argued that the first lady's willingness to embody a carefully cultivated conventional persona was the greatest example of her selflessness and the biggest contribution she made to her husband's campaign. By abandoning the more assertive and progressive stance she had taken her entire life and succumbing to entrenched gender expectations, Obama helped her husband by minimizing opponents' ability to use her against him. As one correspondent explained, "It would have been much tougher for Barack Obama . . . if his wife hadn't morphed into mom-in-chief."[21]

A third way the press portrayed Obama was as a fashion icon who kept herself physically fit. Countless news articles and videos commented on Obama's sense of style, willingness to employ a variety of designers, and ability to carry diverse looks with elegance and poise. These reports asserted, "There is arguably no more powerful influence in American fashion today than the country's stylish, risk-taking first lady."[22] Obama's appearance was reported on so frequently that some journalists recognized their own preoccupation with her looks.[23] In addition to the attention afforded her clothing, there were many commentaries about her physique. Obama's arms were the subject of much debate, with a slew of positive and negative assessments levied. Fitness and women's magazines featured tips on "how to get Michelle Obama's arms"[24] and offered lists of workout music preferred by the first lady.[25]

However, not all media outlets praised the first lady. Many critiqued her as fundamentally unladylike, and others charged that despite her seemingly neutral projects she was actually overstepping the ambiguous boundaries of her position. Conservative pundits reframed her efforts to establish a national mother persona as an overbearing push to restrict Americans' freedoms.[26] Some of the most strident denunciations were racially charged accusations that she did not look enough like a first lady[27] and that she was too "uppity."[28] Right-leaning websites offered unfounded stories questioning Obama's patriotism and reviving concerns about her interest in race relations when she was in college. One news organization complained that her decades-old push for universities to hire more female faculty members and professors of color was an indication of her disdain for white Americans.[29] Some of the negative frames extended beyond politics and became quite personal. For example, talk radio commentator Rush Limbaugh complained that Obama's posterior was too large to be ladylike and referred to her as "Moochelle."[30] Even though much of the press coverage about her was positive, Obama still encountered some extremely negative media portrayals.

Romney, although new to the position of presidential nominee's wife, had spent a considerable amount of time in the public eye over the years as her husband pursued various political positions. By 2012, she had an established public persona reporters used to give context to their assessments of the would-be first lady. Just as commentators frequently mentioned Obama's image evolution, they did the same when it came to the Republican nominee's mate. Contrasting the 2012 version of Romney against the purported "pampered princess"[31] and "daughter of privilege"[32] of past campaigns, reporters vacillated between praising Romney's traditionalism and chiding her for being out of touch with modern American women.

Press renditions of Romney usually presented her as a political mate who embodied conventional views of femininity in a mix of appropriate and inappropriate ways. Described as "traditional, genteel, vulnerable, soothing, [and] earnest,"[33] Romney was a "mother, wife and helpmate . . . the Victorian heroine who civilizes her husband."[34] Journalists routinely mentioned her five sons, her experience as a stay-at-home mom, and her tireless support of her husband and his career ambitions. Most stories focused on how Ann's dutiful homemaking provided Mitt the freedom to pursue his professional and political ambitions, but others actually gave the Republican candidate's wife credit for his enterprising manner. Some commentators called Ann "the purest muse of [Mitt's] aspirations," and others claimed she had pushed her husband to get into politics.[35] For her part, Ann reportedly wanted only to see Mitt "fulfill his destiny."[36]

Romney was both celebrated and condemned for her perspective on womanhood. Journalists wrote several stories delineating the struggles Romney faced caring for five boys and dealing with an often-absent husband. She was applauded for her willingness to sacrifice a career of her own in order to nurture her children, encourage her husband, and volunteer in the community. One writer commended Romney because she "had found a way, at least rhetorically, to define herself in relation to others" and interpreted her home life as a sign of her rebelliousness, explaining that Ann and Mitt "resist[ed] entreaties that they not marry so young and not have so many children."[37] However, the would-be first lady's approach did not always receive media approval.

Reporters also depicted Romney's assumption of submissive feminine roles as a type of self-abnegation. Reviving old charges about her status as an overly yielding Stepford wife, critics in the press accused Ann Romney of lacking autonomy and being too deferential to her husband.[38] She was chastised for saying she and he did not always agree on issues but failing to publicly express her own point of view. The press complained that Romney simply parroted her husband when it came to topics such as the economy and health care. Journalists argued that, in addition to capitulating her own individuality, the Republican standard-bearer's helpmate ignored progressive women's efforts in her church, discounted the struggles of women who had fought to advance females' standing in society, and misrepresented the challenges ordinary American women faced. She was said to have a myopic view of womanhood because she was a "sheltered, well-bred, well-heeled"[39] mother "cocooned in a wealthy, white world"[40] who lacked the experience and imagination necessary to understand other women's lives.

News coverage about Romney was generally a mix of positive and negative commentaries that typified depictions of past candidates' spouses. Treatment of the Republican nominee's wife was akin to that of Gore in that reporters appreciated the friendly mother's personality and accessibility. Romney, like Gore, appeared to enjoy most exchanges with the press and engaged in a variety of interviews. Romney sometimes defended her husband's record and never shied away from sharing personal anecdotes about him and her boys. Much like Gore, Romney relished helping humanize her husband and embraced a persona that touted her as a modern instantiation of the republican mother.

However, Romney's wealth led to a different kind of media representation. In much the same way both Teresa Heinz Kerry and Cindy McCain were lambasted for their expensive tastes and lavish lifestyles, commentators argued that Romney's fiscal resources meant she was disconnected from everyday Americans. Members of the press constantly commented on the price of Romney's clothing, the number of houses she was a homemaker in, and the "couple of Cadillacs" she drove.[41] Her interest in dressage, an expensive equestrian sport likened to horse ballet, provided the most overt and repeated point of contrast between Romney and average Americans. Reporters questioned the sincerity of Romney's proffered public persona as a woman preoccupied with domesticity by juxtaposing the image of the would-be first lady dressed in finery riding a decorated horse against the picture of a fatigued mother of five buried under endless piles of laundry.

Journalists portrayed both Obama and Romney as dutiful wives and doting mothers. Because the press was eager to measure each woman's basic domestic competencies, Obama and Romney were pressured to participate in the usual litany of feminine tests administered in the media. Each woman appeared on daytime talk shows, gave interviews to *Good Housekeeping* magazine, provided tours of their family homes, and submitted a recipe for the *Family Circle* first lady cookie contest. When Obama's white and dark chocolate chip cookies beat out Romney's M&M cookies, the *New York Times, Huffington Post, Slate, ABC News, USA Today, NBC News,* and a host of other outlets reported on the results.

The entertainment media treated the spouses of the presidential nominees much like the news media did. As guests on daytime talk shows such as *The View,* Obama and Romney were asked about being mothers and about their husbands' true personalities. Late-night monologues took humorous jabs at both women: Obama was mocked for her efforts to promote fitness, and Romney was ridiculed for her participation in dressage. On talk radio, the women were variously applauded and critiqued for their public depictions of womanhood. Obama and Romney were each the subject of satirical representations on comedy programs like *Saturday Night Live (SNL)*. In 2012, Romney's likeness appeared on three episodes of *SNL,* each lampooning her naive nature and her unquestioning support of her husband.[42] The skits highlighted her need to humanize him and accentuated her defensiveness of him.[43] Obama was portrayed on *SNL* only once during the campaign. The piece, an allusion to the popular 1980s sitcom *The Cosby Show* that placed the Obamas in the characters' roles, depicted Obama as a working mother who nagged her husband about his diet and exercise.[44]

Obama and Romney also proactively used the media to expand their contributions to their spouses' campaigns. Obama showed up on scripted television shows such as the popular children's sitcom *iCarly,* and Romney cohosted *Good Morning America.* The two also released lists of their families' favorite entertainment programs in an effort to demonstrate their similarities to average Americans, and they shared food and wellness tips in personally penned blogs and magazine stories. Obama and Romney also appeared in social media messages that included text, audio, and video. Most of these messages spotlighted the women's motherly and wifely personas.

The media coverage of Obama and Romney throughout the 2012 presidential campaign relied heavily on archetypal perspectives of women as mothers and wives. Both women were primarily depicted as homemakers, but they were differentiated from each other by the degree of traditionalism each invoked. Obama, although she had given up her professional endeavors, was still portrayed as a working mom who balanced multiple types of responsibilities, and

Romney was presented as a stay-at-home mother with the fiscal means to focus entirely on domestic duties. Each woman was an ardent advocate of her husband and was willing to reveal personal information if it helped promote her mate's agenda. Obama and Romney were both considered charming and gracious, but the press identified Obama as a more influential person by virtue of both her position and her personality. Obama was generally characterized as a revised version of traditional womanhood and Romney as a more orthodox example. Overall, Obama was the more popular of the two women. In late August, 65 percent of Gallup poll respondents held Obama in a favorable light, whereas just 42 percent viewed Romney positively.[45] These opinions reflected the press's argument that Obama was more relatable than Romney and more accurately represented the wide range of experiences of American women.

The media coverage of Obama and Romney depended heavily on republican motherhood imagery and rhetoric just as treatments of past candidates' spouses had, but slight modifications to the old-fashioned trope indicated a small, yet consequential, change in attitudes about women as social and political beings. Obama's favorable portrayal as a *working* mother added a bit of nuance to interpretations of acceptable female attributes. Michelle Obama was not shunned or shamed for her previous ambitions in the same manner Hillary Clinton had been just two decades earlier. Additionally, the public's apparent preference for the mildly assertive, once professionally successful woman (Obama) over the extremely compliant and domestically focused mother and grandmother (Romney) indicated that the electorate expected these public women to show some degree of autonomous self-expression. However, the movement in attitudes was fairly minor. Obama was, after all, praised for embracing her duties as a mother and wife, and Romney was critiqued because of the extreme nature of her apparent docility. The press applications of the republican motherhood ideal to interpret Obama and Romney implied that women generally should regard the needs of their husbands and children as more important than their own. The representations in this cycle also argued that women could and should show a bit of individual drive provided their personal interests did not override their domestic responsibilities.

Party Presentations

The Democratic and Republican Parties upheld their usual perspectives on the spouses of nominees during the 2012 campaign. Each woman's own party considered her a useful asset, and the opposition viewed her as an exploitable liability. Because voters looked more favorably on Obama and Romney than on their respective husbands, the parties frequently deployed these particular campaign surrogates. Each gave speeches, appeared solo at rallies, and participated in numerous mediated events. Midway through the year, Obama had hosted more than fifty fund-raisers, and Romney had made almost two hundred public appearances.[46] Throughout 2012, each major party endeavored to depict its own candidate's mate as the ideal representation of American womanhood while questioning whether the opponent's consort could or should serve as a role model for female citizens.

The Democrats tried to capitalize on Obama's popularity by accentuating her motherly inclinations. They did so by showing her with her own daughters and interacting with various other children. Party leaders touted her maternal bona fides and largely ignored her professional accomplishments. Although they did talk about the first lady as a working mom, they often stressed her preference for mothering and declared that her work life was rooted in fiscal necessity. The Democratic strategy with Obama centered around the idea of continuing to normalize the first lady by underscoring her perceived commonalities with average American women. In many ways, Obama was cast as a reprise of the 1996 soccer mom; she had an advanced education and was successful in the workforce but ultimately prioritized her family over her own career development. Political operatives believed this view of Obama would appeal to a broad, bipartisan swath of voters.

Exploiting Obama to boost her husband's popularity, staffers arranged for the first lady to participate in many supposedly apolitical media events related to her established social agenda. She appeared on television programs such as NBC's highly rated weight-loss show *The Biggest Loser* to talk about maintaining a healthy diet and exercising regularly, she made guest appearances on children's shows to encourage kids to be active, and she was part of social media messaging that promoted healthy living. She also spoke quite a bit about military families and hosted events that drew attention to the sacrifices made by the spouses and children of armed forces personnel. The party's use of Obama throughout the campaign kept her primarily focused on topics that fell squarely within the putatively feminine domain and that purposefully sidestepped controversial subjects. However, rather than simply forcing Obama into a traditional mode that framed her as the compassionate member of the presidential pair, the messaging surrounding the first lady underscored her tendency to entwine personal and political perspectives. She made the case that issues normally dismissed or given little regard because of their connection to private life (topics such as health, fitness, and emotional well-being) deserved more widespread attention from leaders and voters. Democrats touted Obama and her initiatives to demonstrate that they, as a party, were giving voice to the concerns of female voters, a group Democrats claimed was important but regularly ignored. This use of Obama reinforced a narrow view of womanhood by circumscribing women's interests as primarily (or even exclusively) tied to the home.

The Republicans were less enthusiastic about Obama. Using many of the same tactics to critique the Democratic nominee's wife that were employed in

2008, GOP members painted Obama as abnormal in order to urge voters to abandon any affinity they might have felt for her.[47] Party members accused Obama of being an unpatriotic angry black woman. Circulating copies of an old Harvard Law paper she had written about the need to hire more women and minority professors, Republicans argued that her efforts were indicative of her disdain for meritocracy.[48] Furthermore, an email distributed by GOP members included a discredited claim that the first lady disrespected victims of September 11 by complaining "all this for a damned flag" during a memorial service.[49] Party members also complained that Obama had extravagant tastes and indulged them at the taxpayers' expense. One recurring message equated the first lady with Marie Antoinette.[50]

As part of the strategic pillorying of the first lady, individual Republican Party members sent messages to their constituents that denigrated Obama. Using racially charged terminology, a Kansas state representative sent supporters digital messages that referred to "Mrs. Yo' Mama" and jokingly asked whether Obama and the famous Dr. Seuss character the Grinch were twins separated at birth.[51] Another party member implied that Obama was a hypocrite when he chastised the first lady's posterior and contended that its size was evidence she was not as healthy as she forced others to be.[52] Each offender, in turn, made apologies in the press. The initial comments and the additional attention garnered from the public statements of regret spurred discussions about Obama's fitness as the first lady. The slew of GOP recriminations of the first lady offered an unflattering perspective on Obama and her standing as a true representative of American women.[53]

For the Republicans, Romney was the quintessential political mate. A pretty blonde mother and grandmother who had dedicated her life to assisting her husband and raising his sons, Romney was the embodiment of the republican motherhood ideal, a perspective on women the GOP touted as the epitome of proper womanhood. Romney was also considered cheerful, outgoing, and much more likable than her mate. Because she enjoyed talking about her husband and family, party leaders tasked her with humanizing her husband; her job was to tell the stories that made him appear to be more than just a businessman.

Republican strategists considered Romney the key to winning over female voters. As her husband's so-called ambassador to women, Romney's public appearances were tailored toward reaching female-dominated audiences. She spoke to women's groups, appeared on television programming that attracted female viewers, and made comments specifically directed to women during her campaign speeches. Romney was usually introduced as a wife of forty-plus years, a mother of five sons, and a grandmother of eighteen. Party messaging about Romney always spotlighted her work as a stay-at-home mother, her volunteerism, and her standing as a multiple sclerosis and breast cancer survivor. Calling her a more conventional potential first lady than Obama, GOP operatives believed Romney's approach to femininity was a vision of American womanhood voters would find appealing.

Although Romney's public image was relatively benign and noncontroversial, the Democrats still tried to frame her as a political liability for her husband. The most common critique the party launched against the would-be first lady was grounded in her wealth. Party members frequently described Romney as out of touch and elitist. They pointed out her lavish lifestyle, her participation in dressage, and her multiple homes in order to create distance between the GOP standard-bearer's wife and most citizens. Democrats questioned whether Romney's experiences as a homemaker could really be compared to those of average Americans because of the resources at her disposal.

One of the most overt attacks on Romney occurred when a Democratic strategist questioned her standing as her husband's advisor on women's issues. Claiming that the Republican candidate's wife had no understanding of the real struggles of American women because she never held a job, Hillary Rosen created a controversy that found Republicans and Democrats alike defending the hard work and multiple contributions stay-at-home moms make to society. The dig at the GOP leader's spouse benefited both parties and sparked conversations about women's position in society. Republicans were able to accuse Democrats of disregarding a particular subset of women voters while demonstrating their own dedication to established values. Democrats took the opportunity to remind the electorate of the president's humble origins (and his stay-at-home mother) and to underscore their concern for women and women's issues. The discourse instigated by Rosen's comments briefly made perceptions of womanhood a dominant part of both parties' campaign messaging. However, the discussion ultimately devolved into a defense of numerous types of motherhood rather than a dialogue about female citizenship; the ensuing explications of women as political actors were limited to delineating women's choices relative to their reproductive activities rather than expounding on their contributions as independent citizens.

In 2012, the major parties' uses and representations of the nominees' spouses continued the pattern of conflating perceptions of womanhood, motherhood, and wifedom established in previous campaigns. Obama and Romney were defined by their relationships to their husbands and children rather than as autonomous citizens capable of insights that did not rely on their familial bonds. For the parties, each woman's credibility rested on her capacity to effectively meet long-held expectations of femininity. Although the Democrats' version of Obama was a bit more progressive than the Republicans' portrayal of Romney, both renditions relegated the women to submissive, supporting roles. The Democrats' willingness to interpret the personal as political and vice versa gave a bit more gravitas to the compassionate issues assumed to reside in the feminine realm, but it did not significantly alter the party's homogenized view of women and their interests. Based on the ways they presented their own nominee's spouse, each of the parties viewed women voters as domestically focused and preferred traditional feminine iconography when it came to the candidates' wives.

Self-Portrayals

Part of the reason the press and the parties treated the wives of the 2012 presidential nominees in such a conventional fashion is because the women presented themselves in that manner. Obama's experiences in 2008 informed her self-portrayal throughout her time in the White House and during the president's reelection bid. Romney's biography guided her creation of a public persona that matched her view of womanhood as inextricably tied to wifedom and motherhood. Both women seemed to cherish their maternal and spousal roles and appeared to take every opportunity to accentuate their purported femininity. Yet, although each woman cast herself as the ultimate representation of motherhood, the messages by Obama and Romney demonstrated distinctly different perspectives on the proper social and political functions for women as a whole.

Obama embraced many aspects of the republican motherhood ideal and used elements of its rhetoric to describe herself throughout the 2012 presidential election. In interviews, Obama frequently talked about herself as a protective mother. When asked about life in the White House, her initial response referenced the difficulties of "being a mother and trying to keep your kids sane" and wanting "to make sure that my girls come out of this on the other end whole."[54] She also listed maternal activities among her toughest challenges.[55] In a campaign filled with moments when Obama discussed herself in traditionally feminine terms, the most direct self-depiction she offered came in her Democratic National Convention (DNC) address.

In 2012, Obama's DNC speech was highly anticipated because her performance at the 2008 DNC had been exceptionally effective and her popularity had increased significantly since that time. Obama's talk was expected to include several personal anecdotes and to showcase the first lady's engaging personality. The oration was, by most accounts, a success; it showed Obama's humor and humility and allowed her to humanize her husband as she made the case for a second term in the White House.[56] The content of Obama's 2012 address reflects her own strategic use of republican motherhood rhetoric in efforts to both uphold and challenge established gender norms. Throughout the address, she takes on common feminine attributes herself as she rhetorically creates the space for other women to choose their own approaches to womanhood.

Obama's speech contains numerous passages that encourage voters to interpret the first lady as a woman fulfilling duties usually associated with traditionally circumscribed views of female patriotism. She defines herself in a manner that highlights her fealty to her country primarily through her dedication to her family. Obama overtly underscores her national loyalty by explaining "how blessed we are to live in the greatest nation on earth," but her primary self-portrayal as a good citizen is through her actions as a concerned mother and supportive wife.[57] She embraces her own motherhood in the introduction when she thanks the American people for the "incredible kindness and warmth that people have shown me and my family, especially our girls."[58] Obama expands on this maternal perspective at multiple points in her speech. It is evident early on when she places her daughters at the center of her ambivalence about her husband's 2008 campaign. She tells listeners, "Like any mother, I was worried about what it would mean for our girls if he got that chance [to be president]. How would we keep them grounded under the glare of the national spotlight? How would they feel being uprooted from their school, their friends, and the only home they'd ever known?"[59] Here Obama questions her ability to effectively perform her maternal duty to protect her daughters' emotional well-being and to ensure that they become morally upstanding young women. However, in the story as she tells it, Obama's desire to help her husband overrides her apprehensiveness; she enacts the tenets of republican motherhood by submitting herself and her family to a more public lifestyle than she wants in order to buttress her husband's patriotic endeavors.

Throughout the address, Obama repeatedly references her standing as an ordinary wife and mother. She shares details about the early days of her and Barack's courtship when they were "so young, so in love, and so in debt" and how later "a date night for Barack and me was either dinner or a movie, because as an exhausted mom, I couldn't stay awake for both."[60] She spotlights the strength and longevity of the couple's union by confiding, "I love my husband . . . even more than I did 23 years ago, when we first met."[61] Obama also talks about the couple's collective goals as parents, tying the moral lessons she and her husband each learned as children to the values they strive to pass on to their kids. Obama regularly links her experiences and interests as a parent to those of most average Americans through explicit statements such as, "Those are the values Barack and I—and so many of you—are trying to pass on to our own children."[62] The first lady emphasizes her responsibilities as a moral guardian of future generations while illustrating her connection to her husband.

Obama further fortifies her standing as an orthodox female by grounding most arguments she makes in terms related to motherhood or familial connections. She argues that the fundamental promise of the United States is that "you should be able to build a decent life for yourself and an even better life for your kids and grandkids."[63] She also justifies and applauds her husband's political achievements based on their impact on families. She praises her husband's economic policies for helping create "jobs you can raise a family on" and champions health care legislation because "our grandparents should be able to afford their medicine; our kids should be able to see a doctor when they're sick."[64] She argues that most Americans "want something more for your kids and grandkids" and that her husband is the man to create opportunities for future generations.[65]

One of the most memorable parts of Obama's 2012 DNC address is the unequivocal declaration of her dedication to home and family that occurs near the end of the speech. She proclaims, "At the end of the day, my most important title is still 'Mom-in-Chief.'"[66] Defining herself "not just as first lady and not just as a wife" but predominantly as a mother, Obama finishes her speech with a concise statement summarizing the self-portrayal she developed throughout the oration and the campaign.[67] A careful read of the address indicates that Obama's primary loyalty is to her husband, yet her perpetual tendency to tout her maternal standing as her principle source of credibility makes her arguments even more palatable for conservative listeners. Her need to present herself as a representative of traditionalism in order to dissolve the presumed distance between herself and many audience members was particularly acute because Obama could not physically fit the model of first ladydom established by her predecessors as she continually battled racial stereotyping.

Although she takes on the republican mother mantle herself, Obama's speech contains more open-minded interpretations of womanhood and female citizenship than had many of the past speeches by nominees' wives. Unlike McCain and Bush (in 2000), Obama does not generally paint all women with the same restrictive rhetorical brush she uses for her own self-depiction. Even though she does make some assumptions about women's motivations being tied to their actual or prospective motherhood, she also offers interpretations of women that extend beyond the domestic realm. Obama talks about the Lilly Ledbetter Fair Pay Act in terms of fundamental fairness and argues that women deserve equal pay for equal work. She praises the "brave men and women who wear our country's uniform and sacrifice their lives" and reminds listeners that women "dragged to jail for seeking the vote"[68] were just as much a part of securing the American dream as the men who fought in the Revolutionary War. Obama makes a clearly progressive argument in favor of women's autonomy when she says, "Women are more than capable of making our own choices about our bodies and our health care."[69] Rather than advocating for a deferential feminine perspective or making relational connections more important than individual empowerment for women generally, Obama creates a space for women to exist outside of the confines of republican motherhood while simultaneously making it okay for women to choose a more conventional lifestyle. Acting as the ultimate republican mother, Obama sacrifices her own independent identity and voice, defines herself in terms of others, and defers to societal norms in order to make the case for a more enlightened interpretation of women as citizens.

Obama applied republican motherhood rhetoric in a very calculated manner for strategic political purposes, but Romney seemed to employ the trope because she believes heteronormative gender roles are the proper approach to womanhood. Throughout her time in the public eye, Romney considered her duties as a mother to be her primary source of political credibility. She interpreted experiences through a maternal lens and often used pregnancy as a metaphor for activities such as competing in dressage and participating in political campaigns. She repeatedly equated a political contest with gestation, describing it as "very painful. It has a lot of ups and downs. At about nine months, you're saying to yourself, 'How can I get out of this?' But then, you know, it's over."[70] This analogy underscored Romney's tendency to define herself first and foremost as a mother and to offer interpretations of the world from that particular vantage point. Romney's self-depiction was most clearly and concisely articulated in her speech at the Republican National Convention (RNC).

Romney's 2012 RNC address was touted as an homage to American women. However, because she (and many in the Republican Party) viewed womanhood in very traditional ways, the speech is really a panegyric to mothers and wives, with Romney offering herself as the prototypical exemplar of female patriotism. Her self-depiction throughout the speech reinforces a perspective that fuses the terms "woman," "wife," and "mother" and presumes that women's primary interests lie in caring for and nurturing others. Romney presents herself as the ideal woman by being the perfect wife and by discussing political issues from the standpoint of a mother. She begins this approach during the opening of her speech when she says, "I want to talk to you tonight not about politics and not about party. . . . Tonight I want to talk to you about love."[71] Romney tries to reframe the clearly political oration as a personal exploration of a "love so deep only a mother can fathom it."[72] This opening discounts Romney's interest in objective assessments of political policy and suggests that her authority is based solely on her relational connections to others.

Because Romney's speech was promoted as a message of praise for women, it is important to note that she speaks about the particular accomplishments of the men in her life but does not individually mention any of the women. Romney specifically commends her father, father-in-law, and husband for their professional labor and their political activities (her father as a mayor, her husband and his father as governors) and credits the men with providing for their families and being "good fathers teaching their sons and daughters"[73] American values. However, when it comes to women, she talks only generically about the "the moms of this nation—single, married, widowed—who really hold this country together."[74] Romney does not share any details about the lives or work of her own mother, grandmother, or even mother-in-law (who is included as one of Mitt's "two loving parents," while Romney's own mother is not referenced). In spite of telling mothers "we salute you and sing your praises," Romney expresses explicit admiration only for the work of male family members; the value of the females' domestic labor remains unsung.[75] Romney is the only specific woman in the speech whose efforts as a wife and mother are discussed.

Portraying herself as a dedicated matriarch, Romney shares many tales about her home life to underscore her standing as a proper female figure. She begins with anecdotes about her courtship with Mitt and exclaims, "We were determined not to let anything stand in the way of our life together."[76] Discussing the arrival of the couple's first son, Romney tells audience members, "Like every other girl who finds herself in a new life far from family and friends, with a new baby and a new husband, it dawned on me that I had absolutely no idea what I was getting into."[77] She later reminisces about "long, rainy winter afternoons in a house with five boys screaming at once" and briefly mentions Mitt's supportiveness while she battled multiple sclerosis and breast cancer.[78] Ann calls her connection to Mitt "a real marriage" and twice points out the longevity of their union, first as a forty-two-year marriage and second as a forty-seven-year partnership.[79]

Romney's perspective is not only reflected in her personal anecdotes but is also evident in her discussion of political issues. Focusing on reflections about love, she does not explore many policy concerns. Yet the issues she does address are either commonly considered feminine subjects, such as education and health care, or they are broached from a family-oriented perspective. When Romney talks about the economy, a topic ordinarily deemed masculine in orientation, she does so by discussing "working moms who love their jobs but would like to work just a little less to spend more time with the kids" and couples "who would like to have another child, but wonder how will they afford it."[80] She addresses economic problems in terms of their familial impacts when she worries about the "parents who lie awake at night side by side, wondering how they'll be able to pay the mortgage or make the rent."[81] This approach is similar to Obama's contention that politics is personal, but it takes the perspective a step further by meshing the political and the parental.

In a rhetorical gesture similar to Obama's self-designation as mom in chief, Romney declares near the end of her speech, "I can only stand here tonight as a wife, a mother, a grandmother, an American."[82] Although she specifically references her citizenship, the content of the speech leading up to this line indicates that it is only through her conventionally feminine roles that her duties as an American can be fulfilled. Romney accentuates her very traditional point of view and assumes that most other female citizens agree with her perspective on gender norms. At no time in the address does she acknowledge women without explicitly linking them to family members. Women employed outside the home are addressed only as working moms, and unmarried women are referenced as single mothers or widows. She tells no tales of women functioning outside of their duties to others. In fact, Romney specifically defines all females in terms of their relationships when she argues, "We're the mothers, we're the wives, we're the grandmothers, we're the big sisters, we're the little sisters, we're the daughters."[83] In the speech, Romney never recognizes any woman as an autonomous citizen empowered by her individuality. Instead, she depicts all women using the restrictive rhetoric of republican motherhood.

Both Obama and Romney created self-representations that embraced archetypal elements of femininity. Each woman cast herself as a supportive wife and dutiful mother defined exclusively in terms of her relationships with others. Neither woman talked about her own life or accomplishments outside of marriage or motherhood beyond a brief mention of going to college or owing money for a student loan. Obama and Romney addressed political issues from a maternal perspective and claimed to give voice to the worries of mothers across the land. Both women utilized republican motherhood rhetoric extensively. However, Romney's use of the trope appeared simply descriptive, whereas Obama's application of it seemed more tactical. Romney selected the conceit because it accurately described her life and outlook; the first lady chose the construct to help frame herself as a putatively average woman because she needed to normalize her image to overcome underlying racial tensions and stereotypes.

In spite of their similar choice of rhetoric, Obama and Romney each implemented the orthodox female trope in noticeably different ways. Whereas Obama primarily (but not exclusively) administered the confining perspective to herself but afforded other women more flexibility in their enactment of womanhood, Romney rendered all women little more than vassal extensions of their husbands, fathers, and children. Obama argued in favor of some female autonomy. Romney did not. The first lady made domesticity one viable option for women, whereas her prospective replacement presented homemaking as the preferred choice for true female patriots. The distinctions between Obama's and Romney's application of republican motherhood rhetoric reflected significant differences in their points of view regarding women. Obama employed conservative rhetoric to promote a moderately expansive view of women, and Romney simply endorsed a limited view of female citizenship. Still, they both effectively prioritized historically entrenched gender norms and reified conservative outlooks about women as political actors.

Conclusion

Michelle Obama and Ann Romney were not on the ballot in 2012, yet they certainly influenced political dialogue during the presidential contest. Both women fought to present themselves as the quintessential American woman; they did so by accentuating the ways they personally embodied traditional standards of femininity. From emphasizing their roles as wives and mothers to discussing their potential influence as fashion icons, the press and the parties also underscored conventional aspects of these women's lives to evaluate each woman's fitness for the office of first lady of the United States. Consistent with the treatment of past nominees' wives, in 2012 the criteria for judging candidates' spouses were based on republican motherhood ideals.

The public images created by and about Obama and Romney were quite similar on the surface, but they were clearly not the same. Obama was considered a moderately progressive figure because she was perceived as a working mom juggling multiple responsibilities. Romney was a very conservative representative of femininity whose credibility was derived through her domesticity. In the end, the American people seemed to find the woman representing a more modern version of womanhood more appealing. Obama's net favorability in the final poll taken before the 2012 election made her the fourth most popular of the nominees' spouses between 1988 and 2012.[84] Only the amiable and very orthodox Barbara Bush, Laura Bush (in 2004), and Tipper Gore had higher scores. In contrast, Ann Romney's net rating placed her above only Hillary Clinton (in 1992 and 1996) and Teresa Heinz Kerry. It is not unusual for sitting first ladies to have higher ratings than the wives of challengers, but Obama's poll results provide some evidence of the effectiveness of her constructed republican mother persona and of a possible, though slight, shift in Americans' views about women.

Obama's biography aligned her much more closely with the widely disliked Clinton than the generally adored Barbara Bush, but the public mostly perceived Obama positively.[85] This is very likely a result of the creation of an outward image that foregrounded key attributes of traditional female patriotism. Taking cues from republican motherhood and using rhetoric related to the conceit, Obama tapped into long-established assumptions about women's supposedly proper functions to dissolve purported differences between her and some members of the electorate. She proved herself essentially similar to historically idealized visions of American womanhood. Yet, Obama did not discount other women's ability to disrupt norms and violate gender-based expectations. Thus, using republican motherhood rhetoric in her self-depiction but not in her portrayals of other women, Obama offered an appealing blend of conservative and progressive perspectives.

An additional interpretation of Obama's popularity is that her appeal as a well-educated working mom was a sign of the growing acceptance of shifting female roles. In 1992, Clinton was berated for maintaining her career while raising her child, but twenty years later Obama's decision to pursue a profession was accepted as a commonplace choice. By not flaunting her career and generally deflecting public attention away from it, the first lady made her past work life a nonissue. Instead, Obama epitomized the soccer mom trope by having a career but presenting herself as more concerned with her family than her profession. Almost two decades after the suburban working mother was conceptualized as a consequential voter, the first lady was finally permitted to adopt such a persona. The public's preference for the working mom (Obama) over the stay-at-home mother (Romney) reflects a very modest change in women's assumed proper activities.

The 2012 presidential election was interesting for many reasons, not the least of which was the discussion about women that it sparked. The emphasis on motherhood as a fundamental aspect of womanhood dominated much of the dialogue regarding female citizenship because of the conventional depictions of the candidates' wives. In 1992, the mates were two women with contrasting views of womanhood. The 2000 campaign offered two similar women emphasizing their wifely dutifulness. However, the nominees' consorts in 2012 were different women presenting themselves in a similar fashion as they offered comparable interpretations of motherhood but divergent views of womanhood. In many ways, 2012 was the year that conflated the terms "woman," "wife," and "mother" most thoroughly but also offered more wide-ranging views of female citizenship.

The 2016 election shifted the conversation about women's roles as political actors and the treatment of presidential nominees' spouses. The first female presidential nominee brought along with her the first husband of a major party's standard-bearer. This meant the press and the parties faced new challenges framing discussions regarding Bill Clinton and Melania Trump.

8

Bill Clinton and Melania Trump

The Former President and the Model Immigrant (2016)

Several fascinating presidential contests occurred during the time span covered by this book. In 1992, Bill Clinton, a relative newcomer to the national stage, beat out George H. W. Bush, an established statesman, in an election many pundits argued marked a generational shift in national leadership. In 2000, George W. Bush became just the fourth president to assume the Oval Office with an Electoral College win but no popular vote victory to claim. The 2008 competition was arguably the most diverse of any national campaign with a field that included the first African American winner, the oldest-ever Republican standard-bearer, the first woman to effectively contest a major party's nomination, and the first GOP female vice presidential candidate. Yet for all of the notable elements of the seven elections studied in this book, for people interested in women in politics the 2016 contest was possibly the most intriguing of them all.

For the first time ever, a woman won a major party's primary contest and secured its nomination for the US presidency. Hillary Clinton, the much-maligned former first lady, former US senator, and former secretary of state, won thirty-four state elections and caucuses during the Democratic primaries and beat her closest challenger, Vermont senator Bernie Sanders, by almost a thousand delegate votes. During the general election, Clinton faced political newcomer and reality television star Donald Trump. Most politicos initially thought Trump's candidacy was a joke, and many declared Clinton the first female president long before any ballots were counted. Despite criticisms leveled against her, Clinton enjoyed a substantial lead in most opinion polls throughout the later months of the campaign. On election night, as predicted, Clinton made history, but it was not in the manner she desired. She became the second contemporary Democratic nominee to win the popular vote but lose the election. Securing almost 3 million more votes than her opponent, Clinton was the first American woman to win 48.2 percent of the ballots cast in a national election. However, when she earned only 227 Electoral College votes to Trump's 304, she became the fifth candidate to win the popular vote but lose the election; she also earned the dubious distinction of having the largest popular vote margin over her opponent of any losing candidate (she surpassed Al Gore's 2000 mark by more than 2.3 million votes).[1]

Clinton's presidential run was both a boon and a bust for women in politics. Her campaign clearly showed that many Americans were willing to support a female leader in the White House and that multiple voters and voting groups found a blend of feminine and masculine leadership qualities appealing. Clinton also proved that a woman could raise sufficient funds to finance a lengthy national race, finally overcoming the difficulties that ended the efforts of previous female contenders such as Elizabeth Dole. In addition, the results of the presidential election drove many women to consider launching their own political careers. Initiatives like Iowa State University's Ready to Run, a nonpartisan campaign training program, had a spike in female participation in the months following the announcement of the election results and Trump's inauguration.[2]

Although some positives did come out of Clinton's failed run, her efforts brought to light many disheartening attitudes toward women as political actors. The tenor of the campaign and the content of many complaints about the seasoned politician indicated that sex-based stereotypes still permeated many citizens' ideas about what a proper leader should look and act like. There were overt attacks on Clinton's appearance and physical strength that framed her as simultaneously too masculine (wearing pantsuits) and too feminine (purportedly lacking stamina). The more subtle critiques included language that alluded to male physical characteristics, such as conversations about the need for "broad-shouldered leadership" when it comes to foreign policy.[3] As with any politician, there were certainly legitimate critiques to be made about Clinton's perspectives and policy proposals, but the gendered disparagements illustrated that entrenched stereotypes about women's positions in society and politics continued to dominate many Americans' worldviews.

The 2016 campaign contained both the most expansive and constrained perspectives on women as political actors of any US presidential contest. This seemingly schizophrenic approach to female citizenship pervaded several aspects of the campaign, including the treatment of the spouses of the presidential contenders.

The 2016 Presidential Nominees' Spouses

The cast of characters in the 2016 national campaign consisted of a menagerie of unusual and expected individuals. Hillary Clinton's candidacy was clearly historic and garnered a great deal of attention. She chose Tim Kaine, a congenial US senator from Virginia, to complete the Democratic ticket. On the Republican side, Donald Trump beat out fifteen other primary contestants on the strength of his popularity, his status as a Washington outsider and his jingoistic "Make America Great Again" slogan. The real estate mogul with no experience in public service selected Mike Pence, then the governor of Indiana and a past member of the US House of Representatives, as his running mate. The blend of ordinary and extraordinary characters extended beyond the individuals on the ballot and included the spouses of the presidential nominees. There, too, the 2016 contest was noteworthy; the candidates' mates included the familiar past US president Bill Clinton as the first-ever male consort and former model Melania Trump as one of the few foreign-born wives of a candidate.

William Jefferson Blythe III, later known as Bill Clinton, was born on August 19, 1946, in Hope, Arkansas. His father, William Blythe, Jr., died in a car accident a few months before he was born. Bill spent his early years living with his grandparents as his mother, Julia Chester, attended nursing school. In 1950, Chester married a car dealer named Roger Clinton, and the couple soon had a son. Bill and his half-brother were raised together in Hot Springs, Arkansas, where Bill attended school. He started out in a Catholic elementary school program but attained most of his education in the public system. At the age of fifteen, Bill officially assumed his stepfather's last name. During high school, Bill played the saxophone, participated in student government, and was one of his state's representatives to the Boys Nation mock government program. While in Washington, DC, he met President John F. Kennedy, an encounter he frequently identified as a hallmark moment that motivated him to dedicate his life to public service.

In 1968, Clinton earned a bachelor's degree from Georgetown University. He then became a Rhodes Scholar at University College, Oxford. However, because of concerns he would be drafted into the military, he did not complete his studies abroad. Instead, after only one year in England, he accepted an offer to attend Yale Law School. At Yale he met his future wife, Hillary Rodham. She was one class year ahead of him. The two reportedly became inseparable after meeting in 1971. During the summer of 1972, Bill initially followed Hillary to California, but the two ended up moving to Texas together so he could work on George McGovern's ill-fated presidential campaign. During his time in Texas, Clinton began cultivating connections with people like Ron Kirk, Ann Richards, and Steven Spielberg. Clinton earned his JD from Yale in 1973.

After graduation, Clinton returned to Arkansas to teach law and run for elected office. His first race was a failure; he lost a 1974 bid for a US House of Representatives seat. On October 11, 1975, he married Hillary Rodham. The next year, he won the position of Arkansas attorney general. Two years later, Clinton became the governor of Arkansas. The couple's daughter, Chelsea, was born during his first term. That fall, his reelection bid was unsuccessful. Many people blamed his wife for costing him votes from conservative constituents because she did not properly embody the traditional attributes of an Arkansas woman. After reframing both his and his wife's public personas to accommodate constituents' expectations (he became more outgoing and accessible, and she became more conventionally feminine in appearance and attitude), Clinton regained the office in 1982. He remained the governor of Arkansas until his successful 1992 bid for the White House.

Clinton became the forty-second president of the United States on January 20, 1993, and was reelected in 1996. He was not very popular during his first few months in office, but he eventually became a well-liked leader with considerable bipartisan support.[4] During his second term, he faced impeachment charges for perjury and obstruction of justice stemming from an investigation of an alleged extramarital affair with a White House intern named Monica Lewinsky; the US Senate eventually acquitted him. Curiously, Clinton's approval ratings rose after the impeachment hearings, and he ended his presidency with the highest final quarter ratings of any president in the preceding fifty years.[5] After leaving the Oval Office, Clinton built a largely positive outward persona by engaging in different forms of public service. He participated in altruistic programs directly and through the Clinton Foundation, a nonprofit organization designed to assist global philanthropic efforts. In 2004, UN secretary general Kofi Annan appointed Clinton to head relief efforts after a tsunami devastated parts of Asia. The next year, Bill Clinton partnered with former president George H. W. Bush to raise funds for victims of Hurricane Katrina.

Clinton remained active in politics during his postpresidency. He campaigned on behalf of Democrats across the nation, including championing the presidential efforts of Al Gore in 2000 and John Kerry in 2004. Clinton stirred some controversy in 2008 when, as part of his wife's initial presidential bid, he vigorously attacked Barack Obama during the primaries, then touted the Chicagoan as the ideal candidate at the 2008 Democratic National Convention (DNC). In 2012, Clinton fully endorsed the Democratic incumbent for the entirety of the campaign and delivered a compelling address at the DNC that many politicos said helped President Obama secure his second term. In 2016, Clinton was again part of the Democratic candidate's efforts to win the White House. This time, he took on the complicated dual roles of past president and supportive political spouse and broke new ground as the first male mate of a major party nominee.

Melanija Knavs, now known as Melania Trump, was born on April 26, 1970, in Novo Mesto, a town in what is now Slovenia but was then part of Yugoslavia. Her father, Viktor, managed a state-owned car and motorcycle dealership; her mother, Amalija, was a patternmaker for a children's clothing line. Melanija was raised with an older sister and had a half-brother (on her father's side) whom she did not see. The family was financially stable and lived in a modest apartment. At age five, Melanija began modeling.

Melanija spent her teenage years in the towns of Sevnica and Ljubljana. She studied design and photography in secondary school. She also learned to speak English, French, Italian, and German as well as Serbo-Croatian and Slovene. As a sixteen-year-old, she started appearing in commercials and changed her name to the Germanized Melania Knauss. After graduation, she spent one year at the University of Ljubljana before dropping out to pursue a full-time career in modeling. She worked for fashion houses across Europe, including some in the major markets of Paris and Milan. In 1996, she moved to New York and engaged in photo shoots as an undocumented immigrant lacking a proper work visa.[6] Originally considered a second- or third-tier model because of lack of gracefulness in her movements, her career prospects improved considerably after she met her future husband, Donald Trump, at a New York Fashion Week event in September 1998.[7] Shortly after starting to date Donald, Melania began appearing on top-tier magazine covers such as *Vanity Fair* and *Vogue.* In 2001, she earned a US green card by claiming her modeling ability as an extraordinary skill.

Melania had a lengthy courtship with the twice-divorced Donald, who was twenty-four years her senior. They dated for more than five years before becoming engaged and married a year later. The two were wed on January 22, 2005. Bill and Hillary Clinton attended the ceremony and reception along with a host of other celebrities and politicians. Melania gave up modeling upon marrying Donald and became pregnant several months after the wedding. On March 20, 2006, she gave birth to the couple's son, Barron William Trump. It was her first child and Donald's fifth. Following the birth of her son, Trump refused to hire a nanny and declared motherhood her primary occupation; her modeling became limited to family portraits and publicity photos. Trump became an American citizen in July 2006.[8]

In addition to her work as a mother, Trump established multiple philanthropic and business relationships after marrying. She became involved with charities such as the Boys Club of New York and the Police Athletic League.[9] Between 2005 and 2009, Trump served as a Red Cross goodwill ambassador. Her charitable endeavors revolved around helping children, and her commercial associations were primarily connected to the fashion industry. She was the CEO of Melania Marks Accessories Member Corporation[10] and had ties to two skincare product lines.[11] The degree of her actual involvement in the businesses is unclear, but she did promote products from companies bearing her name on various television programs throughout the early 2000s. Leading up to the 2016 presidential election, Trump appeared to reshape her outward persona by scaling back her public activities but retaining her commercial connections.

The biographies of neither Clinton nor Trump fully conformed to or contested the traditionalist perspectives embedded in the republican motherhood ideal. Both consorts of the 2016 presidential contenders in turn challenged and endorsed established gender norms. Clinton, as the first male spouse of a presidential nominee, assumed a somewhat supportive and subordinate posture. From 2000 on, he became the less visible spouse who championed humanitarian causes and helped buoy his mate's political ambitions. Prior to that time,

Clinton was the dominant partner whose desires were paramount. His career path dictated the family's residence and his wife's actions. It was only after his aspirations were realized that his wife's goals were brought to the forefront. For the majority of his life, Clinton embodied the masculine attributes that complement those of the historically idealized female patriot, but in his postpresidency he took on more of the purportedly feminine qualities desired in a political spouse.

Trump was enterprising in her youth, pursuing a challenging career in a competitive industry, breaking international laws in order to improve her professional development, and using romantic connections to enhance her public status. Yet after she married, her life seemed to take a very conventional turn. Trump gave up her work as a model and focused on becoming a consummate wife and mother. She also sought opportunities to engage in charitable causes that dealt largely with children and the needy. Trump's business activities were one way her life as a married woman challenged gender expectations, but because her actual involvement in the companies is difficult to determine, the degree to which she broke with tradition in this manner is uncertain.

The lives Clinton and Trump led prior to the 2016 presidential election demonstrate complex relationships with republican motherhood. They both variously embraced and rejected entrenched gender-based standards. Clinton was at certain times dominant and at other times submissive; Trump was clearly ambitious, yet strategically self-effacing. Despite the unique aspects of this set of candidates' mates, their portrayals were oddly familiar.

Representations of Bill Clinton and Melania Trump

Discussions about Clinton and Trump during the 2016 presidential election highlighted the difficulties the press, the parties, and the spouses themselves had overcoming a stereotypical view of men and women as leaders and helpmates. Because of Clinton's standing as the first husband of a nominee, the spousal representations the media, the parties, and the consorts themselves created in 2016 more explicitly addressed the male characteristics that formed the counterbalance to republican motherhood than they previously had. Rather than focusing on depictions of femininity as measures of fitness for spouses, representations of Clinton overtly explored archetypal aspects of American masculinity.

Media Treatments

Unlike in past presidential campaigns, when two potential first ladies could be interpreted, evaluated, and juxtaposed using standard frames established over many decades, the distinctions between Clinton and Trump made direct comparisons challenging for the press and rendered the exclusive use of feminine expectations difficult. Still, media messaging about these two prevalent political actors was often based on entrenched interpretations of gender norms.[12]

During the primaries and general election, reporters described Clinton and Trump in ways that sometimes seemed quite similar but were actually very different. Both were treated alike in that journalists posed questions regarding their potential White House role should their spouse win the presidency. When speculating about their possible duties, reporters' portrayals of the two highlighted common sex-based stereotypes. For Clinton, the press pondered whether he would serve as a formal advisor, sit on particular committees, or maybe be given a cabinet post.[13] The *New York Times* published a series of articles on the topic in a section titled "If Clinton is Elected, What Should She Do with Bill?," and other news outlets frequently explored the same subject.[14] Some writers argued that, as a past president, Clinton was uniquely qualified to participate in governmental activities.[15] Other commentators pointed out the potential conflicts of interest Clinton would face if he officially served in his wife's administration and the legal problems that could arise from his getting too involved in policy development.[16] Many humorists mocked the idea of Clinton hosting teas and remodeling the White House, suggesting that the usual duties of a presidential mate were too feminine for a male consort. Other commentators used the opportunity to protest the limitations placed on past first ladies.[17]

Discussions about Bill's prospective administrative assignments gave reporters an excuse to remind voters of the disapproval Hillary had garnered while leading failed health care reform efforts during her husband's first term in office.[18] These criticisms often highlighted her reputed unwillingness to behave as a true republican mother should—she refused to be deferential, to prioritize the needs of others, and to shun personal ambition (see Chapters 2 and 3 for more on the press treatment of her as a nominee's spouse and as the first lady). For many members of the press, Bill's masculinity and standing as a former president shielded him from complaints made against many past first ladies regarding their tendency to reach beyond the ambiguous boundaries of their position and to unduly influence policy decisions. Instead, he was presented as a true helpmate who could offer his wife the assistance she might need in order to lead effectively. Such treatments of Bill devalued Hillary's independence and questioned her ability to act as an autonomous citizen.

Most of the coverage about Melania Trump's potential White House ventures focused on what kinds of issues she would be involved in if given the first lady pulpit. Occasionally comparing her to Jacqueline Kennedy, most news outlets cast Trump as largely unconcerned with policy issues and more inclined to simply fill the ceremonial responsibilities generally ascribed to a president's wife.[19] Journalists pondered which causes she might champion as first lady and presumed her activities would fall along conventionally feminine lines. Building off of Trump's experience in the fashion industry, and alluding to Obama's and Kennedy's historic influence, several reporters expected Trump to further solidify the first lady's function as a fashion icon. The press depicted Trump as a consort who would avoid participating in policy discussions, would never be accused of interfering with her husband's decision-making, and would focus on her maternal functions over any sort of government involvement. When discussing her potential White House responsibilities, the media portrayed Trump as a wife who would strive to meet the gender expectations established by the republican mother ideal.

Clinton and Trump also received similar but different treatment by the press regarding their presumed impact on the campaign. In both cases, news stories used republican motherhood to simultaneously applaud the potential presidential helpmates and ridicule them, but the trope was applied to each in distinct ways. Clinton was thought by some to be an asset to his wife's presidential efforts because of his past successes garnering votes from a diverse set of constituents.[20] His own presidential campaigns and his previous efforts on behalf of the incumbent president demonstrated his talent in this area. Reporters were quick to argue that Hillary could benefit from his still significant presidential coattails, particularly when it came to blue-collar workers and folks in rural communities—two demographics Bill won in 1992 and 1996 that Hillary had particular difficulty reaching in 2016. In some cases, journalists credited a potential Democratic victory to the former president.

Although Clinton was considered by many to be a decided asset to his wife's campaign, not all pundits and commentators viewed or treated him favorably. In fact, one of the recurring complaints about Clinton was his history of scandals. Many news reports revived accusations originally made about the nominee's spouse decades before the 2016 contest. Tales of his womanizing returned, including references to an extramarital affair he had when he was the governor of Arkansas, a rape allegation for which he was never charged, and the Lewinsky liaison, which led to his impeachment hearings.[21] In most cases, the stories not only reminded audience members of Bill's tendency to misbehave but also critiqued Hillary by blaming her for her husband's misdeeds. She was accused of condoning his maltreatment of women and of failing to satisfy his sexual needs.[22] Hillary was charged with allowing her personal ambition to prevent her from fulfilling her wifely duties; she was described in Rousseauian terms (see Chapter 1) that framed her as a masculine woman who could not (or would not) manage her husband or take charge of the morality of the family.[23] Bill's past sins did not lead to doubts about his manliness but instead raised concerns about Hillary's womanhood.[24] Although the transgressions were occasionally used to contest his suitability to serve as the president's spouse, they were more frequently employed to argue against his wife's fitness for the presidency.

Trump was also both praised and censured for her potential impact on her husband's campaign. In some news reports, she was lauded for her reticence to speak in public and presumed supportiveness for her husband.[25] Stories from some media outlets portrayed her as a welcome return to less politically assertive first ladies. Attempting to cast Trump as a modern Kennedy because of her perceived poise and fashionable outward appearance, some journalists depicted her as a deferential wife who always acquiesced to her husband's desires and who rarely shared an opinion of her own.[26] Reporters played up this perspective by asking few questions of the potential first lady that did not revolve around her home life. Many conservative reporters in particular touted a submissive and usually quiet wife as a refreshing change from the purportedly more outspoken Obama.[27] Because Trump seemed to fit the requirements set by the republican motherhood ideal, she was viewed by many as either an asset to her husband's campaign or a neutral component of it.

Much like Clinton, Trump also had detractors in the press. Several commentators argued that her mostly seen-but-not-heard participation reflected the dismissive treatment of women by the Republican candidate and his party.[28] Some writers doubted Trump's intellectual ability and claimed that her silence resulted from a lack of knowledge about current events. Others speculated that her submissiveness was a result of intimidation by her husband or her fear of displeasing him.[29] In addition, Trump's ability to serve as an appropriate first lady of the United States was debated when nude photos of her circulated on social media and stories about the pictures made it into the mainstream press. Although the photographs had been taken fifteen years earlier (when she was working as a model), the images resurfaced during both the primary and general elections accompanied by arguments that she lacked the morality necessary to be an effective female role model.[30] Because overt expressions of sexuality run counter to most conceptions of a proper republican mother, the photos were used to chastise the would-be first lady for failing to be a demure, family-focused female. Criticisms about Melania were largely directed toward her and were not particularly tied to Donald; he was not blamed for Melania's past the way Hillary was held accountable for Bill's.

As far as press engagements were concerned, Clinton and Trump fulfilled many of the obligations ascribed to spouses during contemporary campaigns. Some activities, such as giving interviews alongside their mates, occurred as usual. The media modified others because of the uniqueness of the participants. For example, as happened with past candidates' wives, Trump was tasked with giving press members a tour of the family home and was asked about the challenges of parenthood. Clinton did not show off his family's residence, nor was he queried about his views on domesticity, childrearing, or housework. Instead, reporters asked Clinton about the various responsibilities the president faced and his opinions regarding the nominees' abilities to fulfill such leadership duties.

One commonplace campaign event that particularly illustrated the gendered nature of the expectations placed on the two spouses was the *Family Circle* recipe contest.

Initially referred to as the "First Lady Bake-Off," the quadrennial comparison of cookie recipes submitted by presidential contenders' partners was called the "Presidential Cookie Competition" in 2016. Both Clinton and Trump participated. Major news outlets, including the *New York Times, CNN,* and the *Washington Post,* reported on the event and noted that Clinton's recipe was the same one his wife provided in 1992 and 1996. Articles identified her as the originator of the recipe and her husband as the beneficiary of her domestic efforts, both as a lifelong consumer of the cookies and by having a previously victorious entry to submit (she won with it twice). Editors identified them as the "Clinton family's chocolate chip cookies."[31] Meanwhile, Trump's offering was attributed directly to her, as all of the recipes from past nominees' wives had been, and was named "Melania Trump's star cookies."[32] Press coverage emphasized Hillary Clinton's and Melania Trump's presumed domesticity but did not address Bill Clinton's competence in the kitchen. In addition, when reporters speculated about whether Melania Trump had ever actually baked anything at all, they invited readers to judge the GOP nominee's wife based on her homemaking skills.[33] The same metric was never applied to Bill Clinton. In spite of the overall name change, the actual competition and stories about it still demonstrated the deeply entrenched nature of republican motherhood ideals. The male Clinton was not chastised for his potential lack of domestic skills, but the female Trump was. The press portrayed Clinton as a fortunate husband and Trump as a feckless homemaker despite a lack of evidence in support of either depiction.

Entertainment media made references to the would-be presidential helpmates that also employed republican motherhood rhetoric. Satirists such as Stephen Colbert joked about Clinton's potential title and used visuals of him in a woman's evening gown to accentuate the oddity of a male presidential consort. Similarly, comedians mocked Trump's silence, her motivations, and her intellectual ability, particularly after she allegedly plagiarized part of her Republican National Convention (RNC) speech (discussed later in this chapter). Moreover, internet memes and gifs mimicked the content of the news and entertainment depictions of both nominees' spouses, sometimes in humorous ways and other times in scathing rebukes. For example, Bill's womanizing was referenced in anti-Hillary memes proclaiming "Hillary Sucks but not like Monica," and cartoon caricatures showed Hillary standing on Bill's shoulders while he smiled with his pants around his ankles. Again, the criticism was less about Clinton than his wife. Trump was lampooned in online messages that alluded to her past, her nude photos, and her supposedly meager intellect. Memes containing the pictures were intended to create uncertainty about her suitability as a potential first lady. Other social media messages likened her anticipated RNC speech to a performance at a strip club. After the speech, many posts mocked her reported plagiarism as a sign of deficient education and lack of integrity. These negative media representations reinforced conventional and conservative notions that framed purportedly good wives as beacons of virtue and guardians of morality.[34]

Overall, social media messaging amplified rather than altered the depictions of the spouses established by the mainstream media, including their reinforcement of republican motherhood perspectives through rhetoric espousing an assessment based on socially entrenched gender norms. As with the mainstream press, social media content held the wives accountable for the moral rectitude of the family (themselves included). Hillary was maligned for Bill's past bad acts, yet no one blamed Donald for Melania's misdeeds. The uneven application of standards fortified the expectations associated with archetypal female patriotism. In 2016, as had been the case in previous campaigns, such narrow approaches to American womanhood were not limited to the various media outlets.

Party Depictions

The parties' strategic use of Bill Clinton and Melania Trump underscored the continued impact of and reliance on republican motherhood rhetoric in presidential campaigns. The goal was to build identification between the party's potential first couple and the American public and sever potential bonds between voters and the opposition. The party representations of the candidates' mates referenced old-fashioned perspectives on gender; this was particularly surprising for the Democrats because they had nominated a woman for the presidency.

The Democrats had a history of mixed representations of modern political wives, blending traditional (e.g., Gore in 2000 and Obama in 2008 and 2012) with progressive (e.g., Clinton in 1992 and Heinz Kerry in 2004) gender-based portrayals. In 2016, they had the opportunity to set new standards and to encourage more gender-neutral treatment of all future political spouses. But when it came to using Clinton, the party's representations essentially strengthened existing sex-role stereotypes by portraying him in purportedly masculine ways. His standing as a past president contributed to these depictions.

Party leaders generally described Clinton not as a sympathetic spouse but as an elder statesman and accomplished politician. Although past candidates' consorts had regularly been called "secret weapons" for their husbands, there was no clandestine element to Clinton's potential impact. His skill winning over members of the electorate that felt particularly disenfranchised made up for one of the candidate's major shortcomings. Therefore, he was deployed to places such as West Virginia to address audiences that often seemed overlooked by his wife. Clinton also participated, as most spouses have, in a variety of fund-raisers on his spouse's behalf. Moreover, his time in the White House led many party members to promote him as the ultimate presidential helpmate because of the insights he could offer. Some Democratic strategists went so far as to characterize Bill as a potential mentor for Hillary should she win the Oval Office. He would, they said, guide and protect his wife as she negotiated new political terrain as a female president.

Not surprisingly, the Republican Party's version of Bill Clinton was far less kind than that of the Democrats. Much like the press did, the GOP frequently used Clinton's past to discredit his wife. Party operatives repeatedly discussed Bill's sex scandals and used them to refute Hillary's claim to champion feminist principles. The eventual Republican nominee described Bill as someone who preyed on women and called Hillary "an unbelievably nasty, mean enabler"[35] who supported her husband's bad behaviors and worked to destroy the lives of female accusers.[36] A conservative political action committee (PAC) originally called Women against Hillary changed its name to Rape PAC to draw attention to past sexual assault allegations against the Democratic nominee's husband. The organization also labeled Hillary a hypocrite for calling herself a feminist while remaining married to the wolfish Bill.[37] Republican consultant Roger Stone frequently referenced the "Clintons' war on women" when discussing either Hillary or Bill Clinton.[38] Casting Bill Clinton as a habitual abuser of women was a major part of the GOP's depiction of the former president and its campaign against his wife.

Republican Party leaders, particularly Donald Trump, also reframed Bill Clinton's presidency as one of dubious value. They argued that Bill and Hillary Clinton discriminated against African Americans and homosexuals, concocted trade agreements that hurt the US economy, and contributed to the decline of the middle class and traditional family structures.[39] They also highlighted "blemishes on the Clintons' collective record" by reminding the public of unpopular events during his presidency.[40] The GOP's denunciations of Clinton painted him as an assertive male and an ambitious politician. They did not debate his patriotism or address his standing as a supportive partner but instead underscored his manliness. Republican depictions of Hillary Clinton in 1992 and 1996 were much more vitriolic and personally focused than their portrayal of Bill Clinton in 2016. In the 1990s, Republican operatives directly attacked the nominee's spouse to discredit and malign Hillary Clinton. In 2016, they did the same thing—condemned the candidate's spouse to censure Hillary Clinton. Both sets of efforts revolved around proving Hillary Clinton was a heterodox female, but the 2016 attempts used her husband as evidence of her purported rejection of conventional femininity.

Like many candidates' mates before him, Clinton became an easy target for the opposition. However, even though GOP members employed republican motherhood rhetoric as they had with other Democratic consorts, its application here was unique. Instead of stressing Clinton's unwillingness to meet established expectations for candidates' mates, as had become their go-to strategy with most opponents' helpmates during previous cycles, party operatives attacked the Democratic candidate by spotlighting her husband's embrace of orthodox masculinity. By emphasizing Bill's ostensibly manly characteristics, Republican strategists created an image of Hillary that made her appear as either a weak and submissive female who could not manage her husband (and by extension the nation) or as an aberrant woman who was more virile and dominating than her powerful spouse.

The Republican Party treated Trump relatively positively after her husband secured the nomination. During the primary contest, her morality was disputed when the nude photos from her past circulated, but once the early battles ended she was either treated respectfully or was ignored by most party members. Unlike Clinton, who was used by his party in many ways, Trump principally appeared as a background prop in photos and at events, with a couple of notable exceptions. First, she delivered an address at the RNC. The oration was touted as the main event of the gathering's opening evening and garnered a great deal of initial attention because it was Trump's first major campaign speech. It later was scrutinized because of its similarity to Obama's 2008 DNC address. Trump's second significant contribution to the campaign came when her husband faced backlash for video footage from a television show called *Access Hollywood* in which he demonstrated extreme disrespect for women. In a series of seemingly heavily scripted interviews Trump publicly responded to the criticisms of her mate. Similar to Hillary's efforts to defend her husband against accusations of sexual misconduct in 1992, Melania aided Donald by discounting the claims, unequivocally stating her support for him, and reframing her husband's words and actions in an attempt to diminish their impact. Republican leaders cast Trump as an understanding and deferential wife who stood by her husband during difficult times.

The Democrats generally avoided denouncing Trump until after her convention speech, when she made herself a target of derision for plagiarizing parts of Obama's address. Although the White House refused to comment, the speech provided evidence for other Democrats to question Trump's education, morality, and ability to stand up for herself.[41] Mirroring claims made by reporters, many party leaders argued Trump was an unwitting pawn in her husband's political games and someone willing to do whatever she was told in order not to upset her husband. Others portrayed Melania as a complicit liar as devious as Donald. Democrats cited the fact she had bragged about writing every word of the speech herself before the scandal broke as proof that she lacked the integrity necessary to be an effective role model should she become first lady of the United States.[42] The Democrats chided Trump both for meeting the standards of republican motherhood (deferring to her husband and buttressing his efforts) and for failing to do so (lacking the morality necessary to be a true female patriot).

In 2016, the two major parties continued to use republican motherhood rhetoric to shape the personas of the presidential nominees' spouses. Democrats depicted Clinton as a capable consort whose credentials made him an ideal presidential helpmate. Had he been a female, the depiction would have been exceptionally progressive. However, because they were extoling the masculine qualities of a male mate, the Democratic messaging reinforced a historically entrenched perspective on gender that was troublesome for their atypical candidate. Bill's orthodox nature raised questions about Hillary that underscored her heterodox qualities and framed her as a misfit even with her own spouse. Republicans applied the trope in a fashion that preferred traditional and restrictive views of womanhood and accentuated male qualities as essential leadership traits. By presenting the seemingly self-effacing Trump as the model female helpmate and strategically spotlighting Clinton's manliness to degrade his wife's perceived power, GOP strategists created portrayals of the candidates' spouses that prioritized historically feminine social and political functions for women. Both parties favored a view of womanhood that encouraged female citizens to embrace a deferential political perspective.

Self-Portrayals

The spouses of the presidential nominees were distinctly different people with dissimilar backgrounds and contrasting skills as public communicators. Clinton, a Yale-educated lifelong politician, was an experienced interviewee, a confident public speaker, and arguably among the best campaigners of his generation. He held rallies and championed his wife's efforts throughout the primaries and general election. Trump, an immigrant with a heavy accent and uncertain formal education, rarely spoke publicly and played a limited part in her husband's presidential bid. She usually stood silently behind her husband at his rallies and during his speeches. Although the two potential presidential helpmates were obviously unique individuals, they were similar in that both were well known and tended to appeal to voters' more traditional views of men and women through their own self-depictions.

By 2016, Clinton had participated in numerous elections both on his own behalf and as a surrogate supporting others. His long and relatively successful political track record underscored his oratorical skill and his ability to create connections with diverse audiences. Bill was a particularly effective storyteller who often shared tales of his time with Hillary. He frequently attempted to form points of identification between the audience, himself, and his wife by emphasizing the ways he and Hillary had lived a purportedly ordinary American life. Nowhere was this more apparent than in his DNC speech.

Although Clinton was a familiar face at DNC gatherings, having addressed every meeting since 1980, in 2016 he found himself in a new and noteworthy position as the first male spouse of a presidential nominee. Wives had been addressing such gatherings regularly since 1992, but because he was the first husband to deliver such a speech, Clinton had a unique opportunity to reshape the spouse's convention address.[43] Instead, he generally stayed true to many of the established norms for a mate's oration. Like most of the women who had given this type of talk before him, Clinton used personal narratives, emphasized his relational connection to the candidate, and highlighted aspects of the nominee's personal life. Each tactic invited identification building between the speaker, the audience, and the would-be president. Even though it followed the guidelines established by past addresses, Clinton's speech was still distinct from the other mates' orations.

Most previous speeches by candidates' spouses placed the speaker in the subordinate position of a dutiful and deferential wife and highlighted the personal qualities of the candidate to illustrate the nominee's compassionate but strong leadership traits. As a former president, Clinton could not convincingly present himself as docile. His well-known credentials and time in the spotlight prevented him from claiming an inferior or subservient status, and his personal narratives necessarily referenced the various powerful positions he had held. In addition, Bill's reliance on republican motherhood rhetoric to describe his relationship with Hillary presented the female presidential candidate in highly orthodox terms. Although Clinton intended to encourage audience members to perceive his wife as a caring woman who shared listeners' concerns and experiences, he ended up casting the presidential frontrunner as a submissive and supportive helpmate and portrayed himself, the potential first gentleman, as the dominant figure in their marital relationship.

Clinton, as expected based on his status as a nominee's spouse, used his speech to help humanize the party's standard-bearer. Like Barbara Bush, Laura Bush, and Michelle Obama, in the speech Bill Clinton shares personal narratives about his life with the candidate in order to accentuate her personality by providing a more intimate glimpse into her character. Clinton's lengthy address is essentially the tale of the couple's life together. He opens with the line, "In the spring of 1971, I met a girl," then proceeds to detail the pair's meeting, courtship, and partnership.[44] The former president talks about their time at Yale Law School, the multiple marriage proposals he had made and Hillary's rejections of them, and their life as a family after the birth of their daughter, Chelsea. These tales emphasize many of the traditional aspects of the Clintons' relationship.

As he discusses their life together, Bill depicts himself in commonly male terms and frames Hillary using republican mother rhetoric. In one anecdote, he doggedly courts her and she demurely rejects his marriage proposals but indicates her continued attraction by introducing him to her family, seeking his advice regarding key career decisions, and visiting him in Arkansas after he had graduated from law school. Bill highlights his own tenacity and charm and foregrounds his decisiveness when he shares a tale in which he buys a house to convince Hillary to marry him. He reminisces about telling her, "You remember that house you like. . . . While you were gone, I bought it, and you have to marry me now."[45] Here he portrays himself as a loving mate and a competent provider.

Clinton continues to present himself and his wife in conventional terms when he overtly talks about her as a mother. He argues, "Through nursing [sic] school, kindergarten, t-ball, soccer, volleyball, and [Chelsea's] passion for ballet . . . sleepovers, summer camps, family vacations . . . Hillary first and foremost was a mother."[46] Clinton also judges his wife's maternal skill when he says, "My daughter had the best mother in the whole world" and "Hillary has done a pretty fine job of being a mother."[47] Clinton not only focuses on his wife's parental skill but also compares his more emotional parenting style with her seemingly task-oriented approach. He talks about taking Chelsea to college and explains, "There I was . . . staring out the window trying not to cry and there was Hillary on her hands and knees, desperately looking for one more drawer to put that liner paper in."[48] This passage references a common experience many parents might relate to and echoes assertions made by Cindy McCain in 2008 and Ann Romney in 2012 that cast mothers as practical, dutiful parents. Clinton's anecdote reinforces the republican mother perspective that makes women responsible for the day-to-day operations of family life. The tale also frames Clinton as a kindhearted father who, like many men, tries to hide his emotions to maintain a purportedly strong outward persona often equated with mainstream masculinity.

Although Clinton frequently tends to underscore the heteronormative aspects of the couple's relationship, he does occasionally attempt to paint his wife in somewhat less conservative terms while retaining his own perceived virile image. He tells listeners about how she took charge of the situation when he lost his first reelection bid for the governorship of Arkansas. She found the family a house, got him a job, and developed a campaign strategy that regained him the office two years later.[49] Here, Clinton breaks with the republican motherhood ideal to showcase his wife's competence and assertiveness. He positively depicts his mate's response to his failure, saying that as a result of her actions, "We had two fabulous years with Chelsea and in 1982, I became the first governor in the history of our state to become elected, defeated, and elected again. My experience is, it's a pretty good thing to follow [Hillary's] advice."[50] This story initially appears progressive; nevertheless, it is important to note that in Clinton's telling of it, his wife's endeavors were entirely geared toward advancing his career and supporting his goals. Her drive to buttress his aspirations renders her an exemplary helpmate and a sympathetic spouse. In this instance and others, Clinton describes the pair as a couple that occasionally challenges but generally embraces standard gender norms.

In another demonstration of his difficulty moving away from old-fashioned depictions of sex roles, Clinton details his wife's professional accomplishments by delineating his impact on her efforts. He explains that "after I became governor, I asked Hillary to chair a local health committee" and that "when I became president with a commitment to reform health care, Hillary was a natural to head the health care task force."[51] In these passages and others, Clinton continually mentions how his powerful positions translated into opportunities for his wife. Thus, he makes himself appear a thoughtful husband with moderately progressive perspectives on women's abilities and presents his wife as the beneficiary of his open-mindedness. Clinton portrays himself along typical masculine lines that necessarily place his wife, the candidate, in a subordinate position. He does advocate for his wife, but the type of supportiveness he offers is dramatically different from that of most past nominees' mates. Rather than assisting his spouse from a subservient position that accentuates *her* leadership abilities, he presents himself as the dominant and experienced partner and portrays her as the wife in need of her husband's aid.

Trump, unlike Clinton, was new to politics and presidential campaigning. Trump's principal duty during the Republican primaries was to serve as a background prop. She participated in a few interviews and delivered just two notable speeches during the entire 2016 election. In her rare conversations with the press, Trump asserted her independence by indicating that it was her choice to play a minimal role in the campaign.[52] She maintained that she wanted to remain out of politics whenever possible and preferred to focus on her responsibilities as a mother. She did become slightly more vocal beginning with her address at the RNC.

Trump's 2016 RNC speech broke with tradition in minor ways but still relied heavily on rhetoric tied to republican motherhood. Defying the established patterns of past conventions, Trump was welcomed on stage by her husband rather than a family member, a friend, or a well-known female party member. It is not unheard of for the wife of a presidential contender to speak as the lead-in to her husband's nomination acceptance speech; for example, Tipper Gore narrated a short biographical film, then introduced Al Gore for his acceptance address at the 2000 DNC (see Chapter 4). However, in 2016 Donald Trump became the first nominee to introduce his spouse for her address. He appeared briefly on the opening night of the gathering to present his wife to the audience. Describing Melania as "my wife, an amazing mother, and incredible woman," Donald offered an interpretation of the potential future first lady that defined her by her relationships to others and tied her political identity to conventional female roles.[53]

Melania Trump's actual address, a fourteen-minute oration filled with lengthy pauses, was significantly shorter than all of the other spouses' speeches discussed in this book.[54] In spite of its brevity, Trump's address still met many of the expectations of such a speech by a nominee's wife. In it, she praises her husband's patriotism ("he loves this country very much"), loyalty ("Donald is intensely loyal to family, friends, employees, country"), and leadership skills ("Donald has a great and deep and unbounding [sic] determination and a never-give-up attitude") while she introduces herself to the nation.[55] Although Trump does not share any personal stories about her husband, a mainstay in most mates' speeches, she does extol his ability to lead the nation and endorse his character. She proclaims that "he is tough when he has to be, but he's also kind and fair and caring" and contends that "he will make a great and lasting difference."[56] Trump confesses to the audience that her husband's "kindness is not always noted, but it is there for all to see. That is one reason I fell in love with him to begin with."[57] By mentioning her love for her husband, she alludes to a common theme in spouses' speeches that was particularly prevalent in the addresses by Obama and Romney in 2012 (see Chapter 7).

Following the examples set by other presidential nominees' wives, Trump tries to build identification with audience members throughout her address by talking about her own experiences, family, and love for the United States. Early in the speech she explains, "I was born in Slovenia, a small, beautiful, and then-communist country in Central Europe" and later mentions how "after living and working in Milan and Paris, I arrived in New York City 20 years ago, and I saw both the joys and hardships of daily life."[58] She also talks about her various family members and their influence on her personal development. She describes her sister as "an incredible woman and a friend" and introduces her parents by saying, "My elegant and hardworking mother, Amalija, introduced me to fashion and beauty. My father, Viktor, instilled in me a passion for business and travel. Their integrity, compassion, and intelligence reflects [sic] to this day on me and for my love of family and America."[59] Here, Trump overtly ties her patriotism to her familial connections for the first time. The would-be first lady makes this connection again when she claims that love for the United States is a commonality she shares with her husband. She does it once more when she argues that her affinity for the nation motivated her to become an American citizen on July 28, 2006, just a few months after the birth of her son. Throughout the speech, Trump attempts to build connections with voters by depicting herself as a woman whose patriotism is a direct result of her activities as an appreciative daughter, supportive wife, and caring mother.

Trump clearly attempts to depict herself in ways that either explicitly or subtly reference the republican mother trope. As mentioned above, she overtly defines herself in terms of her relationships to others; she is Donald's wife, Barron's mother, and Amalija and Viktor's daughter. Trump repeatedly references her efforts to be a good wife and emphasizes the importance of her work in shaping her son's character. She only once briefly mentions her work outside the home, saying, "I traveled the world while working hard in the incredible arena of fashion."[60] None of her other professional or commercial endeavors are discussed. Trump also meets the trope's ideals by rarely expressing her views on political topics. When she does, she is vague and concentrates on issues frequently associated with feminine or home-based concerns. In the speech, she explains that "one of the many causes dear to my heart is helping children and women" and argues that "we must do our best to ensure that every child can live in comfort and security with the best possible education."[61] This is the full extent of her references to potential policy issues.

Prior to the delivery of her address, in an effort to answer questions about the sincerity of its content and her intellectual skill, Trump told journalists she had written the entire speech herself. However, as viewers (laypeople and pundits alike) began comparing its content to that of Obama's 2008 DNC speech, allegations of plagiarism arose. The campaign at first dismissed the accusations, then later identified a ghostwriter who was credited with authoring the speech and subsequently blamed for the similarities in content with Obama's oration. For several days, Trump was dogged by accusations and mocked on mainstream and social media. Her response was largely to remain quiet on the matter. Within a week or two the focus of the campaign shifted, new political scandals drew the media's attention, and the fervor surrounding Trump's speech faded.

Both Clinton and Trump either alluded to or made explicit statements that condoned historically entrenched perspectives on gender norms and that supported long-held assumptions about appropriate political functions for women and men in society. Clinton bolstered the idea of male dominance and cast his groundbreaking spouse as an old-fashioned wife. Trump painted herself in subordinate female terms and disregarded her past as an ambitious career woman. In both cases, the idea of women as primarily concerned with motherhood and wifedom limits interpretations of females as effective political actors.

Conclusion

The continued reliance on republican motherhood rhetoric to interpret presidential candidates' spouses created distinct difficulties for Clinton and Trump. For Clinton, the use of such standards placed him in a male-dominant frame that forced his candidate-wife into a submissive position that called into question her leadership abilities. Discussions about Clinton as a candidate's spouse accentuated his own masculinity and either played up his wife's femininity or portrayed the candidate as an extremely masculine woman. The trope compelled the couple to appear either as a very traditional pair or as a particularly aberrant twosome.

For Trump, her apparent self-abnegation left voters with no dependable means of assessing her fitness for the position of first lady. Even though she routinely appeared alongside (or behind) her husband, she was the least vocal mate of all presidential consorts examined in this book. Trump and the Republican Party tried to cast the would-be first lady as a conventional mother, yet her minimal and overly scripted public interactions left voters wondering about her intellect, morality, sincerity, English-language skills, and even the status of her marriage. Despite efforts to equate her with first ladies such as Kennedy and Laura Bush by illustrating her deferential nature, desire for privacy, and maternal focus, Trump was more frequently compared with Heinz Kerry, another foreigner who acquired substantial wealth and power through marriage. Ironically, Trump's quiescence led many voters to make assumptions about her that contravened the intended image of her as the quintessential republican mother. For both of the 2016 candidates' life partners, social pressure to meet the gender-based expectations placed on political spouses caused problems.

Clinton and Trump were two of the least liked candidates' mates in modern presidential campaigns. Midway through May 2016, Clinton was suffering from unfavorable ratings that rivaled his wife's record-low marks in 1996.[62] Meanwhile, Trump became the first spouse to register higher unfavorable than favorable scores in preconvention polling.[63] In the final surveys run before the election, the net ratings for Trump and Clinton made them, respectively, the least- and third-least-liked mates of presidential candidates between 1988 and 2016.[64] Trump's score was only the second negative rating within this span of time, the first belonging to Heinz Kerry in 2004. Although many factors contributed to such evaluations by poll respondents, the portrayals of these political figures by the press, the parties, and the consorts themselves certainly influenced how they were perceived.

Forcing these multifaceted individuals to fit into a simplistic interpretive frame based on long-standing assumptions about gender roles limited the ways voters viewed Clinton and Trump. Clinton was regarded as a traditional male despite his history of espousing progressive standpoints and his selection of an unorthodox female mate. He could not shed the mantle of the presidency, and efforts to portray him in a more feminine manner (particularly by the entertainment media) were generally farcical. The rhetorical restrictions surrounding Clinton negatively affected his wife and her ability to stand as a strong, independent candidate in her own right. Trump's challenges relative to meeting the standards of conventional female patriotism were different and indicated a slight potential change in social attitudes toward women. As an often-seen-but-rarely-heard wife, Trump should have been revered based on the most core assumptions of republican motherhood.[65] Her unwavering support for her husband, her apparent passiveness, and her purported dedication to her child should have made her the model political wife. However, she was scorned for her supposedly total submissiveness and chastised for being too docile. Critiques of Trump as too obliging indicate that, perhaps, Americans now actually desire a first lady who meets most established standards but who is also willing to assert her own individuality.

The treatment of Clinton and Trump illustrates how reliance on republican motherhood rhetoric continues to dominate discussions of presidential nominees' spouses. In the following pages, the conclusion of this book discusses the broader implications of the relatively consistent depictions of presidential candidates' spouses by the press, the parties, and the nominees' consorts. It explains how using the deeply entrenched republican motherhood trope constrains perspectives regarding female citizenship and impedes women's progress as fully autonomous political actors.

Conclusion

Reifying Republican Motherhood

In 1776, Abigail Adams wrote a letter to her husband, John Adams, imploring him and other leaders to "Remember the Ladies" when devising the statutes that would guide the development of the new nation.[1] Asking that the founders "not put such unlimited power into the hands of the husbands," she warned that women would protest if not properly considered.[2] After calling Abigail "saucy," John dismissed his wife's concerns by expressing surprise at the potential discontent of females, assuring her that "we know better than to repeal our masculine system" and equating women with other largely ignored subgroups of residents who sought increased privileges in the newly formed democratic republic.[3] In the end, women were left out of the eventually ratified US Constitution. No overwhelming rebellion was fomented as Abigail Adams forewarned, and more than two hundred years later women still endeavor to be perceived as empowered, autonomous citizens. In addition, the wives of prominent politicians continue to struggle against the idea that they are simply vassal-extensions of their husbands.

Many of the contemporary difficulties women face as political actors are grounded in deeply entrenched perspectives that interpret women in exceptionally narrow terms. As explained in detail in Chapter 1, the rhetoric of republican motherhood describes the ostensibly ideal female patriot as domestically focused, self-sacrificial, deferential, and defined by her relationship to others. The trope depicts females as motivated by the needs of others, lacking personal ambition, and having a confined set of interests and abilities. Moreover, it makes women's domesticity their primary means of political contribution and limits women's participation in public deliberations to discussions of issues that fit within a customarily feminine realm. Even though such a restrictive outlook seems antiquated in an era in which women make up a significant portion of the workforce, hold an increasing percentage of advanced educational degrees, and are gaining prominence in many career fields previously closed to them, a careful examination of the standards by which spouses of presidential contenders are judged indicates that heteronormative perspectives still dominate many interpretations of women.

Because presidential helpmates have long been considered "a symbol of American womanhood," the expectations set for individuals who might attain this position speak volumes about how the press, the major political parties, and the people of the United States regard women and their supposedly proper place in society.[4] As several chapters in this book demonstrate, despite the various strides women have made toward establishing equality, assumptions about females that are based on traditional gender norms impede further progress by confining women's perceived political competencies and value. When candidates' wives, often the most visible women in a presidential campaign, are most passionately commended for their unyielding support of their husbands and their dutifulness to their children, are asked to downplay their own professional accomplishments to offer voters a more palatable feminine persona, or are publicly chastised for showing even the slightest personal ambition, a clear message is sent to all American women that prioritizes female acquiescence and self-abnegation over their individual aptitudes or interests. Such treatment denudes women of their power and suggests that independently successful females are an undesirable aberration.

The content of this book illustrates the enduring nature of the republican motherhood ideal and highlights some of the implications of the continued use of rhetoric related to this conceptualization of politically prominent women. The following pages explore the impact historically entrenched interpretations of female patriotism have on the spouses of presidential nominees and on perceptions of American women as political actors. This extended consideration of the reification of conventional gender norms through the application of republican motherhood rhetoric includes specific insights about the rhetorical strategy and the barriers it erects for modern women while also putting forth suggestions for mitigating the republican motherhood ideal's negative impact.

Republican Motherhood: A Paradoxical Rhetorical Tool

With all of the progress women have made increasing their access to social and professional realms once denied them, it might seem odd that the views of womanhood proffered by republican motherhood rhetoric at the time of the nation's founding remain a prominent part of contemporary political dialogue and are a still dominant tool for discussing presidential candidates' mates. However, there are several reasons the conceit endures and is widely employed by the various political entities associated with presidential campaigns. Because it is familiar and built on long-held assumptions about sex roles, republican motherhood is an easy reference point for journalists, political operatives, and the spouses trying to engage potential voters. Its historical roots give it a sense of legitimacy, particularly due to the fact that many of its presumptions are based on biblical interpretations of the sexes (see Chapter 1 for more about the origins of republican motherhood rhetoric). Also, it is such a well-developed, yet malleable, concept that message makers can easily manipulate it to construct positive or negative personas for themselves and others. These elements make republican motherhood an undeniably useful trope, but to understand its impact in an era when women are more independent and autonomous than ever, it is important to look more closely at its assumed benefits and actual drawbacks.

Respect for Caregiving

Since its inception, republican motherhood rhetoric has provided a means for acknowledging the customarily feminine work of caregiving. By talking about women in a traditional, domestic-centered fashion, such dialogue spotlights the contributions of individuals who historically received little attention and gives some political recognition to the people who engage in care work. Rather than belittling or ignoring the difficult duties homemakers perform, this perspective frames home-based activities as a means of political influence and creates a space for respectful public contemplation of the importance of private-sphere activities. When it comes to the treatment of presidential nominees' spouses during campaigns, reverence for caregiving activities takes on amplified importance.

Across the seven election cycles' worth of representations and assessments of candidates' spouses studied here, caregiving is a consistent part of most dialogue about women. Interest in and aptitude for domesticity are major criteria by which the wives of candidates are judged (the lone husband of a candidate was held to markedly different standards—see Chapter 8). In addition, all candidates' spouses are evaluated based on their perceived respect for women who fulfill orthodox feminine functions. As the candidates' wives ostensibly compete to become a national female role model, any hint of disrespect for homemaking becomes fodder for attack. When Hillary Clinton defended her professional career by supposedly insulting housewives, she quickly apologized and spent several weeks baking cookies to confirm her embrace of old-fashioned femininity. Teresa Heinz Kerry was pilloried in the press for suggesting that Laura Bush, a stay-at-home mother, did not understand American women because she had not really worked as an adult. A Democratic commentator's claim that Ann Romney, as a wealthy stay-at-home mother, was too sheltered to serve as her husband's advisor on women's issues drew condemnation from Democrats and Republicans alike. It seems that during a presidential election, any perceived slight toward caregivers is accompanied by a swift and vocal defense of conventionally feminine duties and those who perform them. This responsiveness appears to imply a deep respect for the tasks associated with homemaking and admiration for those (usually women) who act as caregivers.

Although the nation's professed esteem for those who carry out domestic services often assigned to women is reaffirmed during presidential campaigns, this bit of attention does nothing to actually improve the political reach of this group. Instead, the application of republican motherhood rhetoric reinforces stereotypical perspectives regarding who should be responsible for maintaining the home and supports a narrow interpretation of women's interests and aptitudes. It also defines caregiving in an insufficient manner, generally excluding hired care workers and the growing number of male homemakers. The approbation given caregivers during campaigns has some positive aspects, but the hollow praise carries on the original intent of republican motherhood rhetoric by respectfully acknowledging this subset of citizens without actually providing any substantive political empowerment.

The quadrennial defense of home-based female activities creates an atmosphere in which women are coaxed into viewing one another as rivals based on supposedly competing categories such as stay-at-home mothers, working moms, single moms, career women, childless women, and so forth. This division of women encourages perceived infighting among females and offers opportunities for journalists and campaign strategists to fabricate social discord. Political pundits reframe comments, many times abbreviating them or taking them out of context, to manufacture controversies. Clinton's baking cookies comment in 1992 is a prime example. In the full text of her remarks, she defends women's right to choose to work in or out of the home, but the shortened sound bite and descriptions by politicos and the press portrayed her as fervently antihomemaker—a depiction that dogged her throughout her career in public service. This type of political maneuvering is harmful because it fosters ill will among women, minimizes the diversity of women's aptitudes, and distracts females from battling to overcome the shared inequities they all endure.

Furthermore, the quick defense of female caregivers has a chilling effect on dialogue about women and their rights and responsibilities as citizens. When people critique the treatment of women, they must discuss the long-established female caregiver role. However, because the home-focused duties of mothers and wives have long been undervalued and denigrated, it is not uncommon for people to misread assessments of the impact of such depictions as a disparagement of care work or care workers. Academics are often as quick to defend motherhood as political figures are, even when the concept is not actually under attack. This means people attempting to understand the long-term effects that the continued application of established gender-based standards have on society must tread lightly in their analyses or run the risk of condemnation for purportedly disrespecting homemakers. Suppressing conversations about the consequences that follow from the political depictions of caregiving and caregivers, particularly of women and motherhood, leads to slower progress identifying the ways such representations of females contribute to continued political inequality.

Accessing the Political Realm

A second aspect of republican motherhood rhetoric that makes it a pervasive tool is that it provides the grounds for allowing women entry into the political sphere. As explained in Chapter 1, the trope was a central part of women's arguments advocating for educating females and justifying women's public activity during the nineteenth and twentieth centuries. Those using the conceit contended that, to fulfill their obligations as proper female patriots, women needed to be able to develop their intellectual skills and be permitted to publicly discuss political issues that affect the home and family. Even though contemporary applications of the republican mother ideal have moved beyond such basic requests, remnants of those pleas are evident in rhetoric by presidential nominees' spouses.

For many of the spouses studied in this book, republican motherhood rhetoric was not a specifically selected strategy but a means of summarizing their own experiences and points of view. The biographies of Barbara Bush, Laura Bush, Tipper Gore, and Ann Romney, for example, indicate that the concept accurately described their home-focused approach to womanhood and was a natural choice for framing their personas. For other spouses, the rhetorical strategy offered cues for adapting a progressive persona to make it appear more conventional. Clinton tried to transform her image by highlighting her more feminine qualities late in 1992. Both she and Elizabeth Dole used similar strategies to downplay their more modern enactments of womanhood throughout the 1996 election.

Perhaps the most conspicuous example of the prudent employment of republican motherhood rhetoric was by Michelle Obama. After a few missteps with the press, Obama modified her persona to accentuate more socially accepted elements of her femininity starting in 2008 and continuing throughout her time as first lady. A popular working mom turned "mom in chief," Obama exerted the power of the first lady pulpit to advocate for women's right to make their own health care decisions, to serve in the military (and other nontraditional careers), and to demand equal pay for equal work. Her presumed personal embrace of orthodox gender norms allowed her to overcome perceived differences with some voters (see Chapters 6 and 7 for more on Obama's challenges regarding race) and to subtly promote a more expansive approach to understanding women. Obama's use of republican motherhood rhetoric demonstrates its potential usefulness for clever communicators.

The fact that old-fashioned interpretations of female patriotism provide effective tactics for women in the public sphere to create personas that are widely acceptable indicates just how deeply entrenched these restrictive perspectives on gender roles are. When a successful black woman's best opportunity to overcome the race-based challenges she faces appealing to wide swaths of the American public is to amplify her adherence to antiquated and conservative interpretations of womanhood, the complex nature of women's standing in society is revealed.

On the one hand, women's duties as mothers and wives make these experiences a common reference point influential enough to overcome, to a degree, certain racial differences. On the other hand, reinforcing gender stereotypes by claiming relational connections and domestic interests as the basis of political credibility limits the types of topics on which women appear to have expertise. Even though republican motherhood rhetoric gives females a strategy for gaining a sympathetic public ear, its prevalence prevents women from being viewed as fully autonomous individuals capable of contributing to the polis in multiple ways.

Increasing Attention for Feminine Issues

Another potential benefit of republican motherhood rhetoric that might explain its continued use is that it helps draw attention to political affairs commonly regarded as feminine political topics. Such subjects include those considered compassionate in nature and supposedly most directly affect women and children. Education, the environment, and physical and mental health care are commonly considered feminine affairs, whereas the economy, taxes, and national security are usually deemed masculine.[5] These categories illustrate an odd distinction because they are historically linked to what were once common divisions of labor rather than being based on their actual impact on a specific group of citizens. This differentiation is consequential because, with a few notable exceptions such as the ongoing health-care debate, political topics dubbed "feminine" usually garner less attention than those considered "masculine."

Treating presidential nominees' spouses as traditional female patriots often translates into assuming their political interests fall within the boundaries of the feminine realm. This means members of the press, when they actually interview potential first ladies about political issues, usually ask about women's health, education, and other seemingly family-oriented concerns. For their part, the wives of nominees tend to focus their comments in a similarly confined manner.[6] Barbara Bush, Laura Bush, and Cindy McCain championed literacy and early education; Clinton, Dole, Obama, and Romney talked about different aspects of health care; and Gore advocated for advancing mental health initiatives. It is important to note that Bill Clinton, the only male spouse of a presidential candidate, spoke about the economy, job creation, the deficit, health care, national security, and a host of other topics. His standing as a past president and as a male citizen broadened the range of subjects he was asked about and that he had perceived credibility to speak on.

The benefit of so many prominent female political figures discussing frequently undervalued matters is that it legitimizes such interests. When women exploit the strength of the first lady pulpit, either as the sitting first lady or as a contender for the position, they give weight to conversations other speakers cannot. These women actually enhance political dialogue by ensuring that the press, the pundits, and the public think, at least occasionally, about topics often dismissed as personal in nature. They can do this because they have the attention of the media and, as women, they are presumed experts in domestic fields. In some cases, the wives of presidential contenders have even managed to redefine issues by demonstrating how they impact the home and family. Laura Bush made national security and military preparedness a family matter when she talked about mothers worrying about the safety of their children at home and abroad. Obama expanded this idea by becoming a proponent of military families. Romney reframed the economy as a familial concern by talking about the working mothers who want to stay home but cannot afford to do so. These women and others enlarged the realm of acceptable points of deliberation for females and drew attention to feminine features of supposedly masculine subjects. However, there appear to be limits to how far these women can stretch such boundaries.

When the wives of presidential nominees speak about subjects such as the economy, the military, and taxes, unless they couch their conversations in terms of the impact these issues have on the home, either their comments rarely receive attention or the women are censured for reaching beyond the presumed boundaries of feminine expertise. Dole, a former secretary of labor, past secretary of transportation, and previous commissioner of the Federal Trade Commission, was criticized early in her husband's presidential bid when she spoke about the purportedly masculine concerns affiliated with those professional positions. She quickly changed tactics by emphasizing her work at the American Red Cross, giving speeches focused on Bob Dole's personality and character, and denying any interest in influencing policy should she become the first lady. She downplayed her extensive history as a government operative and spotlighted her more acceptably feminine interests. Chastising women who speak about supposedly masculine concerns even though they are verified experts in those areas reinforces problematic perspectives that make it easy to degrade females' credibility and deny them standing as full citizens.

These women's tendency to primarily promote so-called feminine issues supports a limited interpretation of what female citizens' main interests can and should be. Although some political spouses use the tenets of republican motherhood to cleverly shape messages in a manner that allows the speakers to increase the perceived range of socially acceptable points for women to address, continually presenting their own interests in a circumscribed fashion pigeonholes women into gender-restrictive positions and bolsters the idea that females lack the ability and initiative to understand the world outside of their relational connections. Still, because women who do try to break with tradition and directly address reputedly masculine topics are often disregarded and criticized, the savvy employment of republican motherhood rhetoric does at least allow for some widening of women's political reach.

Acknowledging New Political Perspectives

One of the most important positive aspects of republican motherhood rhetoric is that it actually helps legitimize alternative approaches to understanding and participating in politics. By acknowledging different means of contributing to the polis, it opens the opportunity for new perspectives to gain a footing in governance and gives people once considered unconventional political participants a voice. To be clear, the trope is still an oppressive perspective on womanhood that pressures contemporary women to meet unfair and archaic standards of femininity, but by defining maternal and wifely perspectives as recognized political points of view, the rhetoric of republican motherhood does make the case that there is more than one way to access the public sphere.

The spouses of presidential nominees examined in the different chapters of this book frequently, if sometimes unintentionally, advance the idea that a so-called masculine perspective is not the only acceptable approach to politics and leadership. They do this in various ways. As campaign surrogates tasked with humanizing their spouses, the candidates' mates tell stories that demonstrate the compassionate side of their life partners' character. This is even true of Bill Clinton's comments regarding his wife. By accentuating the ostensibly softer side of the would-be leader of the free world, these political spouses imply that cold rationalism and machismo are not the only important traits for a potential president. Furthermore, when the helpmates of presidential contenders remind voters of the multiple ways previously disenfranchised groups overcame barriers, they underscore the nation's heterogeneity and provide hope for groups still struggling to be regarded as politically worthy.

Mirroring the expansion of perceptions proffered by the republican motherhood ideal, some of the messaging by nominees' spouses contained efforts to redefine politics, citizenship, and civic participation. This is particularly evident in the spouses' convention addresses. Barbara Bush reframed the notion of family values and redefined American families to include heterodox arrangements. Her claims implied that some single mothers should be considered proper female patriots. Laura Bush praised female business owners as key contributors to the nation and talked about men who function as caregivers while women serve in the military. Heinz Kerry argued that sex should not be a barrier to political participation and praised caregivers of all genders for their patriotic work. McCain made the case for philanthropic endeavors as a means of serving the nation. Obama explicitly reconceptualized political subjects as personal issues, contending that a good leader should understand the multiple impacts of the decisions he or she makes.

Although republican motherhood rhetoric allows for a reconsideration of what politics should mean, what is and is not political participation, and who should be considered citizens, the conceit actually makes female access to genuine political power more difficult. Because it defines women as necessarily contingent, second-class citizens, the perspective continues to impede women's efforts toward true equality. Still, republican motherhood as an ideal and a rhetorical construct remains pervasive. It is the primary means of discussing and evaluating many female political actors, and it is particularly present in dialogue about and from spouses of presidential contenders. The outcomes from employing this trope appear paradoxical; each advantage is accompanied by an arguably larger disadvantage. The frame offers strategies for women in prominent positions to use when trying to earn widespread support, but the cost of employing such rhetoric is muting the diversity and complexity of women's lived experiences. Therefore, any use of republican motherhood rhetoric necessarily promotes an interpretation of womanhood that is overly constraining and denies women their full sovereignty.

Restrictive Rhetoric and Enduring Barriers

One of the most problematic features of the republican motherhood perspective is that it reinforces the belief that women are a homogeneous group. By conceiving of women as willing and amenable servants of men and assuming that females prefer the purported safety and comfort of a life that is domestically oriented, the outdated viewpoint presents all women as similarly motivated no matter their actual differences. The portrayals of the presidential nominees' spouses illustrate how the use of republican motherhood rhetoric to discuss this group of individuals results in the diminution of their distinctiveness and attempts to classify them in a simplistic and reductive manner.

This book examines seven election cycles and eleven different individuals with various backgrounds, interests, and abilities. The specific pairings involve a grandmotherly first lady and a progressive career woman (1992); two professionally successful women (1996); two stay-at-home mothers (2000); a traditional wife and a powerful, wealthy woman (2004); an affluent white mother and an accomplished black woman (2008); the first African American first lady and a conservative, well-to-do mother of five (2012); and a former president and an immigrant fashion model (2016). The people studied include two women without college diplomas, several people with advanced degrees, four Ivy League–educated attorneys, and a Rhodes scholar. They are white, black, Protestant, Catholic, Mormon, native-born Americans, and immigrants. These people have worked as stay-at-home mothers, librarians, teachers, lawyers, philanthropists, models, governmental agents, and the president of the United States. They do not fit in a single box. Even though their skills and experiences might include being a wife or being a mother, they should not be defined and delimited exclusively by these roles.

Despite the diverse elements that can be explored regarding the spouses of presidential nominees, the public—spurred by the press, the parties, and the spouses themselves—seems preoccupied with evaluating candidates' mates based on their ability to meet outdated standards of femininity (and, in 2016, masculinity). The tendency to interpret candidates' consorts based on their perceived ability and willingness to behave in a gender-normative fashion creates understandings of womanhood that perpetuate the idea that women are, or should be, contingent citizens whose rightful focus is on the needs of others rather than being independent political actors who advocate on their own behalf.

The heavy reliance on republican motherhood rhetoric to describe the would-be presidential helpmates frequently relegates women to two facile categories: good and bad women. The so-called good women are those who meet the ideals of the old-school female patriot by emphasizing their domestic focus, deferential nature, and proclivity for self-sacrifice. The purportedly bad women are those who assert their own power, debate matters that extend beyond the feminine realm, and show signs of personal ambition. These seemingly uncomplicated, oppositional classifications produce difficulties for the spouses of presidential nominees and other females by fortifying interpretive frames that do not accurately reflect the lives of most modern American women.

Narrowly Defining Good Women

According to modern interpretations of American womanhood presented through the rhetoric of republican motherhood and depictions of presidential candidates' spouses, there are three sets of duties a female citizen must perform to be considered a good woman. First, to be an ideal woman, a female must possess an interest in and particular aptitude for domesticity. The spouses of presidential contenders underscore their ability to run a household by discussing personal aspects of their family life in interviews and campaign ads, by giving tours of their family homes, and by sharing humorous anecdotes about developing their housekeeping expertise.

The *Family Circle* cookie recipe contest is one way contemporary media continue to spotlight the conventional femininity of nominees' mates. The event brings homemaking skills to the forefront of conversations about the spouses and makes the candidates' mates overt rivals to be judged based on their domestic talents. The original 1992 event was a direct result of a perceived slight against housewives that inspired the sponsors to ask would-be first ladies to demonstrate their femininity by sharing a cookie recipe they prepared for their families. Every matchup that followed highlighted the homemaking skills, or lack thereof, of presidential candidates' wives and promoted old-fashioned views of women's duties. Even the 2016 competition reinforced stereotypical gender roles. By framing the male submission as a family recipe (i.e., the Clinton family's chocolate chip cookies) rather than linking it to the individual spouse as all of the female offerings did (e.g., Gore's ginger snaps, Dole's pecan rolls, Trump's star cookies, etc.), the contest favored a view of women as bakers and men as beneficiaries of their wives' domestic skill.[7] What is more, the most damning critiques of the female spouses involved accusations that they themselves did not bake, a charge leveled against Margot Perot and Melania Trump, or that they copied their recipe from another source, as McCain and Trump were said to have done. Clinton was exempt from such evaluations and criticisms because he was not expected to enact the characteristics of a good woman.

The second set of responsibilities associated with being a good woman are those connected to motherhood. The republican mother ideal and its rhetoric promulgate the idea that women's political empowerment is derived from their ability to create new generations of patriots. This essential component of the trope is grounded in the Spartan mother ideal, but its American conceptualization contains modifications to the meaning of motherhood. As indicated by the portrayals of presidential spouses and other campaign-related discourse about women, mothers are good women not by virtue of their maternity but because they are self-sacrificing and other-centric. Thus, not all mothers are good women, and some nonchildbearing females can still be considered exemplary if they display specific maternal attributes.

The various mom-based female caricatures of the past few decades help illustrate the actual characteristics of motherhood reviled and revered by republican motherhood rhetoric. Welfare queens are identified as mothers but are not considered good women because they are assumed to be lazy, indifferent to the needs of others, and selfish (see Chapter 1). The vilification of the welfare queen relies on the presumption that such women have children not out of duty to the nation or their (assumed to be nonexistent) husbands but for their own financial benefit. In political discussions, these mothers are bad women. All positive representations of motherhood—the soccer mom, the security mom, and the hockey mom—depict matriarchs whose primary concern is their families even though they often juggle other necessary distractions of modern life. These positive figures might work outside the home, usually to help provide a better life for their families, but their children and husbands take priority over their own professional development. Such women are presented as protective parents willing to advocate on behalf of their children and husbands but not for themselves. Therefore, the commended traits of a good mother have little to do with childbearing and everything to do with a woman's willingness to place her needs as secondary or tertiary to the wants of others.

The fact that actual maternity is less important than enacting particular qualities identified with motherliness when it comes to republican motherhood ideals allows for some flexibility in the application of the concept. Women such as Barbara Bush, Tipper Gore, and Ann Romney were easily framed as ideal women not only because of their multiple children but also due to the fact that each gave up potential careers, moved away from home, and took over the day-to-day practical elements of caring for their brood to allow their husbands to build successful careers. McCain's status as a nurturer was exemplified by her assumption of a parental role with her offspring and her stepchildren, her drive to expand her family through adoption, and her decision to move to Arizona to better care for her children. Conversely, Clinton's maternal credentials were continually questioned because she did not appear to be self-sacrificial, did not quit her professional activities after the birth of her daughter, and rarely talked about her experiences as a mother during the early parts of the 1992 campaign. Even though the republican motherhood ideal touts maternity as the primary means of female participation in politics, rhetoric related to the concept actually applauds females who enact a specific set of characteristics often associated with motherhood regardless of their actual maternal status. This more malleable approach to womanhood allowed Republicans to promote Dole as a good woman in spite of the fact that she never had children of her own.

The third component of a good woman is her willingness and ability to serve as a good wife. Although its name indicates the primacy of the maternal activity outlined above, in practice, republican motherhood foregrounds the performance of traditional wifely functions. Archetypal female patriotism maintains that a good wife is supportive, deferential, and dutiful. She does not dispute her husband in public, she prefers the private realm unless her public activity is necessary to help her husband and family, and she restricts her public comments to statements about home- and family-based concerns. These characteristics are not actually sex-based traits but socially prescribed modes of behavior linked to established gender norms. The expectation that women embrace these features when fulfilling their marital functions is what makes them wifely rather than spousal traits (good husbands face different standards). This perception often includes the other two elements of being a good woman because being an exemplary wife generally means exhibiting aptitude as a homemaker and embracing positive maternal attributes.

For spouses of presidential nominees, being a good mate appears to be of paramount importance because such behaviors seem to gain approval from voters. Many of the most publicly esteemed mates based on national polls are those who have embodied the wifely role prescribed by republican motherhood ideals. Barbara Bush, Laura Bush, and Tipper Gore had the highest net favorability ratings of all presidential nominees' spouses between 1988 and 2016.[8] They were also among the most old-fashioned-seeming mates of the batch. All three gave up any potential professional career upon marrying their spouses, provided assistance as needed during political campaigns, emphasized their preference for privacy over public participation while advocating for their husbands, and addressed so-called feminine issues such as education, literacy, and mental health. The three avoided openly contradicting their husbands and presented themselves as amiable individuals.

On the other end of the favorability scale, Hillary Clinton, Bill Clinton, Teresa Heinz Kerry, and Melania Trump had the lowest scores.[9] Although some efforts were made to present Trump as an ideal wife, her biography and minimal participation in the campaign left doubts about her sincerity and the accuracy of the depiction. Trump's public silence throughout most of the presidential contest made her appear not as a supportive or dutiful wife but as an aloof woman who served as an easily manipulated prop. The other three low-scoring individuals were among the least orthodox of the modern candidates' spouses: Hillary Clinton was openly assertive and extremely politically active, Bill Clinton embraced his masculine standing as a past president, and Teresa Heinz Kerry refused to mollify voters by softening her brash public persona. The fact that Heinz Kerry and Trump were both immigrants who became citizens and acquired great wealth through marriage made them unique among nominees' mates and could have contributed to their low poll numbers. Furthermore, all four of these spouses were embroiled in controversies during their mates' presidential runs.

Based on contemporary applications of the republican mother ideal, the essence of a good woman is inextricably entwined with her willingness to be an effective wife, a self-sacrificing mother, and a skilled homemaker. The link to domesticity is clear, but the proffered attributes extend beyond the practical duties customarily assigned to female members of society and imply attitudes and behaviors that diminish women's ability to advocate for themselves and seek personal or professional fulfillment outside of the home.

Demonizing Unconventional Women

The bad woman is the antithesis of the good woman as typified by the good wife and mother portrayal. Although some depictions assume that bad women are simply ineffectual homemakers, uncaring mothers, and disruptive wives, the denigration of women based on republican motherhood ideals is not limited to such narrow critiques and speaks volumes about contemporary interpretations of American womanhood. In addition to being chastised for lacking interest in or aptitude for duties traditionally assigned to females, spouses of presidential nominees are often reprimanded for appearing to cross socially constructed gender-based boundaries. Wives are harangued when they either appear or act too masculine. This type of charge has been raised against spouses in presidential elections for almost as long as there have been campaigns. Andrew Jackson's wife, Rachel, was castigated for engaging in male pursuits such as riding horses with a western saddle and smoking a pipe. As explained in the introduction of this book, she was considered too rugged (a code word for "masculine") to be able to truly represent American womanhood.

Confidence and fortitude, in appearance and attitude, are welcomed traits in males but become points of critique in females. Of the contemporary candidates' spouses, Hillary Clinton was most fervently accused of embodying too many attributes usually ascribed to males. She wore pantsuits, was too ambitious, asserted her opinion too aggressively, and engaged too eagerly in policy debates. Both the press and the Republican Party vehemently attacked her for these qualities and amplified her perceived violation of gender norms. But Clinton was not the only modern spouse to be admonished for displaying customarily male characteristics. Michelle Obama was rumored to once have been a man and was accused of not appearing ladylike enough because of her stature. Male actors were cast in parodies of Barbara Bush to emphasize her seemingly androgynous body and deep voice, and Teresa Heinz Kerry was mocked for being blunt and authoritative in a way some reporters and voters perceived as threatening.

Furthermore, personal independence and an enterprising spirit are two ideals usually positively connected with US citizenship and frequently equated with the ability to achieve the American dream. However, in wives of presidential nominees these attributes somehow become grounds for censure. Women with impressive personal stories of overcoming challenges and developing successful professional careers are asked to downplay their accomplishments, avoid discussing their achievements, and reframe their life's work in terms of their relational connection to others. Clinton, Dole, Heinz Kerry, and Trump are women who worked hard, took risks, and showed resourcefulness in order to become successful in their various endeavors, but when it came time to campaign by their husbands' sides, they were assessed primarily in terms of their ability, or inability, to meet established measures of femininity and were variously reprimanded for their independent success.

Obama is the most overt example of a woman asked to devalue her own achievements to meet the standards of femininity tied to the republican motherhood ideal. Obama's lower-middle-class upbringing and her race made her attainment of two Ivy League degrees extremely impressive, and her life story was a manifestation of the American dream (a claim usually made about her husband but rarely individually associated with her). Like Clinton and Dole, Obama was an established career woman who often earned more money than her husband. Yet, rather than becoming a beacon of female achievement, Obama deemphasized her work life and presented herself as the nation's mom in chief to avoid the condemnatory frames placed on other successful women. Obama's public persona and its relational focus seemed to contend that winning a husband and having children was the proper and sufficient female enactment of the American dream.

The fact that females who demonstrate some of the same characteristics and motivations praised in males are openly chastised throughout presidential campaigns (and beyond) both illustrates and legitimizes deeply embedded conventional gender norms. Such treatment promotes the idea that there should be clear delineations between the sexes when it comes to political participation despite the distinctions in question being entirely socially constructed. Ambition and resourcefulness are not biologically contingent traits; they are simply interpreted in that manner. Framing successful wives of presidential spouses as quiescent helpmates whose spousal and maternal links are their greatest accomplishments offers inadequate role modeling for American women as a whole. This type of perspective, fortified by republican motherhood rhetoric, encourages women to assume submissive, deferential positions in the home, in society, and in politics.

Reinforcing Contingent (and Subordinate) Female Citizenship

The interpretations of good and bad women posited by the ideals of republican motherhood and reified by the treatment of presidential nominees' spouses are problematic because they help justify perceiving women as second-class citizens in a number of ways. First and foremost, they degrade women's standing as individuals. By limiting women's esteemed aptitudes to skills related to the home, discounting any other talents they might have, and devaluing professional success by females, the traditional approach proffered by republican motherhood asserts that women are unable to function beyond the private sphere and are unwelcome in the public arena. Furthermore, the devaluation of female successes outside the home strips many women of a lifetime of accomplishment and makes them appear ineffectual. Dole, a historic figure with a well-established, independent political career, downplayed her achievements so effectively that many people claimed her own presidential run was built on her popularity as her husband's dutiful wife rather than her extensive experience as a highly effective political functionary.[10] Ignoring the public contributions made by prominent women in a presidential campaign because of their marital connection prompts other women to be reticent about touting their own talents.

Oversimplified depictions of women bolster the idea that they are contingent citizens by amplifying the tendency to understand females only in terms of their relationships to others. For women, such association-based definitional terms make being a mother or wife an essential component of their identity. Being a husband and father is considered something men do; being a wife and mother is treated as something women are. This means men are allowed to be bad husbands and fathers and still retain their status as good Americans. John McCain, Bill Clinton, and Donald Trump allegedly cheated on their wives but were still considered by many to be good men and admirable patriots. Mitt Romney traveled a lot and rarely saw his sons, but he was still called a good man by his wife and others. Women do not have the same freedom; based on the entrenched ideals of republican motherhood, a bad wife or mother is by definition a bad

American. Clinton and Trump stood dutifully by their husbands during public scandals but were deemed bad, unpatriotic women because they did not effectively meet expected standards of femininity in other ways. Heinz Kerry was never accused of infidelity and cared deeply for her children and stepchildren but had her integrity debated because she was forthright, wielded a great amount of power, and refused to be deferential. Tying women's worth to their ability to fulfill familial duties urges them to curtail their own ambitions and divests them of their power as independent beings. It also sets different criteria for men's and women's civic worth.

Nominees' spouses with educational and professional credentials that rival, or even exceed, their husbands' bona fides are often seen talking about a limited set of issues and doing so in a specifically home-oriented manner. Such restricted discussions adversely influence the way the public perceives female political actors and invites future spouses of candidates to engage in similar self-censoring to avoid garnering negative attention. Across the seven election cycles covered in this book, there is ample evidence of spouses learning from others' treatment and abdicating credibility that stems from anything other than their duties as wives and mothers. After four years of the press lambasting Clinton for her lack of traditionalism, in 1996 both Dole and Clinton foregrounded their supportive spouse status and motherly characteristics. Heinz Kerry was frequently rebuked for her assertiveness and brash personality in 2004, so it was not surprising to see McCain and Obama assume softer personas that underscored their credentials as mothers and wives during the next election cycle. Obama's success with the maternal persona in 2008 and throughout her husband's first presidential term offered guidelines that led the 2012 spouses to highlight their good woman standing by focusing on their domesticity. If the mates of presidential contenders are looking to one another for guidance regarding the accepted standards of womanhood, it is likely other women are as well. What these women receive are messages touting the assumed benefits of being self-effacing, deferential, and other-centric.

The depictions of American womanhood proffered by republican motherhood rhetoric as it is applied to presidential nominees' spouses reinforce archaic perceptions of femaleness that erect barriers for women's equal treatment as full autonomous citizens. Defining women in terms of their relationships and their ability to fulfill homemaker duties makes women reliant on others for their identity and severely limits their perceived talents and interests. These factors, combined with the derision of females who show an enterprising nature outside of the home, create clear problems for women who engage in politics at various levels. The impacts of such narrow interpretations of women are generally negative, but there is still hope for overcoming these constraints and encouraging an open-minded view of women as competent, independent political actors.

Mitigating Republican Motherhood's Impacts

Although the press, the parties, and even the presidential contenders' spouses seem particularly intent on retaining some antiquated perspectives on gender norms, a few small but important changes across the seven most recent election cycles indicate that there is the potential for attitudes to evolve. The following pages highlight the shifting perspectives already evident in depictions of presidential nominees' consorts by the press, the parties, and the spouses and suggest ways each can contribute to a more nuanced and comprehensive view of women.

The Press

Despite the dependably conventional approach the mainstream media appear to take when describing and evaluating presidential spouses, advances in communication technologies have created opportunities for more and different perspectives to gain public attention. Since 2008, the number and types of individuals commenting on presidential candidates' spouses have increased, augmenting political dialogue by adding a variety of new points of view and different kinds of assessments. Even though the growing diversity of voices includes more supporters of orthodox gender norms, it also dramatically increases the number of people questioning the restrictive lens commonly placed on prominent women. More reporters, bloggers, and other commentators are now debating the merits of the *Family Circle* cookie recipe contest and decrying the inherent sexism that pervades much of the conversation about potential presidential helpmates. Social media offer voters the option to publish and consume more thorough assessments of the spouses and to learn about aspects of the mates' backstories that often do not get as much mainstream coverage. Admittedly, not all of the information available is always accurate. However, the additional perspectives do provide opportunities for a fuller understanding of the mates and allow for a more complete discussion of the various functions they could or should fulfill in society and government.

Media treatments of the spouses could improve by continuing to increase the amount of attention paid to assorted perspectives when considering prominent women in presidential campaigns. Reporters and commentators should be mindful of their tendency to use constraining and outdated perspectives of womanhood and ought to treat male and female spouses of presidential nominees the way they did Bill Clinton; they should approach all helpmates as individuals with varied backgrounds, interests, and skills. Although there is nothing wrong with appreciating the women who have been stay-at-home moms, journalists need to consciously move away from making traditional gender norms the default criteria for assessments of presidential nominees' spouses.

The Parties

In their modern manifestations, the two major political parties in the United States are often thought to hold strikingly different points of view regarding female citizenship. Contemporary Democrats customarily advocate for sex and gender equality and Republicans, in their words and deeds, usually conceive of women in considerably more circumscribed ways.[11] This distinction in perspective marks a decided shift in philosophy from the historical norms for each party. For many decades, the GOP supported the expansion of women's political participation. In 1872, the Republican Party expressed a desire to be "mindful of its obligations to the loyal women of America for their noble devotion to the cause of freedom," whereas Democrats largely disregarded females as public actors.[12] When woman's suffrage became a prominent issue, a Republican senator proposed what would become the nineteenth amendment to the US Constitution. A few decades later, Republicans overwhelmingly voted in favor of expanding enfranchisement, and Democrats remained split on the issue. When the Democrats again specifically left women out of their party platform in 1968, Republicans openly favored giving "all citizens the opportunity to influence and shape the events of our time."[13] However, during the 1980s, the GOP strategically surrendered its inclusive position to win the backing of socially conservative evangelicals, a move leaders believed would guarantee the party more electoral victories in the long term. Meanwhile, the Democrats evolved from a party focused on earning support from labor organizations to one that embraced demographic diversity. As they made this change, their interest in women and women's rights expanded. By 1992, the GOP had become the party of traditional family values, and the Democrats had turned into a more inclusive group. Most Americans currently associate Democrats with feminism and Republicans with antifeminism.[14]

Despite the contrast in their professed stances regarding women's proper social and political roles, both the Republican and Democratic Parties are complicit in the reification of conventional republican motherhood ideals, particularly when it comes to the use and depiction of presidential candidates' spouses. Although the major parties are opposing entities with seemingly divergent philosophical perspectives, and they go to great lengths to defeat each other every four years, their reliance on rhetoric that characterizes women using familial-based frames is surprisingly similar and consistent. Both the GOP and the Democrats depend on old-fashioned principles to promote their own candidates' spouses and to critique opponents' mates. Modern Republicans are steadfast in their application of archetypal standards and rarely waiver in their conventional view of American womanhood. The Democrats did nominate a female presidential candidate in 2016, thereby expanding dialogue about women's political aptitudes and highlighting some shifts in attitudes about women's presumed proper functions. However, like the Republicans, when it comes to discussions and uses of presidential nominees' spouses, the Democrats still regularly rely on republican motherhood ideals to promote and criticize female figures from both parties during presidential campaigns.

Both parties should reevaluate their perspectives on women and the roles they play in party politics and the nation. Rather than retaining a narrow perspective on women that lags decades behind the actual experiences of most Americans, the parties should recognize that, like men, women are multifaceted individuals with many talents and differing views. Doing so might help each party attract more women members and could diversify their candidate pools at the local, state, and national levels. Furthermore, spotlighting the various skill and knowledge bases of prominent female members would benefit the parties and the nation by presenting more heterogeneous role models for future potential female leaders and by demonstrating a more open-minded interpretation of the half of the nation's citizenry that has long been disregarded.

The Spouses

The spouses of presidential contenders are in an odd position when it comes to their self-representations. They are prominent public figures by virtue of their marriage, and their primary reason for participating in the campaign is because of their duties as spouses. If their mates win, they become even more noteworthy, garner much more attention based on their partners' achievements, and have increased political and social influence despite not having been elected themselves. Although some pundits argue that the spouses have little actual effect on voter preference in elections, studies show that candidates' mates are an important part of many individuals' assessments of nominees.[15] The spouses serve as campaign surrogates, but they lack the independence of other political actors because they are so intimately connected to the candidates. This unique situation creates constraints that are not easily overcome, so the spouses of presidential candidates must be strategic about the public personas they cultivate. On the one hand, they want to put forth a sincere self-portrayal consistent with their biographies, their attitudes, and their beliefs; on the other hand, they must consider their ability to appeal to voters.

Because the US political system still requires a degree of self-abnegation from female political operatives, and many Americans prefer a form of femininity that is deferential, other-centric, and quiescent, challenging entrenched ideals can be costly for nominees' wives. Yet, for women with more progressive biographies and attitudes, failure to confront the problematic features of republican motherhood should be distasteful, making balancing the needs of the campaign against their personal beliefs difficult. Clinton's efforts to contest familiar touchstones earned her the "femi-nazi" label. Her attempts to rehabilitate her persona by publicly embracing motherhood and domesticity then created doubts about her sincerity and authenticity that haunted her throughout her public life. Heinz Kerry managed the conflict between being herself and needing to adapt by simply refusing to conform to the constraining expectations placed on candidates' spouses. A few reporters praised her for showing refreshing candor, but she was mostly harangued and maligned by commentators. Obama learned quickly to embrace the republican motherhood ideal for herself but, through savvy message construction, managed to advocate for a more comprehensive approach to interpreting women generally. She balanced the political needs of her husband with her position as a role model by publicly embracing some conventional standards while rhetorically questioning the foundational assumptions of the republican motherhood trope. More clever approaches like Obama's could help expand dialogue about and by prominent female political actors.

One element of the women's self-portrayals that requires further consideration is the potential increased power incumbent first ladies have to drive conversations about political spouses and American womanhood. Although the analyses in this book assume that all spouses of presidential nominees have a certain degree of access to the so-called first lady pulpit, the women who campaign as presidential nominees' spouses while serving as the first lady certainly can use the full power and force of the unelected office.[16] Because established presidential helpmates' public images seldom change dramatically from one election cycle to the next (Barbara Bush remained the revered grandmother type; Clinton could not shake her antihomemaker persona; and Obama went from everymom to mom in chief), they have little to lose by increasing their advocacy for women.

When incumbent first ladies do present a wider perspective on womanhood, it can be very impactful. Laura Bush went from a seemingly servile cipher in 2000 to a measurably more active citizen in 2004, and her advocacy for women took on new forms. After barely mentioning women in her 2000 Republican National Convention address, Bush offered a considerably more progressive view of gender norms in 2004. The additional attention she gave women's concerns translated into more news coverage about feminine topics and increased conversations regarding the first lady's changed perspective. Future incumbent first ladies should take a cue from her and Obama and use their public platform to augment perceptions of women's skills, interests, and abilities. The first lady should understand the power of the podium and not leave it unused.

Conclusion

Republican motherhood poses a dilemma for political communicators and individuals interested in the gender implications of political rhetoric. The central problem lies in the balance between acknowledging and respecting the routinely undervalued responsibilities women have fulfilled as caregivers and nurturers and understanding the true diversity and richness of contemporary women's lived experiences, which often extend beyond the boundaries of the domestic sphere. The solution lies in a reconceptualization of women that treats them as independent, autonomous beings with the same presumed breadth and depth of potential as men.

Unfortunately, the type of attitudinal sea change necessary to expand attitudes regarding women is difficult to achieve, particularly when traditional perspectives are continually buttressed by the dialogue about and evaluations of prominent women in the political realm. Reliance on this rhetoric is damaging because the frame prioritizes relational connections over individual merit when it comes to valuing women. Multiple chapters of this book demonstrate that the wives of presidential contenders rely heavily on their mates and children as the basis for their own political credibility (even when they have other credentials to tout), but the same is not true of the one husband of a presidential contender. Interpreting male and female spouses of nominees based on this reductive conceit reaffirms the idea that female civic identity is considered conditional in a manner that male civic identity is not.

Although they are the dominant factors assessed in this book, the press, the parties, and the spouses are not the only ones complicit in the reification of republican motherhood ideals. The public also contributes to the reinforcement of this constrictive view of American womanhood. To effect change, various facets of the public must take action. Women need to stop being distracted by the politically constructed controversies that encourage infighting among various groups of females and focus on the hard work of demanding equal treatment not just legally but socially and politically. Rather than factionalizing based on perceived maternal distinctions, women need to cherish and promote the multifaceted nature of womanhood by learning to be more accepting of different approaches to femininity. In addition, men need to recognize the hypocrisy of the "masculine system" John Adams promulgated and work toward realizing the proffered ideals of a democratic republic, which welcome equal participation by all eligible adults. Males must learn that sharing power is not the same as losing power. Rather than men carrying the weight of leadership alone, men and women should shoulder the responsibilities of governance together. The nation would benefit from the diverse perspectives and talents women can bring to the table as fully acknowledged and empowered contributors.

Moreover, all Americans ought to check their own assumptions about the proper roles political spouses play during and after campaigns and acknowledge their own tacit consent to the gender-based stereotyping that regularly accompanies discussions of prominent females in the political sphere. If voters did not appear to hold narrow ideas about women, then party leaders would not create strategies designed to appeal to such attitudes, reporters would quickly find new themes to help shape their stories, and the spouses would be less likely to contort themselves to try to fit an archaic ideal.

Furthermore, scholars need to take the spouses of presidential contenders seriously as political actors to more fully understand the ways they affect voters' perceptions, campaign conversations, and interpretations of power. Rather than dismissing these individuals as peripheral players on the public stage, researchers should work to understand their influence more fully. Some have begun to study these prominent figures, but their research can be expanded. Additional scholarship might include examinations of various portrayals of vice presidential candidates' spouses and the mates of primary contenders. Future scholarly inquiry could help draw attention to the impact of rhetoric by and about these women heretofore seen as rather ancillary political figures.

The rhetoric of republican motherhood is based on a long-standing, ubiquitous, and problematic notion. If women's political power is grounded in their functions as wives and mothers, as the outdated trope contends, then women can never be more than second-class, relationship-contingent members of society. As long as Americans continue to widely use and endorse this oppressive, antiquated interpretation of womanhood, all women will continue to be denied the power and dignity granted to full and autonomous citizens, and they will perpetually struggle to be perceived as anything other than wives, daughters, and moms in chief.

Notes

Introduction: Political Spouses and Presidential Campaigns

1. Theodore Schleifer, "Donald Trump Makes Wild Threat to 'Spill the Beans' on Ted Cruz's Wife," CNN, March 24, 2016, accessed July 24, 2016, http://www.cnn.com/2016/03/22/politics /ted-cruz-melania-trump-twitter-donald-trump-heidi/.

2. Will Cadigan, "Jane Sanders' Former College Closes Doors Citing Burden of Land Deal She Orchestrated," CNN, May 16, 2016, accessed July 24, 2016, http://www.cnn.com/2016/05/16 /politics/jane-sanders-burlington-college/.

3. Glen Kessler, "Trump's Flip-Flop on Whether the Bill Clinton Sex Scandals Are Important," *Washington Post,* May 24, 2016, accessed July 24, 2016, https://www.washington post.com/news/fact-checker/wp/2016/05/24/trumps-flip-flop-on-whether-the-bill-clinton -sex-scandals-are-important/.

4. "First Lady Biography: Dolley Madison," National First Ladies' Library, accessed August 2, 2016, http://www.firstladies.org/biographies/firstladies.aspx?biography=4.

5. Betty Boyd Caroli, *First Ladies: From Martha Washington to Michelle Obama* (New York: Oxford University Press, 2010), 37.

6. Caroli, *First Ladies*, 39.

7. Paul F. Boller, Jr., *Presidential Campaigns: From George Washington to George W. Bush* (New York: Oxford University Press, 2004), 46.

8. Maggie McLean, "Ida McKinley," Civil War Women: Women of the Civil War and Reconstruction Eras, 1849–1877, November 23, 2014, accessed May 19, 2016, http://civilwarwomen blog.com/ida-mckinley/.

9. MaryAnne Borrelli, *The Politics of the President's Wife* (College Station: Texas A&M University Press, 2011), 20.

10. Diane M. Blair, "No Ordinary Time: Eleanor Roosevelt's Address to the 1940 Democratic National Convention," *Rhetoric & Public Affairs* 4 (2001): 203–222, http://dx.doi.org/10.1353 /rap.2001.0021.

11. "Widow of Alf Landon Dies," *New York Times,* July 23, 1996, accessed May 19, 2016, http:// www.nytimes.com/1996/07/23/us/widow-of-alf-landon-dies.html.

12. Evan Andrews, "10 Things You May Not Know about Jacqueline Kennedy Onassis," History.com, July 28, 2014, accessed June 8, 2016, http://www.history.com/news/10-things-you -may-not-know-about-jacqueline-kennedy-onassis.

13. "First Lady Biography: Pat Nixon," National First Ladies' Library, accessed May 19, 2016, http://www.firstladies.org/biographies/firstladies.aspx?biography=38.

14. Caroli, *First Ladies,* 225.

15. Caroli, *First Ladies*, 23.

16. Louisa Thomas, *Louisa: The Extraordinary Life of Mrs. Adams* (New York: Penguin Books, 2016), 294.

17. Carl Anthony, "Electing First Ladies: Presidential Candidate Spouses as Campaign Symbols, Part 1, 1808–1904," National First Ladies' Library, January 12, 2016, accessed May 18, 2016, http://www.firstladies.org/blog/electing-first-ladies-presidential-candidate-spouses-as-cam paign-symbols-part-1.

18. Buchanan was one of only two bachelors elected to the White House. The other was Grover Cleveland, in 1886. Cleveland married two years into his first presidency, whereas Buchanan remained unwed.

19. Paolo E. Coletta, "'Won, 1880: One, 1884': The Courtship of William Jennings Bryan and Mary Elizabeth Baird," *Journal of the Illinois State Historical Society* 50 (1957): 233.

20. Troy A. Murphy, "William Jennings Bryan: Boy Orator, Broken Man, and the 'Evolution' of America's Public Philosophy," *Great Plains Quarterly* 22 (2002): 96.

21. Caroli, *First Ladies,* 115.

22. Anthony, "Electing First Ladies."

23. "Mary Elizabeth Baird Bryan," Arlington National Cemetery website, September 3, 2005, accessed May 18, 2016, http://www.arlingtoncemetery.net/mebbryan.htm.

24. Tammy R. Vigil, *Connecting with Constituents: Identification Building and Blocking in Contemporary National Convention Speeches* (Lanham, MD: Lexington Books, 2015), 279.

25. Lisa R. Barry, "Eleanor Roosevelt: A Rhetorical Reconstruction of First Ladydom," in *Leading Ladies of the White House: Communication Strategies of Notable Twentieth-Century First Ladies,* ed. Molly Meijer Wertheimer (Lanham, MD: Rowman & Littlefield, 2005), 19.

26. Eleanor Roosevelt, "Address to the 1940 Democratic Convention," Eleanor Roosevelt Papers Project, accessed June 25, 2013, http://www.gwu.edu/~erpapers/teachinger/q-and-a/q22-erspeech.cfm.

27. Vigil, *Connecting with Constituents,* 326.

28. Borrelli, *Politics of the President's Wife,* 113.

29. Diana B. Carlin, "Lady Bird Johnson: The Making of a Public First Lady," in *Leading Ladies of the White House: Communication Strategies of Notable Twentieth-Century First Ladies,* ed. Molly Meijer Wertheimer (Lanham, MD: Rowman & Littlefield, 2005), 81.

30. Abigail Adams, Abigail Adams to John Adams, letter, December 23, 1796, Adams Family Papers: An Electronic Archive, Massachusetts Historical Society, accessed January 14, 2016, http://www.masshist.org/digitaladams/archive/doc?id=L17961223aa&bc=%2Fdigitaladams%2Farchive%2Fbrowse%2Fletters_1796_1801.php.

31. Shawn J. Parry-Giles and Diane M. Blair, "The Rise of the Rhetorical First Lady: Politics, Gender Ideology, and Women's Voice, 1789–2002," *Rhetoric & Public Affairs* 4, no. 4 (2002): 565–600, http://dx.doi.org/10.1353/rap.2003.0011.

32. Borrelli, *Politics of the President's Wife,* 3.

33. Carl Anthony, *First Ladies: The Saga of the Presidents' Wives and Their Power, 1789–1961* (New York: Quill/William Morrow, 1990); Caroli, *First Ladies;* Susan Swain, *First Ladies: Presidential Historians on the Lives of 45 Iconic American Women* (New York: Public Affairs, 2015).

34. Tasha N. Dubriwny, "First Ladies and Feminism: Laura Bush as Advocate for Women's and Children's Rights," *Women's Studies in Communication* 28 (2005): 84–114; Myra G. Gutin, *The President's Partner: The First Lady in the Twentieth Century* (Westport, CT: Praeger, 1989).

35. Borrelli, *Politics of the President's Wife;* Barbara Burrell, Laurel Elder, and Brian Frederick, "From Hillary to Michelle: Public Opinion and the Spouses of Presidential Candidates," *Presidential Studies Quarterly* 41 (2011): 156–176, http://dx.doi.org/10.1111/j.1741-5705.2010.03835.x; Cokie Roberts, *Ladies of Liberty: The Women Who Shaped Our Nation* (New York: Harper Perennial, 2008).

36. Karrin Vasby Anderson, "From Spouses to Candidates: Hillary Rodham Clinton, Elizabeth Dole, and the Gendered Office of the U.S. President," *Rhetoric & Public Affairs* 5, no. 1 (2002): 105–132, http://dx.doi.org/10.1353/rap.2002.0001; Rachel B. Friedman and Ronald E. Lee, *The Style and Rhetoric of Elizabeth Dole: Public Persona and Political Discourse* (Lanham, MD: Lexington Books, 2013); Elizabeth J. Natalle and Jenni M. Simon, eds., *Michelle Obama: First Lady, American Rhetor* (Lanham, MD: Lexington Books, 2015), 15–38; Tammy R. Vigil, "Feminine

Views in the Feminine Style: Convention Speeches by Presidential Nominees' Spouses," *Southern Communication Journal* 79, no. 4 (2014): 331, http://dx.doi.org/10.1080/1041794X.2014.916339.

37. Michael X. Delli Carpini and Esther R. Fuchs, "The Year of the Woman? Candidates, Voters, and the 1992 Elections," *Political Science Quarterly* 108 (1993): 32.

38. Delli Carpini and Fuchs, "Year of the Woman?," 32.

39. Vigil, *Connecting with Constituents*, 281.

40. Vigil, *Connecting with Constituents*, 281.

41. Vigil, "Feminine Views," 331.

42. Vigil, "Feminine Views," 342.

43. Borrelli, *Politics of the President's Wife*, 21.

44. Karrin Vasby Anderson, "The First Lady: A Site of 'American Womanhood,'" in *Leading Ladies of the White House: Communication Strategies of Notable Twentieth-Century First Ladies*, ed. Molly Meijer Wertheimer (Lanham, MD: Rowman & Littlefield, 2005), 9.

45. Borrelli, *Politics of the President's Wife*, 15.

46. Shawn J. Parry-Giles and Trevor Parry-Giles, "Gendered Politics and Presidential Image Reconstruction: A Reassessment of the 'Feminine Style,'" *Communication Monographs* 63 (1996): 337–353, http://dx.doi.org/10.1080/03637759609376398.

47. Anderson, "First Lady," 9.

48. Blair, "No Ordinary Time," 209–210.

49. Diane M. Blair and Shawn J. Parry-Giles, "Rosalynn Carter: Crafting a Presidential Partnership Rhetorically," in *Leading Ladies of the White House: Communication Strategies of Notable Twentieth-Century First Ladies*, ed. Molly Meijer Wertheimer (Lanham, MD: Rowman & Littlefield, 2005), 149.

50. Vigil, "Feminine Views," 332.

51. Molly Meijer Wertheimer, "Editor's Introduction: First Ladies' Fundamental Rhetorical Choices: When to Speak? What to Say? When to Remain Silent?" in *Leading Ladies of the White House: Communication Strategies of Notable Twentieth-Century First Ladies*, ed. Molly Meijer Wertheimer (Lanham, MD: Rowman & Littlefield, 2005), xii.

52. Lois W. Banner, *Women in Modern America: A Brief History*, 2nd ed. (San Diego, CA: Harcourt, Brace, Jovanovich, 1984).

53. Burrell, Elder, and Frederick, "From Hillary to Michelle," 160.

54. Vigil, "Feminine Views," 331.

55. Vigil, *Connecting with Constituents*, 282.

Chapter 1. Women as Citizens: The Emergence and Entrenchment of Republican Motherhood

1. Linda Kerber, *Women of the Republic: Intellect and Ideology in Revolutionary America* (Chapel Hill: University of North Carolina Press, 1980), 23.

2. Melody Rose and Mark O. Hattfield, "Republican Motherhood Redux? Women as Contingent Citizens in 21st Century America," *Journal of Women, Politics, and Policy* 29 (2007): 8, http://dx.doi.org/10.1300/J501v29n01_02.

3. Plato, *The Republic*, trans. Desmond Lee (New York: Penguin Books, 1975), 167–178.

4. Plato, *Republic*, 170.

5. Robert Filmer, *Patriarcha; or the Natural Power of Kings*, ed. Johann P. Sommerville (New York: Cambridge University Press, 1991).

6. Lord Henry Home Kame, *Sketches of the History of Man* (Indianapolis, IN: Liberty Fund, 2013); Rose and Hattfield, "Republican Motherhood Redux?," 8.

7. Kerber, *Women of the Republic*, 15.

8. Jean-Jacques Rousseau, *Emile* (1762), 295.

9. Rousseau, *Emile,* 278.

10. Rousseau, *Emile,* 265.

11. Edmund Burke, *Reflections on the Revolution in France,* 1790, ed. Jon Roland, Constitution Society, accessed June 13, 2016, http://www.constitution.org/eb/rev_fran.htm.

12. Joan Hoff, "American Women and the Lingering Implications of Coverture," *Social Science Journal* 44 (2007): 41–55, http://dx.doi.org/10.1016/j.soscij.2006.12.004; Rose and Hattfield, "Republican Motherhood Redux?," 5–30.

13. Linda Kerber, "The Republican Mother: Women and the Enlightenment—an American Perspective," *American Quarterly* 28 (1976): 188, stable url: http://www.jstor.org/stable/2712 349.

14. John Locke, *Two Treatises of Government* and *A Letter Concerning Toleration,* ed. Ian Shapiro (New Haven, CT: Yale University Press, 2003).

15. Charles Louis de Secondat, Baron de Montesquieu, *The Spirit of the Laws,* trans. Thomas Nugent (New York: Colonial Press, 1899), accessed April 2, 2016, Online Library of Liberty, http://oll.libertyfund.org/titles/837.

16. Montesquieu, *Spirit of the Laws.*

17. Thomas Paine, "An Occasional Letter on the Female Sex (1775)," Constitution.org, accessed June 17, 2016, http://www.constitution.org/tp/female.htm.

18. Paine, "Occasional Letter on the Female Sex."

19. Paine, "Occasional Letter on the Female Sex."

20. Connie Titone, "Virtue, Reason, and the False Public Voice: Catharine Macaulay's *Philosophy of Moral Education,*" *Educational Philosophy and Theory* 41, no. 1 (2009): 91–108, http://dx.doi.org/10.1111/j.1469-5812.2007.00365.x.

21. Mary Wollstonecraft, *A Vindication of the Rights of Man and A Vindication of the Rights of Woman* (New York: Cambridge University Press, 1995 [1792]).

22. Wendy Gunther-Canada, "Jean-Jacques Rousseau and Mary Wollstonecraft on the Sexual Politics of Republican Motherhood," *Southeastern Political Review* 27 (1999): 471, http://dx.doi .org/10.1111/j.1747-1346.1999.tb00546.x.

23. Wollstonecraft, *Vindication of the Rights of Woman,* 74, 99, 119.

24. Wollstonecraft, *Vindication of the Rights of Woman,* 74; Gunther-Canada, "Jean-Jacques Rousseau and Mary Wollstonecraft," 475.

25. Montesquieu, *Spirit of the Laws.*

26. Nancy F. Cott, *The Bonds of Womanhood: "Woman's Sphere" in New England, 1780–1835* (New Haven, CT: Yale University Press, 1997), 70.

27. Genesis 2:9 (King James Version).

28. Ephesians 5:22; 5:23 (KJV).

29. Ephesians 5:24 (KJV).

30. Exodus 20:12 (KJV); Deuteronomy 5:16 (KJV).

31. Lois W. Banner, *Women in Modern America: A Brief History,* 2nd ed. (San Diego, CA: Harcourt, Brace, Jovanovich, 1984), v.

32. Cott, *Bonds of Womanhood,* 19.

33. Cott, *Bonds of Womanhood,* 22.

34. Cott, *Bonds of Womanhood,* 71; Kerber, *Women of the Republic,* 25.

35. Cott, *Bonds of Womanhood,* 101.

36. Kerber, *Women of the Republic,* 10.

37. Cott, *Bonds of Womanhood,* 104.

38. Cott, *Bonds of Womanhood,* 105.

39. Hoff, "American Women," 42.

40. Cott, *Bonds of Womanhood,* 5.

41. Kerber, *Women of the Republic,* 148.

42. Kerber, *Women of the Republic,* 139.

43. Cott, *Bonds of Womanhood,* 41.

44. Margaret Fuller, *Woman in the Nineteenth Century and Other Writings* (New York: Oxford University Press, 1994), 15.

45. Fuller, *Woman in the Nineteenth Century,* 15.

46. John Stuart Mill, *On the Subjection of Women* (London: Longmans, Green, Reader, and Dryer, 1869), 39.

47. Mill, *On the Subjection of Women,* 39.

48. Margaret A. Nash, "Rethinking Republican Motherhood: Benjamin Rush and the Young Ladies' Academy of Philadelphia," *Journal of the Early Republic* 17 (1997): 176, http://dx.doi.org/10.2307/3124445.

49. Elizabeth Galewski, "The Strange Case of Women's Capacity to Reason: Judith Sargent Murray's Use of Irony in 'On the Equality of the Sexes,'" *Quarterly Journal of Speech* 93 (2007): 85, http://dx.doi.org/10.1080/00335630701326852.

50. Kerber, *Women of the Republic,* 190.

51. Rosemarie Zagarri, "Morals, Manners, and the Republican Mother," *American Quarterly* 44 (1992): 200, http://dx.doi.org/10.2307/2713040.

52. Cott, *Bonds of Womanhood,* 123.

53. Nash, "Rethinking Republican Motherhood," 177–178.

54. Nash, "Rethinking Republican Motherhood," 179.

55. Cott, *Bonds of Womanhood,* 75.

56. Kerber, *Women of the Republic,* 191.

57. Banner, *Women in Modern America,* 3; Cott, *Bonds of Womanhood,* 125.

58. Gunther-Canada, "Jean-Jacques Rousseau and Mary Wollstonecraft," 471.

59. Banner, *Women in Modern America,* 8.

60. Cott, *Bonds of Womanhood,* 74.

61. Kerber, *Women of the Republic,* 149.

62. Cott, *Bonds of Womanhood,* 20.

63. Kerber, *Women of the Republic,* 163.

64. Hoff, "American Women," 44.

65. Hoff, "American Women," 44.

66. Hoff, "American Women," 44.

67. Zagarri, "Morals, Manners, and the Republican Mother," 210.

68. Kerber, *Women of the Republic,* 11.

69. Kerber, "Republican Mother," 193.

70. Zagarri, "Morals, Manners, and the Republican Mother," 210.

71. Zagarri, "Morals, Manners, and the Republican Mother," 210.

72. Nash, "Rethinking Republican Motherhood," 173.

73. Kerber, "Republican Mother," 188.

74. Kerber, *Women of the Republic,* 193.

75. Cott, *Bonds of Womanhood,* 86.

76. Zagarri, "Morals, Manners, and the Republican Mother," 206.

77. Kerber, *Women of the Republic,* 228.

78. Cott, *Bonds of Womanhood,* 118, 121.

79. Zagarri, "Morals, Manners, and the Republican Mother," 200.

80. Kerber, *Women of the Republic,* 229.

81. Kerber, *Women of the Republic,* 200.

82. Cott, *Bonds of Womanhood,* 64.

83. Cott, *Bonds of Womanhood,* 198.

84. Kerber, *Women of the Republic,* 11.

85. Gunther-Canada, "Jean-Jacques Rousseau and Mary Wollstonecraft," 470.

86. Gunther-Canada, "Jean-Jacques Rousseau and Mary Wollstonecraft," 470.

87. Cott, *Bonds of Womanhood,* 94.

88. Banner, *Women in Modern America,* 51.

89. Nash, "Rethinking Republican Motherhood," 191.

90. Banner, *Women in Modern America,* 40.

91. Gunther-Canada, "Jean-Jacques Rousseau and Mary Wollstonecraft," 473; Kerber, "Republican Mother," 243.

92. Kerber, "Republican Mother," 199.

93. Cott, *Bonds of Womanhood,* 84.

94. Gunther-Canada, "Jean-Jacques Rousseau and Mary Wollstonecraft," 480.

95. Fuller, *Woman in the Nineteenth Century,* 18.

96. Amy Louise Erikson, "Mistresses and Marriage; or, a Short History of the Mrs.," *History Workshop Journal* 78 (2014): 52, http://dx.doi.org/10.1093/hwj/dbt002.

97. Erikson, "Mistresses and Marriage," 56.

98. Cott, *Bonds of Womanhood,* 23.

99. Kathleen Hall Jamieson, *Beyond the Double Bind: Women and Leadership* (New York: Oxford University Press, 1995), 53.

100. Katie Gentile, "What about the Baby? The New Cult of Domesticity and Media Images of Pregnancy," *Studies in Gender and Sexuality* 12, no. 1 (2011): 40, http://dx.doi.org/10.1080/1524 0657.2011.536056.

101. Catharine Esther Beecher and Harriet Beecher Stowe, *The American Woman's Home; or Principles of Domestic Science, Being a Guide to the Formation and Maintenance of Economical, Healthful, Beautiful, and Christian Homes* (New York: J. B. Ford, 1869); Mary Jo Deegan, "Jane Addams, the Hull-House School of Sociology, and Social Justice, 1892 to 1935," *Humanity and Society* 37, no. 3 (2013): 248–258, http://dx.doi.org/10.1177/0160597613493740.

102. Banner, *Women in Modern America,* 38.

103. Banner, *Women in Modern America,* 39.

104. Nash, "Rethinking Republican Motherhood," 175.

105. Banner, *Women in Modern America,* 39.

106. Carolyn Ross Johnston, *Sexual Power: Feminism and the Family in America* (Tuscaloosa: University of Alabama Press, 1992), 22.

107. Dolores Hayden, *The Grand Domestic Revolution: A History of Feminist Designs for American Homes, Neighborhoods, and Cities* (Cambridge: Massachusetts Institute of Technology Press, 1982), 134.

108. Banner, *Women in Modern America,* 117.

109. Banner, *Women in Modern America,* 117.

110. Banner, *Women in Modern America,* 116.

111. Banner, *Women in Modern America,* 118.

112. Suzanne Venker and Phyllis Schlafly, *The Flipside of Feminism: What Conservative Women Know and Men Can't Say* (Washington, DC: WND Books, 2010).

113. Venker and Schlafly, *Flipside of Feminism,* 105.

114. Thomas Vander Ven, *Working Mothers and Juvenile Delinquency* (El Paso, TX: LFB Scholarly, 2003), 24.

115. Carole Pateman, *The Disorder of Women: Democracy, Feminism, and Political Theory* (Palo Alto, CA: Stanford University Press, 1989), 25.

116. F. Carolyn Graglia, *Domestic Tranquility: A Brief against Feminism* (Dallas, TX: Spence, 1998).

117. Cott, *Bonds of Womanhood,* 98.

118. Kerber, *Women of the Republic,* 172.

119. Pateman, *Disorder of Women,* 17.

120. Victoria Irwin, "The Equal Rights Amendment: The Case Against," *Christian Science Monitor,* May 6, 1980, accessed July 12, 2016, http://www.csmonitor.com/1980/0506/050606.html.

121. UShistory.org, "The Equal Rights Amendment," US History Online Textbook, accessed July 12, 2016, http://www.ushistory.org/us/57c.asp.

122. Roberta W. Francis, "The Equal Rights Amendment: Unfinished Business for the Constitution," EqualRightsAmendment.org, accessed July 13, 2016, http://www.equalrightsamendment.org/history.htm.

123. Val Burris, "Who Opposed the ERA? An Analysis of the Social Bases of Antifeminism," *Social Science Quarterly* 64 (June 1983): 314, stable url: http://www.jstor.org/stable/42874034.

124. Cott, *Bonds of Womanhood,* 165.

125. Johnston, *Sexual Power,* 25.

126. Gwendolyn Mink, *The Wages of Motherhood: Inequality in the Welfare State, 1917–1942,* (Ithaca, NY: Cornell University Press, 1998), 7.

127. Suzanne Mettler, *Dividing Citizens: Gender and Federalism in New Deal Public Policy* (Ithaca, NY: Cornell University Press, 1998), 24.

128. Centers for Disease Control and Prevention (CDC), Office of Women's Health, "Leading Causes of Death in Females United States," September 24, 2015, accessed July 14, 2016, http://www.cdc.gov/women/lcod/2013/index.htm.

129. CDC, "Leading Causes of Death in Females United States."

130. Harvard Medical School, "Gender Matters: Heart Disease Risk in Women," *Harvard Health Publications* (September 2006), accessed July 14, 2016, http://www.health.harvard.edu/heart-health/gender-matters-heart-disease-risk-in-women.

131. Rose and Hattfield, "Republican Motherhood Redux?," 8.

132. Celeste Condit, *Decoding Abortion Rhetoric: Communicating Social Change* (Urbana-Champaign: University of Illinois Press, 1990), 23.

133. Condit, *Decoding Abortion Rhetoric,* 208.

134. Rose and Hattfield, "Republican Motherhood Redux?," 8.

135. Rose and Hattfield, "Republican Motherhood Redux?," 8.

136. Mark Baer, "Republicans Are Stripping Away Rights That Others Fought So Hard to Obtain," *Huffington Post,* August 31, 2014, accessed July 14, 2016, http://www.huffingtonpost.com/mark-baer/republican-appointed-supr_b_5549545.html.

137. Zerlina Maxwell, "Reproductive Health Laws Prove GOP 'War on Women' Is No Fiction," *U.S. News and World Report,* April 10, 2012, accessed July 14, 2016, http://www.usnews.com/debate-club/is-there-a-republican-war-on-women/reproductive-health-laws-prove-gop-war-on-women-is-no-fiction.

138. Maxwell, "Reproductive Health Laws Prove GOP 'War on Women' Is No Fiction."

139. Jennifer Haberkorn, "Abortion, Rape Shaped Key Races," *Politico,* November 6, 2012, accessed July 14, 2016, http://www.politico.com/story/2012/11/abortion-rape-shaped-key-races-083449; Margery Eagan, "Lawmakers in Real War on Women," *Boston Herald,* June 16, 2013, accessed July 14, 2016, http://www.bostonherald.com/news_opinion/columnists/margery_eagan/2013/06/eagan_lawmakers_in_real_war_on_women.

140. Amanda Terkel, "Saxby Chambliss Attributes Military Sexual Assault to 'The Hormone Level Created by Nature,'" *Huffington Post,* June 5, 2013, accessed July 14, 2016, http://www.huffingtonpost.com/entry/saxby-chambliss-military-sexual-assault_n_3384286.

141. Danielle Schlanger, "Female Veteran Gives Epic Response to Military Poster Blaming Sexual Assault Victims," *Huffington Post,* August 5, 2013, accessed July 24, 2016, http://www .huffingtonpost.com/entry/military-sexual-assault-poster_n_3709062.

142. Luisita Lopez Torregrosa, "U.S. Culture War with Women at Its Center," *New York Times,* April 3, 2012, accessed July 14, 2016, http://www.nytimes.com/2012/04/04/us/04iht-letter04 .html?_r=0.

143. Banner, *Women in Modern America,* 244.

144. Torregrosa, "U.S. Culture War with Women at Its Center."

145. Rose and Hattfield, "Republican Motherhood Redux?," 10.

146. Graglia, *Domestic Tranquility,* 10.

147. Emilie Stoltzfus, *Citizen, Mother, Worker: Debating Public Responsibility for Child Care after the Second World War* (Chapel Hill: University of North Carolina Press, 2003), 240.

148. Madelyn Cain, *The Childless Revolution: What It Means to Be Childless Today* (New York: Don Congdon Associates, 2001), 3.

149. Cott, *Bonds of Womanhood,* 201.

150. Rose and Hattfield, "Republican Motherhood Redux?," 10.

151. Sharon Hays, *Flat Broke with Children: Women in the Age of Welfare Reform* (New York: Oxford University Press, 2003), 23.

152. Susan Douglas and Meredith Michaels, *The Mommy Myth: The Idealization of Motherhood and How It Has Undermined All Women* (New York: Free Press, 2005), 185, 186.

153. Hays, *Flat Broke with Children,* 23.

154. Hays, *Flat Broke with Children,* 25.

155. Susan J. Carroll, "Voting Choices: The Politics of the Gender Gap," in *Gender and Elections: Shaping the Future of American Politics,* eds. Susan J. Carroll and Richard L. Fox (New York: Cambridge University Press, 2010), 138.

156. Floyd M. Orr, *The Last Horizon: Female Sexuality* (Bloomington, IN: iUniverse, 2002), 41.

157. Katie L. Gibson and Amy L. Heyse, "'The Difference between a Hockey Mom and a Pit Bull': Sarah Palin's Faux Maternal Persona and Performance of a Hegemonic Masculinity at the 2008 Republican National Convention," *Communication Quarterly* 58, no. 3 (2010): 252, http:// dx.doi.org/10.1080/01463373.2010.503151.

158. Karlyn Khors Campbell, "The Rhetorical Presidency: A Two-Person Career," in *Beyond the Rhetorical Presidency,* ed. Martin J. Medhurst (College Station; Texas A&M University Press, 1996), 179–195.

159. Borrelli, *Politics of the President's Wife,* 42, 16.

160. Caroli, *First Ladies,* xxi.

161. Karrin Vasby Anderson, "The First Lady: A Site of 'American Womanhood,'" in *Leading Ladies of the White House: Communication Strategies of Notable Twentieth-Century First Ladies,* ed. Molly Meijer Wertheimer (Lanham, MD: Rowman & Littlefield, 2005), 2.

162. Borrelli, *Politics of the President's Wife,* 12.

163. Anderson, "First Lady," 7.

164. Shawn J. Parry-Giles and Diane M. Blair, "The Rise of the Rhetorical First Lady: Politics, Gender Ideology, and Women's Voice, 1789–2002," *Rhetoric & Public Affairs* 4, no. 4 (2002): 565–600, http://dx.doi.org/10.1353/rap.2003.0011.

165. Borrelli, *Politics of the President's Wife,* 60.

166. Borrelli, *Politics of the President's Wife,* 20.

167. Abigail Adams to John Adams, letter, March 31–April 5, 1776, Adams Family Papers: An Electronic Archive, Massachusetts Historical Society, accessed July 15, 2016, https://www .masshist.org/digitaladams/archive/doc?id =L17760331aa.

168. Hoff, "American Women," 46.

Chapter 2. Barbara Bush and Hillary Rodham Clinton: The Year of the Woman (1992)

1. Barbara Boxer won the regular US Senate election; Dianne Feinstein won a special election for the Senate seat vacated when Alan Cranston retired.

2. Eagleton Institute of Politics, "Fact Sheet: Women Winners for U.S. House Seats, 1970–2014," Center for American Women and Politics, December 2014, accessed January 5, 2017, http://www.cawp.rutgers.edu/sites/default/files/resources/congwin_byseat.pdf.

3. Emma Green, "A Lot Has Changed in the Congress since 1992, the 'Year of the Woman,'" *Atlantic,* September 26, 2013, accessed August 25, 2016, http://www.theatlantic.com/politics /archive/2013/09/a-lot-has-changed-in-congress-since-1992-the-year-of-the-woman/280046/.

4. US House of Representatives, "The Decade of Women, 1992–2002," History, Art, and Archives, accessed August 25, 2016, http://history.house.gov/Exhibitions-and-Publications/WIC /Historical-Essays/Assembling-Amplifying-Ascending/Women-Decade/.

5. Barbara Mikulski, Kay Bailey Hutchinson, Dianne Feinstein, Barbara Boxer, Patty Murray, Olympia Snowe, Susan Collins, Mary Landrieu, and Blanche L. Lincoln, *Nine and Counting: The Women of the Senate* (New York: William Morrow, 2000), 46–50.

6. George H. W. Bush, "Presidential Debate at the University of Richmond," American Presidency Project, October 15, 1992, accessed December 9, 2016, http://www.presidency.ucsb.edu /ws/?pid=21617.

7. Eagleton Institute of Politics, "Fact Sheet: Gender Differences in Voter Turnout," Center for American Women and Politics, October 2015, accessed August 25, 2016, http://www.cawp .rutgers.edu/sites/default/files/resources/genderdiff.pdf.

8. "First Lady Biography: Barbara Bush," National First Ladies' Library, accessed August 25, 2016, http://www.firstladies.org/biographies/firstladies.aspx?biography=42.

9. Diana B. Carlin, "Barbara Pierce Bush: Choosing a Complete Life, 1925–1988," in *A Companion to First Ladies,* ed. Katherine A. S. Sibley (Malden, MA: Wiley-Blackwell, 2016), 604–618.

10. Karen O'Conner, Bernadette Nye, and Laura Van Assendelft, "Wives in the White House: The Political Influence of First Ladies," *Presidential Studies Quarterly* 26 (1996): 835–853, stable url: http://jstor.org/stable/27551636.

11. "First Lady Biography: Barbara Bush."

12. Marjorie Williams, "Barbara's Backlash," *Vanity Fair* (August 1992), accessed September 17, 2016, http://www.vanityfair.com/magazine/1992/08/williams199208; Carlin, "Barbara Pierce Bush: Choosing a Complete Life, 1925–1988," 610.

13. Jeff Girth and Don Van Natta, Jr., *Her Way: The Hopes and Ambitions of Hillary Rodham Clinton* (New York: Little, Brown, 2007).

14. Girth and Van Natta, *Her Way.*

15. Carl Bernstein, *A Woman in Charge: The Life of Hillary Rodham Clinton* (New York: Vintage Books, 2007), 130.

16. Williams, "Barbara's Backlash."

17. Barbara Burrell, Laurel Elder, and Brian Frederick, "From Hillary to Michelle: Public Opinion and the Spouses of Presidential Candidates," *Presidential Studies Quarterly* 41 (2011): 158, http://dx.doi.org/10.1111/j.1741-5705.2010.03835.x.

18. Molly Meijer Wertheimer, "Barbara Bush: Her Rhetorical Development and Appeal," in *Leading Ladies of the White House: Communication Strategies of Notable Twentieth-Century First Ladies,* ed. Molly Meijer Wertheimer (Lanham, MD: Rowman & Littlefield, 2005), 209.

19. Alessandra Stanley, "The 1992 Campaign: Barbara Bush; First Lady on Abortion: Not a Platform Issue," *New York Times,* August 14, 1992, accessed September 17, 2016, http://www .nytimes.com/1992/08/14/us/the-1992-campaign-barbara-bush-first-lady-on-abortion-not -a-platform-issue.html.

20. Jim Miklaszewski, "President George H. W. Bush's Secret Weapon: Barbara Bush," *Today Show,* August 8, 1992, accessed September 17, 2016, https://archives.nbclearn.com/portal /site/k-12/flatview?cuecard=2905.

21. Harry Enten, "Melania Trump Is One of the Least Popular Spouses of a Nominee since 1988," FiveThirtyEight.com, July 19, 2016, accessed September 17, 2016, http://fivethirtyeight .com/features/melania-trump-is-one-of-the-least-popular-spouses-of-a-nominee-since-1988/.

22. John M. Broder, "Column One: First Lady Takes the Gloves Off," *Los Angeles Times,* August 19, 1992, accessed September 17, 2016, http://articles.latimes.com/1992-08-19/news /mn-5603_1_barbara-bush.

23. Williams, "Barbara's Backlash."

24. Susan Baer, "Hillary-Bashing Hot, but May Be Risky," *Baltimore Sun,* August 20, 1992, accessed September 17, 2016, http://articles.baltimoresun.com/1992-08-20/news/1992233028_1 _hillary-clinton-barbara-bush-george-bush; Broder, "Column One"; Miklaszewski, "President George H. W. Bush's Secret Weapon"; Williams, "Barbara's Backlash."

25. Diana B. Carlin, "Barbara Pierce Bush: Choosing a Complete Life, 1988–2015," in *A Companion to First Ladies,* ed. Katherine A. S. Sibley (Malden, MA: Wiley-Blackwell, 2016), 625–628.

26. Donnie Radcliffe, "Barbara Bush in Key Role, Far More Than 'Everybody's Grandmother,'" *Los Angeles Times,* February 16, 1992, accessed October 23, 2016, http://articles.latimes.com /1992-02-16/news/mn-4595_1_barbara-bush.

27. Maureen Dowd, "The 1992 Campaign: Candidate's Wife; Hillary Clinton as Aspiring First Lady—Role Model, or a 'Hall Monitor' Type?" *New York Times,* May 18, 1992, accessed October 23, 2016, http://www.nytimes.com/1992/05/18/us/1992-campaign-candidate-s-wife-hillary-clin ton-aspiring-first-lady-role-model.html?pagewanted=all.

28. Andrew Kaczynski, Ilan Ben-Mir, and Dorsey Shaw, "Watch This Rare, Long-Forgotten Interview with Young Hillary Clinton," *Buzzfeed,* May 12, 2015, accessed October 23, 2016, https://www.buzzfeed.com/andrewkaczynski/hillary-clinton-1979?utm_term=.ysd7D6Bkdo #.fnOM35q9rJ.

29. Dowd, "1992 Campaign: Candidate's Wife."

30. Lloyd Grove, "Hillary Clinton, Trying to Have It All," *Washington Post,* March 10, 1992, accessed October 23, 2016, https://www.washingtonpost.com/archive/lifestyle/1992/03/10 /hillary-clinton-trying-to-have-it-all/bee81ob9-695e-4684-838c-947d327cd758/.

31. Baer, "Hillary-Bashing Hot."

32. Gwen Ifill, "The 1992 Campaign: Democrats; Trapped in a Spotlight, Hillary Clinton Uses It," *New York Times,* February 3, 1992, accessed October 23, 2016, http://www.nytimes .com/1992/02/03/us/the-1992-campaign-democrats-trapped-in-a-spotlight-hillary-clinton -uses-it.html; Dowd, "The 1992 Campaign: Candidate's Wife."

33. Baer, "Hillary-Bashing Hot."

34. Ifill, "1992 Campaign: Democrats; Trapped in a Spotlight."

35. Ifill, "1992 Campaign: Democrats; Trapped in a Spotlight."

36. Robin Toner, "The 1992 Campaign: Political Memo; Backlash for Hillary Clinton Puts Negative Image to Rout," *New York Times,* September 24, 1992, accessed October 23, 2016, http:// www.nytimes.com/1992/09/24/us/1992-campaign-political-memo-backlash-for-hillary-clin ton-puts-negative-image.html?pagewanted=all.

37. Ifill, "1992 Campaign: Democrats."

38. Eleanor Clift, "Hillary Clinton's Not-So-Hidden Agenda," *Newsweek,* September 20, 1992, accessed December 1, 2017, http://www.newsweek.com/hillary-clintons-not-so-hidden -agenda-198398.

39. Dowd, "1992 Campaign: Candidate's Wife."

40. Toner, "1992 Campaign."

41. Dorothee Benz, "The Media Factor behind the 'Hillary Factor,'" *Fair,* October 1, 1992, accessed October 23, 2016, http://fair.org/extra/the-media-factor-behind-the-hillary-factor/.

42. Dowd, "1992 Campaign: Candidate's Wife."

43. Benz, "Media Factor."

44. Gwen Ifill, "The 1992 Campaign: Hillary Clinton Defends Her Conduct in Law Firm," *New York Times,* March 17, 1992, accessed December 15, 2016, http://www.nytimes.com/1992/03/17/us/the-1992-campaign-hillary-clinton-defends-her-conduct-in-law-firm.html.

45. There is some question regarding whether Barbara Bush's recipe was really her own. Ned Zeman, "Cookiegate," *Newsweek,* July 2, 1992, accessed December 21, 2016, http://www.newsweek.com/cookiegate-198220.

46. Karen Lehrman, "Beware the Cookie Monster," *New York Times,* July 18, 1992, accessed December 21, 2016, http://www.nytimes.com/1992/07/18/opinion/beware-the-cookie-monster.html.

47. Marian Burros, "Now Is the Time to Come to the Aid of Your Favorite Cookies," *New York Times,* July 15, 2016, accessed December 21, 2016, http://www.nytimes.com/1992/07/15/garden/now-is-the-time-to-come-to-the-aid-of-your-favorite-cookies.html.

48. Burros, "Now Is the Time."

49. Steve Rushin, "Playing for Laughs," *Sports Illustrated,* September 21, 1992, accessed December 21, 2016, http://www.si.com/vault/1992/09/21/127172/playing-for-laughs-andy-van-slyke-the-pittsburgh-pirates-decidedly-off-center-centerfielder-may-soon-be-a-clown-with-a-batting-crown.

50. Rush Limbaugh, *Rush Limbaugh Show* simulcast, C-SPAN, November 3, 1992, accessed December 21, 2016, https://www.c-span.org/video/?34031-1/rush-limbaugh-show-simulcast.

51. Limbaugh, *Rush Limbaugh Show* simulcast.

52. Jean-Jacques Rousseau, *Emile* (1762), 295.

53. National Broadcasting Company, "The Pat Stevens Show," *Saturday Night Live,* October 10, 1988, accessed December 1, 2017, http://www.nbc.com/saturday-night-live/video/pat-stevens-candidates-wives/2868068.

54. Congressional Quarterly, "1992 Democratic Convention: Call for a New Covenant Tops Off Closing Night," *Congressional Quarterly Almanac,* accessed November 6, 2016, http://library.cqpress.com/cqalmanac/document.php?id=cqal92-845-25178-1106417.

55. Williams, "Barbara's Backlash."

56. Gwen Ifill, "The 1992 Campaign: The Democrats; Clinton Assails G.O.P. Attacks Aimed at Wife," *New York Times,* August 20, 1992, accessed November 6, 2016, http://www.nytimes.com/1992/08/20/news/the-1992-campaign-the-democrats-clinton-assails-gop-attacks-aimed-at-wife.html.

57. David Lauter, "News Analysis: Hillary-Bashing Becoming a Part of the GOP Campaign," *Los Angeles Times,* August 19, 1992, accessed November 5, 2016, http://articles.latimes.com/1992-08-19/news/mn-5607_1_hillary-clinton.

58. Janet Cawley, "First Lady Rips GOP Attack on Hillary Clinton," *Chicago Tribune,* August 14, 1992, accessed November 5, 2016, http://articles.chicagotribune.com/1992-08-14/news/9203130250_1_political-director-mary-matalin-hillary-clinton-barbara-bush.

59. Duncan Lindsey and Rosemary Sarri, "What Hillary Clinton Really Said about Children's Rights and Child Policy," *Children and Youth Services Review* 14 (1992): 473–483.

60. Lindsey and Sarri, "What Hillary Clinton Really Said," 474.

61. Norman Mailer, "By Heaven Inspired," *New Republic,* October 12, 1992, accessed November 5, 2016, https://newrepublic.com/article/78580/heaven-inspired.

62. Patrick Buchanan, "Culture War, August 17, 1992," AmericanRhetoric.com, accessed November 5, 2016, http://www.americanrhetoric.com/speeches/patrickbuchanan1992rnc.htm.

63. Pat Robertson, "1992 Republican Convention," Pat Robertson website, accessed November 5, 2016, http://www.patrobertson.com/Speeches/1992GOPConvention.asp.

64. Marilyn Quayle, "Republican National Convention Address, August 19, 1992," C-SPAN, accessed November 5, 2016, https://www.c-span.org/video/?31358-1/republican-national-con vention-address&start=699.

65. Quayle, "Republican National Convention Address."

66. Maureen Dowd, "The 1992 Campaign: Campaign Trail; From Nixon, Predictions on the Presidential Race," *New York Times,* February 6, 1992, accessed November 6, 2016, http://www .nytimes.com/1992/02/06/us/the-1992-campaign-campaing-trail-from-nixon-predictions-on -the-presidential-race.html.

67. Dowd, "1992 Campaign: Campaign Trail."

68. Rousseau, *Emile,* 265.

69. Dowd, "1992 Campaign: Campaign Trail."

70. Staff Writer, "Profile: If You Vote for Him You Get Her: Hillary Clinton, Would-be First Lady," *Independent,* September 4, 1992, accessed November 6, 2016, http://www.independent .co.uk/voices/profile-if-you-vote-for-him-you-get-her-hilary-clinton-would-be-first -lady-1549590.html.

71. Baer, "Hillary-Bashing Hot."

72. Cawley, "First Lady Rips GOP."

73. Mailer, "By Heaven Inspired."

74. Cable-Satellite Public Affairs Network (C-SPAN), "First Lady on Next First Lady," December 1, 1992, accessed September 17, 2016, https://www.c-span.org/video/?c4541061/bar bara-bush-1992.

75. Cable-Satellite Public Affairs Network (C-SPAN), "Barbara Bush Campaign Interview," July 28, 1992, accessed August 25, 2016, https://www.c-span.org/video/?31214-1/barbara-bush -campaign-interview.

76. MaryAnne Borrelli, *The Politics of the President's Wife* (College Station: Texas A&M University Press, 2011), 171.

77. Tammy R. Vigil, *Connecting with Constituents: Identification Building and Blocking in Contemporary National Convention Addresses* (Lanham, MD: Lexington Books, 2015), 280–281.

78. Connie Cass, "Barbara Bush Set the Stage for Nominees' Wives," Associated Press, August 28, 2012, accessed July 26, 2013, http://news.yahoo.com/barbara-bush-set-stage-nominees -wives-071846208--election.html.

79. Tammy R. Vigil, "Feminine Views in the Feminine Style: Convention Speeches by Presidential Nominees' Spouses," *Southern Communication Journal* 79, no. 4 (2014): 330, http:// dx.doi.org/10.1080/1041794X.2014.916339.

80. Barbara Bush, "1992 RNC Speech," transcript, Speech Vault, August 19, 1992, accessed July 26, 2013, http://www.speeches-usa.com/Transcripts/barbara_bush-1992rnc.html.

81. Bush, "1992 RNC Speech."

82. Bush, "1992 RNC Speech."

83. Bush, "1992 RNC Speech."

84. Bush, "1992 RNC Speech."

85. Bush, "1992 RNC Speech."

86. Bush, "1992 RNC Speech."

87. Bush, "1992 RNC Speech."

88. Josh Burdick, "April 1992 Interview with Hillary Clinton on *Today Show,*" YouTube, September 13, 2015, accessed December 15, 2016, https://www.youtube.com/watch?v=-namImCszCk.

89. Burdick, "April 1992 Interview with Hillary Clinton."

90. "Making Hillary Clinton an Issue," *PBS Frontline,* March 26, 1992, accessed December 15, 2016, http://www.pbs.org/wgbh/pages/frontline/shows/clinton/etc/03261992.html.

91. Ifill, "1992 Campaign: Hillary Clinton Defends."

92. Susan Baer, "More Digestible Hillary Now Offers Cookies: Democratic Convention," *Baltimore Sun,* July 16, 1992, accessed December 15, 2016, http://articles.baltimoresun.com/1992-07-16/news/1992198069_1_hillary-cookies-clinton.

93. Lehrman, "Beware the Cookie Monster."

94. Lehrman, "Beware the Cookie Monster."

95. Karrin Vasby Anderson, "The First Lady: A Site of 'American Womanhood,'" in *Leading Ladies of the White House: Communication Strategies of Notable Twentieth-Century First Ladies,* ed. Molly Meijer Wertheimer (Lanham, MD: Rowman & Littlefield, 2005), 3.

Chapter 3. Hillary Rodham Clinton and Elizabeth Dole: Dutiful (and Accomplished) Wives (1996)

1. Steven Stark, "Gap Politics," *Atlantic,* July 1996, accessed January 6, 2017, http://www.theatlantic.com/magazine/archive/1996/07/gap-politics/305579/.

2. Stark, "Gap Politics."

3. Eagleton Institute of Politics, "Fact Sheet: Summary of Women Candidates for Selected Offices, 1970–2014," Center for American Women and Politics, December 2014, accessed January 5, 2017, http://www.cawp.rutgers.edu/sites/default/files/resources/can_histsum.pdf.

4. Eagleton Institute of Politics, "Fact Sheet: Women Winners for U.S. House Seats, 1970–2014," Center for American Women and Politics, December 2014, accessed January 5, 2017, http://www.cawp.rutgers.edu/sites/default/files/resources/congwin_byseat.pdf.

5. Drew DeSilver, "Women Have a Long History in Congress, but Until Recently There Haven't Been Many," Pew Research Center, January 14, 2015, accessed January 5, 2017, http://www.pewresearch.org/fact-tank/2015/01/14/women-have-long-history-in-congress-but-until-recently-there-havent-been-many/.

6. Susan A. MacManus, "Voter Participation and Turnout: Female Star Power Attracts Women Voters," in *Gender and Elections: Shaping the Future of American Politics,* eds. Susan J. Carroll and Richard L. Fox (New York: Cambridge University Press, 2006), 94–95.

7. Jacob Weisberg, "Soccer Mom Nonsense: The Making of This Year's Election Myth," *Slate,* October 12, 1996, accessed January 6, 2017, http://www.slate.com/articles/news_and_politics/strange_bedfellow/1996/10/soccer_mom_nonsense.html.

8. Mary Douglas Vavrus, "From Women of the Year to 'Soccer Moms': The Case of the Incredible Shrinking Women," *Political Communication* 17 (2000): 194, http://dx.doi.org/10.1080/105846000198477.

9. Michael Tackett, "'Soccer Moms' Tell Why Clinton Gets Backing," *Chicago Tribune,* September 15, 1996, accessed January 6, 2017, http://articles.chicagotribune.com/1996-09-15/news/9609150255_1_bob-dole-soccer-moms-number-of-swing-voters.

10. Susan J. Carroll, "The Disempowerment of the Gender Gap: Soccer Moms and the 1996 Elections," *PS: Political Science and Politics* 32 (1999): 7, http://dx.doi.org/10.2307/420743.

11. Weisberg, "Soccer Mom Nonsense."

12. Carroll, "Disempowerment of the Gender Gap."

13. "The 1996 Presidential Election," Gallup, accessed January 5, 2017, http://library.law.columbia.edu/urlmirror/CLR/100CLR524/ptpreselec.html.

14. Gerhard Peters and John T. Woolley, "Voter Turnout in Presidential Elections: 1828–2012," American Presidency Project, accessed January 9, 2017, http://www.presidency.ucsb.edu/data/turnout.php.

15. Barbara Burrell, Laurel Elder, and Brian Frederick, "From Hillary to Michelle: Public Opinion and the Spouses of Presidential Candidates," *Presidential Studies Quarterly* 41 (2011): 158, http://dx.doi.org/10.1111/j.1741-5705.2010.03835.x.

16. Margaret O'Brien Steinfels, "A New Role for Hillary: Circuit-Riding First Lady," *Commonweal,* December 2, 1994, 5.

17. David A. Graham, "A Short History of Hillary (Rodham) (Clinton)'s Changing Names," *Atlantic,* November 30, 2015, accessed January 12, 2017, https://www.theatlantic.com/politics /archive/2015/11/a-short-history-of-hillary-rodham-clintons-name/418029/.

18. Karrin Vasby Anderson, "From Spouses to Candidates: Hillary Rodham Clinton, Elizabeth Dole, and the Gendered Office of U.S. President," *Rhetoric & Public Affairs* 5 (2002): 106, http:// dx.doi.org/10.1353/rap.2002.0001.

19. Frank Newport, "Clinton's Image at Lowest Point in Two Decades," Gallup, July 25, 2016, accessed January 7, 2017, http://www.gallup.com/poll/193913/clinton-image-lowest-point-two -decades.aspx.

20. Nancy Gibbs and Michael Duffy, "Just Heartbeats Away," *Time,* July 1, 1996, 27.

21. Charles S. Clark, "First Ladies: What Is the Proper Role for the President's Spouse?" *Congressional Quarterly Researcher* 6 (1996): 1.

22. Michael Barone, "Is She a Political Liability?" *U.S. News and World Report,* March 7, 1994, 51.

23. Shawn J. Parry-Giles, *Hillary Clinton in the News: Gender and Authenticity in American Politics* (Urbana-Champaign: University of Illinois Press, 2014), 56.

24. Parry-Giles, *Hillary Clinton in the News,* 56.

25. Linda Feldmann, "First Lady Brings Light — and Heat — to Campaign," *Christian Science Monitor,* August 27, 1996, 1.

26. William Safire, "Essay; Blizzard of Lies," *New York Times,* January 8, 1996, accessed January 12, 2017, http://www.nytimes.com/1996/01/08/opinion/essay-blizzard-of-lies.html.

27. Joan Beck, "Redefining the Role of First Lady," *Chicago Tribune,* January 18, 1996, accessed January 12, 2017, http://articles.chicagotribune.com/1996-01-18/news/9601180059_1_role -of-first-lady-hillary-clinton-elizabeth-dole.

28. Gibbs and Duffy, "Just Heartbeats Away," 25.

29. Gibbs and Duffy, "Just Heartbeats Away," 25.

30. Gibbs and Duffy, "Just Heartbeats Away," 25.

31. Eleanor Clift and Tara Sonenshine, "The Steel Magnolia," *Newsweek,* May 27, 1996, 33.

32. Victoria Pope and Jerelyn Eddings, "An Iron Fist in a Velvet Glove," *U.S. News and World Report,* August 19, 1996, 26.

33. Douglas Frantz, "Blood Bank Politics: A Special Report; Elizabeth Dole and Red Cross: 2 Powers at Work," *New York Times,* May 30, 1996, accessed January 1, 2017, http://www.nytimes .com/1996/05/30/us/blood-bank-politics-special-report-elizabeth-dole-red-cross-2-powers -work.html.

34. Clift and Sonenshine, "Steel Magnolia," 33.

35. Ginger Thompson, "For Dole, Faith without Fanfare: Candidate Described as Devout but Wary of Public Piety," *Baltimore Sun Times,* October 13, 1996, accessed January 1, 2017, http:// articles.baltimoresun.com/1996-10-13/news/1996287023_1_bob-dole-elizabeth-dole-faith.

36. Gibbs and Duffy, "Just Heartbeats Away," 25.

37. Weston Kosova and Michael Isikoff, "The Relentless Mrs. Dole," *Newsweek,* February 5, 1996, 31.

38. Clift and Sonenshine, "Steel Magnolia," 33.

39. David Willman, "Elizabeth Dole Got $875,000 over 4 Years as a Speaker," *Los Angeles Times,* January 25, 1996, accessed January 1, 2017, http://articles.latimes.com/1996-01-25/news /mn-28599_1_elizabeth-dole-got.

40. Frantz, "Blood Bank Politics."

41. Kosova and Isikoff, "Relentless Mrs. Dole," 31.

42. Clift and Sonenshine, "Steel Magnolia," 33.

43. Marcie Bianco, "*SNL*'s Many Faces of Hillary Clinton: What They Say about Us," Women's Media Center, May 8, 2016, accessed January 23, 2017, http://www.womensmediacenter.com /feature/entry/snls-many-faces-of-hillary-clinton-what-they-say-about-us.

44. National Broadcasting Company, "The Barbara Walters Special: Elizabeth Dole," *Saturday Night Live*, October 26, 1996, accessed January 16, 2017, https://www.nbc.com/saturday -night-live/video/barbara-on-liddy/2861298?snl=1.

45. Clark, "First Ladies," 1.

46. Joseph N. Cappella, Joseph Turow, and Kathleen Hall Jamieson, "Call-in Political Talk Radio: Background, Content, Audiences, Portrayal in Mainstream Media," Annenberg Public Policy Center, August 7, 1996, accessed January 1, 2017, http://repository.upenn.edu/cgi/view content.cgi?article=1410&context=asc_papers.

47. Erica Jong, "Hillary's Husband Re-elected: The Clinton Marriage of Politics and Power," *Nation,* November 25, 1996, accessed January 1, 2017, https://www.scribd.com/document /309667569/Hillary-s-Husband-Re-Elected-The-Clinton-Marriage-of-Politics-and-Power.

48. Martha Brant and Eleanor Clift, "Cashing in on Letting Hillary Be Hillary," *Newsweek,* September 2, 1996, 25.

49. Jong, "Hillary's Husband Re-elected."

50. Pope and Eddings, "Iron Fist in a Velvet Glove," 26.

51. Clark, "First Ladies," 3–4.

52. Henry Louis Gates, "Hating Hillary: Hillary's Been Trashed Right and Left—but What's Really Fueling the Furies?" *New Yorker,* February 26, 1996, accessed January 1, 2017, http:// www.newyorker.com/magazine/1996/02/26/hating-hillary.

53. Elizabeth Bumiller, "The Other Dole: A Special Report; Elizabeth Dole Is Eager to Keep Strength Subtle," *New York Times,* July 16, 1996, accessed January 17, 2017, http://www.ny times.com/1996/07/16/us/the-other-dole-a-special-report-elizabeth-dole-is-eager-to-keep -strength-subtle.html.

54. Clark, "First Ladies," 2.

55. Bumiller, "Other Dole."

56. Bumiller, "Other Dole."

57. Feldmann, "First Lady Brings Light," 1.

58. Hillary Clinton, "First Lady Hillary Rodham Clinton Speaks at the Democratic National Convention," *PBS Newshour,* August 27, 1996, accessed July 27, 2013, http://www.pbs.org/news hour/bb/politics/july-dec96/hillary-clinton.html?print.

59. Clinton, "First Lady Hillary Rodham Clinton Speaks."

60. Clinton, "First Lady Hillary Rodham Clinton Speaks."

61. Clinton, "First Lady Hillary Rodham Clinton Speaks."

62. Clinton, "First Lady Hillary Rodham Clinton Speaks."

63. Clinton, "First Lady Hillary Rodham Clinton Speaks."

64. Clinton, "First Lady Hillary Rodham Clinton Speaks."

65. Clinton, "First Lady Hillary Rodham Clinton Speaks."

66. Clinton, "First Lady Hillary Rodham Clinton Speaks."

67. Tammy R. Vigil, "Feminine Views in the Feminine Style: Convention Speeches by Presidential Nominees' Spouses," *Southern Journal of Communication* 79 (2014): 338, http://dx.doi .org/10.1080/1041794X.2014.916339.

68. Elizabeth Dole, "Elizabeth Dole Speaking before the Republican National Convention," *PBS Newshour,* August 14, 1996, accessed July 25, 2013, http://www.pbs.org/newshour/bb /politics/july-dec96/elizabeth_dole_08-14.html.

69. Bumiller, "Other Dole."

70. Dole, "Elizabeth Dole Speaking"

71. Linda Kerber, *Women of the Republic: Intellect and Ideology in Revolutionary America* (Chapel Hill: University of North Carolina Press, 1980), 199.

72. Dole, "Elizabeth Dole Speaking."

73. Clinton, "First Lady Hillary Rodham Clinton Speaks."

Chapter 4. Tipper Gore and Laura Bush: Quintessential Republican Mothers (2000)

1. Kate Taylor, "Why Does Bush Go 'Nucular?'" *Slate,* September 18, 2002, accessed May 1, 2017, http://www.slate.com/articles/news_and_politics/explainer/2002/09/why_does_bush_go_nucular.html.

2. Cynthia B. Costello, Vanessa R. Wight, and Anne J. Stone, "Women in the 107th Congress," in *The American Woman: Daughters of a Revolution-Young Women Today,* eds. Cynthia B. Costello, Vanessa R. Wight, and Anne J. Stone (New York: Palgrave Macmillan, 2002), 351.

3. Eagleton Institute of Politics, "Fact Sheet: Gender Gap in the 2000 Elections," Center for the American Woman and Politics, accessed May 4, 2017, http://www.cawp.rutgers.edu/sites/default/files/resources/pressrelease_12-00_gg2000.pdf.

4. Melinda Henneberger, "Tipper's Dance," *New York Times Magazine,* October 1, 2000, accessed May 7, 2017, http://www.nytimes.com/2000/10/01/magazine/tipper-s-dance.html.

5. Cable News Network (CNN), "Tipper Gore, Bio," July 1996, accessed May 4, 2017, http://www.cnn.com/ALLPOLITICS/1996/conventions/chicago/players/gore/tipper.shtm.

6. Ceci Connolly, "Tipper Gore Details Depression Treatment," *Washington Post,* May 8, 1999, accessed May 7, 2017, http://www.washingtonpost.com/wp-srv/politics/campaigns/wh2000/stories/tipper050899.htm.

7. Cable News Network (CNN), "Who Is Tipper Gore?" June 16, 1999, accessed May 7, 2017, http://www.cnn.com/ALLPOLITICS/stories/1999/06/16/president.2000/mrsgore.biography/.

8. CNN, "Tipper Gore, Bio."

9. Laura Bush, *Spoken from the Heart* (New York: Scribner, 2010).

10. Bush, *Spoken from the Heart.*

11. Joel Achenbach, "Tipper Gore. No, Seriously," *Washington Post,* May 16, 1993, accessed May 7, 2017, https://www.washingtonpost.com/archive/lifestyle/1993/05/16/tipper-gore-no-seriously/3db57953-4cf1-4cff-9b17-9c8345eaf28e/?utm_term=.1895eeaf8288.

12. Helen Peterson, "Gore's Tipper: All-American Cheerleader," *New York Daily News,* August 13, 2000, accessed May 7, 2017, http://www.nydailynews.com/archives/news/gore-tipper-all-american-cheerleader-article-1.882496.

13. Alex S. Jones, "Al Gore's Double Life," *New York Times,* October 25, 1992, accessed May 7, 2017, http://www.nytimes.com/1992/10/25/magazine/al-gore-s-double-life.html?pagewanted=all.

14. Monica Davey, "Tipper Gore Vows She Would Chart Own Course as First Lady," *Chicago Tribune,* August 17, 2000, accessed May 7, 2017, http://articles.chicagotribune.com/2000-08-17/news/0008170483_1_tipper-gore-hillary-clinton-husband-on-key-issues.

15. CNN, "Tipper Gore, Bio."

16. Caryn James, "The Nation: When a Kiss Isn't Just a Kiss," *New York Times,* August 20, 2000, accessed May 7, 2017, http://www.nytimes.com/2000/08/20/weekinreview/the-nation-when-a-kiss-isn-t-just-a-kiss.html.

17. CNN, "Who Is Tipper Gore?"

18. Karen Tumulty, "Democratic Convention: The Women Who Made Al Gore," *Time,*

August 21, 2000, accessed May 7, 2017, http://content.time.com/time/printout/0,8816
,997752,00.html.

19. CNN, "Who Is Tipper Gore?"

20. Maureen Dowd, "Liberties; Tipper's Tiger," *New York Times,* June 2, 1999, accessed May 7,
2017, http://www.nytimes.com/1999/06/02/opinion/liberties-tipper-s-tiger.html.

21. James, "Nation."

22. Lance Murrow, "Gore's Kiss Is So '60s—and Probably Fake," CNN, August 28, 2000, accessed May 15, 2017, http://us.cnn.com/2000/ALLPOLITICS/stories/08/28/morrow8_28.a.tm
/index.html.

23. James, "Nation."

24. Henneberger, "Tipper's Dance."

25. Henneberger, "Tipper's Dance."

26. Davey, "Tipper Gore Vows."

27. Tumulty, "Democratic Convention."

28. Davey, "Tipper Gore Vows."

29. Davey, "Tipper Gore Vows."

30. Katharine Q. Seelye, "The 2000 Campaign: The Vice President's Wife; Tipper Gore Seeks
Privacy under a Public Microscope," *New York Times,* May 19, 2000, accessed May 8, 2017,
http://www.nytimes.com/2000/05/19/us/2000-campaign-vice-president-s-wife-tipper-gore
-seeks-privacy-under-public.html.

31. Tumulty, "Democratic Convention."

32. CNN, "Tipper Gore, Bio."

33. Connolly, "Tipper Gore Details Depression."

34. Skip Hollandsworth, "Reading Laura Bush," *Texas Monthly,* accessed December 31, 2016,
http://www.texasmonthly.com/politics/reading-laura-bush/.

35. Frank Bruni, "Quiet Strength/A Special Report: For Laura Bush, a Direction That She
Never Dreamed Of," *New York Times,* July 31, 2000, accessed May 12, 2017, http://www.ny
times.com/2000/07/31/us/quiet-strength-special-report-for-laura-bush-direction-she-never
-wished-go.html.

36. Allison Mitchell, "The 2000 Campaign: The Governor's Wife—A Political Wallflower Has
a Full Dance Card," *New York Times,* September 21, 2000, accessed May 12, 2017, http://www
.nytimes.com/2000/09/21/us/2000-campaign-governor-s-wife-political-wallflower-has-full
-dance-card.html.

37. Monica Rhor, "Laura Bush a Reluctant Show Stealer," *Miami Herald,* July 31, 2000, 1.

38. John Hanchette, "Laura Welch Bush: Shy No More," *USA Today,* June 23, 2000, accessed
May 12, 2017, https://usatoday30.usatoday.com/news/opinion/e2147.htm.

39. Cable News Network (CNN), "Laura Bush: A Supportive but Behind-the-Scenes Spouse,"
accessed May 13, 2017, https://web.archive.org/web/20080514064711/http://www.cnn.com
/SPECIALS/2000/democracy/bush/stories/laura/.

40. CNN, "Laura Bush."

41. Richard L. Burke, "First Lady of Texas Plays a Firm Second Fiddle," *New York Times,*
August 3, 1999, accessed May 13, 2017, http://www.nytimes.com/1999/08/03/us/first-lady-of
-texas-plays-a-firm-second-fiddle.html; "Laura Bush"; Hanchette, "Laura Welch Bush."

42. Burke, "First Lady of Texas."

43. Bruni, "Quiet Strength."

44. Jessica Reaves, "Now Making Her Bow: The Un-Hillary," CNN, August 1, 2000, accessed
May 13, 2017, https://web.archive.org/web/20081205172343/http://archives.cnn.com/2000
/ALLPOLITICS/stories/08/01/laura8_1.a.tm/.

45. Reaves, "Now Making Her Bow."

46. Mary C. Banwart, Dianne G. Bystrom, and Terry Robertson, "From the Primary to the General: A Comparative Analysis of Candidate Media Coverage in Mixed-Gender 2000 Races for Governor and U.S. Senate," *American Behavioral Scientist* 46 (2003): 658–676, http://dx.doi .org/10.1177/0002764202238491; Brian F. Schaffner, "Priming Gender: Campaigning on Women's Issues in U.S. Senate Elections," *American Journal of Political Science* 49 (2005): 803–817, http://dx.doi.org/10.2307/3647698; Tammy R. Vigil, "Feminine Views in the Feminine Style: Convention Speeches by Presidential Nominees' Spouses," *Southern Communication Journal* 79, no. 4 (2014): 336, http://dx.doi.org/10.1080/1041794X.2014.916339.

47. Burke, "First Lady of Texas."

48. Greg Hitt and James M. Perry, "Republican Convention 2000: Women's Night Reflects One Key to Election Strategy—Bush Camp Sees Advantage in Gore's Tepid Appeal among Female Voters," *Wall Street Journal,* August 1, 2000, accessed May 13, 2017, https://search-pro questcom.ezproxy.bu.edu/docview/398910554?accountid=9676.

49. Barbara Burrell, Laurel Elder, and Brian Frederick, "From Hillary to Michelle: Public Opinion and the Spouses of Presidential Candidates," *Presidential Studies Quarterly* 41 (2011): 156–176, http://dx.doi.org/10.1111/j.1741-5705.2010.03835.x.

50. Cable-Satellite Public Affairs Network (C-SPAN), "Al Gore's 2000 DNC Acceptance Speech," August 17, 2000, accessed May 15, 2017, https://www.c-span.org/video/?c4399462 /al-gores-2000-dnc-acceptance-speech.

51. Mary Elizabeth "Tipper" Gore, "Remarks at the 2000 DNC," Iowa State University Archives of Women's Political Communication, August 18, 2000, accessed May 15, 2017, https://wp.las .iastate.edu/womenspeech/2017/03/21/remarks-at-the-2000-dnc-aug-18-2000/.

52. Gore, "Remarks at the 2000 DNC."

53. Gore, "Remarks at the 2000 DNC."

54. Tammy R. Vigil, *Connecting with Constituents: Identification Building and Blocking in Contemporary National Convention Speeches* (Lanham, MD: Lexington Books, 2015), 62.

55. Laura Bush, "Address to the Republican National Convention," *Vital Speeches of the Day* 66, 21 (August 15, 2000): 650–651.

56. Bush, "Address to the Republican National Convention."

57. Bush, "Address to the Republican National Convention."

58. Bush, "Address to the Republican National Convention."

59. Bush, "Address to the Republican National Convention."

60. Bush, "Address to the Republican National Convention."

61. Bush, "Address to the Republican National Convention."

62. Bush, "Address to the Republican National Convention."

63. Bush, "Address to the Republican National Convention."

64. Lydia Saad, "Melania Trump's Image Less Positive Than Other Spouses," Gallup, July 18, 2016, accessed May 13, 2017, http://www.gallup.com/opinion/polling-matters/193793/mela nia-trump-image-problem-democrats-independents.aspx.

65. Saad, "Melania Trump's Image Less Positive Than Other Spouses."

66. Harry Enten, "Melania Trump Is One of the Least Popular Spouses of a Nominee since 1988," FiveThirtyEight.com, July 19, 2016, accessed May 20, 2017, http://fivethirtyeight.com /features/melania-trump-is-one-of-the-least-popular-spouses-of-a-nominee-since-1988/.

67. Saad, "Melania Trump's Image Less Positive Than Other Spouses."

Chapter 5. Laura Bush and Teresa Heinz Kerry: The All-American Wife and the Assertive Heiress (2004)

1. Steve Friess, "The Father of All Web Campaigns," *Politico,* September 30, 2012, accessed June 4, 2017, http://www.politico.com/story/2012/09/how-deans-wh-bid-gave-birth-to-web -campaigning-081834.

2. Mildred Amer, "Membership of the 109th Congress: A Profile," *CRS Report for Congress,* November 29, 2006, accessed June 4, 2017, https://www.senate.gov/reference/resources/pdf/RS22007.pdf.

3. Katharine Q. Seelye, "Kerry in a Struggle for a Democratic Base: Women," *New York Times,* September 21, 2004, accessed June 3, 2017, http://www.nytimes.com/2004/09/22/politics/campaign/kerry-in-a-struggle-for-a-democratic-base-women.html?_r=0.

4. John Cassidy, "What's up with White Women? They Voted for Romney, Too," *New Yorker,* November 8, 2012, accessed June 4, 2017, http://www.newyorker.com/news/john-cassidy/whats-up-with-white-women-they-voted-for-romney-too.

5. Randy Kennedy, "The 2004 Campaign: The First Lady — the Not-So-Reluctant Bush Campaigner," *New York Times,* August 12, 2004, accessed June 7, 2017, http://www.nytimes.com/2004/08/12/us/the-2004-campaign-the-first-lady-the-not-so-reluctant-bush-campaigner.html?_r=0.

6. "Pennsylvania's Most Politically Powerful Women," *Politics PA,* accessed June 1, 2017, https://web.archive.org/web/20040209095936/http://politicspa.com/features/mostpoliticallypowerfulwomen.htm.

7. Jill Lawrence, "Campaign 2004: With Teresa, Expect an Unconventional Campaign," *USA Today,* May 23, 2004, accessed June 1, 2017, https://usatoday30.usatoday.com/news/politicselections/nation/president/2004-05-23-heinz-kerry-cover_x.htm.

8. Lawrence, "Campaign 2004."

9. Katie Couric, "I'm Not Wild about Being Called First Lady," *Today Show,* February 16, 2004, accessed June 4, 2017, http://www.today.com/news/i-m-not-wild-about-being-called-first-lady-wbn a4276470.

10. Curtis Sittenfeld, "Why I Love Laura Bush," *Salon,* January 29, 2004, accessed June 4, 2017, http://www.salon.com/2004/01/29/laura_2/.

11. Couric, "I'm Not Wild about Being Called First Lady."

12. David Rennie, "Laura Bush Condemns Democrat 'Witch-Hunt,'" *Telegraph,* February 20, 2004, accessed June 4, 2017, http://www.telegraph.co.uk/news/worldnews/northamerica/usa/1454916/Laura-Bush-condemns-Democrat-witch-hunt.html.

13. Tatiana Morales, "Laura Bush: 'The Perfect Wife,'" *CBS News,* January 7, 2004, accessed June 4, 2017, http://www.cbsnews.com/news/laura-bush-the-perfect-wife/.

14. Maureen Dowd, "I Read, I Smoke, I Spin," *New York Times,* February 22, 2004, accessed June 4, 2017, http://www.nytimes.com/2004/02/22/opinion/i-read-i-smoke-i-spin.html?_r=0.

15. Rennie, "Laura Bush Condemns Democrat 'Witch-Hunt.'"

16. Dowd, "I Read, I Smoke, I Spin."

17. Juan Williams, "'W Stands for Women' — but Which Ones?" NPR, May 17, 2004, accessed June 5, 2017, http://www.npr.org/templates/story/story.php?storyId=1899733.

18. Couric, "I'm Not Wild about Being Called First Lady."

19. Darren K. Carlson, "Ideal First Lady: Hillary Clinton or Laura Bush?" Gallup, July 13, 2004, accessed June 3, 2017, http://www.gallup.com/poll/12328/ideal-first-lady-hillary-clinton-laura-bush.aspx.

20. Robin Toner, "The Un-Hillary," *New York Times,* February 15, 2004, accessed June 5, 2017, http://www.nytimes.com/2004/02/15/books/the-un-hillary.html.

21. Ann Gerhart, *The Perfect Wife: The Life Choices of Laura Bush* (New York: Simon & Schuster, 2004).

22. Susan Page, "Public Favors a Traditional, Non-Working First Lady," *USA Today,* October 19, 2004, accessed June 1, 2017, https://usatoday30.usatoday.com/news/politicselections/2004-10-19-first-ladiescover_x.htm.

23. Dick Meyer, "Mrs. Kerry to Reporter: 'Shove It,'" *CBS News,* July 26, 2004, accessed June 7, 2017, http://www.cbsnews.com/news/mrs-kerry-to-reporter-shove-it/.

24. Edward Helmore, "Kerry's Gold," *Guardian,* January 24, 2004, accessed June 1, 2017, https://www.theguardian.com/world/2004/jan/25/usa.uselections2004.

25. Judith Thurman, "The Candidate's Wife," *New Yorker,* September 27, 2004, accessed June 2, 2017, http://www.newyorker.com/magazine/2004/09/27/the-candidates-wife.

26. Helmore, "Kerry's Gold."

27. Thurman, "Candidate's Wife."

28. David Usborne, "Teresa Heinz Kerry: Too Much Attitude for a First Lady?" *Independent,* February 7, 2004, accessed June 5, 2017, http://www.independent.co.uk/news/people/profiles/teresa-heinz-kerry-too-much-attitude-for-a-first-lady-68008.html.

29. Thurman, "Candidate's Wife."

30. Tatiana Morales, "Mama T: Teresa Heinz Kerry," *CBS News,* July 27, 2004, accessed June 4, 2017, http://www.cbsnews.com/news/mama-t-teresa-heinz-kerry/.

31. Thurman, "Candidate's Wife."

32. Pablo Martinez Monsivais, "The Real Running Mates," *USA Today,* October 19, 2004, accessed June 1, 2017, https://usatoday30.usatoday.com/news/politicselections/2004-10-19-teresa_x.htm.

33. Monsivais, "Real Running Mates."

34. Associated Press, "Kerry and Wife Embrace Opulence," *Washington Times,* March 22, 2004, accessed June 6, 2017, http://www.washingtontimes.com/news/2004/mar/22/20040322-104317-3064r/.

35. Michelle Cottle, "The X-Factor," *Atlantic,* October 2004, accessed June 5, 2017, https://www.theatlantic.com/magazine/archive/2004/10/the-x-factor/303499/.

36. National Broadcasting Company, "Kerry Campaign Stop," *Saturday Night Live,* October 2, 2004, accessed June 6, 2017, https://www.nbc.com/saturday-night-live/video/kerry-campaign-stop/n111843?snl=1.

37. Howard Kurtz, "The Making of a Non-President: Behind the Scenes with the Kerry Campaign," *Washington Post,* November 15, 2004, accessed June 1, 2017, http://www.washingtonpost.com/wp-dyn/articles/A49993-2004Nov14.html.

38. Michael Cornfield, "Presidential Campaign Ads Online," Pew Research Center, October 3, 2004, accessed June 8, 2017, http://www.pewinternet.org/2004/10/03/presidential-campaign-ads-online/.

39. Kennedy, "2004 Campaign."

40. Elizabeth MacDonald and Chana R. Schoenberger, "Special Report: The World's 100 Most Powerful Women," *Forbes,* August 20, 2004, accessed June 8, 2017, https://www.forbes.com/home/lists/2004/08/18/04powomland.html.

41. Rennie, "Laura Bush Condemns Democrat 'Witch-Hunt.'"

42. Cottle, "X-Factor."

43. Usborne, "Teresa Heinz Kerry."

44. Helmore, "Kerry's Gold."

45. Jenny Allen, "The Women Bush and Kerry Depend On," *Good Housekeeping,* September 6, 2004, accessed June 4, 2017, http://www.goodhousekeeping.com/life/inspirational-stories/interviews/a16828/women-bush-kerry-octo4/.

46. Allen, "Women Bush and Kerry Depend On."

47. Williams, "'W Stands for Women.'"

48. Laura Bush, "2004 Republican National Convention Address," AmericanRhetoric.com, August 31, 2004, accessed July 27, 2013, http://www.americanrhetoric.com/speeches/PDFFiles/Laura%20Bush%20-%202004%20RNC.pdf.

49. Bush, "2004 Republican National Convention Address."

50. Bush, "2004 Republican National Convention Address."

51. Bush, "2004 Republican National Convention Address."

52. Bush, "2004 Republican National Convention Address."

53. Bush, "2004 Republican National Convention Address."

54. Bush, "2004 Republican National Convention Address."

55. Bush, "2004 Republican National Convention Address."

56. Bush, "2004 Republican National Convention Address."

57. Tammy R. Vigil, "Feminine Views in the Feminine Style: Convention Speeches by Presidential Nominees' Spouses," *Southern Communication Journal* 79, no. 4 (2014): 336, http://dx.doi.org/10.1080/1041794X.2014.916339.

58. Teresa Heinz Kerry, "Teresa Heinz Kerry's Remarks to the Democratic National Convention," *New York Times,* July 27, 2004, accessed July 27, 2013, http://www.nytimes.com/2004/07/27/politics/campaign/27TEXT-TERESA.html.

59. Heinz Kerry, "Teresa Heinz Kerry's Remarks."

60. Heinz Kerry, "Teresa Heinz Kerry's Remarks."

61. Heinz Kerry, "Teresa Heinz Kerry's Remarks."

62. Heinz Kerry, "Teresa Heinz Kerry's Remarks."

63. Heinz Kerry, "Teresa Heinz Kerry's Remarks."

64. Heinz Kerry, "Teresa Heinz Kerry's Remarks."

65. Heinz Kerry, "Teresa Heinz Kerry's Remarks."

66. Heinz Kerry, "Teresa Heinz Kerry's Remarks."

67. Carlson, "Ideal First Lady."

68. Page, "Public Favors a Traditional, Non-Working First Lady."

69. Harry Enten, "Melania Trump Is One of the Least Popular Spouses of a Nominee since 1988," FiveThirtyEight.com, July 19, 2016, accessed May 20, 2017, http://fivethirtyeight.com/features/melania-trump-is-one-of-the-least-popular-spouses-of-a-nominee-since-1988/.

70. Enten, "Melania Trump Is One of the Least Popular Spouses of a Nominee since 1988."

71. Barbara Burrell, Laurel Elder, and Brian Frederick, "From Hillary to Michelle: Public Opinion and the Spouses of Presidential Candidates," *Presidential Studies Quarterly* 41 (2011): 156–176, http://dx.doi.org/10.1111/j.1741-5705.2010.03835.x.

Chapter 6. Cindy McCain and Michelle Obama: Revering Wifedom and Motherhood (2008)

1. Eagleton Institute of Politics, "Fact Sheet: Women Winners for U.S. House Seats, 1970–2014," Center for American Women and Politics, December 2014, accessed January 5, 2017, http://www.cawp.rutgers.edu/sites/default/files/resources/congwin_byseat.pdf.

2. Eagleton Institute of Politics, "Fact Sheet: Gender Differences in Voter Turnout," Center for American Women and Politics, October 2015, accessed August 25, 2016, http://www.cawp.rutgers.edu/sites/default/files/resources/genderdiff.pdf.

3. Bob Dart, "As Candidate's Wife, Cindy McCain Finds Herself in Spotlight," *Statesman,* March 9, 2008, accessed June 19, 2007, https://web.archive.org/web/20080312181334/http://www.statesman.com/news/content/news/stories/nation/03/09/0309cindymccain.html.

4. Dart, "As Candidate's Wife, Cindy McCain Finds Herself in Spotlight."

5. Dart, "As Candidate's Wife, Cindy McCain Finds Herself in Spotlight."

6. Dart, "As Candidate's Wife, Cindy McCain Finds Herself in Spotlight."

7. Leslie Bennetts, "First Lady in Waiting," *Vanity Fair,* December 27, 2007, accessed June 19, 2017, http://www.vanityfair.com/news/2007/12/michelle_obama200712.

8. Peter Slevin, "Michelle Obama: Who She Was before the White House," *New York Times,* April 14, 2015, accessed June 20, 2017, http://nytlive.nytimes.com/womenintheworld/2015/04/14/an-inside-look-at-michelle-obamas-life-before-the-white-house/.

9. David M. Hafbfinger, "For McCains, a Public Path but Private Wealth," *New York Times,* August 22, 2008, accessed June 20, 2017, http://www.nytimes.com/2008/08/23/us/politics /23mccain.html.

10. Julia Reed, "Cindy McCain: Cindy McCain Takes a Moment," *Vogue,* June 1, 2008, accessed June 22, 2017, http://www.vogue.com/article/cindy-mccainbrcindy-mccain-takes-a-moment.

11. Noam Scheiber, "Made Man: How Cindy Hensley Invented John McCain," *New Republic,* August 20, 2008, accessed June 22, 2017, https://newrepublic.com/article/64809/made-man.

12. Associated Press, "Beer Heiress Could Be Next First Lady," *NBC News,* April 3, 2008, accessed June 22, 2017, http://www.nbcnews.com/id/23930780/ns/politics-decision_08/t/beer -heiress-could-be-next-first-lady/#.WUuoFiuQx-U.

13. Justin Rood, "Heiress Wife Is Source of McCain's 'Secret' Millions," *ABC News,* April 18, 2008, accessed June 22, 2017, http://abcnews.go.com/Blotter/story?id=4682970.

14. Associated Press, "Beer Heiress Could Be Next First Lady."

15. Scheiber, "Made Man."

16. Claire Shipman, Susan Rucci, and Imaeyen Ibanga, "Cindy McCain: Mother, Humanitarian, and Potential First Lady," *ABC News,* July 8, 2008, accessed June 22, 2017, http://abcnews .go.com/GMA/story?id=5330040.

17. Sam Dealey, "Cindy McCain Rolls Up Her Sleeves," *Marie Claire,* October 20, 2008, accessed June 22, 2017, http://www.marieclaire.com/politics/news/a2131/cindy-mccain-inter view-election/.

18. Leonard Doyle, "Cindy McCain: Painful Secrets," *Independent,* August 29, 2008, accessed June 22, 2017, http://www.independent.co.uk/news/people/profiles/cindy-mccain-painful -secrets-913247.html.

19. Holly Bailey, "In Search of the Real Cindy McCain," *Newsweek,* June 21, 2008, accessed June 22, 2017, http://www.newsweek.com/holly-bailey-search-real-cindy-mccain-90771. Holly Bailey, "In Search of the Real Cindy McCain," *Newsweek,* June 21, 2008, accessed June 22, 2017, http://www.newsweek.com/holly-bailey-search-real-cindy-mccain-90771.

20. Doyle, "Cindy McCain."

21. Bailey, "In Search of the Real Cindy McCain."

22. Scheiber, "Made Man."

23. Vanessa Grigoriadis, "Black and Blacker: The Racial Politics of the Obama Marriage," *New York Magazine,* August 10, 2008, accessed June 24, 2017, http://nymag.com/news/features /49139/.

24. Stephanie Lysaght, "Michelle Obama: Politics of Fashion," *Los Angeles Times,* June 24, 2008, accessed June 24, 2017, http://www.latimes.com/entertainment/la-et-michelle-obama -fashion-aug292008-pg-photogallery.html.

25. Lauren Collins, "The Other Obama: Michelle Obama and the Politics of Candor," *New Yorker,* March 19, 2008, accessed June 24, 2017, http://www.newyorker.com/magazine/2008 /03/10/the-other-obama.

26. Grigoriadis, "Black and Blacker."

27. Grigoriadis, "Black and Blacker."

28. Grigoriadis, "Black and Blacker."

29. "Michelle Obama's America: Is Barack Obama's Wife His Rock or His Bitter Half?" *Economist,* July 3, 2008, accessed June 24, 2017, http://www.economist.com/node/11670246.

30. Michael Powell and Jodi Kantor, "After Attacks, Michelle Obama Looks for a New Introduction," *New York Times,* June 18, 2008, accessed June 24, 2017, http://www.nytimes .com/2008/06/18/us/politics/18michelle.html.

31. Alex Koppelman, "Fox News Calls Michelle Obama 'Obama's Baby Mama,'" *Salon,* June 12, 2008, accessed June 24, 2017, http://www.salon.com/2008/06/12/fox_obama/.

32. Danny Shea, "Bill O'Reilly Apologizes for Michelle Obama 'Lynching' Remark," *Huffington Post,* March 28, 2008, accessed June 24, 2017, http://www.huffingtonpost.com/2008/02/22/bill-oreilly-apologizes-f_n_87949.html.

33. Powell and Kantor, "After Attacks, Michelle Obama Looks for a New Introduction."

34. Grigoriadis, "Black and Blacker."

35. Collins, "Other Obama."

36. Susan Saulny, "Michelle Obama Thrives in Campaign Trenches," *New York Times,* February 14, 2008, accessed June 24, 2017, http://www.nytimes.com/2008/02/14/us/politics/14michelle.html.

37. "Michelle Obama's America."

38. Collins, "Other Obama."

39. Grigoriadis, "Black and Blacker."

40. Rebecca Traister, "The Momification of Michelle Obama," *Salon,* November 12, 2008, accessed June 24, 2017, http://www.salon.com/2008/11/12/michelle_obama_14/.

41. Saulny, "Michelle Obama Thrives in Campaign Trenches."

42. Betty Hallock, "Cookbook Politics: Democrats, Republicans in the Kitchen," *Los Angeles Times,* August 27, 2008, accessed June 24, 2017, http://www.latimes.com/local/la-fo-cookbooks27-2008aug27-story.html.

43. Leonard Doyle, "How the Cookie Crumbles: The Great First Lady Bake-Off," *Independent,* June 20, 2008, accessed October 22, 2017, http://www.independent.co.uk/news/world/americas/how-the-cookie-crumbles-the-great-first-lady-bake-off-851694.html.

44. National Broadcasting Company (NBC), "The Obama Variety Show," *Saturday Night Live,* October 25, 2008, accessed October 22, 2017, http://www.nbc.com/saturday-night-live/video/obama-address/n12335?snl=1.

45. National Broadcasting Company (NBC), "John McCain and Sarah Palin Do QVC," *Saturday Night Live,* November 1, 2008, accessed October 22, 2017, http://www.nbc.com/saturday-night-live/video/mccain-qvc-open/n12355?snl=1.

46. Jonathan Knuckey and Myunghee Kim, "Evaluations of Michelle Obama as First Lady: The Role of Racial Resentment," *Presidential Studies Quarterly* 46 (2016): 366, http://dx.doi.org/10.1111/psq.12274.

47. Collins, "Other Obama."

48. Collins, "Other Obama."

49. Collins, "Other Obama."

50. Saulny, "Michelle Obama Thrives in Campaign Trenches."

51. Saulny, "Michelle Obama Thrives in Campaign Trenches."

52. Lydia Saad, "Melania Trump's Image Less Positive Than Other Spouses," Gallup, July 18, 2016, accessed May 13, 2017, http://www.gallup.com/opinion/polling-matters/193793/melania-trump-image-problem-democrats-independents.aspx.

53. Cindy McCain, "Text of Cindy McCain's Speech," *Los Angeles Times,* September 4, 2008, accessed July 29, 2013, http://www.latimes.com/news/politics/la-na-cmccaintranscript5 2008sep05,0,4516477.story.

54. McCain, "Text of Cindy McCain's Speech."

55. McCain, "Text of Cindy McCain's Speech."

56. McCain, "Text of Cindy McCain's Speech."

57. McCain, "Text of Cindy McCain's Speech."

58. McCain, "Text of Cindy McCain's Speech."

59. McCain, "Text of Cindy McCain's Speech."

60. McCain, "Text of Cindy McCain's Speech."

61. McCain, "Text of Cindy McCain's Speech."

62. McCain, "Text of Cindy McCain's Speech."

63. McCain, "Text of Cindy McCain's Speech."

64. Michelle Obama, "Transcript: Michelle Obama's 'One Nation,'" CNN, August 25, 2008, accessed June 30, 2013, http://www.cnn.com/2008/POLITICS/08/25/michelle.obama.tran script/.

65. Obama, "Transcript: Michelle Obama's 'One Nation.'"

66. Obama, "Transcript: Michelle Obama's 'One Nation.'"

67. Obama, "Transcript: Michelle Obama's 'One Nation.'"

68. Obama, "Transcript: Michelle Obama's 'One Nation.'"

69. Obama, "Transcript: Michelle Obama's 'One Nation.'"

70. Obama, "Transcript: Michelle Obama's 'One Nation.'"

71. Sojourner Truth, "Ain't I a Woman? (1851)," *Modern History Sourcebook* (August 1997), accessed October 22, 2017, https://sourcebooks.fordham.edu/mod/sojtruth-woman.asp.

72. Tammy R. Vigil, "Conventional and Unconventional Rhetorical Strategies in Michelle Obama's Democratic National Convention Addresses," in *Michelle Obama: First Lady, American Rhetor,* eds. Elizabeth J. Natalle and Jenni M. Simon (Lanham, MD: Lexington Books, 2015), 28.

Chapter 7. Michelle Obama and Ann Romney: Battling for Mom in Chief (2012)

1. Jeffrey M. Jones, "Gender Gap in 2012 Vote Is Largest in Gallup's History," *Gallup News,* November 9, 2012, accessed November 1, 2017, http://news.gallup.com/poll/158588/gender -gap-2012-vote-largest-gallup-history.aspx.

2. Amanda Terkel, "Women in Senate: 2012 Election Ushers in Historic Number of Female Senators," *Huffington Post,* November 11, 2012, accessed November 2, 2017, https://www.huff ingtonpost.com/2012/11/07/women-senate-2012-election_n_2086093.html.

3. Eagleton Institute of Politics, "History of Women Governors," Center for American Women and Politics, accessed November 2, 2017, http://www.cawp.rutgers.edu/history-women-gov ernors.

4. "Bachmann Wins Iowa Straw Poll, Cements Her Top-Tier Status in GOP Race," *Fox News,* August 13, 2011, accessed November 2, 2017, http://www.foxnews.com/politics/2011/08/13 /finally-here-ames-straw-poll-first-test-2012.html.

5. Patrick Condon and Brian Bakst, "Presidential Bid Over, Bachmann Faces Big Decision," *Boston Globe,* January 5, 2012, accessed November 3, 2017, http://archive.boston.com/news /politics/articles/2012/01/05/pres_bid_finished_bachmann_faces_minn_decision/.

6. Elizabeth Dias, "Understanding Michele Bachmann's 'Submission,'" *Time,* August 19, 2011, accessed November 3, 2017, http://swampland.time.com/2011/08/19/understanding-michele -bachmanns-submission/.

7. Shushannah Walshe, "Michelle Bachman 'Submissive' Wife Idea a Matter of Interpreta-tion," *ABC News,* August 12, 2011, accessed November 3, 2017, http://abcnews.go.com/Politics /michele-bachmann-submissive-wife-belief-matter-interpretation/story?id=14292494.

8. Bobbie L. Kyle, "10 Things You Didn't Know about Ann Romney," *U.S. News and World Report,* December 12, 2007, accessed July 13, 2017, https://www.usnews.com/news/national /articles/2007/12/12/10-things-you-didnt-know-about-ann-romney.

9. Susan Page, "Michelle Obama on Her Garden, Her Future, and the Campaign," *USA To-day,* May 29, 2012, accessed July 14, 2017, https://usatoday30.usatoday.com/news/washington /story/2012-05-28/white-house-garden-book-michelle-obama-obesity/55249152/1.

10. Michelle Cottle, "Battle of the First Ladies: Michelle Obama vs. Ann Romney," *News-week,* November 9, 2012, accessed July 14, 2017, http://www.newsweek.com/battle-first-ladies -michelle-obama-vs-ann-romney-63859.

11. Cottle, "Battle of the First Ladies."

12. Amy Sullivan, "Michelle Obama's Most Important Title Really Is Mom-in-Chief," *New Republic,* September 5, 2012, accessed July 14, 2017, https://newrepublic.com/article/106954 /michelle-obamas-most-important-title-really-mom-chief.

13. Kate Dailey, "Michelle Obama: Her Four-Year Evolution," BBC, September 4, 2012, accessed July 14, 2017, http://www.bbc.com/news/magazine-19431000.

14. Leslie Marshall, "Michelle Obama Is the President's Secret Weapon," *U.S. News and World Report,* September 5, 2012, accessed July 14, 2017, https://www.usnews.com/opinion/blogs /leslie-marshall/2012/09/05/michelle-obama-is-the-presidents-secret-weapon.

15. Sullivan, "Michelle Obama's Most Important Title Really Is Mom-in-Chief."

16. Dailey, "Michelle Obama."

17. Page, "Michelle Obama on Her Garden, Her Future, and the Campaign."

18. Elizabeth J. Natalle, "Michelle Obama's Ethos and Let's Move!" in *Michelle Obama: First Lady, American Rhetor,* eds. Elizabeth J. Natalle and Jenni M. Simon (Lanham, MD: Lexington Books, 2015), 70.

19. Dailey, "Michelle Obama."

20. Curtis Sittenfeld, "Give the First Lady a Break," *Guardian,* October 13, 2012, accessed July 14, 2017, https://www.theguardian.com/world/2012/oct/14/obama-presidency-verdict -curtis-sittenfeld.

21. Sullivan, "Michelle Obama's Most Important Title Really Is Mom-in-Chief."

22. Bee-Shyuan Chang, "Wooing the First Dresser," *New York Times,* February 10, 2012, accessed July 14, 2017, http://www.nytimes.com/2012/02/12/fashion/michelle-obama-wooing -the-first-dresser.html.

23. "Michelle Obama 'Doesn't Look or Act' Like a First Lady, Says Virginia Voter Bobbie Lussier," *Huffington Post,* September 28, 2012, accessed July 14, 2017, http://www.huffingtonpost .com/2012/09/28/michelle-obama-look-like-a-first-lady-bobbie-lussier_n_1922236.html.

24. Devin Dwyer, "Michelle Obama Makes Cameo in Nickelodeon's *iCarly,*" *ABC News,* January 13, 2012, accessed July 14, 2017, http://abcnews.go.com/blogs/politics/2012/01/mi chelle-obama-makes-cameo-in-nickelodeons-icarly/.

25. "Michelle Obama's Workout Playlist," *Women's Health,* May 11, 2012, accessed June 14, 2017, http://www.womenshealthmag.com/fitness/michelle-obama-and-fitness.

26. Page, "Michelle Obama on Her Garden, Her Future, and the Campaign."

27. "Michelle Obama 'Doesn't Look or Act' Like a First Lady."

28. Jonathan P. Hicks, "Commentary: Insulting Michelle Obama Seems to Be the New Sport of the Right," BET, January 9, 2012, accessed July 14, 2017, http://www.bet.com/news/na tional/2012/01/09/commentary-insulting-michelle-obama-seems-to-be-the-new-sport-of-the -right.html.

29. Charles Johnson, "Michelle Obama Harvard Essay Surfaces," *Fox News,* August 15, 2012, accessed July 14, 2017, http://nation.foxnews.com/michelle-obama/2012/08/15/michelle -obama-harvard-essay-surfaces.

30. Hicks, "Commentary."

31. Ruth La Ferla, "Writing Her Own Dress Code," *New York Times,* June 13, 2012, accessed July 16, 2017, http://www.nytimes.com/2012/06/14/fashion/ann-romney-is-writing-her-own -dress-code.html?_r=1&smid=tw-nytimes&seid=auto&pagewanted=all.

32. Irin Carmon, "The Real Ann Romney," *Salon,* August 8, 2012, accessed July 16, 2017, http://www.salon.com/2012/08/08/the_real_ann_romney/.

33. Cottle, "Battle of the First Ladies."

34. Carmon, "Real Ann Romney."

35. Carmon, "Real Ann Romney."

36. Carmon, "Real Ann Romney."

37. Carmon, "Real Ann Romney."

38. Chris McGreal, "Ann Romney: The Privileged Housewife Worth More to Mitt Than His Millions," *Guardian,* April 28, 2012, accessed July 16, 2017, https://www.theguardian.com/world/2012/apr/28/ann-mitt-romney-republicans.

39. Cottle, "Battle of the First Ladies."

40. McGreal, "Ann Romney."

41. Trip Gabriel, "In Rarefied Sport, a View of the Romney's World," *New York Times,* May 26, 2012, accessed July 16, 2017, http://www.nytimes.com/2012/05/27/us/politics/ann-romneys-hobby-spotlights-world-of-dressage.html.

42. National Broadcasting Company (NBC), "Mitt Romney Reflects on His Loss," *Saturday Night Live,* November 10, 2012, accessed October 29, 2017, http://www.nbc.com/saturday-night-live/video/mitt-romney-on-a-balcony-cold-open/n28751?snl=1.

43. National Broadcasting Company (NBC), "Weekend Update: Ann Romney on Her Husband's Critics," *Saturday Night Live,* September 22, 2012, accessed October 29, 2017, http://www.nbc.com/saturday-night-live/video/weekend-update-ann-romney/n27700?snl=1.

44. National Broadcasting Company (NBC), "The Obama Show," *Saturday Night Live,* February 18, 2012, accessed October 29, 2017, http://www.nbc.com/saturday-night-live/video/cosby-obama/n13405?snl=1.

45. "Favorability: People in the News," *Gallup News,* accessed October 29, 2017, http://news.gallup.com/poll/1618/favorability-people-news.aspx.

46. Page, "Michelle Obama on Her Garden, Her Future, and the Campaign"; La Ferla, "Writing Her Own Dress Code."

47. Jonathan Knuckey and Myunghee Kim, "Evaluations of Michelle Obama as First Lady: The Role of Racial Resentment," *Presidential Studies Quarterly* 46 (2016): 367, http://dx.doi.org/10.1111/psq.12274.

48. Johnson, "Michelle Obama Harvard Essay Surfaces."

49. Bill Adair, "Chain Email Says River School Lip-Reading Instructor Confirms First Lady Michelle Obama Said 'All This for a Damn Flag' at 9/11 Ceremonies," Politifact, June 26, 2012, accessed July 14, 2017, http://www.politifact.com/truth-o-meter/statements/2012/jun/26/chain-email/river-school-lip-reading-damn-flag-first-lady/.

50. Hicks, "Commentary."

51. Hicks, "Commentary."

52. Hicks, "Commentary."

53. Knuckey and Kim, "Evaluations of Michelle Obama as First Lady," 367.

54. "Michelle Obama: No Tension with Husband's Aids," *CBS News,* January 11, 2012, accessed July 14, 2017, http://www.cbsnews.com/news/michelle-obama-no-tension-with-husbands-aides/.

55. Rosemary Ellis, "*Good Housekeeping* Talks with Michelle Obama," *Good Housekeeping,* October 11, 2012, accessed July 14, 2017, http://www.goodhousekeeping.com/life/inspirational-stories/interviews/a19484/michelle-obama-interview-2012-election/.

56. Tammy R. Vigil, "Conventional and Unconventional Rhetorical Strategies in Michelle Obama's Democratic National Convention Addresses," in *Michelle Obama: First Lady, American Rhetor,* eds. Elizabeth J. Natalle and Jenni M. Simon (Lanham, MD: Lexington Books, 2015), 15–38.

57. Michelle Obama, "Michelle Obama's Democratic Convention Speech," *ABC News,* September 4, 2012, accesses July 29, 2013, http://abcnews.go.com/Politics/OTUS/transcript-michelle-obamas-democratic-convention-speech/story?id=17155898.

58. Obama, "Michelle Obama's Democratic Convention Speech."

59. Obama, "Michelle Obama's Democratic Convention Speech."
60. Obama, "Michelle Obama's Democratic Convention Speech."
61. Obama, "Michelle Obama's Democratic Convention Speech."
62. Obama, "Michelle Obama's Democratic Convention Speech."
63. Obama, "Michelle Obama's Democratic Convention Speech."
64. Obama, "Michelle Obama's Democratic Convention Speech."
65. Obama, "Michelle Obama's Democratic Convention Speech."
66. Obama, "Michelle Obama's Democratic Convention Speech."
67. Obama, "Michelle Obama's Democratic Convention Speech."
68. Obama, "Michelle Obama's Democratic Convention Speech."
69. Obama, "Michelle Obama's Democratic Convention Speech."
70. Carmon, "Real Ann Romney."

71. Ann Romney, "Ann Romney RNC Speech," *Politico,* August 29, 2012, accessed July 29, 2013, http://www.politico.com/news/stories/0812/80346.html.

72. Romney, "Ann Romney RNC Speech."
73. Romney, "Ann Romney RNC Speech."
74. Romney, "Ann Romney RNC Speech."
75. Romney, "Ann Romney RNC Speech."
76. Romney, "Ann Romney RNC Speech."
77. Romney, "Ann Romney RNC Speech."
78. Romney, "Ann Romney RNC Speech."
79. Romney, "Ann Romney RNC Speech."
80. Romney, "Ann Romney RNC Speech."
81. Romney, "Ann Romney RNC Speech."
82. Romney, "Ann Romney RNC Speech."
83. Romney, "Ann Romney RNC Speech."

84. Harry Enten, "Melania Trump Is One of the Least Popular Spouses of a Nominee since 1988," FiveThirtyEight.com, July 19, 2016, accessed May 20, 2017, http://fivethirtyeight.com /features/melania-trump-is-one-of-the-least-popular-spouses-of-a-nominee-since-1988/.

85. Laurel Elder and Brian Frederick, "Perceptions of Candidate Spouses in the 2012 Presidential Election: The Role of Gender, Race, Religion, and Partisanship," *Politics, Groups, and Identities* (2017): 9, http://dx.doi.org/10.1080/21565503.2017.1338969.

Chapter 8. Bill Clinton and Melania Trump: The Former President and the Model Immigrant (2016)

1. Federal Election Commission, "Official 2016 Presidential General Election Results," accessed August 5, 2017, https://www.fec.gov/pubrec/fe2016/2016presgeresults.pdf.

2. "Record Number of Participants Attend Ready to Run Iowa," Carrie Chapman Catt Center for Women and Politics, March 2017, accessed August 20, 2017, https://cattcenter.iastate .edu/2017/03/13/record-number-of-participants-attend-ready-to-run-iowa/.

3. Nick Gass, "Pence Fires Back at Clinton's 'Amateurish' Foreign Policy," *Politico,* September 1, 2016, accessed November 10, 2017, https://www.politico.com/story/2016/09/mike -pence-clinton-amateur-227646.

4. "Presidential Approval Ratings—Bill Clinton," *Gallup News,* accessed November 10, 2017, http://news.gallup.com/poll/116584/presidential-approval-ratings-bill-clinton.aspx.

5. David W. Moore, "Clinton Leaves Office with Mixed Public Reaction," Gallup, January 12, 2001, accessed July 31, 2017, http://www.gallup.com/poll/2125/clinton-leaves-office-mixed -public-reaction.aspx.

6. Ben Schreckinger and Gabriel Debebetetti, "Gaps in Melania Trump's Immigration Story

Raise Questions," *Politico,* August 4, 2016, accessed November 10, 2017, https://www.politico.com/story/2016/08/melania-trump-immigration-donald-226648.

7. Schreckinger and Debebetti, "Gaps in Melania Trump's Immigration Story Raise Questions."

8. "Melania Trump," Biography.com, accessed November 10, 2017, https://www.biography.com/people/melania-trump-812016.

9. Caroline Simon, "Melania Trump Spoke at the GOP Convention—Here Are 10 Things You Might Not Know about Her," *Business Insider,* July 18, 2016, accessed July 31, 2017, http://www.businessinsider.com/10-things-you-might-not-know-about-melania-trump-2016-7.

10. "Melania Marks Accessories Member Corp," FindNYCorp.com, accessed November 10, 2017, http://findnycorp.com/corporation.php?id=3807093.

11. Julie Bykowicz, "Melania Trump Still Involved in Businesses and Branding, Court Documents Show," *Washington Times,* February 8, 2017, accessed July 31, 2017, http://www.washingtontimes.com/news/2017/feb/8/melania-trump-still-involved-businesses-and-brandi/.

12. Roseann M. Mandziuk, "Whither the Good Wife? 2016 Presidential Candidate Spouses in the Gendered Spaces of Contemporary Politics," *Quarterly Journal of Speech* 103 (2017): 138, http://dx.doi.org/10.1080/00335630.2016.1233350.

13. Margaret Talbot, "What Bill Clinton Should Do as First Gentleman," *New Yorker,* November 2, 2016, accessed February 22, 2017, http://www.newyorker.com/news/daily-comment/what-bill-clinton-should-do-as-first-gentleman.

14. This segment ran on the *New York Times* opinion page on July 28, 2016. It included seven different articles; http://www.nytimes.com/roomfordebate/2016/07/28/if-clinton-is-elected-what-should-she-do-with-bill.

15. Liz Kreutz, "Bill Clinton Would Be 'in Charge of Revitalizing the Economy,' Hillary Clinton Says," *ABC News,* May 15, 2016, accessed February 22, 2017, http://abcnews.go.com/Politics/bill-clinton-charge-revitalizing-economy-hillary-clinton/story?id=39132832; Letty Cottin Pogrebin, "Bill Clinton Would Be an Ideal Middle East Envoy," *New York Times,* July 28, 2016, accessed February 22, 2017, http://www.nytimes.com/roomfordebate/2016/07/28/if-clinton-is-elected-what-should-she-do-with-bill/bill-clinton-would-be-an-ideal-middle-east-envoy?smid=tw-share.

16. Cathleen Decker, "An Asset or a Disruption? What the White House Might Look Like with Bill Clinton in the East Wing," *Los Angeles Times,* July 26, 2016, accessed February 23, 2017, http://www.latimes.com/politics/la-na-pol-bill-clinton-20160726-snap-story.html.

17. Jennifer Gilmore, "Listen, Cookie, the First Spouse Has Better Things to Do," *Los Angeles Times,* July 28, 2016, accessed February 22, 2017, http://www.latimes.com/politics/la-na-pol-bill-clinton-20160726-snap-story.html.

18. Carl Bernstein, "A Second Co-Presidency, without So Much Controversy," *New York Times,* July 28, 2016, accessed February 22, 2017, http://www.nytimes.com/roomfordebate/2016/07/28/if-clinton-is-elected-what-should-she-do-with-bill/a-second-co-presidency-without-so-much-controversy?smid=tw-share.

19. Anna Caldwell, "The Other Race to the White House: Bill Clinton versus Melania Trump," *Herald Sun,* July 23, 2016, accessed February 23, 2016, http://www.heraldsun.com.au/news/world/the-other-race-to-the-white-house-bill-clinton-versus-melania-trump/news-story/6e560919a385bdf145daco4e40c6d063.

20. Robin Abcarian, "Bill Clinton, the Natural, Reaches Out to Voters in Places That Love Trump," *Los Angeles Times,* November 4, 2016, accessed February 22, 2016, http://www.latimes.com/politics/la-na-pol-bill-clinton-campaigning-20161105-story.html.

21. Eric Bradner, "Bill Clinton's Alleged Sexual Misconduct: Who You Need to Know," CNN, October 9, 2016, accessed February 23, 2016, http://www.latimes.com/politics/la-na-pol-bill

-clinton-campaigning-20161105-story.html; Ryan Girdusky, "A Millennial's Guide to Bill Clinton's 20+ Sex Scandals," *Fox News,* December 29, 2015, accessed March 20, 2017, http://nation.foxnews.com/2015/12/29/millennials-guide-bill-clintons-20-sex-scandals.

22. Eddie Scarry, "Media Omit Hillary's Role in Bill's Sex Scandal," *Washington Examiner,* October 1, 2016, accessed March 20, 2017, http://www.washingtonexaminer.com/media-omit-hillarys-role-in-bills-sex-scandal/article/2603336.

23. Shawn Boburg, "Enabler or Family Defender? How Hillary Clinton Responded to Husband's Accusers," *Washington Post,* September 28, 2016, accessed March 20, 2017, https://www.washingtonpost.com/local/enabler-or-family-defender-how-hillary-clinton-responded-to-husbands-accusers/2016/09/28/58dad5d4-6fb1-11e6-8533-6b0b0ded0253_story.html?utm_term=.9156e6512a63.

24. Rich Lowry, "Yes, Hillary Was an Enabler," *National Review,* May 27, 2016, accessed March 20, 2017, http://www.nationalreview.com/article/435941/hillary-clinton-enabled-bill-clintons-abuse-women-her-own-standards.

25. Guy Trebay, "Melania Trump, the Silent Partner," *New York Times,* September 30, 2015, accessed February 22, 2017, https://www.nytimes.com/2015/10/01/fashion/melania-trump-the-silent-partner.html?_r=0.

26. Lisa Suhay, "Is Melania Trump the Next Jackie Kennedy?" *Christian Science Monitor,* March 23, 2016, accessed March 20, 2017, http://www.csmonitor.com/USA/Politics/2016/0323/Is-Melania-Trump-the-next-Jackie-Kennedy-video.

27. Jennifer Harper, "Melania Trump: Poise, Grace, and Style through the Campaign, Right into the White House," *Washington Times,* January 19, 2017, accessed March 20, 2017, http://www.washingtontimes.com/news/2017/jan/19/melania-trump-showed-poise-during-long-campaign-tr/.

28. Emily Jane Fox, "The Quiet Tragedy of Melania Trump," *Vanity Fair,* October 14, 2016, accessed March 20, 2017, http://www.vanityfair.com/news/2016/10/quiet-tragedy-of-melania-trump.

29. Elspeth Reeve, "The Horror of Being Melania Trump," *New Republic,* May 13, 2016, accessed February 22, 2017, https://newrepublic.com/article/133471/horror-melania-trump.

30. Jennifer Weiner, "Naked Lady Politics," *New York Times,* March 26, 2016, accessed February 22, 2017, https://www.nytimes.com/2016/03/27/opinion/campaign-stops/naked-lady-politics.html?smid=tw-share.

31. *"Family Circle* 2016 Presidential Cookie Poll," *Family Circle,* accessed March 20, 2017, http://www.familycircle.com/recipes/desserts/cookies/family-circle-2016-presidential-cookie-poll/?page=2.

32. *"Family Circle* 2016 Presidential Cookie Poll."

33. Michelle Ward Trainor, "Melania Trump and Bill Clinton Square Off in What Used to Be Called the 'First Lady Cookie Contest,'" *People,* August 19, 2016, accessed March 20, 2017, http://people.com/food/melania-trump-bill-clinton-family-circle-cookie-contest/.

34. Mandziuk, "Whither the Good Wife?," 139.

35. Jill Abramson, "Hillary Clinton, a 'Nasty, Mean Enabler'? The Claim Is Ludicrous," *Guardian,* May 9, 2016, accessed November 11, 2017, https://www.theguardian.com/commentisfree/2016/may/09/hillary-clinton-enabler-bill-donald-trump-presidential-campaign.

36. Amy Chozick, "'90s Scandals Threaten to Erode Hillary Clinton's Strength with Women," *New York Times,* January 20, 2016, accessed November 11, 2017, https://www.nytimes.com/2016/01/21/us/politics/90s-scandals-threaten-to-erode-hillary-clintons-strength-with-women.html.

37. Abramson, "Hillary Clinton."

38. Abramson, "Hillary Clinton."

39. Heidi M. Przybyla, "Trump's Problem with Attacking Bill Clinton on Economy? His Own

Words," *USA Today,* May 17, 2016, accessed November 11, 2017, https://www.usatoday.com/story/news/politics/elections/2016/05/17/donald-trump-bill-clinton-economy/84500518/.

40. Javier Panzar, "The GOP Reacts to Bill Clinton and the Democrats on Social Media," *Los Angeles Times,* July 27, 2016, accessed November 11, 2017, http://www.latimes.com/nation/politics/trailguide/la-na-democratic-convention-2016-live-the-gop-reacts-to-bill-clinton-and-the-1469592120-htmlstory.html.

41. David Nakamura, "White House Declines to Respond to Melania Trump's Convention Speech," *Washington Post,* July 19, 2016, accessed November 11, 2017, https://www.washingtonpost.com/news/post-politics/wp/2016/07/19/white-house-declines-to-respond-to-melania-trumps-convention-speech/?utm_term=.1d7fb935d2ec.

42. Aliyah Frumin, "'Brazen' and 'Outrageous': Ex-Obama Speechwriters React to Melania Trump's Speech," *NBC News,* July 19, 2016, accessed November 11, 2017, https://www.nbcnews.com/news/us-news/brazen-outrageous-ex-obama-speechwriters-react-melania-trump-s-speech-n612436.

43. Tammy R. Vigil, "Feminine Views in the Feminine Style: Convention Speeches by Presidential Nominees' Spouses," *Southern Communication Journal* 79, no. 4 (2014): 336, http://dx.doi.org/10.1080/1041794X.2014.916339.

44. Bill Clinton, "Full Text: Bill Clinton's DNC Speech," *Politico,* July 27, 2016, accessed February 22, 2017, http://www.politico.com/story/2016/07full-text-bill-clinton-dnc-speech-226269.

45. Clinton, "Full Text: Bill Clinton's DNC Speech."

46. Clinton, "Full Text: Bill Clinton's DNC Speech."

47. Clinton, "Full Text: Bill Clinton's DNC Speech."

48. Clinton, "Full Text: Bill Clinton's DNC Speech."

49. Clinton, "Full Text: Bill Clinton's DNC Speech."

50. Clinton, "Full Text: Bill Clinton's DNC Speech."

51. Clinton, "Full Text: Bill Clinton's DNC Speech."

52. Alex Kuczynski, "Melania Trump's American Dream," *Harper's Bazaar,* January 6, 2016, accessed November 11, 2017, http://www.harpersbazaar.com/culture/features/a13529/melania-trump-interview-0216/.

53. "Melania Trump's Full Speech at the 2016 Republican National Convention," *PBS NewsHour,* July 18, 2016, accessed August 1, 2016, https://www.youtube.com/watch?v=Jt_9yb4FSYA.

54. Tipper Gore's 2000 DNC appearance did not include a full speech. See Chapter 4.

55. Will Drubhold, "Watch Melania Trump's Speech at the Republican Convention," *Time,* July 18, 2016, accessed August 1, 2016, http://time.com/4412008/republican-convention-melania-trump-2/.

56. Drubhold, "Watch Melania Trump's Speech at the Republican Convention."

57. Drubhold, "Watch Melania Trump's Speech at the Republican Convention."

58. Drubhold, "Watch Melania Trump's Speech at the Republican Convention."

59. Drubhold, "Watch Melania Trump's Speech at the Republican Convention."

60. Drubhold, "Watch Melania Trump's Speech at the Republican Convention."

61. Drubhold, "Watch Melania Trump's Speech at the Republican Convention."

62. Brian Frederick and Laurel Elder, "Presidential Candidate Spouses May Have Record Unfavorable Ratings in 2016," *Huffington Post,* May 20, 2016, accessed February 22, 2016, http://www.huffingtonpost.com/brian-frederick2/presidential-candidate-sp_b_10067098.html.

63. Frederick and Elder, "Presidential Candidate Spouses May Have Record Unfavorable Ratings in 2016."

64. Harry Enten, "Melania Trump Is One of the Least Popular Spouses of a Nominee since 1988," FiveThirtyEight.com, July 19, 2016, accessed May 20, 2017, http://fivethirtyeight.com/features/melania-trump-is-one-of-the-least-popular-spouses-of-a-nominee-since-1988/.

65. Mandziuk, "Whither the Good Wife?," 145.

Conclusion: Reifying Republican Motherhood

1. Abigail Adams to John Adams, letter, March 31–April 5, 1776, Adams Family Papers: An Electronic Archive, Massachusetts Historical Society, accessed July 15, 2016, https://www.masshist.org/digitaladams/archive/doc?id =L17760331aa.

2. Abigail Adams to John Adams, March 31–April 5, 1776.

3. John Adams to Abigail Adams, letter, April 14, 1776, Adams Family Papers: An Electronic Archive, Massachusetts Historical Society, accessed August 20, 2017, http://www.masshist.org/digitaladams/archive/doc?id=L17760414ja&bc=%2Fdigitaladams%2Farchive%2Fbrowse%2Fletters_1774_1777.php.

4. Karrin Vasby Anderson, "The First Lady: A Site of 'American Womanhood,'" in *Leading Ladies of the White House: Communication Strategies of Notable Twentieth-Century First Ladies,* ed. Molly Meijer Wertheimer (Lanham, MD: Rowman & Littlefield, 2005), 3.

5. Mary C. Banwart, Dianne G. Bystrom, and Terry Robertson, "From the Primary to the General: A Comparative Analysis of Candidate Media Coverage in Mixed-Gender 2000 Races for Governor and U.S. Senate," *American Behavioral Scientist* 46 (2003): 658–676, http://dx.doi.org/10.1177/0002764202238491; Brian F. Schaffner, "Priming Gender: Campaigning on Women's Issues in U.S. Senate Elections," *American Journal of Political Science* 49 (2005): 803–817, http://dx.doi.org/10.2307/3647698.

6. Tammy R. Vigil, "Feminine Views in the Feminine Style: Convention Speeches by Presidential Nominees' Spouses," *Southern Communication Journal* 79, no. 4 (2014): 336, http://dx.doi.org/10.1080/1041794X.2014.916339.

7. Maura Judkis, "The 2016 First Lady Cookie Contest Is Just as Weird as the Rest of the Election," *Washington Post,* August 18, 2016, accessed August 23, 2017, https://www.washingtonpost.com/lifestyle/food/the-2016-first-lady-cookie-contest-is-just-as-the-rest-of-the-election/2016/08/17/2c0fb4fa-63c9-11e6-8b27-bb8ba39497a2_story.html?utm_term=.8af39383b695.

8. Harry Enten, "Melania Trump Is One of the Least Popular Spouses of a Nominee since 1988," FiveThirtyEight.com, July 19, 2016, accessed May 20, 2017, http://fivethirtyeight.com/features/melania-trump-is-one-of-the-least-popular-spouses-of-a-nominee-since-1988/.

9. Enten, "Melania Trump Is One of the Least Popular Spouses of a Nominee since 1988."

10. Karrin Vasby Anderson, "From Spouses to Candidates: Hillary Rodham Clinton, Elizabeth Dole, and the Gendered Office of U.S. President," *Rhetoric & Public Affairs* 5 (2002): 105–132, http://dx.doi.org/10.1353/rap.2002.0001.

11. Christina Wolbrecht, *The Politics of Women's Rights: Parties, Positions, and Change* (Princeton, NJ: Princeton University Press, 2000).

12. "Republican Party Platform of 1872," American Presidency Project, June 5, 1872, accessed March 15, 2018, http://www.presidency.ucsb.edu/ws/?pid=29623.

13. "Republican Party Platform of 1968," American Presidency Project, August 5, 1968, accessed March 15, 2017, http://www.presidency.ucsb.edu/ws/?pid=25841.

14. Jo Freeman, *We Will Be Heard: Women's Struggles for Political Power in the United States* (Lanham, MD: Rowman & Littlefield, 2008), 137.

15. Barbara Burrell, Laurel Elder, and Brian Frederick, "From Hillary to Michelle: Public Opinion and the Spouses of Presidential Candidates," *Presidential Studies Quarterly* 41 (2011): 156–176, http://dx.doi.org/10.1111/j.1741-5705.2010.03835.x.

16. Laurel Elder and Brian Frederick, "Perceptions of Candidate Spouses in the 2012 Presidential Election: The Role of Gender, Race, Religion, and Partisanship," *Politics, Groups, and Identities* (2017): 9, http://dx.doi.org/10.1080/21565503.2017.1338969.

Selected Bibliography

"The 1996 Presidential Election." Gallup. Accessed January 5, 2017. http://library.law.colum
bia.edu/urlmirror/CLR/100CLR524/ptpreselec.html.

Adams, Abigail to John Adams, letter, March 31–April 5, 1776. Adams Family Papers: An Electronic Archive. Massachusetts Historical Society. Accessed July 15, 2016. https://www
.masshist.org/digitaladams/archive/doc?id =L17760331aa.

Adams, Abigail to John Adams, letter, December 23, 1796. Adams Family Papers: An Electronic
Archive. Massachusetts Historical Society. Accessed January 14, 2016. http://www.mass
hist.org/digitaladams/archive/doc?id=L17961223aa&bc=%2Fdigitaladams%2Farchive%2
Fbrowse%2Fletters_1796_1801.php.

Adams, John to Abigail Adams, letter, April 14, 1776. Adams Family Papers: An Electronic Archive. Massachusetts Historical Society. Accessed August 20, 2017. http://www.masshist
.org/digitaladams/archive/doc?id=L17760414ja&bc= %2Fdigitaladams%2Farchive%2Fbr
owse%2Fletters_1774_1777.php.

Amer, Mildred. "Membership of the 109th Congress: A Profile." *CRS Report for Congress,* November 29, 2006. Accessed June 4, 2017. https://www.senate.gov/reference/resources/pdf
/RS22007.pdf.

Anderson, Karrin Vasby. "The First Lady: A Site of 'American Womanhood.'" Pp. 1–15 in *Leading
Ladies of the White House: Communication Strategies of Notable Twentieth-Century First Ladies.* Edited by Molly Meijer Wertheimer. Lanham, MD: Rowman & Littlefield, 2005.

———. "From Spouses to Candidates: Hillary Rodham Clinton, Elizabeth Dole, and the Gendered Office of the U.S. President." *Rhetoric & Public Affairs* 5, no. 1 (2002): 105–132. http://
dx.doi.org/10.1353/rap.2002.0001.

Anthony, Carl. "Electing First Ladies: Presidential Candidate Spouses as Campaign Symbols,
Part 1, 1808–1904." National First Ladies' Library, January 12, 2016. Accessed May 18, 2016.
http://www.firstladies.org/blog/electing-first-ladies-presidential-candidate-spouses-as
-campaign-symbols-part-1/.

———. *First Ladies: The Saga of the Presidents' Wives and Their Power, 1789–1961.* New York:
Quill/William Morrow, 1990.

Bailey, Holly. "In Search of the Real Cindy McCain." *Newsweek,* June 21, 2008. Accessed June 22,
2017. http://www.newsweek.com/holly-bailey-search-real-cindy-mccain-90771.

Banner, Lois W. *Women in Modern America: A Brief History,* 2nd ed. San Diego: Harcourt, Brace,
Jovanovich, 1984.

Banwart, Mary C., Dianne G. Bystrom, and Terry Robertson. "From the Primary to the General: A Comparative Analysis of Candidate Media Coverage in Mixed-Gender 2000 Races for
Governor and U.S. Senate." *American Behavioral Scientist* 46 (2003): 658–676. http://dx.doi
.org/10.1177/0002764202238491.

Barone, Michael. "Is She a Political Liability?" *U.S. News and World Report,* March 7, 1994, 51.

Barry, Lisa R. "Eleanor Roosevelt: A Rhetorical Reconstruction of First Ladydom." Pp. 16–40 in
*Leading Ladies of the White House: Communication Strategies of Notable Twentieth-Century
First Ladies.* Edited by Molly Meijer Wertheimer. Lanham, MD: Rowman & Littlefield, 2005.

Beecher, Catharine Esther, and Harriet Beecher Stowe. *The American Woman's Home; or*

Principles of Domestic Science, Being a Guide to the Formation and Maintenance of Economical, Healthful, Beautiful, and Christian Homes. New York: J. B. Ford, 1869.

Bennetts, Leslie. "First Lady in Waiting." *Vanity Fair,* December 27, 2007. Accessed June 19, 2017. http://www.vanityfair.com/news/2007/12/michelle_obama200712.

Benz, Dorothee. "The Media Factor behind the 'Hillary Factor.'" *Fair,* October 1, 1992. Accessed October 23, 2016. http://fair.org/extra/the-media-factor-behind-the-hillary-factor/.

Bernstein, Carl. *A Woman in Charge: The Life of Hillary Rodham Clinton.* New York: Vintage Books, 2007.

Bianco, Marcie. "*SNL*'s Many Faces of Hillary Clinton: What They Say about Us." Women's Media Center, May 8, 2016. Accessed January 23, 2017. http://www.womensmediacenter.com/feature/entry/snls-many-faces-of-hillary-clinton-what-they-say-about-us.

Blair, Diane M. "No Ordinary Time: Eleanor Roosevelt's Address to the 1940 Democratic National Convention." *Rhetoric & Public Affairs* 4 (2001): 203–222. http://dx.doi.org/10.1353/rap.2001.0021.

Blair, Diane M., and Shawn J. Parry-Giles. "Rosalynn Carter: Crafting a Presidential Partnership Rhetorically." Pp. 140–164 in *Leading Ladies of the White House: Communication Strategies of Notable Twentieth-Century First Ladies.* Edited by Molly Meijer Wertheimer. Lanham, MD: Rowman & Littlefield, 2005.

Boller, Paul F., Jr. *Presidential Campaigns: From George Washington to George W. Bush.* New York: Oxford University Press, 2004.

Borrelli, MaryAnne. *The Politics of the President's Wife.* College Station: Texas A&M University Press, 2011.

Buchanan, Patrick. "Culture War, August 17, 1992." AmericanRhetoric.com. Accessed November 5, 2016. http://www.americanrhetoric.com/speeches/patrickbuchanan1992rnc.htm.

Burke, Edmund. *Reflections on the Revolution in France* (1790). Edited by Jon Roland. Constitution Society. Accessed June 13, 2016. http://www.constitution.org/eb/rev_fran.htm.

Burrell, Barbara, Laurel Elder, and Brian Frederick. "From Hillary to Michelle: Public Opinion and the Spouses of Presidential Candidates." *Presidential Studies Quarterly* 41 (2011): 156–176. http://dx.doi.org/10.1111/j.1741-5705.2010.03835.x.

Burris, Val. "Who Opposed the ERA? An Analysis of the Social Bases of Antifeminism." *Social Science Quarterly* 64 (Jue 1983): 305–317. Stable url: http://www.jstor.org/stable/42874034.

Bush, Barbara. "1992 RNC Speech Transcript." Speech Vault, August 19, 1992. Accessed July 26, 2013. http://www.speeches-usa.com/Transcripts/barbara_bush-1992rnc.html.

Bush, George H. W. "Presidential Debate at the University of Richmond." American Presidency Project, October 15, 1992. Accessed December 9, 2016. http://www.presidency.ucsb.edu/ws/?pid=21617.

Bush, Laura. "2004 Republican National Convention Address." AmericanRhetoric.com, August 31, 2004. Accessed July 27, 2013. http://www.americanrhetoric.com/speeches/PDFFiles/Laura%20Bush%20-%202004%20RNC.pdf.

———. "Address to the Republican National Convention." *Vital Speeches of the Day* 66, no. 21 (August 15, 2000): 650–651.

———. *Spoken from the Heart.* New York: Scribner, 2010.

Cable-Satellite Public Affairs Network (C-SPAN), "Barbara Bush Campaign Interview." July 28, 1992. Accessed August 25, 2016. https://www.c-span.org/video/?31214-1/barbara-bush-campaign-interview.

Cain, Madelyn. *The Childless Revolution: What It Means to be Childless Today.* New York: Don Congdon Associates, 2001.

Campbell, Karlyn Khors. "The Rhetorical Presidency: A Two-Person Career." Pp. 179–198 in

Beyond the Rhetorical Presidency. Edited by Martin J. Medhurst. College Station: Texas A&M University Press, 1996.

Cappella, Joseph N., Joseph Turow, and Kathleen Hall Jamieson. "Call-in Political Talk Radio: Background, Content, Audiences, Portrayal in Mainstream Media." Annenberg Public Policy Center, August 7, 1996. Accessed January 1, 2017. http://repository.upenn.edu/cgi/view content.cgi?article=1410&context=asc_papers.

Carlin, Diana B. "Barbara Pierce Bush: Choosing a Complete Life, 1925–1988." Pp. 604–620 in *A Companion to First Ladies.* Edited by Katherine A. S. Sibley. Malden, MA: Wiley-Blackwell, 2016.

———. "Barbara Pierce Bush: Choosing a Complete Life, 1988–2015." Pp. 621–634 in *A Companion to First Ladies.* Edited by Katherine A. S. Sibley. Malden, MA: Wiley-Blackwell, 2016.

———. "Lady Bird Johnson: The Making of a Public First Lady." Pp. 71–94 in *Leading Ladies of the White House: Communication Strategies of Notable Twentieth-Century First Ladies.* Edited by Molly Meijer Wertheimer. Lanham, MD: Rowman & Littlefield, 2005.

Carlson, Darren K. "Ideal First Lady: Hillary Clinton or Laura Bush?" Gallup, July 13, 2004. Accessed June 3, 2017. http://www.gallup.com/poll/12328/ideal-first-lady-hillary-clinton -laura-bush.aspx.

Carmon, Irin. "The Real Ann Romney." *Salon,* August 8, 2012. Accessed July 16, 2017. http:// www.salon.com/2012/08/08/the_real_ann_romney/.

Caroli, Betty Boyd. *First Ladies: From Martha Washington to Michelle Obama.* New York: Oxford University Press, 2010.

Carroll, Susan J. "The Disempowerment of the Gender Gap: Soccer Moms and the 1996 Elections." *PS: Political Science and Politics* 32 (1999): 7–11. http://dx.doi.org/10.2307/420743.

———. "Voting Choices: The Politics of the Gender Gap." Pp. 117–143 in *Gender and Elections: Shaping the Future of American Politics.* Edited by Susan J. Carroll and Richard L. Fox. New York: Cambridge University Press, 2010.

Cass, Connie. "Barbara Bush Set the Stage for Nominees' Wives." Associated Press, August 28, 2012. Accessed July 26, 2013. http://news.yahoo.com/barbara-bush-set-stage-nominees -wives-071846208--election.html.

Centers for Disease Control and Prevention, Office of Women's Health. "Leading Causes of Death in Females United States." September 24, 2015. Accessed July 14, 2016. http://www .cdc.gov/women/lcod/2013/index.htm.

Clark, Charles S. "First Ladies: What Is the Proper Role for the President's Spouse?" *Congressional Quarterly Researcher* 6 (1996): 1.

Clift, Eleanor, and Tara Sonenshine. "The Steel Magnolia." *Newsweek,* May 27, 1996, 33.

Clinton, Bill. "Full Text: Bill Clinton's DNC Speech." *Politico,* July 27, 2016. Accessed February 22, 2017. http://www.politico.com/story/2016/07/full-text-bill-clinton-dnc-speech-226269.

Clinton, Hillary. "First Lady Hillary Rodham Clinton Speaks at the Democratic National Convention." *PBS Newshour,* August 27, 1996. Accessed July 27, 2013. http://www.pbs.org/news hour/bb/politics/july-dec96/hillary-clinton.html?print.

Coletta, Paolo E. "'Won, 1880: One, 1884': The Courtship of William Jennings Bryan and Mary Elizabeth Baird." *Journal of the Illinois State Historical Society* 50 (1957): 231–242.

Collins, Lauren. "The Other Obama: Michelle Obama and the Politics of Candor." *New Yorker,* March 19, 2008. Accessed June 24, 2017. http://www.newyorker.com/magazine/2008/03/10 /the-other-obama.

Condit, Celeste. *Decoding Abortion Rhetoric: Communicating Social Change.* Urbana-Champaign: University of Illinois Press, 1990.

Congressional Quarterly. "1992 Democratic Convention: Call for a New Covenant Tops Off

Closing Night." *Congressional Quarterly Almanac,* July 18, 1992. Accessed November 6, 2016. http://library.cqpress.com/cqalmanac/document.php?id=cqa192-845-25178-1106417.

Cornfield, Michael. "Presidential Campaign Ads Online." Pew Research Center, October 3, 2004. Accessed June 8, 2017. http://www.pewinternet.org/2004/10/03/presidential-campaign-ads-online/.

Costello, Cynthia B., Vanessa R. Wight, and Anne J. Stone. "Women in the 107th Congress." Pp. 351–381 in *The American Woman: Daughters of a Revolution — Young Women Today.* Edited by Cynthia B. Costello, Vanessa R. Wight, and Anne J. Stone. New York: Palgrave Macmillan, 2002.

Cott, Nancy F. *The Bonds of Womanhood: "Woman's Sphere" in New England, 1780–1835.* New Haven, CT: Yale University Press, 1997.

Cottle, Michelle. "Battle of the First Ladies: Michelle Obama vs. Ann Romney." *Newsweek,* November 9, 2012. Accessed July 14, 2017. http://www.newsweek.com/battle-first-ladies-michelle-obama-vs-ann-romney-63859.

———. "The X-Factor." *Atlantic,* October 2004. Accessed June 5, 2017. https://www.theatlantic.com/magazine/archive/2004/10/the-x-factor/303499/.

Dailey, Kate. "Michelle Obama: Her Four-Year Evolution." BBC, September 4, 2012. Accessed July 14, 2017. http://www.bbc.com/news/magazine-19431000.

Dealey, Sam. "Cindy McCain Rolls Up Her Sleeves." *Marie Claire,* October 20, 2008. Accessed June 22, 2017. http://www.marieclaire.com/politics/news/a2131/cindy-mccain-interview-election/.

Deegan, Mary Jo. "Jane Addams, the Hull-House School of Sociology, and Social Justice, 1892 to 1935." *Humanity and Society* 37, no. 3 (2013): 248–258. http://dx.doi.org/10.1177/01605976 13493740.

Delli Carpini, Michael X., and Esther R. Fuchs. "The Year of the Woman? Candidates, Voters, and the 1992 Elections." *Political Science Quarterly* 108 (1993): 29–36.

DeSilver, Drew. "Women Have a Long History in Congress, but Until Recently There Haven't Been Many." Pew Research Center, January 14, 2015. Accessed January 5, 2017. http://www.pewresearch.org/fact-tank/2015/01/14/women-have-long-history-in-congress-but-until-recently-there-havent-been-many/.

Dole, Elizabeth. "Elizabeth Dole Speaking before the Republican National Convention." *PBS Newshour,* August 14, 1996. Accessed July 25, 2013. http://www.pbs.org/newshour/bb/politics/july-dec96/elizabeth_dole_08-14.html.

Douglas, Susan, and Meredith Michaels. *The Mommy Myth: The Idealization of Motherhood and How It Has Undermined All Women.* New York: Free Press, 2005.

Drubhold, Will. "Watch Melania Trump's Speech at the Republican Convention." *Time,* July 18, 2016. Accessed August 1, 2016. http://time.com/4412008/republican-convention-melania-trump-2/.

Dubriwny, Tasha N. "First Ladies and Feminism: Laura Bush as Advocate for Women's and Children's Rights." *Women's Studies in Communication* 28 (2005): 84–114.

Eagleton Institute of Politics, Center for American Women and Politics. "Fact Sheet: Gender Differences in Voter Turnout." October 2015. Accessed August 25, 2016. http://www.cawp.rutgers.edu/sites/default/files/resources/genderdiff.pdf.

———. "Fact Sheet: Gender Gap in the 2000 Elections." Accessed May 4, 2017. http://www.cawp.rutgers.edu/sites/default/files/resources/pressrelease_12-00_gg2000.pdf.

———. "Fact Sheet: Summary of Women Candidates for Selected Offices, 1970–2014." December 2014. Accessed January 5, 2017. http://www.cawp.rutgers.edu/sites/default/files/resources/can_histsum.pdf.

———. "Fact Sheet: Women Winners for U.S. House Seats, 1970–2014." December 2014.

Accessed January 5, 2017. http://www.cawp.rutgers.edu/sites/default/files/resources
/congwin_byseat.pdf.

———. "History of Women Governors." Accessed November 2, 2017. http://www.cawp.rutgers
.edu/history-women-governors.

Elder, Laurel, and Brian Frederick. "Perceptions of Candidate Spouses in the 2012 Presidential
Election: The Role of Gender, Race, Religion, and Partisanship." *Politics, Groups, and Identities* (2017): 1–22. http://dx.doi.org/10.1080/21565503.2017.1338969.

Enten, Harry. "Melania Trump Is One of the Least Popular Spouses of a Nominee since 1988."
FiveThirtyEight.com, July 19, 2016. Accessed September 17, 2016. http://fivethirtyeight.com
/features/melania-trump-is-one-of-the-least-popular-spouses-of-a-nominee-since-1988/.

Equal Rights Amendment. US History Online Textbook. UShistory.org. Accessed July 12, 2016.
http://www.ushistory.org/us/57c.asp.

Erikson, Amy Louise. "Mistresses and Marriage; or, a Short History of the Mrs." *History Workshop Journal* 78 (2014): 39–57. http://dx.doi.org/10.1093/hwj/dbt002.

"Favorability: People in the News." *Gallup News.* Accessed October 29, 2017. http://news.gallup
.com/poll/1618/favorability-people-news.aspx.

Federal Election Commission. "Official 2016 Presidential General Election Results." Accessed
August 5, 2017. https://www.fec.gov/pubrec/fe2016/2016presgeresults.pdf.

Filmer, Robert. *Patriarcha; or the Natural Power of Kings.* Edited by Johann P. Sommerville. New
York: Cambridge University Press, 1991.

"First Lady Biography: Barbara Bush." National First Ladies' Library. Accessed August 25, 2016.
http://www.firstladies.org/biographies/firstladies.aspx?biography=42.

"First Lady Biography: Dolley Madison." National First Ladies' Library. Accessed August 2, 2016.
http://www.firstladies.org/biographies/firstladies.aspx?biography=4.

"First Lady Biography: Pat Nixon." National First Ladies' Library. Accessed May 19, 2016. http://
www.firstladies.org/biographies/firstladies.aspx?biography=38.

Fox, Emily Jane. "The Quiet Tragedy of Melania Trump." *Vanity Fair,* October 14, 2016. Accessed
March 20, 2017. http://www.vanityfair.com/news/2016/10/quiet-tragedy-of-melania-trump.

Francis, Roberta W. "The Equal Rights Amendment: Unfinished Business for the Constitution."
EqualRightsAmendment.org. Accessed July 13, 2016. http://www.equalrightsamendment
.org/history.htm.

Frederick, Brian, and Laurel Elder. "Presidential Candidate Spouses May Have Record Unfavorable Ratings in 2016." *Huffington Post,* May 20, 2016. Accessed February 22, 2016. http://
www.huffingtonpost.com/brian-frederick2/presidential-candidate-sp_b_10067098.html.

Freeman, Jo. *We Will Be Heard: Women's Struggles for Political Power in the United States.* Lanham, MD: Rowman & Littlefield, 2008.

Friedman, Rachel B., and Ronald E. Lee. *The Style and Rhetoric of Elizabeth Dole: Public Persona
and Political Discourse.* Lanham, MD: Lexington Books, 2013.

Fuller, Margaret. *Woman in the Nineteenth Century and Other Writings.* New York: Oxford University Press, 1994.

Galewski, Elizabeth. "The Strange Case of Women's Capacity to Reason: Judith Sargent Murray's Use of Irony in 'On the Equality of the Sexes.'" *Quarterly Journal of Speech* 93 (2007):
84–108. http://dx.doi.org/10.1080/00335630701326852.

Gates, Henry Louis. "Hating Hillary: Hillary's Been Trashed Right and Left—but What's Really
Fueling the Furies?" *New Yorker,* February 26, 1996. Accessed January 1, 2017. http://www
.newyorker.com/magazine/1996/02/26/hating-hillary.

Gentile, Katie. "What about the Baby? The New Cult of Domesticity and Media Images of Pregnancy." *Studies in Gender and Sexuality* 12 (2011): 38–58. http://dx.doi.org/10.1080/152406
57.2011.536056.

Gerhart, Ann. *The Perfect Wife: The Life Choices of Laura Bush.* New York: Simon & Schuster, 2004.

Gibson, Katie L., and Amy L. Heyse. "'The Difference between a Hockey Mom and a Pit Bull': Sarah Palin's Faux Maternal Persona and Performance of a Hegemonic Masculinity at the 2008 Republican National Convention." *Communication Quarterly* 58, no. 3 (2010): 235–256. http://dx.doi.org/10.1080/01463373.2010.503151.

Girth, Jeff, and Don Van Natta, Jr. *Her Way: The Hopes and Ambitions of Hillary Rodham Clinton.* New York: Little, Brown, 2007.

Gore, Mary Elizabeth "Tipper." "Remarks at the 2000 DNC." Iowa State University Archives of Women's Political Communication, August 18, 2000. Accessed May 15, 2017. https://wp.las .iastate.edu/womenspeech/2017/03/21/remarks-at-the-2000-dnc-aug-18-2000/.

Graglia, F. Carolyn. *Domestic Tranquility: A Brief against Feminism.* Dallas, TX: Spence, 1998.

Grigoriadis, Vanessa. "Black and Blacker: The Racial Politics of the Obama Marriage." *New York Magazine,* August 10, 2008. Accessed June 24, 2017. http://nymag.com/news/features /49139/.

Gunther-Canada, Wendy. "Jean-Jacques Rousseau and Mary Wollstonecraft on the Sexual Politics of Republican Motherhood." *Southeastern Political Review* 27 (1999): 469–490. http:// dx.doi.org/10.1111/j.1747-1346.1999.tb00546.x.

Gutin, Myra G. *The President's Partner: The First Lady in the Twentieth Century.* Westport, CT: Praeger, 1989.

Harvard Medical School. "Gender Matters: Heart Disease Risk in Women." *Harvard Health Publications,* September 2006. Accessed July 14, 2016. http://www.health.harvard.edu/heart -health/gender-matters-heart-disease-risk-in-women.

Hayden, Dolores. *The Grand Domestic Revolution: A History of Feminist Designs for American Homes, Neighborhoods, and Cities.* Cambridge: Massachusetts Institute of Technology Press, 1982.

Hays, Sharon. *Flat Broke with Children: Women in the Age of Welfare Reform.* New York: Oxford University Press, 2003.

Hicks, Jonathan P. "Commentary: Insulting Michelle Obama Seems to Be the New Sport of the Right." BET, January 9, 2012. Accessed July 14, 2017. http://www.bet.com/news/na tional/2012/01/09/commentary-insulting-michelle-obama-seems-to-be-the-new-sport-of -the-right.html.

Hoff, Joan. "American Women and the Lingering Implications of Coverture." *Social Science Journal* 44 (2007): 41–55. http://dx.doi.org/10.1016/j.soscij.2006.12.004.

Hollandsworth, Skip. "Reading Laura Bush." *Texas Monthly.* Accessed December 31, 2016. http://www.texasmonthly.com/politics/reading-laura-bush/.

Jamieson, Kathleen Hall. *Beyond the Double Bind: Women and Leadership.* New York: Oxford University Press, 1995.

Johnston, Carolyn Ross. *Sexual Power: Feminism and the Family in America.* Tuscaloosa: University of Alabama Press, 1992.

Jones, Jeffrey M. "Gender Gap in 2012 Vote Is Largest in Gallup's History." *Gallup News,* November 9, 2012. Accessed November 1, 2017. http://news.gallup.com/poll/158588/gender-gap -2012-vote-largest-gallup-history.aspx.

Jong, Erica. "Hillary's Husband Re-elected: The Clinton Marriage of Politics and Power." *Nation,* November 25, 1996. Accessed January 1, 2017. https://www.scribd.com/document/30966 7569/Hillary-s-Husband-Re-Elected-The-Clinton-Marriage-of-Politics-and-Power.

Kames, Lord Henry Home. *Sketches of the History of Man.* Indianapolis, IN: Liberty Fund, 2013.

Kerber, Linda. "The Republican Mother: Women and the Enlightenment—an American

Perspective." *American Quarterly* 28 (1976): 187–205. Stable url: http://www.jstor.org/stable /2712349.

———. *Women of the Republic: Intellect and Ideology in Revolutionary America.* Chapel Hill: University of North Carolina Press, 1980.

Kerry, Teresa Heinz. "Teresa Heinz Kerry's Remarks to the Democratic National Convention." *New York Times,* July 27, 2004. Accessed July 27, 2013. http://www.nytimes.com/2004/07/27 /politics/campaign/27TEXT-TERESA.html.

Knuckey, Jonathan, and Myunghee Kim. "Evaluations of Michelle Obama as First Lady: The Role of Racial Resentment." *Presidential Studies Quarterly* 46 (2016): 365–386. http:// dx.doi.org/10.1111/psq.12274.

Kuczynski, Alex. "Melania Trump's American Dream." *Harper's Bazaar,* January 6, 2016. Accessed November 11, 2017. http://www.harpersbazaar.com/culture/features/a13529/mela nia-trump-interview-0216/.

Limbaugh, Rush. *Rush Limbaugh Show* simulcast. C-SPAN, November 3, 1992. Accessed December 21, 2016. https://www.c-span.org/video/?34031-1/rush-limbaugh-show-simulcast.

Lindsey, Duncan, and Rosemary Sarri. "What Hillary Clinton Really Said about Children's Rights and Child Policy." *Children and Youth Services Review* 14 (1992): 473–483.

Locke, John. *Two Treatises of Government* and *A Letter Concerning Toleration.* Edited by Ian Shapiro. New Haven, CT: Yale University Press, 2003.

MacDonald, Elizabeth, and Chana R. Schoenberger. "Special Report: The World's 100 Most Powerful Women." *Forbes,* August 20, 2004. Accessed June 8, 2017. https://www.forbes .com/home/lists/2004/08/18/04powomland.html.

MacManus, Susan A. "Voter Participation and Turnout: Female Star Power Attracts Women Voters." Pp. 78–116 in *Gender and Elections: Shaping the Future of American Politics.* Edited by Susan J. Carroll and Richard L. Fox. New York: Cambridge University Press, 2006.

"Making Hillary Clinton an Issue." *PBS Frontline,* March 26, 1992. Accessed December 15, 2016. http://www.pbs.org/wgbh/pages/frontline/shows/clinton/etc/03261992.html.

Mandziuk, Roseann M. "Whither the Good Wife? 2016 Presidential Candidate Spouses in the Gendered Spaces of Contemporary Politics." *Quarterly Journal of Speech* 103 (2017): 136–159. http://dx.doi.org/10.1080/00335630.2016.1233350.

"Mary Elizabeth Baird Bryan." Arlington National Cemetery Website, September 3, 2005. Accessed May 18, 2016. http://www.arlingtoncemetery.net/mebbryan.htm.

Maxwell, Zerlina. "Reproductive Health Laws Prove GOP 'War on Women' Is No Fiction." *U.S. News and World Report,* April 10, 2012. Accessed July 14, 2016. http://www.usnews.com/de bate-club/is-there-a-republican-war-on-women/reproductive-health-laws-prove-gop-war -on-women-is-no-fiction.

McCain, Cindy. "Text of Cindy McCain's Speech." *Los Angeles Times,* September 4, 2008. Accessed July 29, 2013. http://www.latimes.com/news/politics/la-na-cmccaintranscript5 2008sep05,0,4516477.story.

McGreal, Chris. "Ann Romney: The Privileged Housewife Worth More to Mitt Than His Millions." *Guardian,* April 28, 2012. Accessed July 16, 2017. https://www.theguardian.com /world/2012/apr/28/ann-mitt-romney-republicans.

McLean, Maggie. "Ida McKinley." Civil War Women: Women of the Civil War and Reconstruction Eras, 1849–1877, November 23, 2014. Accessed May 19, 2016, http://civilwarwomenblog .com/ida-mckinley/.

"Melania Trump." Biography.com. Accessed November 10, 2017. https://www.biography.com /people/melania-trump-812016.

"Melania Trump's Full Speech at the 2016 Republican National Convention." *PBS Newshour,*

July 18, 2016. Accessed August 1, 2016. https://www.youtube.com/watch?v=Jt_9yb4 FSYA.

Mettler, Suzanne. *Dividing Citizens: Gender and Federalism in New Deal Public Policy*. Ithaca, NY: Cornell University Press, 1998.

"Michelle Obama's America: Is Barack Obama's Wife His Rock or His Bitter Half?" *Economist*, July 3, 2008. Accessed June 24, 2017. http://www.economist.com/node/11670246.

Mikulski, Barbara, Kay Bailey Hutchinson, Dianne Feinstein, Barbara Boxer, Patty Murray, Olympia Snowe, Susan Collins, Mary Landrieu, and Blanche L. Lincoln. *Nine and Counting: The Women of the Senate*. New York: William Morrow, 2000.

Mill, John Stuart. *On the Subjection of Women*. London: Longmans, Green, Reader, and Dryer, 1869.

Mink, Gwendolyn. *The Wages of Motherhood: Inequality in the Welfare State, 1917–1942*. Ithaca, NY: Cornell University Press, 1998.

Montesquieu, Charles Louis de Secondat, Baron de. *The Spirit of the Laws*. Translated by Thomas Nugent. Online Library of Liberty. Accessed April 2, 2016. http://oll.libertyfund.org/titles/837.

Moore, David W. "Clinton Leaves Office with Mixed Public Reaction." Gallup, January 12, 2001. Accessed July 31, 2017. http://www.gallup.com/poll/2125/clinton-leaves-office-mixed-public-reaction.aspx.

Morales, Tatiana. "Laura Bush: 'The Perfect Wife.'" *CBS News*, January 7, 2004. Accessed June 4, 2017. http://www.cbsnews.com/news/laura-bush-the-perfect-wife/.

———. "Mama T: Teresa Heinz Kerry." *CBS News*, July 27, 2004. Accessed June 4, 2017. http://www.cbsnews.com/news/mama-t-teresa-heinz-kerry/.

Murphy, Troy A. "William Jennings Bryan: Boy Orator, Broken Man, and the 'Evolution' of America's Public Philosophy." *Great Plains Quarterly* 22 (2002): 83–98.

Nash, Margaret A. "Rethinking Republican Motherhood: Benjamin Rush and the Young Ladies' Academy of Philadelphia." *Journal of the Early Republic* 17 (1997): 171–191. http://dx.doi.org/10.2307/3124445.

Natalle, Elizabeth J. "Michelle Obama's Ethos and Let's Move!" Pp. 61–84 in *Michelle Obama: First Lady, American Rhetor*. Edited by Elizabeth J. Natalle and Jenni M. Simon. Lanham, MD: Lexington Books, 2015.

Natalle, Elizabeth J., and Jenni M. Simon, eds. *Michelle Obama: First Lady, American Rhetor*. Lanham, MD: Lexington Books, 2015.

National Broadcasting Company. "The Barbara Walters Special: Elizabeth Dole." *Saturday Night Live*, October 26, 1996. Accessed January 16, 2017. https://www.nbc.com/saturday-night-live/video/barbara-on-liddy/2861298?snl=1.

———. "John McCain and Sarah Palin Do QVC." *Saturday Night Live*, November 1, 2008. Accessed October 22, 2017. http://www.nbc.com/saturday-night-live/video/mccain-qvc-open/n12355?snl=1.

———. "Kerry Campaign Stop." *Saturday Night Live*, October 2, 2004. Accessed June 6, 2017. https://www.nbc.com/saturday-night-live/video/kerry-campaign-stop/n11843?snl=1.

———. "Mitt Romney Reflects on His Loss." *Saturday Night Live*, November 10, 2012. Accessed October 29, 2017. http://www.nbc.com/saturday-night-live/video/mitt-romney-on-a-balcony-cold-open/n28751?snl=1.

———. "The Obama Show." *Saturday Night Live*, February 18, 2012. Accessed October 29, 2017. http://www.nbc.com/saturday-night-live/video/cosby-obama/n13405?snl=1.

———. "The Obama Variety Show." *Saturday Night Live*, October 25, 2008. Accessed October 22, 2017. http://www.nbc.com/saturday-night-live/video/obama-address/n12335?snl=1.

———. "The Pat Stevens Show." *Saturday Night Live*, October 10, 1988. Accessed December 1,

2017. http://www.nbc.com/saturday-night-live/video/pat-stevens-candidates-wives/2868
068.

———. "Weekend Update: Ann Romney on Her Husband's Critics." *Saturday Night Live*, September 22, 2012. Accessed October 29, 2017. http://www.nbc.com/saturday-night-live/video/weekend-update-ann-romney/n27700?snl=1.

Newport, Frank. "Clinton's Image at Lowest Point in Two Decades." Gallup, July 25, 2016. Accessed January 7, 2017. http://www.gallup.com/poll/193913/clinton-image-lowest-point-two-decades.aspx.

Obama, Michelle. "Michelle Obama's Democratic Convention Speech." *ABC News,* September 4, 2012. Accesses July 29, 2013. http://abcnews.go.com/Politics/OTUS/transcript-michelle-obamas-democratic-convention-speech/story?id=17155898.

———. "Michelle Obama's 'One Nation.'" Transcript. CNN, August 25, 2008. Accessed June 30, 2013. http://www.cnn.com/2008/POLITICS/08/25/michelle.obama.transcript/.

O'Conner, Karen, Bernadette Nye, and Laura Van Assendelft. "Wives in the White House: The Political Influence of First Ladies." *Presidential Studies Quarterly* 26 (1996): 835–853. Stable url: http://jstor.org/stable/27551636.

Orr, Floyd M. *The Last Horizon: Female Sexuality.* Bloomington, IN: iUniverse, 2002.

Paine, Thomas. "An Occasional Letter on the Female Sex (1775)." Constitution.org. Accessed June 17, 2016. http://www.constitution.org/tp/female.htm.

Parry-Giles, Shawn J. *Hillary Clinton in the News: Gender and Authenticity in American Politics.* Urbana-Champaign: University of Illinois Press, 2014.

Parry-Giles, Shawn J., and Diane M. Blair. "The Rise of the Rhetorical First Lady: Politics, Gender Ideology, and Women's Voice, 1789–2002." *Rhetoric & Public Affairs* 4, no. 4 (2002): 565–600. http://dx.doi.org/10.1353/rap.2003.0011.

Parry-Giles, Shawn J., and Trevor Parry-Giles. "Gendered Politics and Presidential Image Reconstruction: A Reassessment of the 'Feminine Style.'" *Communication Monographs* 63 (1996): 337–353. http://dx.doi.org/10.1080/03637759609376398.

Pateman, Carole. *The Disorder of Women: Democracy, Feminism, and Political Theory.* Palo Alto, CA: Stanford University Press, 1989.

"Pennsylvania's Most Politically Powerful Women." *Politics PA.* Accessed June 1, 2017. https://web.archive.org/web/20040209095936/http://politicspa.com/features/mostpoliticallypowerfulwomen.htm.

Peters, Gerhard, and John T. Woolley. "Voter Turnout in Presidential Elections: 1828–2012." American Presidency Project. Accessed January 9, 2017. http://www.presidency.ucsb.edu/data/turnout.php.

Plato. *The Republic.* Translated by Desmond Lee. New York: Penguin Books, 1975.

"Presidential Approval Ratings—Bill Clinton." *Gallup News.* Accessed November 10, 2017. http://news.gallup.com/poll/116584/presidential-approval-ratings-bill-clinton.aspx.

Quayle, Marilyn. "Republican National Convention Address, August 19, 1992." C-SPAN. Accessed November 5, 2016. https://www.c-span.org/video/?31358-1/republican-national-convention-address&start=699.

Reaves, Jessica. "Now Making Her Bow: The Un-Hillary." CNN, August 1, 2000. Accessed May 13, 2017. http://content.time.com/time/magazine/article/0,9171,51517,00.html.

"Record Number of Participants Attend Ready to Run Iowa." Carrie Chapman Catt Center for Women and Politics, March 2017. Accessed August 20, 2017. https://cattcenter.iastate.edu/2017/03/13/record-number-of-participants-attend-ready-to-run-iowa/.

Reed, Julia. "Cindy McCain: Cindy McCain Takes a Moment." *Vogue,* June 1, 2008. Accessed June 22, 2017. http://www.vogue.com/article/cindy-mccainbrcindy-mccain-takes-a-moment.

"Republican Party Platform of 1872." American Presidency Project, June 5, 1872. Accessed March 15, 2018. http://www.presidency.ucsb.edu/ws/?pid=29623.

"Republican Party Platform of 1968." American Presidency Project, August 5, 1968. Accessed March 15, 2017. http://www.presidency.ucsb.edu/ws/?pid=25841.

Roberts, Cokie. *Ladies of Liberty: The Women Who Shaped Our Nation.* New York: Harper Perennial, 2008.

Robertson, Pat. "1992 Republican Convention." Pat Robertson website. Accessed November 5, 2016. http://www.patrobertson.com/Speeches/1992GOPConvention.asp.

Romney, Ann. "Ann Romney RNC Speech." *Politico,* August 29, 2012. Accessed July 29, 2013. http://www.politico.com/news/stories/0812/80346.html.

Roosevelt, Eleanor. "Address to the 1940 Democratic Convention." Eleanor Roosevelt Papers Project. Accessed June 25, 2013. http://www.gwu.edu/~erpapers/teachinger/q-and-a/q22-erspeech.cfm.

Rose, Melody, and Mark O. Hattfield. "Republican Motherhood Redux? Women as Contingent Citizens in 21st Century America." *Journal of Women, Politics, and Policy* 29 (2007): 5–30. http://dx.doi.org/10.1300/J501v29n01_02.

Rousseau, Jean-Jacques. *Emile.* 1762.

Saad, Lydia. "Melania Trump's Image Less Positive Than Other Spouses." Gallup. July 18, 2016. Accessed May 13, 2017. http://www.gallup.com/opinion/polling-matters/193793/melania-trump-image-problem-democrats-independents.aspx.

Schaffner, Brian F. "Priming Gender: Campaigning on Women's Issues in U.S. Senate Elections." *American Journal of Political Science* 49 (2005): 803–817. http://dx.doi.org/10.2307/3647698.

Shipman, Claire, Susan Rucci, and Imaeyen Ibanga. "Cindy McCain: Mother, Humanitarian, and Potential First Lady." *ABC News,* July 8, 2008. Accessed June 22, 2017. http://abcnews.go.com/GMA/story?id=5330040.

Stark, Steven. "Gap Politics." *Atlantic,* July 1996. Accessed January 6, 2017. http://www.theatlantic.com/magazine/archive/1996/07/gap-politics/305579/.

Steinfels, Margaret O'Brien. "A New Role for Hillary: Circuit-Riding First Lady." *Commonweal,* December 2, 1994, 5.

Stoltzfus, Emilie. *Citizen, Mother, Worker: Debating Public Responsibility for Child Care after the Second World War.* Chapel Hill: University of North Carolina Press, 2003.

Sullivan, Amy. "Michelle Obama's Most Important Title Really Is Mom-in-Chief." *New Republic,* September 5, 2012. Accessed July 14, 2017. https://newrepublic.com/article/106954/michelle-obamas-most-important-title-really-mom-chief.

Swain, Susan. *First Ladies: Presidential Historians on the Lives of 45 Iconic American Women.* New York: Public Affairs, 2015.

Terkel, Amanda. "Saxby Chambliss Attributes Military Sexual Assault to 'The Hormone Level Created by Nature.'" *Huffington Post,* June 5, 2013. Accessed July 14, 2016. http://www.huffingtonpost.com/entry/saxby-chambliss-military-sexual-assault_n_3384286.

———. "Women in Senate: 2012 Election Ushers in Historic Number of Female Senators." *Huffington Post,* November 11, 2012. Accessed November 2, 2017. https://www.huffingtonpost.com/2012/11/07/women-senate-2012-election_n_2086093.html.

Thomas, Louisa. *Louisa: The Extraordinary Life of Mrs. Adams.* New York: Penguin Books, 2016.

Thurman, Judith. "The Candidate's Wife." *New Yorker,* September 27, 2004. Accessed June 2, 2017. http://www.newyorker.com/magazine/2004/09/27/the-candidates-wife.

Titone, Connie. "Virtue, Reason, and the False Public Voice: Catharine Macaulay's *Philosophy of Moral Education.*" *Educational Philosophy and Theory* 41, no. 1 (2009): 91–108. http://dx.doi.org/10.1111/j.1469-5812.2007.00365.x.

Trainor, Michelle Ward. "Melania Trump and Bill Clinton Square Off in What Used to Be Called the 'First Lady Cookie Contest.'" *People,* August 19, 2016. Accessed March 20, 2017. http://people.com/food/melania-trump-bill-clinton-family-circle-cookie-contest/.

Traister, Rebecca. "The Momification of Michelle Obama." *Salon,* November 12, 2008. Accessed June 24, 2017. http://www.salon.com/2008/11/12/michelle_obama_14/.

Truth, Sojourner. "Ain't I a Woman? (1851)." *Modern History Sourcebook* (August 1997). Accessed October 22, 2017. https://sourcebooks.fordham.edu/mod/sojtruth-woman.asp.

Tumulty, Karen. "Democratic Convention: The Women Who Made Al Gore." *Time,* August 21, 2000. Accessed May 7, 2017. http://content.time.com/time/printout/0,8816,997752,00.html.

US House of Representatives. "The Decade of Women, 1992–2002." History, Art, and Archives. Accessed August 25, 2016. http://history.house.gov/Exhibitions-and-Publications/WIC/Historical-Essays/Assembling-Amplifying-Ascending/Women-Decade/.

Vander Ven, Thomas. *Working Mothers and Juvenile Delinquency.* El Paso, TX: LFB Scholarly, 2003.

Vavrus, Mary Douglas. "From Women of the Year to 'Soccer Moms': The Case of the Incredible Shrinking Women." *Political Communication* 17 (2000): 193–213. http://dx.doi.org/10.1080/105846000198477.

Venker, Suzanne, and Phyllis Schlafly. *The Flipside of Feminism: What Conservative Women Know and Men Can't Say.* Washington, DC: WND Books, 2010.

Vigil, Tammy R. *Connecting with Constituents: Identification Building and Blocking in Contemporary National Convention Speeches.* Lanham, MD: Lexington Books, 2015.

———. "Conventional and Unconventional Rhetorical Strategies in Michelle Obama's Democratic National Convention Addresses." Pp. 15–38 in *Michelle Obama: First Lady, American Rhetor.* Edited by Elizabeth J. Natalle and Jenni M. Simon. Lanham, MD: Lexington Books, 2015.

———. "Feminine Views in the Feminine Style: Convention Speeches by Presidential Nominees' Spouses." *Southern Communication Journal* 79, no. 4 (2014): 327–346. http://dx.doi.org/10.1080/1041794X.2014.916339.

Weisberg, Jacob. "Soccer Mom Nonsense: The Making of This Year's Election Myth." *Slate,* October 12, 1996. Accessed January 6, 2017. http://www.slate.com/articles/news_and_politics/strange_bedfellow/1996/10/soccer_mom_nonsense.html.

Wertheimer, Molly Meijer. "Barbara Bush: Her Rhetorical Development and Appeal." Pp. 187–216 in *Leading Ladies of the White House: Communication Strategies of Notable Twentieth-Century First Ladies.* Edited by Molly Meijer Wertheimer. Lanham, MD: Rowman & Littlefield, 2005.

———. "Editor's Introduction: First Ladies' Fundamental Rhetorical Choices: When to Speak? What to Say? When to Remain Silent?" Pp. i–xii in *Leading Ladies of the White House: Communication Strategies of Notable Twentieth-Century First Ladies.* Edited by Molly Meijer Wertheimer. Lanham, MD: Rowman & Littlefield, 2005.

Williams, Marjorie. "Barbara's Backlash." *Vanity Fair* (August 1992). Accessed September 17, 2016. http://www.vanityfair.com/magazine/1992/08/williams199208.

Wolbrecht, Christina. *The Politics of Women's Rights: Parties, Positions, and Change.* Princeton, NJ: Princeton University Press, 2000.

Wollstonecraft, Mary. *A Vindication of the Rights of Man and A Vindication of the Rights of Women.* New York: Cambridge University Press, 1995 [1792].

Zagarri, Rosemarie. "Morals, Manners, and the Republican Mother." *American Quarterly* 44 (1992): 192–215. http://dx.doi.org/10.2307/2713040.

Index

Cruz, Heidi, 1
Cruz, Ted, 1

Dean, Howard, 101
Democratic National Convention (DNC), 52,
    58, 69, 93–94, 171
    and Eleanor Roosevelt, 6, 9–10, 75
    Gore kiss, 85, 89, 94
    and Helen Taft, 6
    spouses' addresses, 72–74, 118–121, 141–143,
        160–162, 181–184
divorce
    laws affecting women, 24–25
    presidential nominees, 64, 126, 172
    Rachel Jackson scandal, 3
Dole, Bob, 62, 64, 71
Dole, Elizabeth "Liddy," 93, 141, 193, 194,
    200, 204
    1996 RNC speech, 75–76
    American Red Cross, 64–65, 70, 75, 195
    biography, 64
    cabinet posts, 64, 195
    governmental operative, 69–70, 80, 144,
        202, 203
    presidential candidate, 80, 81, 169
    scandals, 68, 78
domestic feminism, 31–32, 38, 97, 99
domesticity. See women's domesticity
drug abuse
    anti-drug campaigns, 39
    Cindy McCain's addiction, 126, 138
    feminine political topic, 10

economy
    Ann Romney, 156, 164, 195
    feminine frames, 164, 195
    masculine political topic, 113, 116, 164, 194
education
    for females, 18–19, 21, 23–24, 31
    feminine political topic, 10, 46, 59, 64, 164,
        194, 200
    as political cause, 57, 73, 88, 95, 115, 186
    as women's work, 24, 91
Edwards, John, 102
enfranchisement, 18, 20, 30, 33, 37, 43, 206
Equal Rights Amendment (ERA), 33–34

Family Circle, 49. See also First Lady Bake-
    Off; Presidential Cookie Competition
family values, 37, 82, 179, 196
Feinstein, Dianne, 42
female citizenship, perspectives on

Democratic Party, 42–43, 206–207
post–Revolutionary War era, 22–25, 121
Republican Party, 42–43, 206–207
female governmental representation
    governors, 146
    US House of Representatives, 42, 61, 80,
        125, 146
    US Senate, 42, 61, 80, 125
female political tropes, 37–38, 199
    hockey moms, 36, 40, 147
    security moms, 113, 117
    soccer moms, 61–62, 66, 77–79, 91, 157, 166
    welfare queens, 37, 199
feme sole, 22, 24
feminine political topics. See childcare; drug
    abuse; education; health care; highway
    beautification; literacy; mental health
Filmer, Robert, 17
First Lady Bake-Off, 88, 109, 155
    competition controversy, 135, 199
    name change, 177
    origins, 49
    sexism in, 177, 205
    spotlighting conventional femininity, 11,
        69, 89, 113, 198
    See also Presidential Cookie Competition
first lady pulpit, 39, 106, 174, 193–194, 208
Ford, Betty, 6, 7
Freemont, Jessie, 5, 7
Fuller, Margaret, 23

gender gap, political
    candidate preference, 102, 146
    voting, 80, 125
Good Housekeeping, 155
Good Morning America, 155
good woman
    antithesis of bad woman, 199, 201–203
    conventional enactments, 50, 110–112, 133,
        138, 139, 204
    definition, 54, 198–201
Gore, Al
    presidential candidate, 80, 81, 92, 168, 171
    vice presidential candidate, 43, 52, 62
Gore, Tipper (Mary Elizabeth), 144, 149, 193,
    194, 199
    2000 DNC appearance, 85, 93–95, 184
    biography, 82
    favorability ratings, 98, 166, 200
    Parents Music Resource Center (PMRC),
        82, 86
    See also mental health